Multi-dimensional sociology

Multi-dimensional sociology

Adam Podgórecki and Maria Łoś

Routledge & Kegan Paul

London, Boston and Henley

First published in 1979
by Routledge & Kegan Paul Ltd
39 Store Street, London WC1E 7DD,
Broadway House, Newtown Road,
Henley-on-Thames, Oxon RG9 1EN and
9 Park Street, Boston, Mass. 02108, USA
Set in English Times
and printed in Great Britain by
Ebenezer Baylis and Son, Ltd.,
The Trinity Press,
Worcester, and London

British Library Cataloguing in Publication Data

Podgórecki, Adam

Multi-dimensional sociology. – (International
library of sociology).
1. Sociology
I. Title II. Łoś, Maria W
III. Series
301   HM51   79-40585.

ISBN 0 7100 0296 3

Contents

Acknowledgments

Both authors wish to acknowledge their debt to their former colleagues at the Centre for Sociology of Norms and Social Pathology at Warsaw University where in the years 1975-6 the initial idea of this book originated and was discussed.

Adam Podgórecki would like to thank the Netherlands Institute for Advanced Studies in Humanities and the Social Sciences in Wassenaar for giving him the opportunity to prepare the first version of his part of the book, and Ms Kathrine Murphy for typing it. He also wishes to express his gratitude to the SSRC Centre for Socio-Legal Studies in Oxford for allowing him to work further on the text and to Ms Lorna Pollock for typing it.

Maria Łoś wishes to thank the members of the Centre for Criminological Studies and of the Faculty of Law at the University of Sheffield for the privilege of working in their stimulating intellectual and friendly atmosphere. She wants to thank especially Professor Anthony Bottoms, Professor Graham Battersby and Mr Paul Wiles for their continuous support and Mr Vaughan Bevan for invaluable advice and help in preparing the final version of the text. She is also very grateful to Mrs Vera Marsh for her help in typing the manuscript.

The authors and publisher would like to thank the editors of *Oficyna Poetó* for permission to use copyright material from no.1 (48), 1978, pp. 31-6, 'Intelligentsia of all countries unite', and no. 3, 1978, pp. 58-9 and the editors of *Polish Sociological Bulletin* for permission to use copyright material from no. 3-4 (39-40), 1977, 'Global Ethics'. The authors would like to thank Routledge & Kegan Paul Ltd for permission to use copyright material from Karl Popper, *The Open Society and its Enemies*, 1962 and Sir Isaiah Berlin for permission to publish his letter of 28 March 1978.

A.P.
M.Ł.

Introduction

Our intention in writing this book has been to make sociology aware of its own riches. Coming from a country where pluralism in social science is somewhat restricted we appreciate the potential and indeed the necessity of varied orientations and methods in sociology. However, we also realize that some important steps have to be taken if this multiplicity is not going to lead us towards unselective eclecticism or futile competition. A strategy to bring about required change may lead to the discovery of a completely new paradigm which adequately accommodates various perspectives. Or, it may be far less spectacular, humbly piecemeal and rather painstaking. We have realistically chosen the second approach. As a consequence, we have attempted to accomplish the following objectives leading eventually to the establishment of a thorough basis for development of 'multi-dimensional sociology':
(1) Systematic scrutiny of the epistemological and ontological (or political) assumptions of various distinctive theoretical perspectives within sociology;
(2) Assessment of the consequences of these assumptions – focusing on the necessary implications, and not on the developments which are only accidentally connected with the given perspective or attributed to it by its critics;
(3) Confrontation of the obtained results with each other, leading to a cognitive vision of the 'multi-dimensional human society' approximating the configurations of features determined by the selected perspectives (contradictions being accepted as consistent with the very nature of human society as well as with the present development of our cognitive faculties);
(4) Assessment of the lessons drawn from such an exercise with a view to a possible re-evaluation and redefinition of divisions between various perspectives;

(5) Proposal of a method (certainly one of many) of uniting those
    carefully scrutinized and refined perspectives (related to certain
    dimensions of the above proposed reconstruction of human
    society) into the 'multi-dimensional sociology'.

It should be emphasized that the proposed survey of the selected
orientations should be - at least to a significant extent - conducted
on 'their own terms'. It means that, for instance, phenomenology is
not supposed to be criticized for being inconsistent with the positivistic methodology. It also means that it would not be seen as a
rival perspective which has to be eliminated at all costs (by, for
instance, attacking its grossly distorted version or its side-tracks
and temporary disturbances) - which is a common practice in
'friendly' sociological battles. It does not mean, however, that
criticism is precluded. It is in fact indispensable as far as it points to
the unjustified inadequacies, corrosions and fallacies within the
particular perspective judged more or less by its own criteria and
programme. Wherever the criticism goes beyond that, it should be
warranted by the inner logic of discussion and/or the fact that the
criteria mentioned above may not be so absolutely clear after all.
Another kind of required criticism should point to the unfulfilled
potential, biases or limitations of the given perspective unjustified
by its basic assumptions.

Our discussion of multi-dimensional sociology does not stop
here. First of all, we are afraid that our theoretical explorations
might be too dry or even somewhat boring if they were not supplemented by some considerations on a less abstract level. Second, we
think that the controversy around the mysterious relations between
the 'objective' structural dimension and 'subjective' cognitive one
is somewhat exaggerated by contemporary sociology. There are, in
fact, many concepts which cannot be understood at all if they are
confined to a one-dimensional perspective (for instance, 'objective'
or 'subjective' one). Indeed, most of the recognized perspectives
are not of this nature at all (contrary to the wishes and imputations
of their opponents). For example, the marxist sociology does not
exclude consciousness, and symbolic interactionism surely does not
ignore the 'objective' social reality. They both attempt to elaborate
dialectical vision allowing for theoretical reconciliation of
contradictions.

Thus, in the second part of the book we try to discuss, redefine
and indeed propose some of the concepts which are relevant from
the point of view of the controversy mentioned above. They seek to
grasp both dimensions in some unique points of their inevitable
convergence. They show clearly that despite the spurious battles
between the various perspectives the sociological concepts refuse to
be confined to any narrowly defined, antagonistic camps. Having

2

stated that, we should emphasize that this spontaneous vivacity of the sociological concepts cannot be authentically beneficial if it is not curbed by the conscious development of the 'multi-dimensional sociology'. Its body of concepts may evolve into something more than a simple collection of concepts developed within the separate perspectives. It should eventually take the shape of a network of dialectical concepts which would be fed by the knowledge generated by various theoretical approaches. Naturally, these concepts would incorporate the unresolved dilemmas and mysteries of the ontological and epistemological nature. They would not settle them. They would simply reveal the unpretentious realism of the appreciation of the mysterious and intricate nature of the social world.

The final part of the book contains some reflections on the nature of links between social thought and social practice. This extremely complex area is approached from several angles but the outcome is far from satisfying. It seems that a fuller development of the 'multi-dimensional' sociological quest is the necessary condition for more mature progress in this domain. Nevertheless, independently of the level of advancement of theoretical sociology, there is and always will be a political and moral aspect which intimidates the development of the practice-oriented sociology. It is mainly this dimension which attracts most of our attention in the third part of the book.

There are still several remarks (or warnings) to be made. The book has been written by two Polish sociologists who did not want to shy away from their direct experience in that particular country. Nor did they wish to undermine the unique and rich body of the Polish sociological literature (unfortunately largely unknown outside). Thus the reader has to expect quite frequent references to the Polish sociological researches as well as to more intuitive insights into the texture of that society.

With such an enormous task as this, one has arbitrarily to limit and select the material to be systematically scrutinized. Having decided to discuss several influential theoretical perspectives, we certainly could not discuss in any detail works of particular authors. Thus it may disappoint some that the great masters of sociology - Durkheim, Weber, Parsons and so forth - are only briefly mentioned. We believe, however, that the amount of written work focused on their theoretical systems justifies the assumption that the reader is fairly familiar with their thoughts.

A last remark which remains to be made is the obvious fact that one author's thoughts are not always consistent with those of the other. Indeed, the probability of inconsistencies, disagreements and divergent commitments is significantly increased in the case of

co-authorship. We realize that we have not fully succeeded in compelling each other to give up personal views and style for the sake of
the coherence of the book. In fact, the measure of disagreement
between us may offer the reader a choice of opinions and it confirms our conviction that no single study of sociology can be a
simple, coherent answer to all problems.

M.Ł.
A.P.

Part one

Sociological schools

1 General systems theory: its implications for sociology

Maria Łoś

> . . . we always pay for generality by sacrificing content, and all we can say about practically everything is almost nothing. Somewhere however between the specific that has no meaning and the general that has no content there must be, for each purpose and at each level of abstraction, an optimum degree of generality.
>
> Kenneth E. Boulding (1968)

In considerations of the main trends of theoretical sociology it is difficult to omit theories which lend sociologists a certain perspective and theoretical framework without being sociological theories *sensu stricto*. These are formal theories which assume a certain theoretical form in which are denoted the various contents of different scientific disciplines. To such theories may be reckoned structuralism and the general systems theory. The latter classifies systems according to their organizational principles and systematizes the laws governing the behaviour and the processes of development of given types of systems. The development of this theory constituted a reaction to narrow specialization and lack of a flow of information between disciplines hedged off from others by their hermetic semantics and specific methodology. It opposed the growing isolation of individual fields of knowledge leading to squandering scientific discoveries, to doubled efforts, to failure to draw useful inspiration from the investigations of varied phenomena and to neglecting the rules of analogy where its application may be justified. According to one of its co-creators and propagators, the general systems theory holds the 'promise of re-establishing holistic approaches to knowledge without abandoning scientific rigor' (Rapoport, 1968, xxi).

The ideas of the biologist Ludwig von Bertalanffy (see Bertalanffy, 1950, 1951, 1952, 1962, 1968), coupled with simultaneously developing cybernetics, the theory of information, the game theory, the decision-making theory, constitute the basis of the so-called contemporary systems theory which has gained many adherents, continuators and popularizers. In Bertalanffy's conception, the systems theory is a basic science the counterparts of which in the field of applied science are: system engineering (scientific planning, designing, assessment and construction of systems composed of people and machines), operative research (scientific control of existing systems composed of people and machines, materials, etc.), human engineering (the scientific adaptation of systems, mainly of machines, in order to attain maximum output with the minimum financial expenditures and other input), etc. At present the systems theory has found vast application in the management of complex organizations. An extensive literature has made many-sided analyses – with different degrees of formalization – of the conditions for the effectiveness of system management. However, in accordance with the theoretical aim of this part of the book the present considerations omit the questions connected with the systems theory as an applied science and focus only on certain of its general theoretical assumptions and on some of its implications for the development of theory in sociology.

Two main currents may be distinguished in the orientation of the general systems theory:

(1) Analysis of various types of phenomena which would help to grasp more general phenomena to be found in different fields and the construction of a general theoretical model adequate for the description of these phenomena (e.g. models of the individual's – or unit's – interaction with its environment, applicable in natural, physical, geological, social research, etc.).

(2) Attempts at the hierarchical ordering of various empirical fields according to the organizational complexity of their basic units or their modes of behaviour as well as attempts to determine the level of generalization appropriate for their analysis. There are thus distinguished:

(a) the static level – the 'geography' and 'anatomy' of the given field;

(b) the simple dynamic system, symbolically comparable to the 'clock' (e.g. Leibniz's monads) – completely foreseeable, homogeneous, ordered functioning;

(c) control mechanisms or the cybernetic system, symbolically comparable to a 'thermostat', in which equilibrium is not a constant, invariable state like the movement of a watch, but a state attained by adjusting mechanisms put into motion in situations of changed conditions;

(d) an open or self-regulating system, symbolically comparable to a 'cell', which retains its distinctness (individuality) and reproductive capacity despite its organic and indispensable link with the external world;

(e) the genetico-social level, symbolically comparable to a 'plant', characterized by the division of labour between cells and the existence of a 'society of cells' composed of differentiated and interrelated parts;

(f)   the 'animal' level characterized by higher and greater mobility, purposeful behaviour and self-consciousness. On this level appear developed receptors of information leading to a tremendous growth of the volume of received information and an internally developed system of the transmission and organization of information;

(g)   the 'human' level conceiving every human being as a discrete system. On this level appears self-awareness of a higher order, or awareness of self-consciousness – associated with the development of language, reception and interpretation of symbols (as distinct signs characteristic of the animal level). There appears also the awareness of time, processes, relations, etc.;

(h)   the level of social organization, the basic components of which are not individuals (people) but their social roles, or those aspects of the individual which are essential to the given organized social situation;

(i)   transcendental systems – pertaining to certain ultimate, absolute, unknowable phenomena, etc. (Boulding, 1968, pp. 5–10).

In Boulding's opinion,

> The General Systems Theory is the skeleton of science in the sense that it aims to provide a framework or structure of systems on which to hang the flesh and blood of particular disciplines and particular subject matters in an orderly and coherent corpus of knowledge (Boulding, 1968, p. 10).

It seems that the *skeleton* stimulates the development of science primarily by making us aware of its underdevelopment. Thus an analysis of many psychological conceptions (some versions of the learning theory, for example) may easily lead to the conclusion that they are rather adequate for systems of a lower order (the cell system, for instance) than for the human or social level – just as many sociological theories have adequate relevance to phenomena of the genetico-social level, or even the static level, rather than the level of social organization.

Another merit of the systems theory is that it shifted the accent from the static description of structures to the analysis of processes and change. This was of great significance to sociological research, for it suggested the conception of society as a complex, multi-aspected, changing whole based on co-operation and antagonism, on association and dissociation. 'The "structure" is an abstract construct, not something distinct from the ongoing interactive process but rather a temporary, accommodative representation of it at any one time' (Buckley, 1967, p. 18).

On the basis of the above assumptions one may criticize sociological theories which are built around the notion of social system's tendency to maintain a state of equilibrium ('social consensus' theories) as well as the psychological theories which treat the need to reduce tension as a main determinant of behaviour. Referring to the above distinctions, it may be said that those theories accept the principle of the 'thermostat' as being characteristic of complex human societies. There are many - quite unacceptable with respect to the social systems - consequences of such an assumption. According to Deutsch, for example, a social system is in a state of equilibrium when:

(1) it returns to the starting-point in case of some perturbation,
(2) all perturbations originate outside the system,
(3) the stronger the perturbance the greater is the force displayed by the system in the effort to restore the previous state,
(4) whatever the rate of change calculated to restore a previous state, it does not cause any tension, complications or new perturbations (see Deutsch, 1951).

Many authors have noted the great significance to sociological considerations of such concepts as feed-back loop or return information mechanisms - key concepts of contemporary systems theory. They help to perceive social processes in a more realistic way, and to recognize the important consequences of processes of reaction and adaptation for further complication of the conditions which stimulated them in the first place. It is an attempt to decipher the play between the changing and the changed, their mutual inter-actions and enforcement.

One example of the interpretation of social processes by means of the feed-back concept is the conception of deviance which was proposed by Wilkins (1964). It conceives social control as processes stimulating both conformist and order as well as deviance and disorder. And it broadens that concept by also including among their designates interactions between those which interpret them in various ways. These interactions may contribute to strenghtening conformist and deviance, which in turn may either maintain the prevailing normative order or influence its modification.

Deviance is a systemic product generated out of a network of ongoing events or processes that involve the historically

generated institutional and cultural structure, with its vested
interests and 'moral entrepreneurs'; the matrix of
interpersonal transactions within this structure whereby the
strains of everyday role-playing generate adjustments,
bargainings, and random or trial deviations which, in a
context of 'societal reactions', may lead to a 'labelling' and
consequent definition of the self as deviant; the resultant build
up of career deviant – whether aggregates of the mentally ill or
the unusually creative, subcultures of the alienated or of
political activists, or formal organizations of criminals; and
finally, the feedback of the reactions of these groups, directly
and indirectly, into the sociocultural structure, to contribute
to its elaboration or disintegration (Buckley, 1967, pp. 167-8).

The feed-back problem is directly associated with that of the so-
called open systems. Societies – though it is often obscured by
simplified analysis – are open systems and only by considering the
consequences of this fact is it possible to apply to them laws and
methods worked out by contemporary systems theory. Open
systems were characterized by Buckley as follows:
(1) their characteristic features depend on certain internal para-
    meters and variable criteria maintained within certain given
    limits;
(2) their organization develops as selective responsiveness, or
    patterns of relations to things and events in the environment
    which are essential from the viewpoint of the above criteria;
(3) their receptive apparatuses are able to apprehend all deviations
    from the system's internal order;
(4) the feed-back mechanism guarantees that information received
    by the receptive apparatus is transmitted to behaviour directing
    centres which are able to react in the direction of reduction of
    deviations (in the case of negative effects) or of their reinforce-
    ment (in the case of positive effects) (see Buckley, 1967, p. 53).
These seem to be minimal conditions met also by much simpler
systems than social organizations. The further distinction of open
systems (sometimes made) into goal-*oriented* systems and systems
directed by goals may prove useful. The former are characterized
by a certain automatism and a mechanism of adaptation to the
take-off programme. The latter – in which is also reckoned society –
are in a position to modify their goals and manner of their realization in the event of changing conditions: tensions, crises, etc. Their
development does not depend on some original, starting-point plan
prepared in advance. It regrettably appears that systems theory is
not quite adequate while applied to such complicated systems, with
so many unknowns and such a complex course of collisions of

manifold, often accidental, factors. Nor are the tools of analysis – provided by cybernetics, game theory or theory of information – really applicable in this context.

The quest of development phases for systems of various types (or systems of one type), characteristic of systems theory, also had its essential consequences for the development of certain directions of sociological research. By way of example may be mentioned the theory of needs (see Maslow, also Kocowski, 1973, 1975), the theory of the evolution of societies (Sorokin or Moore), the theory of the basic mechanisms conditioning the stability of societies (Parsons or Homans). These theories have had tremendous influence on the interpretation of social phenomena on various levels. We may also mention in this context other conceptions frequently appearing in various fields of sociology such as: the so-called natural histories of various phenomena – for instance social problems, economic cycles, institutionalization processes, processes of accumulation of knowledge, etc. The conception of the purposeful (useful for action) accumulation of knowledge, proposed by Campbell (1959), may serve as an example. Besides the processes of adaptation and biological selection, Campbell distinguishes the following higher levels of knowledge:

(1) the method of trial and error,
(2) learning – or utilizing the effects of the first method to familiar situations,
(3) perception – the visual investigation of potential alternative actions,
(4) observational learning – based on observing attempts and results of action by others,
(5) imitation – the observation and imitation of the behaviour of others,
(6) verbal instruction – reception of verbal information from others,
(7) thought – symbolic confrontation of possible behaviour with an adopted model of reality,
(8) collective decision-making on the basis of observation of reality made by many people under the same conditions.

That approach is of course associated with the widely developed subject-matter of the circulation and social distribution of information and the selectivity of its receptors in social organizations. This conception appears in an intuitive phenomenological version (see Schutz's theory of structure of knowledge, 1970), in positivist empirical sociology, as well as in the shape of extremely formalized mathematical models. Equally important from the viewpoint of general systems orientation are the conceptions of the flow and utilization of energy within and between systems (see, for instance,

a sociological analysis of this phenomenon as applying to the industrial organizations – Matejko, 1968).

A frequently cited example of certain basic assumptions of contemporary systems theory (particularly cybernetics) is Mead's symbolic interactionism. The best interpretation, from the viewpoint of its importance for systems analysis in sociology, was made by Tamotsu Shibutani. 'Behaviour is seen not as response to stimulation, as relief from tension, nor as the accomplishment of symbolized intent; it is something that is constructed in a succession of self-correcting adjustments to changing life conditions' (Shibutani, 1968, p. 331).

To understand that conception it is necessary to investigate the pertinent meaning of such concepts as 'temporariness', the 'current time' or the 'change'. It is also necessary to regard behaviour as a category which cannot be isolated from some more general process. One of its aspects is perception. Mead emphasizes that not all objects and occurrences in the individual's environment are encompassed in perception, but he is sensitive only to the reception of those signals which are essential to immediate or planned action. The meanings he attaches to the things are not latent in the things themselves, but are characteristic of the relations between the individual and those things because of given aims. The aims may be those of individuals, but they are as a rule modified or stimulated by group aims; gratification associated with the attainment of aims is also primarily of an interpersonal character. Aim attainment is made possible by feed-back processes, particularly in the spheres of thought and symbolic interaction. The feed-back is expressed in the fact that an individual's behaviour is associated with its experience and world view and the effects of that behaviour influence further activity. Thinking enables one to envision probing for and testing the best solutions. Symbolic interaction shapes the individual's social ego, which owing to the ability of conscious interaction with tself is in a position to link the opinions, reactions and image of cthers in the modification of his autoperception, which is in turn of essential significance to further behaviour. This conception undoubtedly depicts quite accurately the character of interpersonal control and the flow of information in a system of such a unique level of complication as human organization.

It is difficult to make a convincing synthesis and to evaluate contemporary systems theory by only signalizing some problems and threads of sociological quests developed under its influence. It seems to be rather a certain way of thinking linked with a given conceptual web and methodological preferences than a theory or a scientific school. It should be stressed that the general philosophical principles at the foundation of this current may lead to highly varied, often contradictory interpretations of the social reality (e.g. the marxist theory and Parsons's theory). Acceptance of its general methodological guidelines may similarly lead to departing far from that current's philosophical and epistemological foundations (by reducing complicated systems to excessively simplified models of a lower level, by developing static structural models instead of models of processes, or carrying to absurdity the use of specialized and hermetic language, in quests conducted under a common denomination). It may hence be in place to indicate – after Buckley (1967, p. 39) – the possible benefits of applying the systems approach in the social sciences:

(1) a common terminology unifying several behavioural disciplines;
(2) a technique of investigation of large and complex organizations;
(3) a synthetic approach excluding fragmentary analysis in view of the internal links between the parts which cannot be investigated outside the context of the whole;
(4) a viewpoint enabling one to analyse basic sociological problems, i.e. to investigate socio-cultural systems in terms of the transmission of information and course of communications;
(5) the investigation of *relations* rather than of *entities*, with emphasis on process and the probability of change;
(6) possibility of operative, objective, not anthropomorphic investigation of goal-orientation and goal-oriented systems of behaviour, symbolic cognitive processes, social consciousness, self-consciousness, socio-cultural states of emergency, etc.

Sociology does not seem to have fully utilized the possibilities latent in contemporary systems theory. But this is partly due to the fact that an abstract formal theory does not provide any particular indicators of how to penetrate complex human society, realizing all its general postulates.

It should be noted that in spite of the general systems theory's potential applicability to (and compatibility with) various orientations in social sciences, its influence upon the functionalist sociology was probably the most remarkable. It stimulated and inspired the functionalist insight into the nature of society, contributing greatly to the perfection of its methodology. However, its misleading, one-sided interpretation was also used as a support for the functionalist ideology and, in fact, contributed significantly to the domination of 'system paradigm' in sociology. It may be argued that its more adequate and sensitive understanding would rather lead to an earlier appreciation of the change and conflict dimension.

Naturally, the general systems theory's stress on analogy as well as its assumption of similarity of various aspects of different systems may suggest that the positivist methodology constitutes the only approach compatible with it. It seems, however, that the 'analogy' assumption does not necessarily result from the postulate of unity of methods. If properly interpreted, the general systems theory could probably help to develop a sociology which would combine the uniqueness of its method of studying society with a 'global' perspective, unifying social systems with the 'non-social' rest of the world.

Bibliography

Bertalanffy, Ludwig von (1950), 'The Theory of Open Systems in Physics and Biology', *Science*, no. 3.

Bertalanffy, Ludwig von (1951), 'Problems of General System Theory', *Human Biology*, vol. 23.

Bertalanffy, Ludwig von (1952), *Problems of Life: An Evaluation of Modern Biological Thought*, New York: Wiley.

Bertalanffy, Ludwig von (1962), 'General System Theory - A Critical Review', *General Systems, Yearbook of the Society for General Systems Research*, vol. 7.

Bertalanffy, Ludwig von (1968), *General Systems Theory: Foundations, Development, Applications*, New York: Braziller.

Boulding, Kenneth E. (1968), 'General Systems Theory - The Skeleton of Science', in Buckley (1968), pp. 3–11.

Buckley, Walter (1967), *Sociology and Modern Systems Theory*, Englewood Cliffs, N.J.: Prentice-Hall.

Buckley, Walter (1968) (ed.), *Modern Systems Research for the Behavioural Scientist*, Chicago: Aldine.

Campbell, Donald T. (1959), 'Methodological Suggestions from a Comparative Psychology of Knowledge Processes', *Inquiry*, no. 2.

Deutsch, Karl W. (1951), 'Mechanism, Teleology and Mind', *Philosophy and Phenomenological Research*, no. 12.

Kocowski, Tomasz (1973), 'A System Theory of Human Needs and Sociotechnics', report at the First Conference of the Research Committee on Sociotechnics, I.S.A., Loughborough.

Kocowski, Tomasz (1975), 'Needs and Hierarchies of Personal Values', Wroclaw: The Prognostic Research Centre of Wroclaw Polytechnique, Communication no. 73.

Matejko, Aleksander (1968), 'Przydatność socjotechniczna analizy strukturalno-funkcjonalnej zakladu pracy' ('The Suitability of Sociotechnical Structural-Functional Analysis of a Production Plant'), in A. Podgórecki (ed.), *Socjotechnika: Praktyczne Zastosowania Socjologii (Sociotechnics: Practical Application of Sociology)*, Warsaw: Książka i Wiedza.

Rapoport, Anatol (1968), Foreword to Buckley (1968).

Schutz, Alfred (1970), *On Phenomenology and Social Relations* (ed. H. R. Wagner), Chicago and London: University of Chicago Press.

Shibutani, Tamotsu (1968), 'A Cybernetic Approach to Motivation', in Buckley (1968).

Wilkins, Leslie T. (1964), *Social Deviance*, Englewood Cliffs, N.J.: Prentice-Hall.

2 Functionalism
Adam Podgórecki

> The trouble with functional theory is not that it is false, but
> that it is simply not theory.
>
> George C. Homans

Semantic introduction

Devastating harm was done to the 'functional method'. It seems
that now is the proper time to give 'the honours' back to it and try
to explain the roots of existing misunderstandings. In short – one
should not simply blame 'functional method' for not fulfilling
improperly directed expectations which have been orientated
towards it. Additionally, one should not attribute to this method
ideas which did not originally belong to it. Nevertheless, before
such an attempt at 'rehabilitation' is presented it might be useful to
recall the main features of this method.

The so-called theory of functionalism is defined in various ways.
It is sometimes called 'functionalism' or 'structural functionalism'
and at times 'functional orientation' or 'functional approach'.[1]

The term 'function', basic to that sociological trend, has many
meanings. H. Stasiak distinguishes the following ones:

> First, all authors cited by us define function as a given effect
> or as a process of activity with precisely that effect. . . .
> Secondly, that effect is considered in relation to the frame of
> reference regarded as a 'whole', a 'system', sometimes as a
> 'structure', explicitly or in the social conjecture. . . . Thirdly,
> that effect is considered in respect of the given state of the
> given system or of the given process transpiring in that
> system. . . . Fourthly, some authors clearly assert that the
> positive effect in relation to the given state (process) of the
> system must be evoked by an element of that particular
> system (Stasiak, 1964, pp. 247–8).

It seems to be advisable – in order to assess properly the potential
of the functional method – to detach it from those elements which

have been, apparently for accidental though important reasons, artificially associated with it. Therefore it might be useful to analyse to what extent the link between the functional method and the structural approach is justified.

It should be made clear that the structural approach (which is different from structuralism) deals, in principle, with the social type of structure which is supposed to exist in the given society. This type of approach is interested mainly in the substantive characteristics of the social system in question. This type of approach may imply that the given social system is characterized by social 'equilibrium'. It may additionally specify the essential features of equilibrium of the given type. It also may ascertain that the social equilibrium (as such) constitutes the basic feature of all possible social systems, etc. Although it is disputable to which extent these assumptions are, indeed, supported by the testable data, nevertheless, it seems to be clear enough that they belong to a methodologically different category. Thus, functional method should not be 'victimized' when those assumptions appear not to be well grounded, for their implications, as was stated, are of an entirely different logical category.

Nevertheless more detailed considerations concerning the different meaning of the concept 'function' and its possible application are needed before one may, in a legitimized way, secure a divorce between functional method and structured approach.

The term 'function' is thus ambiguous, and that influences its multi-form uses in the functional trend. And all the more so, since such phrases are used as functional method, as conceptual networks of a functional character or functional theory. The multiplicity of its meanings necessitates an additional - taken from the well known authority in the field - semantic analysis of the term 'function'.

According to E. Nagel, that term may have six meanings: (1) To state a relation or correlation between a certain number of variable elements ('variables') which may be measurable or not measurable. (2) The term 'function' is used to designate a complex of processes occurring within some whole (or the action of that whole), regardless of the effects exerted on that whole or on some other whole. (3) The term signifies a 'living function', hence complex types of processes transpiring in living organisms (the term has been used in this meaning by biologists). (4) It is used to signify the given commonly known utilization or application of some object or the generally expected effect of its utilization. (5) The term 'function' is used to indicate the more or less broad range of consequences evoked by a given thing or action from the viewpoint of the 'total system' of which the given thing or activity is a part. (6)

The term designates the contribution of a given object or activity (or the potential contribution) to maintaining the properties or state of affairs of a given system (see Nagel, 1961, pp. 522-6).

The above review of the meanings associated with the term 'function' also indicates how variously it could have been used when the functional trend in sociology was in bud. The anthropologists B. Malinowski and A. R. Radcliffe-Brown are considered the fathers of the functionalist conception in the social sciences. E. Durkheim may also to some extent be considered its precursor. He wrote in 1919:

> When, then the explanation of social phenomena is undertaken, we must seek separately the efficient cause which produces it and the function it fulfils. We use the word 'function' in preference to 'end' or 'purpose' precisely because social phenomena do not generally exist for the useful results they produce. We must determine whether there is a correspondence between the fact under consideration and the general needs of the social organisation, and in what this correspondence consists, without occupying oneself with whether it has been intentional or not. All these questions are too subjective to allow of scientific treatment (Durkheim, 1938, p. 95).

Despite certain threads of functionalism in Durkheim's works, Malinowski and Radcliffe-Brown are regarded as the most conscious creators of functionalism. Here are their standard formulations:

Malinowski asserted that the functional analysis of culture

> aims at the explanation of anthropological facts at all levels of development by their function, by the part which they play within the integral system of culture, by the manner in which they are related to each other within the system, and by the manner in which this system is related to the physical surroundings. . . . The functional view of culture insists therefore upon the principle that in every type of civilization, every custom, material object, idea and belief fulfills some vital function, has some task to accomplish, represents an indispensable part within a working whole (Malinowski, 1936, pp. 132-3).

Following are basic statements of Radcliffe-Brown:

> To turn from organic life to social life, if we examine such a community as an African or Australian tribe we can recognize the existence of a social structure. Individual human beings,

19

the essential units in this instance, are connected by a definite set of social relations into an integrated whole. The continuity of the social structure, like that of an organic structure, is not destroyed by changes in the units. Individuals may leave the society, by death or otherwise; others may enter it. The continuity of structure is maintained by the process of social life, which consists of the activities and inter-actions of the individual human beings and of the organized groups into which they are united. The social life of the community is here defined as the 'functioning' of the social structure. The function of any recurrent activity, such as the punishment of a crime, or a funeral ceremony, is the part it plays in the social life as a whole and therefore the contribution it makes to the maintenance of the structural continuity (Radcliffe-Brown, 1952, pp. 179-80).

The ideas formulated above were accepted by many anthropologists and sociologists. A number of works appeared representing that trend. R. Merton and T. Parsons are at present regarded as the principal representatives of structural-functional analysis in sociology. But the conceptions of these two scholars pertaining to functionalism should be treated separately. While Merton placed the main emphasis on a developed functional methodology which could serve as an efficient tool for various middle-range inquiries, Parsons applied methods of functional analyses to the investigation of social structures in general or of various elements of concrete social structures (e.g. Germany, Japan, USA). This is the neglected face of T. Parsons.

Merton worked out the most developed pattern (paradigm) of functional analysis. Although it is functional analysis in its fullest conception, that paradigm is relatively little known and is consciously used only in a distorted manner. It consists of eleven elements and its canons are the following:

(1) A phenomenon to which some function is attributed ought to be accurately designated. The basic question is: Which data should enter the focus of observation in order to be submitted to systematic functional analysis in connection with the designated phenomenon?

(2) Conceptions pertaining to subjective dispositions (motives, aims). The basic question is: What types of analyses provide an adequate foundation to treat the observed motivation, which data and what types of motivation ought to be regarded as problematical - as deriving from other data?

(3) Conceptions pertaining to objective consequences (function, dysfunction). The basic question is: What are the effects of the

conversion of functions previously regarded as concealed (concealed functions - those unintended nor initially recognized as the effects of activity) into avowed and open functions?

(4) Conceptions pertaining to the determination of elements aiding the cognition of given functions.

(5) Conceptions regarding functional requirements (needs). The basic question is: What is necessary to establish the importance of such a variable (functionally) as requirements (claims, demands) in situations where it is practically impossible to apply scientific experiments?

(6) Conceptions pertaining to the mechanisms by means of which functions are materialized. The basic question is: Is it already possible to make an inventory of social mechanisms on the model of the catalogue of psychological mechanisms?

(7) Conceptions pertaining to functional alternatives (equivalent functions of substitutes). The basic question is: Since scientifically investigated equivalents of given functions would require precise experimental investigations and since such research is very difficult in various macro-situations, what practical research procedure is applicable here?

(8) Conceptions pertaining to the structural context (or structural limitations). The basic question is: To what extent does the given structural context limit the range of possibilities of analysis of the phenomenon (problems) which could fulfil the functional requirements?

(9) Conceptions pertaining to social changes and their dynamics. The basic question is: Whether the excessive interest devoted by functional analysers to social equilibrium does not distract their attention from problems connected with the lack of social equilibrium?

(10) Problems associated with the general evaluation of functional analysis. The basic question is: To what degree is functional analysis cognitively limited by difficulties in the choice of adequate samples of social systems which could be the subject of comparative research?

(11) Problems associated with the ideological implications of functional analysis. The basic question is: How do we establish the ideological colouring of the effects of functional analysis and to what extent is the given ideology derived from the basic principles otherwise acknowledged by the given sociologist? (See Merton, 1967, pp. 50-4.)

The above complicated Mertonian paradigm is presented in a simplified but didactically lucid manner by P. Sztompka.

Let us try to formulate, for example, several such rules. The most general – if not the basic – directive of the functional trend could be expressed as follows: if you wish to find an explanation for a given social phenomenon look for the function it fulfills in the broader social or cultural context. A more particular rule suggested by the famous Mertonian distinction between open and concealed functions may be put as follows: if you wish to find an explanation for a given social phenomenon seek not only those of its effects which are intended and perceivable, but also – perhaps even first of all – side effects, unanticipated. Another rule of this type, formulated on the basis of counter-posing function and dysfunction, may be expressed thus: if you wish to find an explanation for some given social phenomenon seek not only that phenomenon's positive effects on the social or cultural system, but also its negative consequences (Sztompka, 1972, pp. 276–7).

Three examples

On the whole, functional analysis is a valuable general directive applicable in research on various problems of the social sciences. Below are three examples of application of that type of analysis. They pertain to incest, the so-called 'second life' and some problems of social stratification.

Example 1

The interesting research of G. Murdock, based on data collected in 250 different communities (mostly primitive societies), enabled the following generalizations with reference to incest: (1) prohibition of sexual intercourse between mother and son, father and daughter as well as between siblings (the nuclear family) is obligatory in all investigated societies; (2) as concerns the family broader than the nuclear, the prohibition of incest is obligatory on a varying scale; (3) prohibition of incest is nowhere limited to the nuclear family, but also applies to the broader family; (4) the prohibition is associated with particularly strong emotional and social reactions; (5) prohibition of incest is the most universal social norm acknowledged in varied societies (see Murdock, 1949).

There are various hypotheses interpreting the 'taboo' of incest. According to one interpretation, this prohibition stems from biological considerations: the offspring from incestuous relations are supposed to be subject to various biological defects, which are explicable by the accumulation of disease susceptibility among biologically related individuals. Another attempted interpretation is to the effect that failure to prohibit incest would militate against the diffusion of technical and organizational innovations carried over from one environment to another. This essentially means that if incest were not prohibited families maintaining sexual relations within their own circles would not tend to establish contact with members of other families and would thus be unable to transmit their experience or become acquainted with the innovative ideas of others. Hypotheses pertaining to the dissemination of information undoubtedly belong to those which genetically derive from the inspiration of functional analysis. However, the most probable interpretation – also of a functional character – is the role, the function, which the prohibition of incest plays within the nuclear family (or the family approximating it). Evidently, if incest were not prohibited, unions could arise within the nuclear family between father and daughter, mother and son, or among siblings. Such unions would run counter to parental authority, the basic element of children's socialization in the family. Parental authority transmits the cultural values absorbed from the broader environment to the new generation. Lack of incest prohibition would thus infringe upon that basic social function which is in the interest of the entire society, of which the family is the principal element.

Example 2

Various sociological researches have disclosed that some educational or corrective institutions are endangered by certain elements of the so-called 'second life'. What characterizes this 'second life' was at first unknown. The educators and teachers in these educational or corrective institutions possessed only fragmentary, incomplete and haphazard knowledge about this phenomenon. Sociological research disclosed that where such a 'second life' existed, the lives of those incarcerated in such institutions are split into two basic realms: (1) an official life associated with school activity, activity controlled by guardians, and (2) a closed life, governed by its own specific laws. The essence of that 'second life' in the Polish institutions consists of the inmates' particular stratification which is basically reducible to 'people' and 'suckers'. The former are equals and differ only in the degree of acceptance of the patterns of behaviour in relation to the second life ritual. The latter are 'dirty' individuals with whom no physical contact (except instrumental-homosexual) or social contact is maintained. The 'people' are independent and dominate the 'suckers'.

The above is a pretty unique picture of social stratification.

Functional analysis suggested the quest for the 'concealed functions' of that type of stratification. As an interpretive hypothesis of the above phenomenon appeared the idea of 'artificial social stratification'. According to this conception, there is a constant feeling of stress and aggression in the situation of the isolated institution. But the world of people living in that kind of situation is not in a state of ceaseless mutual aggression and continuous chaos. An informal community subject to oppression and frustration also requires a certain order. Mutual aggression hence petrifies according to certain schemes. A structure constituted by a 'second life' comes into existence as the established order. For the 'second life' transforms the mutuality of punishment into a stratified and ordered system of penalty and reward. Relegation into a lower position is a penalty, rising in the hierarchy is a reward. Functional analysis thus discloses that members of isolated institutions bring into being an 'artificial stratification' which enables them to reorder their lives into another disposition of punishment and rewards, a disposition more adequate to the conditions of informal life existing in such institutions (Podgórecki, 1971, pp. 281-302).

Example 3

Functional analysis has occupied itself primarily with problems of social structure. One of the more interesting conceptions in regard to the question of social stratification is that of Davis and Moore. W. Wesołowski made an interesting critical analysis of that conception. He called attention to the fact that the basic elements of social stratification on which Davis and Moore focused, thus narrowing the field of research, are material benefits and prestige. Pointing to the omission of such an important factor as power, Wesołowski stated:

> The same functional aspect or kind of power to be found in industry exists also in the state organism as an administrative organism. It appears in every state, class and classless, democratic and despotic, with slow and rapid rotation of leaders. That functional aspect of government will of course develop in socialist and communist societies as societies of a high degree of organised and planned course of economic and social processes (Wesołowski, 1962, pp. 113-15).

It is possible to quote many other examples which would show the usefulness of functional method. The cases presented above are only intended to make it clear that: (1) the functional method tries to identify those factors which do not manifest themselves easily –

which do not appear on the surface of social life but which usually play strategic roles behind the social scene; (2) this method may be useful to analyse social processes not only on the micro-level but also – and especially – on the macro-level; (3) the cognitive potential of this method is *neutral* – it might serve, in its consequences, as a convenient instrument for strengthening or disrupting existing bonds of the social order, thus to support or unmask the existing establishment. In this context it may be interesting to note that several representatives of Polish marxists adopted the Parsonian approach as a suitable theoretical framework which was supposed to enrich the thin internal structure of marxist world view. Some of these attempts, mainly due to political reasons, were later labelled 'revisionistic'. Some others, nevertheless, became the inherent elements of marxist *Weltanschauung*.

Before this point – that it is essential that one's understanding of functionalism is not distorted – is elaborated more extensively, let us turn to the short presentation of functionalism in its most mature form, to the Parsonian version.

The essence of Parsons's contribution

The conception of structural-functional analysis was further developed by Parsons. Thus he elaborated a number of additional conceptual instruments which served, in his opinion, to present a fuller picture of the investigated society's structure. Among the more essential of these concepts may be reckoned the following five so-called basic dilemmas: (1) affectiveness as against affective neutrality (the actor in public activity may take some action to satisfy his emotional needs or to give them expression – he may be also instrumentally disposed, in particular in relation to given tasks); (2) orientation geared to self-interests or towards interests of others; (3) the universalist as against the particularist attitude (the public actor of a universalist disposition solves problems according to generally accepted standards, while one with a particularist attitude is guided by the interests of the family, a clique, superiors, etc.); (4) quality as against procedure of activity (important in relation to quality is who the actor is, whereas when the procedure of activity is under consideration what counts is how the public actor carries out his activity); (5) specificity as against generality (important in the case of the former is how the actor assumes his role from the viewpoint of his strictly defined position; essential in the case of the latter is how the actor comports himself as a complete person, irrespective of particular roles he may fulfil).

Another of Parsons's conceptions widely applied in the analysis of varied social systems is that of social systems' four basic functions. He distinguishes the following: (1) *Aim determination.* One of the basic functions is that of fixing the aims of the given social system and of successively analysing the means appropriate to their realization. (2) *Adaptation.* The second function of a social system is ever more elastically and efficiently to adjust to external conditions (the environment) and to the system's internal conditions. (3) *Elaboration of standards of activity.* The third function of a social system is to streamline the existing, and innovatively seek out new standards of, individual and collective activity. (4) *Integration.* The fourth basic function of social systems is to integrate their infrastructure in such a manner as to create a state of loyalty and feeling of affiliation between the members of the systems, thus counteracting tendencies of members or parts of the systems to break away.

Parsons's conception of social systems is based on the idea of social equilibrium. He expresses that idea explicitly;

> It is certainly contrary to much of the common sense of the social sciences, but it will nevertheless be assumed that the maintenance of the complementarity of role-expectations, once established, is not *problematical*, in other words, that the tendency to maintain the interaction process is the *first law* of *social process* . . . Another way of stating this is to say that no *special mechanisms* are required for the explanation of the maintenance of complementary interaction-orientation (Parsons, 1951, p. 205).

Discussion and criticism

The above conceptions of Parsons have met with much criticism of late. The critics stress that they exaggerate the roles of stability, harmony and unity of social systems. They reproach Parsons for basing his conceptions on equilibrium and overlooking the role of social or class conflicts. This is associated with the supposition systematically maintained by Parsons that existing social institutions are primarily of a morally benevolent character. He is further accused of an unhistorical approach to the problems of analysis of social systems and of his conceptions having a conservative colouring, since he separates institutions from their social milieu and assumes that they are 'natural' and given. It is finally charged that Parsons's theoretical conceptions do not provide an adequate basis for formulating theories of social change (Buckley, 1967; the especially vigorous attack by Gouldner, 1970; Zeitlin, 1973 and others).

M. Ossowska repeatedly criticized functional analysis for its methodological limitations. In her conception, the quest for certain functions of a given social system or of its institutions implies the assumption that these functions satisfy some need. And she pointed many times to the ambiguity of the very conception 'needs' (the ambiguity of the term 'function' was indicated above). Thus in Ossowska's opinion, over-extension of the conception of the term 'need' makes the results of functional analysis banal – in that state of affairs all social institutions or systems satisfy some need. While in its narrow meaning the term 'need' gives rise to various problems in connection with the definitional discord between the terms 'function' and 'need' (Ossowska, 1963, pp. 131-59). Thus, Ossowska's contribution to the general theoretical sociology gives an interesting illustration of what can be gained if general theoretical considerations become more closely connected with a particular subdiscipline of sociology. In this case: sociology of morals.

It may be said in general that functional analysis is in many cases a useful method in the social sciences of conducting research and analysing its findings. But it cannot in any case be maintained that it occupies the rank of theory. For this conception is unable to produce a body of general propositions which would tie into a whole a complex of empirically verified hypotheses pertaining to social systems. Functional analysis essentially developed a world of concepts specific to that method. But in many cases the conceptual network seems to veil the analysed social material. And despite its structuralist intentions, it sometimes treats the conceptual world shaped by it as independent social reality.

'Harm' was inflicted on functional method by two main strokes. The first one consists of treating this method as a theory. Then, by implication, it is supposed to support 'the establishment', 'the system', different types of social reality, etc. Wrong assumptions of this type give leeway to several inferences which otherwise would be – with more visibility – addressed in a different direction. Although it is true that this method is usually associated with assumptions of this type, nevertheless it is necessary to notice that those assumptions belong to a different sphere of reality: they obviously express certain ideas about the nature of social objects. Functional method in its pure form abstains from making such presumptions. In its proper usage it might be applied only as an instrument designed to analyse social reality, to diagnose it, but not, by any means, to interject into this reality ideas about the character of this reality.

The second stroke, producing more vulnerable effects, is closely linked with the previous one. An assumption that functional method has a conservative nature is, as has already been said, methodologically wrong and misleading, because, by the same token, it could also have several 'progressive' implications. Methods of this type may not only be used to support the existing system or to show in which way certain social, economic or political institutions play the role of strengthening this system (providing policy-makers with the relevant knowledge to utilize those institutions in order to make the system stronger or more resistant to possible changes). It may also be used to show *dysfunctions* in certain social, economic or political institutions – unmasking in this way procedures which otherwise would be unrecognizable or hidden. This unmasking, uncovering role of sociology in general and the functional method in particular seems to be systematically overlooked when they are (and especially the latter) accused of their, presumably, conservative consequences. This point raises separate problems which should be analysed in full independently: sociologies as they exist in different countries have been generated in various social environments. Without any doubt the character of these surroundings does imprint the main ideas of a given sociology in its own peculiar way. In this context it may be worth mentioning that Polish sociology (even if it developed itself later – since 1945 – in a different direction) originally had a critical and unmasking character.

It should be noticed in conclusion that the term 'functional method', in fact, has a different meaning in sociology from its use in other contexts. The term 'method' generally is applied in the social sciences as a systematically repeatable means of enabling data of a given type to be acquired. Without going into a detailed consideration of the differences between methods and techniques, it only needs to be noted that a whole gamut of methods and techniques is constantly used in the social sciences. Among them may be reckoned: the experimental method, the method of participant observation, the technique of statistical analysis, the public opinion poll technique, etc. Nevertheless, the functional method should hence be distinguished from the above, since it is intended to be a method of a higher order – a meta-method. For the functional method shows how to co-ordinate various traditional methods and techniques in order to obtain essential scientific results. It hence constitutes a general orientation, a general directive for fixing the basic direction of research strategy.

In conclusion one may say that the functional method – according to its nature – did not produce, since it was not its design, a body of testifiable empirical propositions. Nor is it supposed to generate a consistent framework of the hypotheses of higher order – hypotheses which would undertake the task of systematization of propositions under question. For its task is complementary – instrumental. Therefore, functional method may only serve as a useful tool to help to discover propositions which have not yet been recognized or which have been hidden until now in a less or more skilful way. Due to its character, this method is constructed to give prescriptions for means of analysing social reality. Those prescriptions have in the most mature way been formulated by Merton.

Nevertheless one may venture a conjecture that functionalism seems to be the final articulation of British Fabianism. It is quite interesting to notice that Fabianism with all its pragmatic devices like summer schools, manifestos, journals devoted to social problems, links with the trade unions, abilities to appeal to public opinion, the establishment of a practically-oriented college (London School of Economics), with all its concern about social justice and social arithmetic, with all its impact on the creation of the Labour Party – was not able to formulate its own social philosophy. Functionalism may be regarded as the kernel of this ideological and social movement. But a separate study should show if this guess is a proper one.

Note

1 Due to several subtle emphases associated with the term 'functionalism' it seems to be advisable to start the analysis of this notion with the exposition of several possible usages. Again, in order to avoid additional problems connected with possible differences in interpretation, it seems to be reasonable to rely mainly on the original quotations adopted from the quoted authors.

Bibliography

Buckley, W. (1967), *Sociology and Modern Systems Theory*, Englewood Cliffs, N.J., Prentice-Hall.

Durkheim, E. (1938), *The Rules of Sociological Method*, University of Chicago Press.

Gouldner, A. (1970), *The Coming Crisis of Western Sociology*, New York: Basic Books.

Malinowski, B. (1936), 'Anthropology', in *Encyclopaedia Britannica*, Suppl. Vol. 1., New York and London.

Merton, R. (1967), *Social Theory and Social Structure*, Chicago: The Free Press.

Murdock, G. (1949), *Social Structure*, New York: Macmillan.

Nagel, E. (1961), *The Structure of Science,* London: Routledge & Kegan Paul.

Ossowska, M. (1963), *Socjologia moralnosci (The Sociology of Morality)* Warsaw: PWN.

Parsons, T. (1951), *The Social Systems*, Chicago: The Free Press.
Podgórecki, A. (1971), *Zarys socjologii prawa (Outline of the Sociology of Law)*, Warsaw: PWN.
Radcliffe-Brown, A. (1952), *Structure and Function in Primitive Society*, London: Cohen & West.
Stasiak, H. (1964), 'Pojecia zwiazane z terminem "funkcja" w socjologii' ('Conceptions Associated with the Term "Function" in Sociology'), *Studia Socjologiczne*, no. 13.
Sztompka, P. (1972), 'Funkcjonalizm socjologiczny/teoria, schemat pojeciowy, metoda' ('Sociological Functionalism/Theory, Conceptual Scheme, Method'), in *Studia z zakresu sociologii, etnografii i historii, ofiarowane Kazimierzowi Dobrowolskiemu (Studies in the Fields of Sociology, Ethnography and History in Honour of Kazimierz Dobrowolski)*, Cracow Literary Publishers.
Wesołowski, W. (1962), 'Funkcjonalna teoria stratyfikacji Davisa i Moore'a' ('The Davis and Moore Functional Theory of Stratification'), *Studia Socjologiczne*, no. 7.
Zeitlin, I. (1973), *Rethinking Sociology*, New York: Appleton-Century-Crofts.

3 Structuralism
Adam Podgórecki

> In rough approximation structure is - a system of changes which, as a system, has its laws (in contrast to the properties of its elements) and it maintains or enriches itself owing to the very play of its transformations; except that the changes do not transcend the boundaries of the system nor do they have to invoke external elements. In a word, structure is of a triple character: a whole, change and self-steering.
>
> Jean Piaget

Structuralism is without doubt one of the most esoteric and flourishing theoretical trends in modern sociology. It is as vague in its origins as in its basic principles. Its central thesis is the idea that essential for social aggregates are not the causal connections operating with them (relations between various variables) but the shaping of various compositions of individual elements and different systems of these elements into certain social wholes.

Structuralism is a multi-aspected trend of thought. The following characterization provides one of the best syntheses of its trends of thought and the propositions they project:[1]

> Structuralism may of course be conceived broadly and narrowly. But if we wanted to define it in a way which would pertain to structural linguistics, the psychology of character and to the anthropology of culture (not cultural anthropology) we would have to establish that structuralism is a standpoint according to which: (1) an investigated object constitutes a certain whole or consists of elements of systems, (2) a whole is not only a combination, a complex of parts, (3) a whole is defined by describing the system of its parts, apprehension of the parts is acquired by relating them to the whole (or in the mereological conception - in reference to the other parts involved), (4) the development of something should be investigated (explained) by considering the structures of its developmental phases, (5) the ultimate meaning of anything is designated by its place (role) in a given system, in a certain whole, (6) sometimes that which renders meaning is concealed, unconscious (Stepień, 1971, p. 578).

Structuralism is a relatively young trend of thought. *Panorama of Contemporary Ideas* - a kaleidoscope of currents of thought - a book which appeared in France in 1957 did not consider structuralism at all. Its origins are traceable to various analyses by psychologists, mathematicians (the so-called Bourbaki school) and linguists. Best known are the relations between the contemporary anthropological structuralism of Lévi-Strauss and various considerations in the sphere of linguistic analysis. But few people remember that the development of structuralism was strictly speaking derived from the formalistic Russian Stylistic School of the early twentieth century (1916–30). Although the original ideas of that school were not uniform and possessed many threads, the intellectual impact of its considerations on various scholars was considerable.

In order to present the basic ideas of structuralism let us use an analogy which may be a clue for grasping structuralism's essential feature.

As in a sonata, one tune may persistently repeat itself in a different scale of tones, so, in a similar manner, structuralism tries to find its way (and recognition) through various already established products of human activities. It tries to gain its identification not so much through the establishment of a set of acceptable (or testable) propositions, but rather through its indirect or even artificial references to previously generated forms of cognitive data. Consequently, structuralism takes as its fabric different areas of cultural or cognitive realities: linguistics, history, anthropology, culture itself, marxism, etc. This being so, let us try to trace those eager attempts to find its own uniqueness. Are they, in its final analysis, successful?

Structuralism versus linguistics and historicism

It might be useful to cite some statements of that school's representatives in order to indicate their varied views and point to their initial ideas which were later developed. R. Jakobson, one of the principal representatives of that school, in earlier years stated: 'We inevitably understand every fact of poetic language against the background of three moments – the prevailing poetic tradition, modern practical language and the future poetic trend opened up by the given fact' (Jakobson, 1921, p. 4). The Russian Stylistic School, which seems to have been the source of inspiration for the development of structuralism, was historically oriented, unlike later structuralism as such:

> Art is an uninterrupted process, therefore its investigation
> not as an historical phenomenon with its own laws of
> development, but as a projection of the individual
> 'temperament' is the same as investigating the problem of

time by means of the dial of a clock (Eichenbaum, 1924, p.
257).

The most extreme and at the same time paradoxical formulation of
some ideas generated by this school was the manifest article of
Opoyazu (Society for Research on Poetical Language, founded in
1916 and in existence until 1930) of 1923:

> The social role of poetry cannot be understood as an analysis
> of its individual characteristics and customs. Indispensable is
> an investigation on a mass scale of all the devices of the
> poetic craft, their differences from the proximate fields of
> human endeavour, of the laws of their historical development.
> Pushkin is not the creator of a school, but its principal
> representative. If there were no Pushkin, *Eugene Onegin*
> would have been written anyway. America would have been
> discovered without Columbus. . . . The poet-craftsman of the
> word serves his class, his social group, with the creative word.
> The reader prompts him what to write about. Poets do not
> think up themes, they cull them from the surrounding
> environment (quoted by Mayenowa, 1970, n. 47).

But the Russian Stylistic School was not entirely uniform in
respect of its historical orientation. Voloshinow, perhaps philo-
sophically its most adroit representative, attempted in 1930 to give
the group the most general orientation. His main propositions
(summarized by M. Mayenowa) are as follows:
(1) every ideology has the character of a symbol;
(2) individual awareness may realize itself and become an actual
    fact only when embodied in sign materials;
(3) a sign is a form of reality common to the individual psyche and
    to ideology (Mayenowa, 1970, p. 50). Chomsky, after
    Voloshinow, developed that idea and made it famous
    (Chomsky, 1957).
Lévi-Strauss, the leading representative of structuralism in the
domain of the social sciences, maintains outright that linguistics is
the model on which the other social sciences ought to base themselves. Linguistics is for him also the main source of inspiration. He
thus states:

> In the complex of social sciences, to which it undoubtedly
> belongs, linguistics occupies an exceptional place; it is not a
> social science like others, but the one which has made the
> greatest progress. It is perhaps the only one which can pretend
> to the status of a scientific approach and which has managed
> to formulate a positive method and at the same time cognize
> the nature of facts analysed by it (Lévi-Strauss, 1968).

Lévi-Strauss not only shows respect for linguistics as a formal science occupied with the internal analysis of its component elements, but also shows disrespect for historical analysis. He considers that various situations in the different historical epochs are characterized – simply and primarily – by varied configurations of given elements, in relation to the current system of elements. Lévi-Strauss furthermore maintains that anthropological research discloses variously disposed systems of elements in different societies investigated today. Thus, in his opinion, diachronic and synchronic analyses are two variants of the more basic analysis, namely structural analysis. He writes:

> The anthropologist respects history, but he does not accord it special value. He conceives it as a study complementary to his own: one of them unfurls the range of human societies in time, the other in space. And the difference is even less great than it might seem, since the historian strives to reconstruct the picture of vanished societies as they were at the points which for them corresponded to the present, while the ethnographer does his best to reconstruct the historical stages which temporally preceded their existing form (Lévi-Strauss, 1974, p. 256).

Emphasizing the disposition (structure) of elements within a given distinct whole, Lévi-Strauss does not attach particular importance to casual analysis of social phenomena. He consistently attacks functionalism as a trend which aims to seek out various social variables. He criticizes the application of functionalism in various situations and charges it with the danger of banality. He cites Boas's view that there is always the danger of broad generalizations deduced from an investigation of cultural integration turning out commonplaces. And he continues sarcastically:

> But what have we learned about the 'institution of gardening' when we are told that it is 'universally found wherever the environment is favourable to the cultivation of the soil and the level of culture sufficiently high to allow it'? Or about the outrigger canoe, its multiple forms, and its peculiar distribution, when it is defined as a canoe whose 'arrangement creates stability, seaworthiness and manageability, considering the limitations in material and in technical handicraft of the oceanic cultures' (Lévi-Strauss, 1968, p. 13).

In analysing relations between the members of various societies, the symbols and languages they use, Lévi-Strauss carefully avoids generalizations which would directly reveal his philosophical and methodological principles. His few remarks pertaining to general premises formulate only some normative, wishful-thinking, trivial postulates. He writes:

> Finally, I would say that between culture and language there cannot be *no* relations at all, and there cannot be 100 per cent correlations either. Both situations are impossible to conceive. So the conclusion which seems to me the most likely is that some kind of correlation exists between certain things on certain levels and our main task is to determine what these things are and what these levels are (Lévi-Strauss, 1968, p. 79).

The above clearly indicates that the author in question is deeply convinced of the unchangeability of the human intellect, regardless of historical and social circumstances. But the above considerations also show that this leading structuralist is - despite his own intentions - really a functionalist when he draws generalizations from his research programme. For he states that it is necessary to grasp 'the unconscious structure latent in each institution and every custom' in order to rightly understand external symbols. Is this not the modified Mertonian question of latent functions?

In his search for basic aprioristic forms which, according to his assumptions, should be materialized in various configurations against the background of varied social contexts, Lévi-Strauss turns - with an intention to elaborate it further - to the principle of mutuality (again a proposition previously formulated by the functionalist Malinowski). The author in question states:

> This approach was fully validated by the demonstration, reached by pure deduction, that the mechanisms of reciprocity known to classical anthropology - namely, those based on dual organization and exchange - marriage between two partners or partners whose number is a multiple of two - are but a special instance of a wider kind of reciprocity between any number of partners (Lévi-Strauss, 1968, p. 60).

E. Leach, perhaps the best authority on Lévi-Strauss's structuralism, thus applies his conception of mutuality to explain Lévi-Strauss's other propositions pertaining to the stability of political systems which among primitive people is supposed to depend on 'the sustained continuity of affinity between small family groups'. The mutual exchange of women creates this affinity: thus a brother hands over his sisters and a father his daughters. According to that conception, women are regarded as wealth of a very high, if not the highest, rank. But if men had to agree to give up their women in order to maintain a stable socio-political structure, then some social device had to compel their agreement to resign their 'natural rights'. Hence exogamy and incest prohibition are basic postulates assuring the stable functioning of the societies concerned (Leach, 1973, p. 65). But the insistent question again appears: even if we accept this peculiar construction which reduces women to the role of property subject to social circulation according to the principle of mutuality, then functionalism reappears immediately, for is not the introduction of the conception of incest prohibition as the explanation of why that kind of property circulation becomes possible the functional principle of applying the conception of incest to disclose its (actual or apparent) hidden functions?

The ambiguity (or, if one wishes, the originality) of Lévi-Strauss's structuralist conceptions is revealed even more glaringly by an analysis of the myth phenomenon treated as a sacral tale. With regard to the riddle of the Sphinx, Lévi-Strauss claims that it is in the nature of things that a mythical riddle should have no answer. It is also in the nature of things that a mother should not marry her own son. Oedipus contradicts nature by answering the riddle; he also contradicts nature by marrying his mother.

Now if we define a mythical riddle as 'a question which postulates that there is no answer' then the converse would be 'an answer for which there was no question'.

In the Oedipus stories disaster ensues because someone answers the unanswerable question; in another class of myths of world-wide distribution, disaster ensues because someone fails to ask the answerable question. Lévi-Strauss cites as examples the death of Buddha because Ananda failed to ask him to remain alive, and the disasters of the Fisher-King which are the consequence of Gawain-Percival's failing to ask about the nature of the Holy Grail.

> This kind of juggling with a generalized formula is quite typical of Lévi-Strauss' hypothesis-forming procedure, but such methods cannot show us the truth; they only lead into a world where all things are possible and nothing sure (Leach, 1973, p. 86).

The structuralists' considerations explain relatively little. The hypotheses concerning public control or social norms of various kinds are pretty abstract. The idea that social compulsion and social norms result from the structural requirements of given social aggregates is nevertheless original. But not all structuralists point to the possible consequences of that thought. As Piaget states:

> If structure is a system of change, which as a whole has its own laws, and the kind of laws which assure it self-control, then various investigations - even the most diverse - pertaining

to society lead to one or another structuralism, since social systems or subsystems impress themselves directly as totalities. This is because these totalities are in turn dynamic and because their self-control is expressed through the particular social fact of the existence of all kinds of compulsion and norms or rules imposed by the social group (Piaget, 1972, p. 126).

Structuralism versus marxism

A comprehensive symbiosis of different 'theoretical' strategies of exploration seems to be quite evident in cases of links between structuralism and marxism. For one may come finally to the conclusion that structuralism does not have its own cognitive merits but that this approach to sociology may be methodologically 'profitable' *only* when combined with another supportive point of view. So, marxism proposes several theoretical hypotheses. They may have some explanatory potential. Nevertheless, the traditional configuration of marxist propositions is built mainly on political grounds. Thus, the general marxist thesis that the 'base' determines the content of 'superstructure' contains a considerable amount of revolutionary force. But this thesis is not necessarily - methodologically and theoretically - correct, though it aims to establish links among different hypotheses on the basis of its political potentialities. For these reasons, structuralism might be indispensable for marxism in an attempt to clarify its theoretical basis. Because in consequence it provides the large (but methodologically disintegrated) body of marxist theoretical propositions with a scheme which tries to put them into a unified framework. This is why Althusser's contribution to marxism seems to be, for many scholars, so attractive and illuminating. If this is the case, then the real contribution to marxist sociology, and not so much to sociology at large, does not comes from its initiator, Lévi-Strauss, but from Althusser. A detailed analysis of this issue concludes:

In a sense, his weakness [Althusser's] is also his strength. He realises many of the most fundamental problems in Marxist theory and tries to overcome them, and that he is not entirely successful in providing alternatives does not mean that he should be rejected. For example, he realises the need for a Theory of theory and of the production of knowledge in historical materialism; his critique of evolutionism and historicism leads him to suggest concepts appropriate to a synchronic analysis, and his rejection of determinism, both economic and idealist, is combined with the beginnings of a much more flexible analysis of the social formation, which conceives of different types of internal relationships between its constituent elements. All concepts used in this: differential experience of time, separate development of elements, dominance levels, instances, relative autonomy, metonymy, weightings, are all of obvious relevance to sociology. From a Marxist point of view, Althusser is to be seen as giving the basis for a philosophical critique of the remaining strands of Hegelism in Marxism, and of continuing Lenin and Gramsci's critique of academicism, determinism and empiricism and presenting an elaborate understanding of the relationship between theoretical and political practice (Glucksmann, 1974, pp. 137–8).

Conclusion

It appears that structuralism is on the whole an attractive conception, but one which has not gone beyond the phase of intellectual ferment. It has thus far been unable to denote its own specific subject-matter. That conception has moreover neither been able to present a stock of propositions or hypotheses of its own nor to propose methods not reducible into other, better known and developed research orientations. It would nevertheless be going too far to maintain that structuralism is only a pretentious, inflated antic. For the idea that the elements of a social whole acquire their specific social sense by the place they occupy in the social structure can – when a synthetic diagnosis or reliable prognosis for sociotechnics is required – indicate new research problems and open up new perspectives. In the present stage of its scientific fructification this idea is the precursor of some meta-method of research which could later emerge from it.

Be that as it may, Runciman's characterization of that trend of thought may serve as the conclusion of general considerations of structuralism. He writes:

> But if my argument is at all well founded, it suggests that 'structuralism' whether in its Anglo-Saxon or Gallic version, should not be claimed to constitute a novel, coherent and comprehensive paradigm for sociological and anthropological theory. . . . I merely have been concerned to suggest that 'structuralist' theory may not be distinctive to quite the degree that is apt to be claimed for it (Runciman, 1970, p. 58).

As a general conclusion one may say that structuralism being not a sociological school in the proper sense (lack of body of systematized propositions) proposes an interesting meta-method which might be utilized to analyse more closely interrelations which take place in the given social entity; being in this way a subsidiary approach, it helps to put together hypotheses already built on the basis of an approach of a different type. Thus structuralism may be especially useful in discovering social distances, positions, replacements, mobilities, diffusions, distortions, and other interplays among many relevant elements which exist in the given society. And since whole societies seem to be the proper subjects of sociological analyses, then structuralism, as a way of introducing some cognitive order into the diagnosis of divergent points of elements of whole entities, may be quite useful as a comprehensive approach to studying societies as a whole.

In conclusion one may regard structuralism as an autotelic exercise in prestidigitation of various elements of social life.

Note

1 As with the case of functionalism, it seems to be advisable to summarize the basic ideas of structuralism in a special way, by relying on original quotations from appropriate authors. This is because the present author regards structuralism as the type of approach to sociology which is blown up out of all proportion.

Bibliography

Althusser, L. (1969), *For Marx* (translated by Ben Brewster), London: Allen Lane, the Penguin Press.

Badcock, C. R. (1975), *Lévi-Strauss, Structuralism and Social Theory*, London: Hutchinson.

Chomsky, N. (1957), *Syntactic Structures*, The Hague: Mouton.

Eichenbaum, B. (1924), *Niekrasow*, in the collection 'By Means of Literature' (in Russian), Leningrad.

Giddens, A. (ed.) (1974), *Positivism and Sociology*, London: Heinemann.

Glucksmann, A., 'The Althusserian Theatre', *New Left Review*, vol. 72.

Glucksmann, M. (1974), *Structuralist Analysis in Contemporary Social Thought*, London: Routledge & Kegan Paul.

Jakobson, R. (1921), *The Latest Russian Poetry* (in Russian), Prague.

Leach, E. (1973), *Lévi-Strauss*, Glasgow: Fontana.

Lévi-Strauss, C. (1968), *Structural Anthropology*, London: Allen Lane.

Lévi-Strauss, C. (1974), *The Savage Mind*, London, Weidenfeld & Nicolson.

Mayenowa, M. R. (1970), 'Rosyjskie propozycje teoretyczne w zakrasie form poetyckich 1916–1930' ('Russian Theoretical Propositions in the Sphere of Poetic Forms, 1916–1930') in *Rosyjska szkola stylistyki (The Russian Stylistic School)*, Warsaw: PIW.

Mullins, N. C. (1973), *Theories and Theory Groups in Contemporary American Sociology*, New York: Harper & Row.

Ricoeur, P., and Lévi-Strauss, C., 'A Confrontation over Myths', *New Left Review*, vol. 62.

Robey, D. (ed.) (1973), *Structuralism*, Oxford: Clarendon Press.

Runciman, W. (1970), *Sociology in its Place*, Cambridge University Press.

Runciman, W. (1969), 'What is Structuralism?', *British Journal of Sociology*.

Saussure, F. de (1931), *Cours de linguistique générale*, Paris: C. Bally and Secretary with A. Riedlinger.

Stepień, J. (1971), 'Structura i pojecia pokrewne', *Znak*, no. 5, Krakow.

Veltmeyer, H. (1975), 'Marx, Lévi-Strauss and Althusser', *Science and Society*, spring.

Voloshinow, W. (1930), *Markism i filozofia jezyka (Marxism and the Philosophy of Language)*, Second Russian ed., Leningrad.

4 The sociological content of historical materialism
Adam Podgórecki

> Hitherto, sociologists have found difficulty in distinguishing in the complex network of social phenomena which phenomena are important and which unimportant (that is the root of subjectivism in sociology) and had been unable to discover any object criterion for such a distinction. Materialism has provided an absolutely objective criterion by singling out the 'relations of production' as the structure of society, and by making it possible to apply to these relations that general scientific criterion of repetition whose applicability to sociology the subjectivists denied.
>
> Lenin, 1943, p. 419

> And now as to myself, no credit is due to me for discovering the existence of classes in modern society, nor yet the struggle between them. Long before me, bourgeois historians had described the historical development of this class struggle, and bourgeois economists the economic anatomy of the classes. What I did that was new was to prove: (1) that the existence of classes is only bound up with particular historical phases in the development of production (historische Entwicklungsphasen der Produktion); (2) that the class struggle necessarily leads to the dictatorship of the proletariat; (3) that this dictatorship itself only constitutes the transition to the abolition of all classes and to a classless society.
>
> Karl Marx

> There is a tale of a man who specialized in manufacturing anti-earthquake pills who, when their efficiency was questioned, answered: 'Have you anything better to offer?'

The analysis of some conceptions pertaining to the sociological content of historical materialism presented below requires a number of preliminary reservations. In the Polish sociological literature – which, being an insider tries, at the same time, to be also an outsider – a wide variety of attempts have been made to classify and illuminate basic marxist concepts in more precise formulations and confront them with empirical evidence. This is why the main sources of this elaboration stem from Polish sociology.[1]

The essential difficulty which is encountered in the analysis of the sociological content of historical materialism stems from the fact that the marxist world view encompasses very many inter-related questions in the fields of philosophy, political economy, political science, law, culture, psychology and so forth. Generally speaking, marxist ideas aspire to provide a comprehensive *Weltanschauung*. But each of these questions – accumulating an immense literature on the subject – constitutes a special problem in itself; and it is impossible to synthesize and embrace all these questions in a work which is not entirely devoted to marxism. Nevertheless, it is not possible to omit considerations of the laws of social development elaborated by Marxist-Leninist thought in any theoretical work on sociology.

While aware of the fact that marxism has become the ideology of a considerable part of the working masses of different continents and that the marxist *Weltanschauung* is additionally the intentional instrument for accomplishing various fundamental social transformations, the present analysis restricts itself to two basic questions. These are: (1) to what extent marxism may be regarded as a scientifically proved body of knowledge concerning the social reality? (2) To what extent is the appeal of marxism addressed to human cognitive abilities or rather to what extent does it gain its momentum from emotional residues of the human psyche?

But still another qualification needs to be made before proceeding. Considering the great multiplicity of works in the field of historical materialism and particularly in marxist philosophy, it seems to be advisable to limit the present analysis to the essential propositions in the sphere of dynamics of social processes. This limitation is additionally justified by the scholastic character of the bulk of marxist works. Therefore the following analysis is concentrated on the theory of social change as it is elaborated by historical materialism. Five basic components (crucial for this orientation) of that theory have been singled out: (1) the theory of correlation between people's real-life situations and their ideology, which is associated with given types of social situation; (2) the conception of society as a structure composed of classes and strata with contradictory interests; (3) the very conception of change occurring in various kinds of social structures; (4) the migration of ideas as factors which may inspire or manipulate social changes; and (5) the processes associated with the formation of personality most desired by the socialist system.

I The first of these five fields of the marxist theory of social change pertains to what is generally called *the relation between the base and the superstructure*. This relation may be formulated in such simple terms as 'being determines consciousness'. However, in more sophisticated semantics, this relationship may be described as follows: *Historical development consists of the transition from one socio-economic formation to the next (higher) formation*. By *formation* is understood the totality of social relations at any given time and place. Social formulations are distinguished in relation to their corresponding economic systems (the economic base) and in respect of the ideological and institutional superstructure subordinate to the given economic system: for example, slave and Asiatic societies, feudal and bourgeois – all of them are supposed to be based on private property containing contradictions between the base and the superstructure. The *base* is defined as 'the totality of production relations at the given stage of social development' (Kania, 1974, p. 72). The *superstructure* is correspondingly understood as

> institutionalised social relations and forms of social awareness which are characterised by the following two traits: they are shaped under the powerful influence of the given type of production relations and they are not passive toward those relations – and particularly toward the given form of ownership of the means of production – but play an active role either in their preservation or abolition. The superstructure is primarily composed of such institutions as the state and political parties and such forms of social consciousness as political and philosophical views or, generally speaking, ideology (Kania, 1974, pp. 72–3).

Some further elaboration was given to the above-mentioned conceptions. Thus, the fundamental – for marxism – conception of *mode of production* was replaced by three more specific, detailed notions as they have been proposed by J. Hochfeld:

(a) mode of production in the sense of a simple model of an 'ideal type' – a theoretical category serving analysis which does not appear in history in that shape but may be abstracted for the purpose of analysis and then, consecutively, used for the sociological analysis of history;

(b) the economic system of a socio-economic formation (also called the economic base or the base of that formation) in which the dominant mode of production – hence the most characteristic mode of production for the given formation – appears in certain relations with other modes of production which as a result always modify it in relation to the ideal type;

(c) the economic system should be understood as the real, modified effect of relations with other economic systems within the base, the shape of the mode of production (Hochfeld, 1963, pp. 168–9).

The above considerations, together with Krzywicki's conceptions of social progress, enabled Wiatr to formulate more detailed propositions on the relations between the base and the superstructure:

(1) The spontaneous development of productive forces leads in each system to the emergence of new material relations (the level and character of the productive forces, elements of new production relations) which were not previously planned or postulated. In this sense economic development forges ahead of development of the superstructures.

(2) The new material relations correspond to the interests of given strata and classes but meet – at the same time – obstacles in the prevailing institutions and views representing the interests of classes and strata which are interested in maintaining the existing system of production relations. The superstructure acts in this case as an important force checking social development.

(3) Contradictory class interests are reflected in the social awareness which characterizes the emergence of particular views, ideas, feelings, which at their inception are immature and uncrystallized. These contradictory class interests create a social 'psyche' susceptible to the progressive aspirations: thus the rise of ideology, which sparks the previously isolated aspirations and renders them a mature form. 'Ideology is the shreds of social psychology', according to Bucharin's controversial definition.

(4) The progressive force, interested in the development of new, more advanced productive forces and production relations, creates not only a given system of views but also institutions serving their realization. The class struggle then assumes a non-spontaneous, conscious character, although its results may be spontaneous in the sense that they are not planned by people and that the outcome may differ from those they had imagined and even desired.

(5) Resistance by institutions of the old superstructure leads to the necessity of a revolutionary change in policy, as a result of which a new superstructure may delay the destruction of the regressive economic base, but in doing so it proclaims the necessity of a violent revolution (Wiatr, 1972, pp. 73-4).

The above concepts and propositions suggest further propositions in the sphere of the marxist theory of social change:

> (6) A social group (a class) does not accept given ideologies
>   if their acceptance would require the members of the
>   group to relinquish their privileges.[2]

This proposition pertains to the relations between the conditions of social being and the ideologies associated with those conditions. It may be modified by introducing certain additional concepts. One of them is the conception of 'false consciousness' which was described by Marx as ideology which is not – during its functioning – submitted to scientific control of its own adherents, adherents who, on the grounds of certain very definite socio-historical realities, consider these ideological illusions as finally secured and accurate knowledge of permanent factual conditions existing everywhere. Although this concept should be regarded as one of the most interesting ones, it is still not clear enough: who is finally entitled to judge the truth and functionality of a given type of consciousness? Nevertheless, adoption of the idea of *false consciousness* leads to the further proposition:

> (7) A social group (class) may under certain circumstances
>   adopt as its own a given ideology, if that ideology
>   assumes the shape of 'false consciousness'.

In connection with this proposition it may be reasonable to distinguish the conception of 'class in itself' from the conception of 'class for itself'. By the former is understood a collectivity of individuals who find themselves in the same objective conditions designated by the dominant mode of production, but who do not possess a consciousness of their essential mutual interests. On the other hand, 'class for itself' signifies the definite sense of communion, organization, and consciousness arising from the possession of similar, objective, social relations and the ability to purposefully shape that community of interests, organization and consciousness. Thus, class in itself may not possess consciousness on its own, and hence may mistakenly accept an alien, false awareness. But simultaneously with the sharpening of antagonistic contradictions within a class formation, opposing tendencies will appear encouraging the abandonment of the prevailing false ideology. The social groups that desire to relinquish that kind of ideology may be described by the following proposition:

> (8) Social groups (classes) deprived of the enjoyment of given
>   privileges tend to develop an ideology directed to
>   combating the groups which enjoy those privileges. [Not,
>   as is said quite often, 'the system which gives them those
>   privileges' – since the 'hypostatic' terms are excluded!]

A desire to fight against the privileges of antagonistic classes may arise spontaneously or it may arise by way of developing a contrary ideology. Various peasant rebellions and workers' strikes and their leaders are examples of the spontaneously shaped elements of class ideology of this type. These various elements are moulded into a whole by political leaders and thinkers; they then appear in various forms of more or less organized ideologies. The ideology, system of thought, which most adequately corresponds to the prevailing mode of production is accepted as the ideological expression of the social groups whose interests it represents. The following proposition presents the polarization which occurs within antagonistic formations alongside the sharpening of the ideological struggle:

(9) If social groups (classes) start through their representatives to consolidate their positions and to extend the range of their privileges by developing and propagating given ideologies (and their philosophical, religious, scientific, and artistic ramifications), then the adherents of already established commitments will have a tendency to oppose those privileges and ideologies of the corresponding antagonistic groups (classes).

The further propositions describe the situation which occurs when abstract ideology is confronted by conflicting interests of real social and economic life:

(10) In the case of a conflict arising inside the given social system between established interests and acknowledged ideology in situations where dominant interests are retained, when at the same time there is no official change in the obligatory ideology, members of this social system will behave in accordance with socio-economic pressures and not according to ideology.

and:

(11) In the event of an extended conflict between the essential interests of a class or social group, and its ideology (or some of its elements), then that ideology will transform itself into 'false consciousness' or its elements will undergo modification in the direction of adaptation to the dominant interests.

II   The second of the spheres of the marxist theory of social change distinguished above pertains to the conception of society as a structure composed of classes with conflicting interests. It should be noted here that historical materialism distinguishes between antagonistic formations and formations based on non-antagonistic contradictory interests. According to this idea the conflict in the former basically leads to its abolition, in the latter it may contribute to the general welfare: 'in the process of replacement of social systems clearly appears the second general law of transition of socialist into communist, namely, the utilization by society of the inequalities existing under socialism as the most important levers hastening the motion of equality' (Rutkiewicz and Filipow, 1975, p. 243). Social systems based on antagonistic contradictions are the slave, feudal and bourgeois formations. It may therefore be asserted that

> (12) Antagonistic societies are divided into classes on the basis of conflicting interests.

It may be stated, in reference to formations not based on antagonistic contradictions (socialistic societies are regarded by Polish marxist theoreticians as such – an example of 'meta false consciousness'?), that

> (13) In non-antagonistic societies, the interests of social classes and strata are not in conflict.

Anyway, if the last proposition is applicable to the analysis of contemporary Polish society, it still does not provide direct deductions useful for the analysis of that society's social structure. P. Tobera (1972, pp. 31–5) clearly distinguishes four basic viewpoints on this matter. According to the first, Polish society is composed of distinct classes (though their understanding differs from the marxist tradition); according to this understanding, these classes are regarded as socially not antagonistic, since the economic and social premises of class antagonism – as it is claimed – have been eliminated in Poland. (This corresponds with the view of S. Widerszpil, among others.)

According to the second viewpoint, the Polish social structure is primarily one of strata. In the Marxist-Leninist understanding, classes wither away under socialism. The very conception of non-antagonistic classes contains an internal contradiction, since the essence of a social class consists by definition of its antagonistic relations with opposing classes. So, instead of classes, different social strata are emerging and are maintained. This view is echoed by J. Wiatr.

The third view is that the socialist social structure is comprised of a mixture of both class and stratum characteristics. The class-stream conception constitutes an intermediate approach. Such views are represented by K. Słomczyński and W. Wesołowski.

The fourth conception of Polish society and its social structure is based on the category of occupation as the deciding factor. Adherents of that conception, J. Chałasiński and J. Ulatowski, reject the conception of social classes and strata as inadequate for the social conditions existing in Poland. Factors associated with occupation, i.e. the nature of one's work, vocational/professional qualifications and professional role, are of deciding importance in their view. It should be noted that the emphasis which is put on these factors shifts attention away from the main problem - specific to the socialist countries – which is the discrepancy between the new structure of ruling administrative operators and the secondary one – different models of social stratification. One may additionally mention that this thesis was formulated during the seminars of the Warsaw 'flying university' in 1950-51 much earlier than the well-known statement by Djilas.

If one turns back to the previous considerations concerning so-called antagonistic social formations the following propositions may appear:

(14) The owners of means of production have interests contrary to the interests of those who are deprived of means of production belonging to others. Ownership of means of production differs in degree. A considerable sphere of private property in means of production leads to the phenomenon of class rule (domination). Thus those who own particular large stocks of means of production are in a position to exercise class domination over those who do not own or use others' means of production (Wesołowski, 1961, pp. 67-105).

According to this conception, class rule has three essential segments: (a) the economic dimension pertains to domination over the labour process, the means of production, and the products of labour; (b) the political dimension is the degree of possible influence over government; (c) the ideological dimension is the degree of possible influence over the acceptance by the given society of the ideology of the ruling class. This conception of the dimensions of class rule tends to provide a possibility to diagnose, with at least a certain approximation, the social situations within which class rule might be regarded either as stronger or weaker. Class domination is thus stronger where these three dimensions are merged and weaker when they act in isolation from each other.
III The third sphere in the marxist theory of social change pertains to the processes and changes occurring in various types of social structures. The following propositions may be formulated regarding these changes:

(15) If the representatives of social classes, guided by immediate, direct interests and the discovery and application of new modes of production, begin to develop new organizational conceptions and thus contribute to the development of production relations within the base, they will then be able to influence the social structure in such a manner as to increase the social importance of those classes while simultaneously lowering that of other classes.

As is known, the marxist conception of social change assumes progressive development. According to this conception progress is conditioned by changes in the social base and in the relations between that base and its superstructure. Given types of relations between the base and the superstructure may hamper social progress in some cases and stimulate it in others; the following proposition attempts to apprehend the empirical sense of that idea:

(16) Of the antagonistic social classes confronting each other in a given society, that one prevails whose direct interests correspond with the interest of economic progress expressed by the productive forces.

IV, V   The fourth and fifth spheres of the marxist conception of social change pertain to the migration of ideas or processes in the moulding of the new personality pattern – the personality model of the socialist man. Thus

(17) If a class (or group) which represents the interests of economic progress in a given society is confronted with political and legal patterns of life (institutions, organizations, governmental, and administrative doctrines) which limit the possibility of promoting its interests, then the members of this class (or group) will have a tendency to spread ideas which underline the need to change the prevailing political and legal relations.

Ideals of social change may be transferred – according to marxism, transplanted – from one social system to another. As L. Krzywicki wrote:

When an idea is born and exists not as the fantasy of an individual and flighty thought but as an historic watchword of entire strata, then the problem gradually created by life is so far advanced as to arouse ideas of the most proper ways of solving it. While in some other country only elements of that complex of material relations may emerge which elsewhere has already given rise to new ideas as conscious formulations of

their needs. The ideas of one country penetrate another
retarded in its development and begin to influence thought
(Krzywicki, 1936).

That same year Petrażycki – taking as the point of departure views
opposite to marxism – developed a somewhat more elaborated idea:

> In the case of contact of various levels of economic activity
> there takes place (naturally and unavoidably) such an
> economic choice and adaptation that the representatives of the
> higher economic culture and initiative fulfil a higher economic
> function, that which requires a higher level of economic
> sophistication and a more developed spirit of enterprise. If,
> additionally, we divide economically useful occupations into
> two types – physico-technical (cultivating the soil, breeding
> cattle, handicrafts, etc.) and psycho-juridical (legal,
> merchandising, credit transactions, and similar activities) –
> then it is clear a priori and it can be anticipated that the
> activity of the representatives of a higher economic culture
> must be directed primarily in the second, the psycho-juridical,
> credit, etc., sphere. Consequently it is possible to separate the
> activities and functions of the first kind (physico-technical)
> into two categories: (1) common routine, occupied with long
> existing vocations in mining, stock breeding, grain cultivation,
> manufacturing, traditional handicrafts, etc., inherited from
> forefathers, involving the application of inherited customs and
> routines, and (2) innovative activity. One may characterize the
> innovative activity as the introduction of new brands and
> varieties of industrial production in general – a new type of
> enterprise carrying out their former functions but with new
> progressive forms of organization or techniques. If so, then it
> is possible to foresee that the representatives of higher
> economic culture also in the physico-technical sphere will be
> concentrated in the innovative sphere (Petrażycki, 1936, pp.
> 6–7).

Although Petrażycki and marxist ideas deal in certain areas with
similar matters, it might be interesting to note that according to
Petrażycki socio-psychological elements (like, for example,
organizational abilities) play a crucial role while economic factors,
according to him, only depend on them. The above digression is
intended to show that the practically unknown ideas of Petrażycki
have, at least in this area, more explanatory power than constantly
repeated marxist reflections. They seem to be especially revealing as
far as so-called socialistic systems are concerned. These ideas show
that in socialism economic factors play a secondary role when

psychological factors (mainly meta-attitudes) decisively shape the structure of this type of society. Quite often force and fear stick behind these psychological factors – a point which is often hidden or overlooked.

Coming back to marxist conceptions regarding the migration of ideas, it is possible to formulate the following hypothesis:

(18) An idea grafted into one social system from another, if in harmony with interests supporting the further development of production relations (determined by the base), is capable of contributing to the qualitative leap of that society by effecting qualitative changes first in the superstructure and then in the base itself.

A neglected field of analysis which could throw much light on the question of accepting migrating ideas and corresponding institutional forms in the alien society is the adoption of one society's legal system by another. The change of Japanese law is an interesting example in this respect:

The initial acceptance of Western law in Japan during the Medji period [1868-1913] was necessary to realize national policy which aimed to overtake the capitalist countries. The reaction to the transfer of law ran from approval to rejection, with many intermediate states. Furthermore, the traditional divisions in class and other social positions had an essential effect on the development of legal awareness and of rights of the individual. Attitudes to law depended on whether a person occupied with it belonged to the ruling classes, was a merchant or a peasant, a landowner or a tenant, etc. . . . By accepting legal codes Western ideas undoubtedly stimulated awareness of the law and of individual rights as well as influenced economic development. Remote and agricultural parts of the country were of course subjected to weaker influences. Factory workers and tenant farmers whose rights were not protected by the Civil Code gradually became aware of the fact – regardless of whether the Code granted them these rights or not – that the law is also their concern. As a result, many demands and struggles to assure their rights took place which consequently went far beyond the range fixed by the Civil Code (Fukushima, 1975, pp. 12-13).

It is assumed by Polish marxist theoreticians that social changes transpiring in socialist societies regarded by them – in a questionable manner – as non-antagonistic, lead to the emergence of new normative patterns. One of these is the pattern of a 'personality of socialist man', which supposedly combines the following traits:

many-sided development of the personality, active recognition of the interests of socialist society as the basic guideline for activity, the constant raising of one's knowledge and occupational aptitudes, firmly grounded ethical principles, highly developed ideological consciousness and rational attitudes (Białyszewski, 1974, pp. 332-4). Such patterns after additional 'refinement' jump from the 'is reality' into 'ought reality' and intend to disclose a general pattern of the ideal personality of socialist man. Such a personality would then contain the following traits: (1) a socialist attitude to work, understood primarily as its conversion into a personal need and a form of expression which is motivated by the desire to participate in and improve the working environment; (2) an attitude to property, based on thrift and responsibility for public ownership; (3) a civic attitude, based on a belief in egalitarianism and democracy and the desire to overcome egoism and bourgeois individualism; (4) an attitude based on involvement in the political defence of the socialist system and its further development; (5) patriotism and internationalism; (6) socialist ethical principles, like: humanism, respect for human dignity, sensitivity to social inequality, guidance by the principle of social justice; (7) friendly and helpful attitudes in interpersonal relations, family relations based on emotional ties and co-operation; (8) involvement in public activity; (9) the taste-oriented effort to shape a scientific world view; (10) personal self-realization and development of the need for the creative expression of the personality in socially useful activity (Jasińska and Siemińska, 1975, pp. 125–6). The above mixture of descriptive and normative statements suggests the following hypothesis of a hybrid nature as those mixing together descriptive and normative elements:

> (19) The non-antagonistic concurrence of the base and superstructure leads not only to changes in both which mutually consolidate the two, but also leads to the emergence of a normative pattern of personality which emerges as a synthetic integration of both of them.

The members of societies resting on non-antagonistic foundations become collectivities 'on which are based the attainments of science and technology . . . a collectivity of mutual individual development – a society of developing individuals' (Richta, 1971, pp. 309-10). From this follows the next hypothesis of the same questionable hybrid character:

> (20) A non-antagonistic superstructure and base not only favours mutually stimulating changes in both; it induces not only the emergence of socially benevolent individual patterns of behaviour but also of the collective ones.

The hypotheses listed above do not exhaust basic propositions deducible from marxist thoughts. They pertain mainly to questions associated with the laws of social change which may undergo empirical tests. They are, nevertheless, systematically proved only in a few instances. This avoidance of empirical tests is apparently linked with the tendency to transform marxist ideas into an attractive political force rather than into a body of methodologically reliable knowledge.

Generally speaking one may say that:

(1) Marxist propositions are based on the assumption of possible conflicts and contradictions between various social groups. Such conflicts are particularly sharp between opposing classes within an antagonistic social system. They do not rest on conceptions of accord and harmony or on the equilibrium of interests. On the whole, they seem to seek a vision of an optional society, they propose an analytical conceptual scheme which intends to specify contradictory interests and tendencies inside the existing antagonistic social systems, and they suggest, at the same time, the possible directions of desired social change.

(2) The above propositions are based on an intention (of exceptional importance to sociology) to explain phenomena which are not evidenced and externalized by direct observations and are therefore difficult to grasp by empirical analyses. These concealed features if revealed are claimed to have a unique validity, since they purportedly constitute factors which may have the strategic importance in introducing the desired social changes. Their identification is thus crucial since it is assumed that only knowledge of these elements leads to deep diagnoses and consequently to extrapolations pertaining to the transformations of the existing society.

(3) The propositions presented above are designed to apply to various societies taken as integral wholes. In contrast, hypotheses generated by 'rival' social theories appear as fragmented and dispersed generalizations, formulated by various branches of social sciences which are not united. Since they do not usually have a general frame of reference, these hypotheses do not provide a structurally consistent picture of a given society. Marxism hence aspires to apprehend diffused propositions in a systematically ordered whole which seems to be potentially ready to give answers to a large spectrum of questions relating to important social matters.

(4) Marxist sociology, on the basis of a large body of propositions, claims to provide the foundations for the critical analysis of

other social philosophies and sociological trends and schools. They are criticized for approaching social problems in a fragmentary manner, focusing, as a rule, their diagnostical potentials on the questions which are at the centre of present public interest. On the contrary, the holistic comprehensives which are claimed by marxism and which arise from the tendency to furnish the 'masses' with a global *Weltanschauung* try mainly to 'digest' methodological reservations by para-scientific argumentation. This argumentation appeals mainly to those who are interested not so much in the cognitive truth, but in the acute questions of social justice.

(5) The body of propositions presented above, with certain additional specifications, intends to match the political needs calling for an integral, centrally co-ordinated, programme of macro-social transformations based on 'scientific evidence'.

In conclusion it seems to be clear that: (1) historical materialism offers a large, comprehensive, interlinked spectrum of propositions which purport to be scientifically proven; (2) they pretend to be scientifically proven since they use the empirical evidence only as exemplary material – accumulated according to selective criteria; (3) marxism appeals not so much to empirical evidence as to social and political emotions and seems to have a holistic explanation of complicated problems of social reality; (4) marxism suggests a kaleidoscope of different strategies for social and political actions; and, finally (5) marxism tries, utilizing present-day highly developed mass media apparatus, to satisfy the widespread hunger and cry for social justice by its own package of normative vision of the 'happy society'.

Notes

1 Nevertheless, there are additional reasons for doing it. Some of them are: (1) Polish interpretation of marxism is not well known to the reader from outside; (2) this interpretation is representative of the published literature on the subject in the Eastern Bloc; (3) this interpretation tries to fulfil a very difficult task - to be orthodox and original at the same time; (4) this interpretation is not so heavily emotionally loaded as those which were originated by several socio-political move-emnts in so-called underdeveloped countries, and (5) claims to be the most sophisticated one inside the sphere of 'orthodoxy'.

2 Propositions 1-5 are taken from J. Wiatr (1972); propositions 6-13 from A. Malewski (1957); proposition 14 from W. Wesołowski (1961); propositions 15-16 from A. Malewski (1957); propositions 17-18 were formulated on the basis of the work of A. Jasińska and R. Siemińska (1975), and R. Richta (1971). It is worthwhile to note that Malewski's methodologically sound proposal to digest extensive marxist literature to a list of theoretical propositions accessible to empirical testing was not upheld later by Polish specialists in this field. Anyway, the list of

propositions is formulated according to this type of recommendation. They are articulated in a manner which tends to exclude all 'hypostatic' terms (those not reducible to empirical verification), although this manner is not inherent in the marxist way of thinking.

Bibliography

Białyszewski, H. (1974), 'Osobowość a społeczeństwo. Rozwój osobowości w socjalizmie' ('The Personality and Society. Development of the Personality Under Socialism'), in S. Widerszpil (ed.), *Wybrane problemy socjologii marksistowskiej (Selected Problems of Marxist Sociology)*, Warsaw: Książka i Wiedza.

Fukushima, M. (1975), 'Reception of Western Law and Japan's Modernization'. Report at the Conference on the Sociology of Law at Hakone, Japan.

Hochfeld, J. (1963), *Studia o marksistowskiej teorii społeczeństwa (A Study of the Marxist Theory of Society)*, Warsaw: PWN.

Jasińska, A., and Siemińska, R. (1975), *Wzory osobowe socjalizmu (Socialist Personality Patterns)*, Warsaw: Omega, Wiedza Powszechna.

Kania, A. (1974), 'Podstawowe prawa rozwoju społecznego' ('The Principal Laws of Social Development'), in *Selected Problems*, *op. cit.*

Krzywicki, L. (1936), 'Idea a życie' ('Ideas and Life') in *Dzieła*, vols 1–5, Polska Akademia Nauk.

Lenin, V. I. (1943), 'What the "Friends of the People" Are', *Selected Works*, vol. XI, New York: International Publishers, p. 419.

Malewski, A. (1957), 'Empiryczny sens teorii materializmu historycznego' ('The Empirical Sense of the Theory of Historical Materialism'), *Studia Filozoficzne*, no. 2.

Petrażycki, L. (1936), *O dopełniajacych prawach kulturalnych i prawach rozwoju handlu (On the Correlation of Cultural Currents and the Laws of Development of Trade)*, Warsaw: pp. 617.

Richta, R. (1971), *Cywilizacja na rozdrozu (Civilization at the Crossroads)*, Warsaw: Książka i Wiedza.

Rutkiewicz, M., and Filipow, F. (1975), *Przemieszczenia społeczne (Social Developments)*, Warsaw: Książka i Wiedza.

Tobera, P. (1972), *Zróżnicowanie społeczne pracowników przemysłu (The Social Differentiation of Industrial Workers)*, Warsaw: PWN.

Wesołowski, W. (1961), 'Marksistowska Teoria Panowania Klasowego a Teoria Wadzy Grupi Interesów' ('The Marxist Theory of Class Domination and the Theory of Interest Groups'), *Kultura i Społeczénstwo*, no. 1.

Wiatr, J. (1972), *Szkice o materializmie historycznym i socjologii (Sketches on Historical Materialism and Sociology)*, Warsaw: Książka i Wiedza.

5 Critical sociology:
the 'Frankfurt School'
Adam Podgórecki

Like the concept of society cannot be deduced from any
individual facts or itself be grasped as such a fact, we cannot
ascertain any social fact that was not determined by society as a
whole.

Theodor W. Adorno

If we looked for an ideological justification of the situation in
which people function as something more than the gears in their
own machinery, we might admit without exaggeration that
contemporary people serve as such an ideology for their own
existence, when they pursue their own free will in order to
perpetuate what is obviously a perversion of real life.

Theodor W. Adorno

It is a difficult task to reconstruct the scope of concerns of the so-
called Frankfurt School – perhaps beyond anybody's means. For
the 'Frankfurt School' appears to have been more of a legend than
reality. What is labelled with this name, arose from the activities of
the Institute of Social Research in Frankfurt (Institut für
Sozialforschung an der Universität Frankfurt am Main). The
institute was established on 3 February 1923. Its first director was
Carl Grünberg who defined himself in his opening lecture as an
adherent of marxism, intending to introduce significant elements of
marxism into the methodology of the social sciences. Grünberg was
sometimes considered to be one of the founders of the so-called
Austro-marxism. The working of the institute was based, in the
initial phase, on a private foundation of Hermann Weil, a
businessman who allotted large funds to start the institute. The
intention was to bypass the university routines and to develop
researches independently of academic and official control. The two
first research projects dealt with the history of labour movements
and the origin of Anti-Semitism. In January 1931, M. Horkheimer
took over as the director of the institute. Under his rule, the
institute planned to analyse attitudes of workers and employers
towards a number of important German and European issues. The
institute grouped such eminent scholars as S. Kracauer, W.
Benjamin, M. Horkheimer, E. Fromm, H. Marcuse, E. Frenkel-
Brunswik and L. Löwenthal. Under the impact of the wave of

Nazism and in anticipation of what was looming, they moved, one after another, to Paris, Geneva or Oxford; also the funds and archives of the institute were transferred abroad. Horkheimer went to the USA in 1934 and became director of the Institute of Social Research at Columbia University. Fromm had moved even earlier to the USA and he was followed by other members of the Frankfurt group. Horkheimer returned to Frankfurt in 1949 (together with Adorno) to reconstruct the institute. Later (in 1954), however, he went back to the USA to take the chair of sociology at Chicago University. Adorno remained in Frankfurt, gaining popularity until the tragic breakdown in 1968, when during the student upsurge he was attacked for his more and more eager attachment to the 'establishment'. Those migrations and biographical entanglements have essentially contributed to the myth of the scientific school allegedly constituted by what was at the outset a loose group of personalities. The group was loose, however, in terms of the scientific concerns, but not in terms of the ideological commitments, of its members. Today, it is relatively easy to identify those who belonged to the Frankfurt group, but it is extremely difficult to bring out a synthesis of the essential ideas or problems that have been actually the group's focal concerns.

It is said sometimes that the so-called Frankfurt School is characterized by its critical approach, but we can hardly find any other developed school in the social sciences that would not be critical, especially towards other sociological schools. It is also said that the Frankfurt School is a version of marxism or Freudism, but we can hardly find today a sociological school that would not make use of some concepts or themes deriving from Freudism or marxism. What, then, are the common and peculiar features of the Frankfurt School? This question cannot be answered in an unambiguous manner. There seem to be no obvious features by which this group of scholars is distinct from other ones. However, a broad recognition of the Frankfurt School as an entity in the sociology of science is a hard fact and thus we have to consider what are the characteristics distinguishing it from other contemporary trends in sociological theory.

One of the concepts that appear to have been the starting-points for the development of the 'Frankfurt School' is the idea of the authoritarian personality. It constitutes a complex pattern of characteristics:

The most crucial result of the present study, as it seems to its authors, is the demonstration of close correspondence in the type of approach and outlook a subject is likely to have in a great variety of areas, ranging from the most intimate features

of family and sex adjustment through relationships to other
people in general, to religion and to social and political
philosophy. Thus a basically hierarchical, authoritarian,
exploitive parent-child relationship is apt to carry over into a
power-oriented, exploitively dependent attitude towards one's
sex partner and one's God and may well culminate in a
political philosophy and social outlook which has no room for
anything but a desperate clinging to what appears to be strong
and a disdainful rejection of whatever is relegated to the
bottom. The inherent dramatization likewise extends from the
parent-child dichotomy to the dichotomous conception of sex
roles and moral values, as well as to a dichotomous handling
of social relations as manifested especially in the formation of
stereotypes and of ingroup-outgroup cleavages.
Conventionality, rigidity, repressive denial, and the ensuing
break-through of one's weakness, fear and dependency are
but other aspects of the same fundamental personality
pattern, and they can be observed in personal life as well as in
attitudes toward religion and social issues (Adorno *et al.*,
1950, p. 971).

The concept of the authoritarian personality eventually won a great
vogue in social psychology, psychology and sociology and it
contributed to many attempts at explaining the peculiarities of the
German nation and society. It was also subject to critical remarks,
as for example by another member of the Frankfurt School –
Habermas. Analysing his contemporary epoch he declared that the
concept of the authoritarian personality did not seem to be a useful
explanatory term. 'From the psycho-social point of view, the
authoritarian personality is something less adequate for the
contemporary epoch than the conception of destructuralized super-
ego' (Habermas, 1974, p. 107). Indeed, in order to explain the
socio-political situation in Germany after the Second World War
other concepts seem to be more adequate. One of them is the
notion of 'fatherless society' coined by A. Mitscherlich. Sons
deprived of their fathers' care (absence during the War, loss of
their prestige, intense professional life after the war, etc.) have not
been influenced properly by these 'natural' socializing agents.
The idea of the authoritarian personality was criticized for its
inconsistent usage in writings of 'Frankfurters'. We are told that
authoritarian attitudes are of decisive influence on the shaping of a
family in contemporary societies (and, in particular, of the German
family before the Second World War), while, on the other hand, it
is maintained that the role of the family and its inherent structure
are diminishing in the contemporary world. Another objection

against the concept of the authoritarian personality was that the patterns of obedience relied on in Wilhelm's Germany and in Nazi Germany had been altogether different. In still another argument, if political and economic conservatism was in fact linked with authoritarianism (as some members of the Frankfurt group maintained), then why was it not, for example, attributed to those who expressed the demand for state socialism - this being limited only to so-called conservatists. In effect, the charge was raised against those who investigated the authoritarian personality that their own political allegiances had 'coloured' the results of their investigations (Jay, 1973, pp. 245-8).

While searching for the link between various authors belonging to the Frankfurt circle, we encounter now and again the concept of dominance. According to Adorno, not only the common sense, but also empirical investigations in the social sciences, aim at the reinforcement of the prevailing institutions. This is because the institutions already functioning in a society are taken for granted and self-explanatory. Adorno attempted to grasp the latent modes of dominance (not easily seen by mere observation of the surrounding social arrangements and facts) by applying a peculiar dialectics. Such dialectics relies on the postulate of the reflexive bent of mind. Besides thinking of a subject, we should be aware of our thinking; awareness and self-awareness ought to be coextensive. The mind, however, tends to produce illusions as to its own autonomy. This is because it cannot possibly be aware all the time of the fact that it is aware of something else and thus it is naturally apt to get sunk in the subject of its analysis. If we grant this, then the thought has reached the point at which it identifies itself delusively with what it analyses. Adorno says:

> Integration goes even further than that: adjustment of people to the social processes and relationships constituted by history (and without which people could hardly exist at all) has put its hallmark on the mere possibility to break through (without sharp institutional conflicts), even if carried out at the level of thought only - so that the breaking through has become a little probable and unrealistic. People have become - and this is the triumph of integration - identical with their inherent patterns of behaviour and with their fates in contemporary society.

According to Adorno (1969-70), the dominance of society over an individual has gone so far that an individual, having lost his freedom, believes that the contemporary society has provided him with all opportunities to develop most freely.

Marcuse picked up the conception of Adorno and related it, in the spirit of the German tradition, to Weber's idea of rationalization. Marcuse believes that 'rationalization' represents not only the rational relationship between ends and means, but that it also furtively brings in unrecognized elements of political domination. Since the relation between ends and means, dealt with in the concept of rationalization, is mainly a technological relationship, Marcuse sorts out the notion of 'technological reasons' for further analysis. He says: '[the] very concept of technical reason is perhaps ideological. Not only an application of technology, but technology itself is domination (of nature and man) – methodical, scientific, calculating control' (Marcuse, 1968, p. 223).

According to Marcuse, not only technology, but also science performs the dominative function, in a more or less overt manner. Marcuse says:

> The principles of modern science were a priori structured in such a way that they could serve as conceptual instruments for a universe of selfpropelling, productive control; theoretical operationalism came to correspond to practical operationalism. The scientific method which led to the ever-more-effective domination of nature thus came to provide the pure concepts as well as the instrumentalities for the ever-more-effective domination of man by man *through* the domination of nature. . . . Today, domination perpetuates and extends itself not only through technology but *as* technology, and the latter provides the great legitimation of the expanding political power, which absorbs all spheres of culture (Marcuse, 1968, p. 130).

Both Marcuse and Habermas regard the concept of rationalization as crucial for the understanding of domination. We are told that in contemporary industrial societies the concept of rationalization has not only retained its primary sense of indicating the appropriate means towards defined ends, but it has also the meaning given to it by Freud. In the latter sense, rationalization consists in concealing the obsolete forms of domination by resort to purposeful rational imperatives. Another application of the concept of rationalization to the understanding of contemporary domination is connected with its two special uses, 'rationalization from below' and 'rationalization from above'. Rationalization from below takes place by the cumulation of all kinds of technological and organizational developments, their diffusion, generalization, planned extension, etc. Rationalization from above, on the other hand, is introduced by rational explanatory patterns, provided as vindications of the dominating political power. Social systems are submerged in the broader natural environment. Domination encompasses nature not only because man has mastered the world of things, or that he has mastered other men by means of his mastery of things, but also because he has formed an approach to nature as vulnerable to possible technological control. He thereby forgets that he might treat nature, not as the subject of his exploitation, but as something with which to contract a brotherly alliance.

Habermas took the effort of applying these concepts to the analysis of industrial societies. He discerned two types of social systems: those with the predomination of purposive-rational behaviours, and those in which symbolic human interactions are the most significant. The purposive-rational systems are characterized by the following features: predomination of technical rules; language without emotional contents; conditional (end-dependent) imperatives; education towards skills and qualifications; problem-solving orientation; a fear of inefficiency; emphasis on the growth of productive potentialities. Social systems based on symbolic interactions are marked by the prevalence of social-oriented norms; intersubjectively intelligible language; mutual expectations; internalization of social roles; sustaining the existing institutions; emancipation; individualism; the tendency to communicate rather than to dominate.

The purposive-rational system prevalent in today's industrial societies is marked, in addition, by five characteristics:

(1) The apparently independent development of science and technology is in fact an independent variable in the process of economic growth. The ideals attached to the pursuing and developing of pure science are essentially instrumentally related to economic expansion.

(2) Conflicts tend to be transferred to the marginal regions of social life. For example, the racial conflict, very acute in the USA has become socially conspicuous, while the more essential (economic) conflict is shaded by other, artificially blown up ones.

(3) Manipulative endeavours come to the fore as the predominating type of interaction.

Today the psychotechnic manipulation of behaviour can already liquidate the old-fashioned detour through norms that are internalized but capable of reflection. Behavioural control could be instituted at an even deeper level tomorrow through biotechnic intervention in the endocrine regulating system, not to mention the even greater consequences of intervening in the genetic transmission of inherited information. If this occurred, old regions of consciousness developed in ordinary-language communication would of necessity completely dry up. At this stage of human engineering, if the end of psychological manipulation could be spoken of in the same sense as the end of ideology is today, the spontaneous alienation derived from the uncontrolled lag of the institutional framework would be overcome. But the self-objectivation of man would have fulfilled itself in planned alienation – men would make their history with will, but without consciousness (Habermas, 1971, p. 118).

(4) Technology and science are accepted as generalized and self-sufficient outlooks, appropriate to reconcile incompatible political and ideological views and in the end to be substituted for these views. The end of the age of ideology is avowed. Those features of the industrial society acknowledged to be remarkable are related to the ramified processes of *active adaptation*, whereby individuals skilfully adjust to the organizational and technological conditions of social life, as well as to those of *passive adaptation* to which organizations and institutions are subject. In fact, individuals can adapt themselves actively, while institutions and organizations do not take conscious or planned measures aiming at the change of social reality, but on the contrary, they are expanded, modified or liquidated by social processes. All these processes converge in the science and technology-based ideology as justifying the prevailing state of affairs.

(5) In contemporary industrial societies various kinds of audiences can be identified, such as the sophisticated, the plebeian and the affirmative-applauding audiences. The increasing significance of the third type of audience is most remarkable for those societies. The mass media, owing to their huge impact, are in fact a restrictive factor in the genuine communication among the members of society. They are so restrictive partly on account of their selective informational contents. It is necessary to remember that these interesting remarks lost, at least partially, their validity in view of the events of the late 1960s (massive anti-poverty programme in the USA, students' movements, anti-establishment terrorist activities, etc.).

In considerations of the so-called critical school, the question arises again and again, what are its significantly novel contributions to sociological knowledge? Certainly its characteristic critical attitude has been taken over from marxism. But it departs from Marxism. Marxism-oriented sociologist, P. Slater, gives in this respect a penetrating and informative analysis and critique of the Frankfurt School. His work on the subject intends to grasp changeable relations between the flexible socio-political reality and the constantly drifting ideology of this school into a coherent order. His general conclusion is:

> the Frankfurt School of the 1930s and early 1940s made a serious contribution to the elucidation and articulation of historical materialism but, *at the same time*, failed to achieve the relation to praxis which is central to the marxist project.
>
> Thus, the present study attempts a metacritique of the Frankfurt School's social theory in its formative years. It is worth stating, in anticipation, that a metacritique is a critique framed within a context that transcends the object under scrutiny. In the case of the Frankfurt School, such a procedure is both complex and problematical: they acknowledged as their frame of reference the method, categories, and political orientation of historical materialism, yet their analyses fail to concretise these categories, particularly as regards the problems of economic manipulation and revolutionary social praxis. Thus, immanent critique and metacritique, in the case of an analysis of the Frankfurt School, fuse (Slater, 1977, pp. xii–xiv).

The search for the latent factors of change is derived from marxism and freudism. The idea of social facts as 'things' put forth by Horkheimer and Adorno is certainly borrowed from Durkheim. Considerations to the effect that what is treated as a social fact has been prepared as such a fact by various kinds of selections (political, economic, organizational, etc.), and the idea that entities treated as facts are more or less ostensibly related to ethical and ideological values, are also not quite new conceptions, although they have been forcefully applied in the criticism of positivism. However, this criticism was not very revealing with respect to what was crucial for positivism, i.e. in the field of the methods and techniques of social research being unable to produce an alternative option on its own. Reflections concerning the philosophical or epistemological assumptions of the social sciences and their methods, although interesting, have also failed to bring very fruitful ideas. Moreover, the so-called critical school, in its analysis of the concept of rationality and in the search for analogies between science-based technology and methods of influencing social life, creates an essential fallacy. It considers the science-based technology as a convenient ground of reference for comparisons with the functioning of various techniques in social life. Such comparisons are illusory and ungrounded in the present phase of development of the social sciences. The techniques of organization of social life still remain on the level of pre-scientific witchcraft. Until now, there has been no generally accepted methodology for the practical (i.e. applied) social sciences. Ideas concerning management, organization and control of social life are only in a minor degree based on systematic empirical investigations, or on any strict methodical principles, while they rely mainly on intuition, professional experience and economic pressures. Another weak point of the so-called critical school is connected with what was intended to give it its main impetus: the postulate of studying the society as a whole. The rise and development of Nazism impelled German intellectuals to look for answers to questions about the character of the emerging social system. Investigations of family (carried out by Fromm) and studies on the authoritarian personality (summed up by Adorno and others) were efforts aimed towards this goal. Members of the so-called Frankfurt School made many critical remarks about the established sociology; they postulated the need for overall social analyses and expressed their negative attitude towards fragmented and minor contributions. However, the school could not, in spite of its own postulates, produce a convincing diagnosis of the German society. Nevertheless, it should be stressed that it generated a very interesting postulate that society should be studied as a whole: in its totality. But by asking far too much (why experimental?), Adorno in the same statement rejects his own claim!

> Central to the refutation process is the role of tests in research procedures. Adorno argues that if the notion of discrete individual facts is rejected and replaced by facts existing in a dialectical relationship with societal totalities, then no experimental procedure can be instituted which examines the dependence of some phenomenon upon a societal totality, since this very totality itself could never exist in an experimental research procedure (Frisby, 1974, p. 215).

And:

> In contrast, a dialectical theory of society insists that the coherence of theoretical statements rests upon the very societal process to which sociological research itself belongs. It must be related to the societal totality of which it is a moment (Frisby, 1974, p. 217).

The Frankfurt School claimed thus that a given social process should be analysed in the context in which it is situated, but not only in the given context but also in the society at large. Neither the first postulate (the Frankfurt School did not produce the comprehensive diagnosis of its own society) nor the second postulate was fulfilled (the phenomenon of authoritarian personality was not consistently and systematically related to a different - from German - structure). Moreover, it could not even elaborate the methods that might be helpful in preparing such a synthetic diagnosis. Among the lasting contributions of the critical school there seem to remain the interesting theme of considerations on the origin and character of the encompassing domination of society over an individual, as well as some elements of the analysis of contemporary industrial society. The postulate, picked by the school, although not invented by it, of the style of social studies aimed at overall, synthetic, empirical and theoretical diagnoses, also remains to be an important practical directive.

According to Horkheimer, the so-called Frankfurt School was kept together by its critical approach: 'What united them was the critical approach to existing society' (in the introduction to Jay, 1973, p. xi). However, this life philosophy was not consequently realized, at least at the level of personal relevance. Jay, perhaps the best expert on the Frankfurt School and its apologetic critic, wrote about Horkheimer:

> After his resettlement in the early fifties, Horkheimer was lionized by a Frankfurt community grateful for the recapture of at least one survivor of Weimar culture. He rubbed shoulders with Konrad Adenauer and made frequent appearances on radio and television, and in the press (Jay, 1973, p. 287).

The sudden collapse of the 'school' and its almost total disappearance from the German academic kaleidoscope still waits for its comprehensive evaluation and a convincing explanation. At the present moment one may tentatively accept as instructive and interesting the appreciation of the school by Habermas. Trying to identify the peculiar features of the Frankfurt School, he defines them in negative terms:

> (1) Confronted with the objectivism of the behavioural sciences – critical sociology is opposed to the reduction of intentional activity to behaviour. (2) Confronted with idealism of hermeneutics developed in the disciplines dealing with thought – critical sociology is opposed to the reduction of meaningful, socially subsisting objectified complexes to the contents of cultural tradition. (3) Confronted with universalism of overall theories of social systems – critical sociology is opposed to the reduction of all social conflicts to what can be defined as unsolved problems inherent in self-regulating systems. (4) Finally, confronted with the dogmatic inheritance of history – critical sociology must defend itself

> against the tyranny of concepts of reflexive philosophy
> (Habermas, 1974, pp. 10-13).

Critical sociology was deeply involved in a methodological fight with positivism. Positivism was viewed by it as narrow-minded – due to its insistence on relying on empirically tested methods. These standardized methods were regarded by critical sociology as limited tools which are only able to grasp tangible knowledge about social reality (as it is additionally shown by phenomenology or ethnomethodology). If social reality is seen as it is pictured by these methods, then, according to the Frankfurt School, this reality is distorted or invented and structured by arbitrarily selected techniques (Adorno *et al.*, 1976). Critical sociology took as its main critical target this version of positivism which has been so skilfully elaborated by Karl Popper. It might be interesting to notice that, despite this seemingly damaging attack, in his book *Unended Quest*, which is a sort of summary of his *Weltanschauung*, Karl Popper does not mention the Frankfurt School or its representatives at all.

One may say in general that critical sociology had an 'intention' in its search to find the real causes of social progress and changes – to go beyond the boundaries which are established by the research techniques of the accessible fabric of the social world. Although this type of approach is an interesting one and sometimes quite fruitful (it might reveal at least a possibility of overlooking these essential and strategic aspects of social life which are too complicated, subtle, or too 'obvious' for standardized measures), nevertheless at the same time it is too often misused by those who, being not methodologically mature, have a temptation to reject all reliable tests of social investigation in order to be free to profess various types of speculative or spectacular political ideas.

It seems useful – although against the spirit of critical sociology – to distil from the bulk of reflections attributed to this approach some general, important, hypotheses. These are:

(1) It is possible to specify the essential features of authoritarian personalities: the more an individual is authoritarian, the more he is dominant (or associated with dominant forces) and consequently more rigid and contemptuous in his social attitudes.

(2) Domination is exercised not only through the crude economic power: the captivity of super-ego composes the crucial element of this domination – the less it is visible, the more it is oppressive.

(3) Reinterpreted marxist 'superstructure' not only plays the role of a dependent variable. Being transformed into a system

66

(establishment), it plays the role of a strategic element which captures the human awareness in a way which is useful for this system.

(4) In the short run, domination is exercised by manipulation which (in an unconscious way) restricts the individual freedom but also pushes an individual towards options which only spuriously seem to be profitable for him.

(5) In the long run, domination is exercised by reified elements of ideology. Those being alienated from the individual are, at the same time, 'natural' for him (then he is not aware of any other options, neither is he able to imagine them).

Those hypotheses give an interesting general starting-point for an analysis of the basic social processes and changes in a given society. They are not so much concerned with the specific tangible factors (like marxist economic ones), but they try to locate the power (crucial element of social life) as it is structured in the social system which is under consideration.

It is a pity that the 'Frankfurt School' lost its intellectual momentum so fast. Its political, psychological, autobiographical, cognitive and historical ramifications were so fascinating that this scientific legend may be regarded as even more interesting and in-structive than several 'real' sociological schools!

Bibliography

Adorno, T. (1969–70), 'Society', *Salmagundi*, no. 10–11 Autumn 1969–Winter 1970.

Adorno, T. (1973), *The Jargon of Authenticity*, London: Routledge & Kegan Paul.

Adorno, T., Frenkel-Brunswik, E., Levinson, D., and Sandford, R. (1950), *The Authoritarian Personality*, New York: Norton.

Adorno, T., Albert, H., Habermas, J., Popper, K. and Pilot, T. (1976), *The Positivist Dispute in German Sociology*, London: Heinemann.

Frisby, D. (1974), 'The Frankfurt School: Critical Theory and Positivism', in J. Rex (ed.), *Approaches to Sociology*, London: Routledge & Kegan Paul.

Fromm, E. (1942), *Fear of Freedom*, London: Kegan Paul.

Fromm, E. (1955), *The Sane Society*, New York.

Habermas, J. (1971), *Toward a Rational Society*, London: Heinemann.

Habermas, J. (1974), *Theory and Practice*, London: Heinemann.

Horkheimer, M. (1939), 'The Social Function of Philosophy', SPSS, VIII, p. 3.

Jay, M. (1973), *The Dialectical Imagination*, London: Heinemann.

Marcuse, H. (1968), *One-Dimensional Man*, London: Sphere Books.

Popper, K. (1979), *Unended Quest*, Illinois.

Slater, P. (1977), *Origin and Significance of the Frankfurt School*, London: Routledge & Kegan Paul.

6 The 'Hermeneutic' sociology
Adam Podgórecki

An activity manifested in uttering a sentence, writing a poem, making a horseshoe, putting money into a deposit, proposing marriage to a girl, electing an official, performing a religious ritual – as empirically given, is the thing contained in the experience of the speaker and his listeners, of the poet and his readers, of the blacksmith and the owner of the horse, of the lover and the courted girl, of the electorate and the elected official, of the religious persons participating in the ritual. A student who wishes to investigate those actions in the inductive manner, must take them as they are in the experience of people – of the actor and those on whom he reacts; those data are his empirical data, besides being their empirical data. I have already put forth this view by saying that the data of this kind possess the 'humanistic coefficient' for the person who studies them.

F. Znaniecki

Understanding gains the insight . . . into the vital expressions of others by transpositions of one's own experience.

W. Dilthey

What the 'hermeneutic sociology' is about, is – at the same time – one of the most crucial, but also one of the most elusive cognitive enigmas. How one looks on the 'hermeneutic sociology' depends on many, for the most part tacit, assumptions. It depends, in the first place, on the general definition of sociology. On one stipulation, sociology is

the science about human collectives . . . [describing] the phenomena and processes whereby arise various forms of collective life of people, the structures of such collectives arising from mutual human interaction, the forces that bring them together or disrupt them, their changes and transformations (Szczepański, 1970, p. 12).

By sociology can also be meant the comparative analysis of social structures. Max Weber who accepted this type definition of sociology used to describe himself as a student of 'comparative history' and rejected the label of a 'sociologist', purporting that he did not know its meaning (personal information from A. Salomon, member of Weber's circle, in Wrong, 1970, pp. 12-13). On still another definition, sociology is 'the study of human actions' (Aron, 1970, p. 270). These and other definitions of sociology limit its scope in different ways. The approaches of Szczepański and

Aron obviously confine it – being sociologically 'conformistic' – to the human social behaviours. Weber's definition ('comparative history'), apparently more adequate to the broader perceptions of the whole, does not put such a limitation on it and the implications of this definition, the appearances notwithstanding, are far reaching indeed. For if sociology is meant – and recent studies on animal social groups seem to indicate that it is – as a study dealing with social structures, that are present also in the animal world, how could one establish, then, the eventual syntony of the perception of a certain action by non-human individuals among themselves? And how could one relate these possible meanings to the human understanding? A discussion on the understanding of sociology thus is involved, from the very outset, in the essential, epistemological problems of social sciences in general.

In some ways it is easier to say what 'hermeneutic sociology' does not mean.

Certainly it is not a subdivision of general sociology or, as one may proclaim, a subdivision of the sociology of knowledge (which methodologically would be a more appropriate category) because hermeneutic sociology pretends to play the role of a predecessor of all possible sociology. Thus, sociology seems to be involved in two particular types of vicious circles. (1) Sociological inquiries intend to elucidate human relations through enlarging the existing scope of their perception; the adequate notion of this perception should be acquired after several existential approximations to social reality; nevertheless social reality is not a one-dimensional world; in order to grasp it as a whole it is necessary to have access to all its entities; but how is it possible without *a priori* knowledge of the structure of the whole reality to single out the chance of omitting its element (or elements)? (2) Only after the entrance into social reality of the notions relevant to it becomes 'familiar', 'obvious', 'natural'; thus, direct, intuitive acquiescence of this reality seems to be only a precondition to its real, conceptual recognition. But when is the entrance into it 'deep' enough? When is it adequate? And when is it not submerged by utopia or illusion?

Neither is 'hermeneutic sociology' a 'humanistic sociology'. Although such a label seems to be attractive (it may link the cognitive dimension of a human being to other ones: emotional, volitional, unconscious, etc.), it seems to be still too narrow. It is easy to observe that it omits the social worlds of animals (or – living creatures at large) which paradoxically enough quite often disclose human relations in a more transparent way than the human world itself!

Hermeneutic sociology claims that it should be treated as a general introduction to all possible sociological approaches (are they methods, 'schools' or, more or less, real schools?) due to its attempt to elucidate those notions of social reality which are regarded as basic. From this point of view the present development of 'hermeneutic sociology' does not seem to be satisfactory: although it tries to find its own specific subject, nevertheless it is not able to scrutinize all those concepts which are in everyday sociological use.

To grasp what the 'hermeneutic sociology' avows, is by no means made easy by the texts of its founder and chief propagator. According to him:

> Let us first summarise the results of the preceding investigations about the interrelatedness of the human studies. This rests on the relationship between experience and understanding from which three main principles have emerged. Our knowledge of what is given in experience is extended though the interpretation of the objectification of life and its interpretation, in turn, is only made possible by plumbing the depths of subjective experience. Similarly, understanding of the particular depends on the knowledge of the general, which, in turn, presupposes understanding. Finally a part of the historical course of events can only be understood completely in terms of its relation to the whole and a universal-historical survey of the whole presupposes the understanding of the parts united in it (Dilthey, 1976, pp. 195-6).

The above points taken from Dilthey's 'poetics' can be interpreted in too many ways. It can be suggested that 'understanding' should be referred to a given man only ('depths of subjective experience') but it can also be argued that it entails other living creatures too ('the objectification of life'); by another guess, the mental states of other individuals are analysed by empathy aimed at the above mentioned 'depths of subjective experience', but perhaps the phenomenological insight is also possible into the other historical epochs ('part of the historical course of events'). Understanding may refer, on one reading, to one's own culture which is existentially close to the understanding subject, but on a different reading it may also refer to remote cultures (the knowledge of the general). Those ambiguities call for a closer analysis of the key concept of understanding. Graff summarizes Husserl's (the chief ancestor of this idea) points on the subject in the following manner:

> In the personalistic attitude it can be seen how physical characteristics are strangely tied up with the body: they cannot be traced to any of its parts, but they are motivationally

connected with it. . . . I treat the world as my human
surroundings, rather than as the biological environment; those
surroundings are inhabited by intentional entities, such as
persons, institutions, their products, etc. I also treat myself as
a person, as long as I see myself in the surroundings. The
world of a person is not the world in itself, but for me it is
what I know about. The stimuli are experienced by a person
as motivational, rather than sensed as causal; his things are
not physical objects, but experienced intentional objects of
personal consciousness. The natural personalistic set is
practical in the broadest sense: it is always relevant to 'the
acting' and 'experiencing I'. In fact, other people are
sometimes treated as things – but the set is then shifted from
personalistic to nature-oriented.

And:

A community is constituted by the fact that the I turns
towards others as to subjects who react to his turning towards
them. 'By these acts a higher unity of consciousness is
produced among persons who already "know" each other; the
surrounding world of things, including physical ones, is also
comprised in this unity as the common environment of those
persons.' 'The communicating parties belong mutually for
each other to the surrounding world.' They all constitute
together 'the world of these subjects, i.e. the world of social
objects'. Communities, too, can communicate, understand
and experience one another. The surrounding world is
'spiritually meaningful' [geistige Bedeutung hat], because it is
constituted by spiritual acts of understanding and agreement.
The common world of different subjects is, 'on the lowest
level, the intersubjective material nature as the common field
of actual and possible experience of individual spirits,
individually or in experiencing togetherness'. Here belong
individual bodies, sensual experiences, emotions and drives.
On the higher level, nature in the field of activities and
evaluations, i.e. of 'activities performed by spirits on various
levels of socialisation' (Graff, 1977, pp. 14-15).

Generally speaking, the concept of 'hermeneutics' can, indeed,
be variously understood. On one account, it allows for some kind
of intersubjective test; on another, it does not. It can be perceived
as: (1) the semantic understanding of a given notion; (2) one
utilizing an analysis of logical consequences of related concepts; (3)
one based on empirical findings and (4) one grounded on structural
interrelations. These understandings are only to a limited degree

intersubjectively controlled. On the one hand, the understandings based on the empathy used in anthropological, or cultural, investigations escape, as a rule, intersubjectively oriented tests.

On the other hand, it might be worthwhile to state that the semantic understanding on some occasions could undergo relatively simple verification procedures. For example, if a given individual cannot recognize the practical consequences of definite symbols and behaves in the given area in incompatible, or in self-contradictory ways, being otherwise subjectively convinced about his integrity, thus accepting internally obvious contradictions, then it may be assumed that the individual fails to understand the given terms or concepts. He is not, then, able to understand the code in which that concept has been elucidated by, as Dilthey sometimes says, 'the objectification of life'. An interesting picture of such a failure was given by a professor of literature who wrote in his native language a number of vague, and therefore perceived as deep, books on Shakespeare, whose works he knew only from translations. That professor was eventually invited to lecture at Yale University and it then turned out that his ingenious ideas about Shakespeare did not result from his insight and originality, but from semantic misunderstandings brought about by the medley of translations, a 'combination' of them allowing for interpretations far remote from the original.

The understanding of logical constructions can be most readily observed when analysing deductive systems, mathematical formulas, statistical reports, etc. In general, the understanding of logical constructions depends less on the ability to use some broad patterns of thought and more on the ability to apply the basic rules of logical thinking. If we make a distinction between the 'narrow' and 'broader' positivism, or between positivism as making weaker and strong claims, we can say that the understanding of logical constructions remains within the domain of positivism in its narrower scope. Whereas positivism in its broader version consists of an approach which accepts only those statements which are based (or reducible to) empirically obtained data (the inability to distinguish between these two versions of positivism leads to many misunderstandings - the attack on positivism launched by the 'Frankfurt School' is one of them). Critical remarks concerning the assumed detrimental influence exerted on the social sciences by the predominance of the broader version of positivism are controversial, but are not justified at all as far as its narrower version is concerned. For the rules of thought; the directives of constructing and testing of propositions; the techniques which inform how to use the indicators; the rules of inductive thinking - these are the main instruments which contribute to the growth of the number of intersubjectively controllable beliefs. The positivism in the narrower sense is simply a set of abstract skills of efficient and controllable thinking about the empirical reality.

Understanding grounded in empirical findings is rather more elusive than the former kinds. If someone does not know that each aggression is a manifestation of some frustration; he is apt to see an actual case of aggressive behaviour as the 'holy ire', a righteous moral indignation, a reformatory zeal, or hostility and envy, etc. He may also consider it as something absolute and autotelic, or as a phenomenon without any psycho-social causes. But if such a person is told, and convinced by the relevant empirical data, that each aggression reflects some frustration (although not every frustration is manifested by aggressive behaviour), he is apt to seek for factors that tend to bring about aggression, or for the causes of frustration. But, of course, it cannot be excluded that a given individual will learn intuitively (or by a phenomenological insight), without any knowledge of empirical data, that aggression is related to frustration. The understanding based on empirical evidence can thus help to grasp the meaning of definite social phenomena. Nevertheless, this type of understanding (based on empirical findings) is still elusive, because someone may, quite rightly, notice that the understanding of this category is grounded in some arbitrary definitions regulating the meanings of relevant terms.

The understanding based on the placing of the given social phenomena within some broader structure also is subject, to some degree, to controlled testing. For example, we cannot understand the peculiarities of the social milieu of the Polish intelligentsia if we do not see it against the background of the general social structure of Polish society. This social class – originating from the gentry, deprived of its original position by large expulsions performed by foreign governments which divided the Polish state, marked additionally by the anticipatory fear of further loss of status, compelled to withdraw from services which it earlier performed for the nation, still ready for messianic missions – was treated in Polish society by other social strata as a basic reference group. It may be fully understood only within the social system in which it has existed. Thus, in situations where the holistic point of view is needed, the given social phenomenon can only be properly (i.e. in the intersubjectively controllable manner) understood if it is placed within the more general pattern of the analysed system.

The intuitive or empathetic understanding is sometimes very penetrating, but even more often it is wholly misleading. The semantic acrobatics of the 'inclusive empathy' (understanding based on inductive analysis of the set of indicators informing about the scope of inquiry) may be fallacious in a double manner: they not only fail to explain what kind of 'empathy' accounts for the sampling of certain indicators rather than of others, but also a neck-breaking leap is indeed made by taking for granted that the given set of indicators is adequate with respect to the whole contents of the analysed object. Weber's 'empirical-empathetic' abilities, which may be used here as a good example, made him seek the meaning of the concept of understanding (*Verstehen*) in the idea of the scheme relating ends to means. According to Weber's scheme, all actions should be explained by indicating that they constitute the means towards the actor's ends. If an actor accepts certain ends, it can be assumed, from his own perspective, that he is apt to seek the appropriate means of their realization.

The last meaning of understanding which may be used in hermeneutic sociology is the understanding of definite cultural entities. If one is ignorant of the Chinese culture, one does not know that a certain type of smile of a Chinese does not mean approval or confirmation but an anticipatory expression of negation, designed to release the forthcoming uneasiness. If one does not know the peculiar Japanese idea of 'giri' (the obligation to help those belonging to the family or local circle with an implication, in this respect, that those excluded are not regarded as partners in social relationships), one will not understand why in Japan practically nobody would feel obliged to answer a stranger's questions. According to the principle of seniority, functioning in Japanese culture, a woman must on no occasion take a bath before a man in the same premises. The distance between cultures makes isolated fragments of an alien culture seem strange without their broader contexts. But it is very difficult to see those broader frames of reference, for it requires a renouncement of one's own cultural perspective and an acquiring of that prevailing in the studied culture. It should be remarked that in anthropological and sociological investigations the understanding of the meaning of alien cultural phenomena is the most significant part of the cognitive task. But it is in this domain that the traps of subjectivism are the most abundant.

It can be noted that the introduction of the concept of 'understanding', or of the 'human coefficient', enhances the phenomenon of subjectivism which is common for all the social sciences and particularly significant in sociology.

Subjectivism indeed may have several cognitively important virtues: (1) it may give a chance to construe a new social reality; (2) it may design and build an unprecedented world of ideas and values; (3) it may transform separated individual environmental elements into a uniquely perceived entity; it may, in short, 'enrich' the scope of human perceptiveness. The main task of hermeneutic sociology is to elucidate those earlier unrecognized realms of human existence. But hermeneutic sociology, perceived in such a manner, faces an antinomy which seems to be inherent in all social sciences. For those sciences do not seek only to multiply subjective, in principle irreducible, standpoints, but they 'work' towards an establishment of an objective platform, from which the social regularities can be grasped without subjective colouring. Additionally, methodological individualism as represented by hermeneutic sociology is opposed to the holistic or organicist approach in sociology. The organicist view assumes that societies are 'wholes', at least in the sense that some of the macro-scale behaviours are ruled by specific sociological macro-laws, i.e. such that cannot be explained as regularities or tendencies being mere net results of individual behaviours. On the other hand, it is individual behaviours which are, at least in part, explained in terms of such laws (on the holistic account), eventually in conjunction with explanations of individuals' roles within institutions and the functions of institutions within the whole social system (Nagel, 1961, p. 463). Subjectivism can be thus counterbalanced by construing objective regularities holding for the larger societal bodies. But again the problem arises, do objective regularities exist at all, or are they rather some generalized, collectively accepted rationalizations. Or, possibly, they are the products of 'false consciousness' which interjects them into social reality in order to have it understood systematically in accordance with the interests of those who produce the relevant paradigms. It does not seem easy for the hermeneutic sociology to get disentangled from antinomies of this kind, for the vicious circle is always there: who understands properly (and how?) the given elements of 'understanding'?

However, the hermeneutic sociology has certain achievements, in that it offers some generalizations which although based on intuitive entrances into social reality give some valuable concepts of a general nature. Interesting analyses of this kind have been offered by M. Weber.

Weber saw bureaucracy as the aggregate of organizations rationally geared together and adjusted to definite ends; bureaucracy, according to him, is a precise hierarchy of orders coming from the top to the bottom; it involves a neat division of tasks and their assigned roles; it requires definite skills for the performance of these roles; it has fixed mechanisms of advancement and retirement; it imposes impersonal standards of behaviour from its personnel towards the clients; positions within its structures are occupied irrespective of the privileges of property or birth; the work in bureaucracy is treated as a vocation for life. It is quite well known that such a description of bureaucracy does not reflect any definite social reality, but it represents a so-called 'ideal type'. This model fails altogether to take into account the subservient role of bureaucracy in relation to the ruling classes, the problem of anti-functional formalism, existence of pressure groups which are present in many bureaucratic systems, the operations of white-collar subcultures, the frequent phenomenon of the 'dirty togetherness', and, finally, it neglects the processes described by Parkinson's law in which work gets extended so as to fill the time scheduled for it. The analytical model of bureaucracy briefly presented above can serve as a convenient starting-point for more detailed investigations of bureaucracies which actually exist.

Interesting, too, is Weber's classification into three types of legitimization: rational-legal, traditional and charismatic. The traditional type of legitimization of a definite system of power is based on established customs ('what was good enough for my father is good enough for me', or 'things have always been done like that'). In this way, power is made legitimate by the 'eternal yesterday'. Power is grounded in rational-and-legal premises, if the sustenance of a system of law is the reason of existence of the power (although power has often called forth legal systems for that purpose); the rational means entailed by the law as instructions for the bureaucracy are also thereby vindicated. The charismatic type of power, according to this approach, is a revolutionary challenge for the *status quo*. The charismatic power is associated with the charismatic leader. He has virtues of the 'higher order' and the splendour of actual or pretended heroic deeds; pointing out his mission, he demands obedience from his followers because of his extraordinary personality. Weber classifies additionally human activities into customary, affective, purposive and axiological. It was noticed that the correspondences can be established between the customary activity and traditional power, affective activity and charismatic power, purposive activity and rational-legal power, but a power corresponding to the type of activity based on values is lacking from the scheme (Aron, 1970, p. 186). This omission may be easily corrected if one will take into account the power which refers to 'natural law' as its possible justification.

Again, the distinction between the ethics of responsibility and the ethics of ultimate ends is useful for the explanation of social phenomena. According to Weber, the ethics of absolute ends consists in raising a definite pattern of behaviour, with reference to some accepted value, to the rank of the standard for all the relevant behaviours; the ethics of responsibility take into account the 'ultimate historical objectives of the given cause and it admits of the necessity to act instrumentally towards this objective' (Wrong,

1970, p. 60). The parallelism between these two types of ethics and the idea of ethics as based on instrumental and principled attitudes can be readily seen (see Chapter 12, 'The Concept of Meta-Attitudes').

The standpoint represented by the hermeneutic sociology thus ought to be treated as one which enlarges the scope of epistemological potentialities in social sciences. It represents the middle way between barren abstraction fed by arbitrary conceptual artefacts, on the one hand, and the 'gluey hard facts' forbidding any generalizations beyond the empirical evidence, on the other. The ideas of Weber presented above seem to offer a way out from the dilemma, which is better than none at all.

The conception of the hermeneutic sociology is also itself an interesting problem for the sociology of knowledge, for the question remains open. What social and individual factors determine a given cognitive outlook on social reality which, in turn, may attribute a definite meaning to hermeneutic perspective of understanding? Is it true, as Max Weber used to say, that 'one need not be Julius Caesar to understand Caesar', or is Wrong correct when he says: 'It may take a thief to catch a thief, but surely a thief's goals are intelligible to an honest man' (Wrong, 1970, pp. 19-20).

It should be finally noted that the most interesting situations may emerge from a hermeneutic sociological point of view, when social, political, economic, ideological entities appear which are not completely defined, and when it is difficult to know where do they lead, what sort of significance do they carry? (Are they going to be the leading ideologies in a given society or social group or are they just remainders and relics of outdated attitudes and values?) Hermeneutic sociology may innovatively – through elaboration of various rationalizations – also play an important cognitive role; it could elucidate new trends in social life or evolve new ideas in the social sciences, attaching to these trends or ideas significance which might be not otherwise recognized. But, and let us make it clear, the hermeneutic sociology may perversely play also quite a dangerous role: it could attach a scientistic charisma to oppressive or backward ideas.

Bibliography

Aron, R. (1970), *Main Currents in Sociological Thought 2*, Harmondsworth: Penguin.
Dilthey, W. (1976), *Selected Writings*, Cambridge University Press.

Gerth, H., and Mills, C. W. (1972), 'From Max Weber', in M. Brinker-hoff and P. Kunz (eds), *Complex Organizations and Their Environments*, Iowa: Wm. C. Brown.

Graff, P. (1977), 'Phenomenology as an Esoteric Doctrine' (unpublished manuscript).

Husserl, E. C. (1964a), *The Idea of Phenomenology*, The Hague:

Husserl, E. C. (1964b), *The Paris Lectures*, The Hague:

Husserl, E. C. (1970), *Logical Investigations*, London: Routledge & Kegan Paul.

Mokrzycki, E. (1971), *Założenia socjologii humanistycznej (Principles of Humanistic Sociology)*, Warsaw: PWN.

Nagel, E. (1961), *The Structure of Science*, London: Routledge & Kegan Paul.

Szczepański, J. (1970), *Elementarne pojecia socjologii (Elementary Concepts of Sociology)*, Warsaw: PWN.

Weber, M. (1962), *Basic Concepts in Sociology*, London: P. Owen.

Weber, M. (1964), *The Theory of Social and Economic Organization*, London: Free Press.

Wrong, D. (ed.) (1970), *Max Weber*, Englewood Cliffs, N.J.: Prentice-Hall Inc.

Znaniecki, F. (1957), 'Social Action', in L. Coser and B. Rosenberg (eds), *Sociological Theory*, New York: Macmillan.

7 Phenomenological sociology
Maria Łoś

Phenomenological thought in sociology - like symbolic interactionism in social psychology - constituted a reaction against the
methodological premises of the behavioural orientation in social
sciences. Schutz, who initiated the phenomenological perspective in
sociology, did not question the good intentions of the behavioural
researchers, but was convinced that their assumptions about the
methodological unity of social and 'natural' sciences were
completely inaccurate. He believed that it led them towards a
gradual substitution of a fictitious world for the true social reality.
It is worth noting that there is some difference between his view on
this matter and that of Weber. To Weber, the methodology of
natural sciences could be successfully applied to the study of
society, although he himself recommended a different method as
more desirable. He saw the qualitative, individualized methods
(particularly that of interpretative understanding) as likely to bring
a more interesting and revealing insight into social reality. He did
not discard the quantitative, nomothetic approach, but regarded it
as bringing only a limited knowledge to certain aspects of society. It
seems that what Weber had in mind is exactly these aspects of
intersubjective reality which Schutz described as the main subject-
matter of his phenomenological sociology. Those mundane,
regular patterns, which Schutz attempted to analyse by the
phenomenological method, were to Weber a vital but banal and
uninteresting part of social life, which may be studied in the
fashion characteristic to natural sciences.

In fact, one of the most persistent themes of contemporary
critiques of Schutz's phenomenology is the annoying tediousness
and relatively small importance of the phenomena which he
scrupulously studied for most of his life. Naturally, one possible
reaction to such a critique is that his studies give us a good insight

into one broad plane of the social world, and that instead of criticizing him we should rather concentrate on the application of phenomenological method to other planes in order to obtain a complete picture. There are, however, many other points which can be raised in response to such critiques.

First of all, discovering what is obvious and taken for granted by the members of the given society allows us to comprehend more fully what is treated by them as problematic, or threatening to their common-sense life world, and why it is treated as such. In this task, a comparative perspective is the most fruitful method. Schutz's phenomenology should be perceived as sociology of everyday knowledge. It deals with the content of social consciousness. A generally accepted, but rather over-simplified interpretation would consider the content of 'group unconsciousness' as an absurd concept in the light of Schutz's main epistemological assumptions. If we, however, accept the obvious fact that there exist more than one group and that they interact with each other as well as with their common environment, the concept may assume a new meaning. If we agree that the actions of the members of one hypothetical group are influenced by the content of their consciousness, we should also predict that those actions will influence and change the environment as well as some aspects of the situation of other groups. It is this subjective-objective reality which is usually passed unnoticed by the defenders of either side of the old controversy within social sciences. The subjective stand may be illustrated by Husserl's thesis on the intentionality of consciousness which defines as existing only what is intentionally perceived. Let us discuss this postulate. The individual or the group members perceive intentionally various things which remain unnoticed by other individuals or groups interacting with him, or with them. However, these facts are very likely to produce some changes in the behaviour of our 'conscious' individuals and, probably, in their interactions with others. In this way, those others – unaware of the initial 'facts' – are nevertheless affected by them indirectly. They would define the new situation in some ways and those definitions would be crucial for their subsequent actions, but an observer may be able to go beyond their subjectivity and trace the 'objective' causes in the subjective intentional consciousness of other people (individuals, social classes, power elites, etc.). Needless to say, those complex processes of 'interaction' may be transmitted, distorted or facilitated by material objects and by the peculiar relations of the various groups and individuals to them. Moreover, the definitions of the situation by the affected party – usually conditioned by previous experience and agreed meanings – may also be intentionally manipulated by the party initiating change or imposing conditions. We can thus speak – contrary to the prevailing opinion on this matter – about the basic compatibility of the marxist concept of 'false consciousness' with the phenomenological vision of society. It seems that all the above mentioned phenomena and meaningful social processes can be studied adequately within Schutz's methodological perspective. There is no need for limiting the applicability of his approach to those aspects of the social world which he had chosen to describe in detail and to which he adjusted his method and conceptual framework.

Schutz realized that before any advanced research could be undertaken his main task was to search for valid explanations of the very foundations of social life and, consequently, of sociological concepts. He attempted to answer some primary questions as to the nature of communication among people, the essence of social associations, social norms, etc. He hoped to discover some universal, elementary features of the social world – the general conditions necessary for the existence of a society and which open and define its inner horizon. However, his method may be also successfully applied to the studies of concrete societies and various groups within them. Schutz's analysis of the inevitability of the existence of the unnoticed and 'taken for granted' network of social patterns may, for instance, inspire research on the scope of those unified, routine spheres within various societies. Are they shared by various social classes, ethnic groups, age categories, etc.? What are the consequences and/or correlates of the various degrees of routinization of social behaviour and of the occurrence of the naïve attitude in everyday life? Again, what are the prevalent nature and content of assumed factors of social reality under different political and economic systems?

It seems, for instance, that in the centralized 'socialist' countries the 'taken for granted' margin is very thoroughly permeated by political and ideological factors. Among the routine, automatic aspects of the everyday lives of the people in those countries are: a deeply internalized fear, an assumption of the existence of an omnipotent 'they' who are against 'us', habitualized double language and meaningless verbal tributes to the existing order, and a defensive sense of humour, which functions as a symbolic counterbalance to the constant threat to one's dignity and integrity. The majority of the adult population tend (perhaps subconsciously) to push these unavoidable and more or less constant factors into the sphere of the 'obvious' and 'normal'. Those who suspend these assumptions and adopt a more reflective attitude towards the obvious aspects of 'natural life world' are punished, not only by the formal system, but also by the informal social reaction. The latter would label them promptly as unrealistic, desperate, immature, unstable and so forth. They would be viewed as a threat to the taken for granted global submission to the unreflective attitude which is justified and imposed by the external circumstances. Needless to say, the centralized formal system may skilfully stimulate these informal labelling mechanisms, securing in this way continuity of the taken for granted world of the 'hypnotized' society.

On the other hand, the 'welfare' states by their standardized packages of offered opportunities and incentives strengthen significantly the whole range of the 'obvious' values, the necessary biographical stages, 'natural' aspirations and expectations, etc. More systematic analyses of the hidden mechanisms pushing those various factors into the sphere of the taken for granted reality in the different societies or social classes (groups) might bring about very interesting findings. However most of the positivist style research focuses on much more verbalized and consciously defined social phenomena. Unfortunately most of the phenomenological (and ethnomethodological) work in this area overlooks the political and ideological dimensions, trying to be faithful to the considerably contorted belief that only the most trivial and standardized aspects of social life deserve our attention. Moreover, the phenomenologists are often so overwhelmed with the idea of studying the 'naïve' attitude that they themselves fall into the trap of naïvety. The processes of social institutionalization of the selected patterns, ideas and values which contribute to the content of the naïvely taken for granted world are by no means so 'innocent', spontaneous and egalitarian as the phenomenologically orientated sociologists often assume. They are socially imposed upon the 'common' people by those who are better educated, or who have access to the power, media, charisma, truth, various institutions, control agencies, etc. All these people (individuals, social strata, classes, agencies, etc.) are interlinked by highly differentiated relationships and they mould the processes of construction of everyday reality within the framework of the given present time, historical past and the economic and political system. Their contributions are incorporated into these processes only, if, and in so far as they can actually help to mould the attitudes consistent with the resultant definition (or definitions) of the mission of the common people in the given socio-cultural system and the given historical stage of the society. Such definitions are characterized by continuity as well as by change. And they do not simply mirror the subjective perceptions and meanings of those influential people, but rather absorb their suitable redefined forms which may be successfully sunk into the 'natural' world.

Let us come back for a moment to the social reality of the

'socialist' countries. In the centralized systems, characterized by direct ideological control, by censorship and by relative cultural isolation, the natural attitude absorbs many rather frightening and cruel features of the social reality. They cannot be helped by the people, nor can they be negated or overpowered; they can only be 'naturalized' or 'normalized' by their incorporation into the sphere of unquestioned, unavoidable reality. Needless to say, those phenomena are welcome and encouraged by the political managers of the systems in question. In order to make this hypothesis less abstract let us imagine a Polish citizen who goes to a butcher and sees piles of meat and no trace of a queue. His surprise would be great, he would try to find out what had actually happened and he would surely tell all his friends about this rather startling and unusual experience. Let us take another example of the taken for granted expectations. Someone, say a Polish worker, stands up during a crew meeting and says that he does not approve of the one-party political system. Everybody is shocked. It is generally taken for granted that one simply does not say such things in public. They ask each other whether he is drunk or, perhaps, crazy. Let us further suppose that the worker has not been sacked from his job, neither has he been formally punished in any other way. His fellow workers are puzzled. It is so obvious that one is punished in such circumstances. If one is not – then why do we all keep silent? Well, it is obviously too risky to speak up. It just cannot be true that it was simply passed by 'them' unnoticed. And so, they begin to suspect some ugly deals, humiliating denials of his views and self-criticism, or a promise of some dubious collaboration on the part of the unfortunate fellow. It is self-evident that he must have done something of this sort. And – whether he has or not – he will get his punishment, informally, owing to the familiar, naïve, natural attitude.

Perhaps one can learn something interesting about the working of the macro-system by studying this 'soft' world of everyday routine reality which is so often neglected and so often ridiculed. However, reading Schutz's apologia of the naïve attitude and finding similar tones in the writings of his followers, one becomes truly amazed how innocent and unsuspicious some of our fellow social scientists can be.

Another problem, mentioned before briefly, is the controversial question whether the pre-given, taken for granted life-world could be better described and explained by the 'objective', positivist methods. Schutz passed over the 'transcendental reduction', by means of which Husserl had been attempting to achieve objective insight into the essences of things. In his concept of transcendental ego Husserl hoped to overcome the limits of any individual subjectivity and to reach objective apodictic knowledge without abandoning the subjective perspective. Schutz turns his attention towards the subjective-naïve attitude of average people in everyday 'life-world'. Its peculiar form of epoché implies – in contradistinction to the epoché of phenomenological reduction – suspension of every doubt concerning the existence of the outer world and its objects. This is epoché of the cognitive style of average people, and it is Schutz's intention to see the world through their eyes. Even more, he desires to discover not only what they see, but also what they do not actually perceive any more because it is so obvious that it forms an invisible background to all their activities. They are, however, conscious of it, in a passive, natural way, which can be easily proved by the fact that they become alert and puzzled as soon as the anticipated patterns do not occur, or assume different forms.

We may suppose that Schutz did not believe that the understanding of social life can be achieved by the abstract, detached, transcendental ego which operates within the cognitive style completely alien and, in fact, opposite to that typical of the members of the society in their intersubjective, shared with others, biographically conditioned, paramount reality. This world would be meaningless to them if they did not believe that it is similarly experienced and interpreted within the same subjective meaning-context by their fellow-men. And it would be equally meaningless to the sociologist if he suspends his belief in the existence of society, communication among the people and the social construction of meanings. However, in order to get insight into this world he is expected to use Husserl's method of 'philosophical reduction' by suspending the unquestioning, 'naïve' attitude and facing directly these very features of the social life which are commonly treated by the people as obvious and not deserving of any systematic attention.

The social scientist is supposed to study this self-evident, paramount reality of common people. Not being preoccupied with the pragmatic interests and pursuits as they usually are, he may reflect upon their everyday 'life-world' and grasp its true meaning as it is expressed in their subjective meaning-contexts. In this sense, Schutz argues, phenomenological knowledge revealed in sociological ideal types is objective. It is also consistent with the main directives of phenomenological perspective since its source and significant starting-point is located in the pre-scientific reality of everyday life, as also is its language – free of any assumptions except those accepted within the studied world. The cognitive interest of the researcher – as opposed to the practical interests of the people in their everyday life – and his detachment from his biographical situation, are supposed to guarantee the objective nature of the thought constructs of the second order which he builds up on the basis of common-sense constructs found in every-day reality. This is Schutz's modest, and perhaps more realistic version of Husserl's transcendental ego. Instead of reading the 'essences' of objects, his sociologist is expected to grasp (from some neutral observation point) the prevailing typifications which make life easier for the members of the given group, by channelling and standardizing their mutual expectations, ways of communication, etc. Basically, the same task is performed by the common people when they abandon their convenient, 'naïve' attitude and reflect upon some usually taken for granted patterns, types, habits, etc. However, as the sociologist is better equipped methodologically and more persistent in his cognitive efforts, he is more likely to produce a fuller and more systematic map of the socially agreed upon typifications.

Is this type of knowledge objective? According to Schutz its source is subjective, but it is objectively organized into a coherent and complete system of ideal types. Of course, one may reject such objectivity. But, what about the objectivity of behavioural positivist empiricism? Does it not try to make sense out of 'empirical', 'objective' data in the most subjective way, by inventing some coherent interpretations, by imputing some motivations, meanings or other rather vague forces, thus making possible organization of the data in some constructive way? The situation is simply reversed in the case of Schutz's phenomenological sociology. The problem is that it is, in practice, rather difficult to determine what the objectivity in sociology can possibly mean. It has apparently more than one meaning, and it is difficult to say which one is meant by each of the critics who reproach Schutz with lack of objectivity or with the doubtful quality of objectivity (for instance, Gorman, 1977). Nor is it clear what Schutz himself meant when he claimed that his sociological constructs conform to some basic requirement of objectivity and empirical verification. Is not this mysterious concept of objectivity a kind of fiction naïvely taken for granted by the social scientists? If so, let it serve as yet another example of how perverse the naïve attitude can be - as it has been normally for ideological or competitive purposes that the concept of 'objectivity' has been used. It has often served as a self-evident weapon in the efforts to discredit the opposed theoretical and methodological orientations as well as in argument for the superiority of one's own approach.

It is worthwhile to note at least some of the meanings of 'objectivity' occurring in those sophisticated skirmishes. For Schutz 'objective' is the knowledge produced by a 'detached' observer and organized according to the basic rules of logic. For the positivist, objective is 'empirical' knowledge – i.e. knowledge intersubjectively verifiable (which means that another researcher using the same techniques would arrive at the same conclusions; the possibility of a bias of the particular technique or the agreed upon sociological paradigm not being questioned). For marxists, 'objective' is synonymous with Marx's inspired vision of historical materialism known for its scant respect to the actual 'empirical evidence'. In addition, epistemological meaning of 'objective' is often confused with the ontological stand on the nature of the social world (to Schutz, for instance, the world of everyday life is in a way objective) and on the nature of forces shaping human behaviour and social development as well as on the 'freedom-determinism' controversy.

Moreover, 'objective' occurs in yet another context in the discussions on the neutrality or value-involvement of social sciences. This controversy has managed to produce even more confusion and miscommunication among various points of view than the previously mentioned ones.

In this situation, the defenders of the superiority of the positivist sociology would have to refer to more specifically defined advantages of their approach in order to enable a methodologically meaningful confrontation with the phenomenological social science. It seems that the most serious obstacle in the further development of positivistic perspective has been the inability to account for the dialectic nature of social processes and relationships between individual and society. Questions to be answered by the techniques accepted within the positivist methodological tradition cannot be confronted with a simultaneous 'yes' and 'no' response without risking a complete frustration of the computer (or a computer-like research scheme).

Phenomenological sociology seems to be much more flexible in this respect. It allows for various contradictions, apparently in the belief that the dialectical nature of the social world is better reflected in this way. Unfortunately, most of the critics do not recognize this unorthodox methodological approach, expecting unequivocal declarations on the classical controversies around such issues as: 'objective'-'subjective', 'individual freedom'-'social determinism', 'pure' and 'praxis-related' science, etc.

It is, naturally, true that Schutz's man is free only to obey – as Gorman (1977) has bitterly summed it up – but we should not forget how complex is the reality we are talking about. First of all, Schutz spoke about the plane of social life which constitutes the common framework of taken for granted typifications and behavioural patterns. From the point of view of Schutz's inquiry, it is indeed the most important plane, as it not only forms a real foundation for development of group life but also opens possibilities for more advanced forms of social communication, interaction and structure construction. Whether we like it or not, without some basic stock of common signs, symbols, ways of communication, norms, etc., social life would be clearly unthinkable. From the subjective perspective of the average people, however, it is not necessarily the most meaningful life plane (although it is certainly the paramount and basic one), since it is handled by them in a routine, partially automatic and 'habitualized' way. Perhaps this is the very condition enabling them to reflect upon other things in life, to develop more spontaneous and meaningful relationships with chosen individuals or groups, to plan, to select, to achieve, to imagine, to rebel, etc. If they were (like Schutz's 'stranger') really consciously involved in all those small decisions and choices which they are faced with in every minute of their complicated lives (in 'existentialist' fashion), they would not be able to notice anything else but the intricate procedure of buying a bottle of milk, travelling by bus, analysing rhetorical remarks of their fellow workers, etc.

It is, then, tempting to see this freedom to obey in the area of mundane, petty activities as a gate to freedom to choose within more significant spheres of human life (a possibility completely overlooked by critics like Smart, Gorman and others). Nevertheless, a more penetrating analysis of this statement may lead to some more sceptical questions. Can we be really sure that what is contained in the routine and mundane life-world is actually relatively less significant for the development of human potentialities? What sort of criteria enable us to make such judgments or to create such a hierarchy? Can we really assume that an unreflexive, naïve attitude in everyday life does not, in fact, produce a habit or readiness to behave similarly in other, less routinized, planes of life, encouraging basically passive, obedient and conformist orientations? Should we not suspect that the taken for granted assumptions about the everyday life-world influence and condition the vision and attitudes also outside this mundane sphere? Do they not, indeed, become a part of the 'objective' reality, framing people's aspirations, evaluations, expectations, etc.?

This contradiction contains quite weighty practical and political aspects. On the one hand, the preoccupation and full involvement in coping with everyday reality may divert attention from more problematic political and social questions (the strategy rather successfully introduced in the 'socialist' countries). On the other hand, however, a carefree concentration on the 'higher' regions of human existence represents also some considerable threat to the individual's freedom and integrity. As the scope and content of the taken for granted world of everyday life is socially inherited and/or unreflexively acquired by the individual, it is exactly through this area of social consciousness (or 'unconsciousness') that the members of society can be most easily manipulated and pro-grammed by the dominating culture, ideology and economic interests. That is why – independently of the scholarly reasons given by Schutz – a profound, critical insight into the mundane, banal and uninteresting might be seen as a rather vital and urgent task.

Bibliography

Berger, P. L., Berger, B., and Kellner, H. (1974), *The Homeless Mind*, Harmondsworth: Penguin.

Berger, P. L., and Luckmann, T. (1966), *The Social Construction of Reality*, Garden City, New York: Doubleday.

Filmer, P., Phillipson, M., Silverman, D., and Walsh, D. (eds) (1972), *New Directions in Sociology*, London: Collier-Macmillan.

Gorman, R. (1977), *The Dual Vision*, London: Routledge & Kegan Paul.

Husserl, E. (1962), *Ideas*, London: Allen & Unwin (revised edition).

Husserl, E. (1965), *Phenomenology and the Crisis of Philosophy*, New York: Harper & Row.

Husserl, E. (1970), *The Crisis of European Sciences and Transcendental Phenomenology*, Evanston, Ill.: Northwestern University Press.

Mullins, N. C. (1973), *Theories and Theory Groups in Contemporary American Sociology*, New York: Harper & Row.

Psathas, G. (ed.) (1973), *Phenomenological Sociology. Issues and Applications*, New York: Wiley.

Schutz, A. (1962), *Collected Papers I: The Problem of Social Reality*, ed. M. Natanson, The Hague: Nijhoff.

Schutz, A. (1964), *Collected Papers II: Studies in Social Theory*, ed. A. Brodersen, The Hague: Nijhoff.

Schutz, A. (1966), *Collected Papers III: Studies in Phenomenological Philosophy*, ed. Ilse Schutz, The Hague: Nijhoff.

Schutz, A. (1970), *On Phenomenology and Social Relations*, ed. H. R. Wagner, Chicago and London: University of Chicago Press.

Schutz, A., and Luckmann, T. (1974), *The Structure of the Life World*, London: Heinemann Educational Books.

Smart, B. (1976), *Sociology, Phenomenology and Marxian Analysis*, London: Routledge & Kegan Paul.

Weber, M. (1947), *The Theory of Social and Economic Organization*, William Hodge.

8 Ethnomethodology[1]
Adam Podgórecki

In opposition to the age-old argument that sociology deals with
obvious problems, we propose that it dealt with the obvious as a
problem. We believe that domain of everyday life, while
providing sociology with various research topics, is itself very
rarely an independent research subject.

Zimmermann and Pollner

Until recently ethnomethodology had been an 'invisible college'
with quite distinct social features. At the outset, ethnomethodologists published very little, not because they did not try, but because American sociological journals tended to turn away their
typescripts. This fact, as well as other peculiarities of the 'invisible
college', made them develop a very efficient system of distributing
their mimeographed writings by mail to anyone who asked to be on
the mailing list – thus, in fact, to the relatively few 'insiders'.
Ethnomethodology is sometimes defined in terms of three specific
traits related to its organization as a scientific school, namely: (1)
emphasis on the central axiom, to the effect that all social science is
derived from, or is secondary with respect to, everyday social
knowledge; (2) a strong rejection reaction on the part of the
parental discipline; (3) intensive exchange of texts, almost
exclusively within the group (Mullins, 1973, p. 196). Any critic who
refused to yield to their arguments and stuck to his own opinions
was likely to hear their familiar rebuke: 'If you haven't been
trained to understand these ideas, you cannot expect to understand
them.' According to Mullins, the group who initiated
ethnomethodology was active at the beginning in southern
California (in 1964, of about twenty-five persons who were apt to
identify themselves as ethnomethodologists, eleven worked there).

The recognized founders and intellectual leaders of this trend in
sociology are H. Garfinkel, A. V. Cicourel[2], and H. Sacks; the first
two mentioned are also considered its organizational leaders. It is
remarkable that the work by Garfinkel (1967a), 'Some Rules of
Correct Decision Making That Jurors Respect', admittedly one of
the most successful pieces of writing in the field, had been for a
long time circulated in mimeographed form only (Mullins, 1973, p.
183), to be finally published as Chapter 4 of his *Studies in
Ethnomethodology* (Garfinkel, 1967b).

89

The emergence of this term 'ethnomethodology' is interesting too. Garfinkel explains that he coined it as he was trying to find an adequate label for his studies in the sociology of law. He was then occupied with the analysis of interviews and statements by jurors, made after their actual deliberations in court had been tape-recorded. Garfinkel was struck, as he writes, by the fact that the jurors who were laymen and thus could exert their common sense only, styled their statements in language aping that of professional lawyers. Garfinkel wanted ethnomethodology to include everyday, grass-roots knowledge ('ethno') and to use the methods which are different from the formal and petrified ones of the established social sciences ('methodology'). The term alluded to the fact that the basic concerns of ethnomethodology have been studies in practical activity, analyses of common-sense knowledge and considerations of the specific ways of thought which emerge from practical organizational involvement.

Ethnomethodology is one of those American trends which are essentially rooted in European thought. Many of its ideas have been drawn from the works of the German sociologist and philosopher, Alfred Schutz. (Alfred Schutz, a scholarly clerk, left Germany in 1939 and took a job as a bank official in New York. Since 1943 he has been lecturing on philosophy and the principles of the social sciences in the New York School for Social Research. His status of university lecturer earned him an academic conspicuity, after waiting twenty years for the emergence of a new trend in sociology.)

It would not be correct to assess that Garfinkel developed ethnomethodology out of obscure and unfashionable origins, whereas, in fact, he did it probably only after his disappointment with the existing state of sociological theory. He did his Ph.D. at Harvard (with T. Parsons as his supervisor), being interested in classical sociological problems, like the problem of social order and especially the relationship between social order as a concrete external existence and its subjective perception. This important stimulus of ethnomethodological development should not be ignored. It is particularly notable that Garfinkel and Sudnow, at one moment, played with an idea of substituting 'neopraxiology' for 'ethnomethodology'. Indeed, some affinities between ethnomethodology and praxiology appear to be obvious. While praxiology deals mainly with scientific rules of all efficient action (without neglecting all sorts of everyday wisdom), ethnomethodology is occupied, although not exclusively, with similar problems, with more emphasis on the commonsensical sources of this kind of knowledge. However, the general pattern of events is remarkable from the point of view of the development of science (and from that of the sociology of science); a germ of a new school arises and seeks for authorities in the philosophical and social past; various choices are open (mostly European); ultimately, ideas of the German-American phenomenologist take the upper hand over those of a Polish philosopher, T. Kotarbiński, founder of praxiology and a less internationally conspicuous academic personality.

Schutz's basic idea is that there is an insurmountable barrier between the world of scientific knowledge and everyday experience. According to him, an expert in social science can practically never enter 'here and now' into the world of the common man. One reason is that the rational models of action and the actual models realized by people in their practical endeavours are incompatible. According to Schutz, a sociologist has no privileged access to what a common man is and what he does. A social expert can only speculate in his abstract analyses of his own conceptual constructs (Schutz, 1963).

The essential for an ethnomethodological reasoning concept of the common man and his everyday activity has a significant consequence for the methodology of social research. We are told (by Garfinkel and others) that each individual takes for granted, according to principles (such as the principle of trust), various more or less overt or latent assumptions for his thoughts and actions. Following Denzin - although he is controversial among some representatives of ethnomethodology - eight such assumptions can be distinguished: (1) human interactions are time-sequenced, and human events cannot be properly understood without taking the past and current occurrences into account; (2) individuals talk on various matters in various situations, but many elements of those talks have their covert meanings which are taken for granted and never mentioned expressly; (3) ordinary events have obvious meanings and relevances, hardly set in doubt in individual contacts; (4) a situation with a defined meaning sustains such meaning among contacts or their sequences among the individuals involved; (5) 'any object present in the situation is what it is presented as being'; (6) a meaning given to an object in a human contact tends to be sustained, unless the situation gets changed; (7) individuals interrelated by their activities give uniform terms, symbols and labels to definite objects; (8) since individuals tend to define situations with reference to their own biographies and experiences, several discrepancies emerging in the course of their contacts and brought about by their different respective experience remain unresolved ('suspended'). It is worthwhile to add that this 'crippled decalogue' is not only theoretically interesting. It might also have some practical validity as an instruction which would inform interviewers about psychological and social settings of those sociological inquiries which are carried on by direct conversations.

Situations are defined mainly in the course and in terms of interaction processes: this is one reason why people often feel the public and private definitions of many terms to be incompatible and believe there is a right to sustain such discrepancies (Denzin, 1969, p. 927).

It is indicated that methodological innovations of ethnomethodologists do not aim at improving or correcting the recognized techniques and methods of social research, particularly those applying to questionnaires and interviews. In regard to this problem, Cicourel is ambiguous, as he sometimes seems to imply that ethnomethodology can 'repair' or improve existing, already established, methods. But in general ethnomethodologists claim that their analyses aim at the elaboration of independent principles and rules of social research (Coulter, 1974).

They claim also that the findings which they produce are essentially different from those which are generated by traditional sociology:

> The study of the operations of practical reasoning, then, does not produce 'findings' which resemble those of traditional sociologies, and it should be abundantly clear that ethnomethodology is not an alternative 'methodology' aimed at a more effective solution of traditionally formulated problems. Focusing upon the accomplished character of action scenes, it necessarily develops a style of research and argument responsive to its elected subject matter. In noting that for members a 'real world' is indubitably *just there*, without reference to its accomplished character, the last thing it has in mind is to cast systematic doubt upon the 'existence of a real world.' On the contrary, that there is an observable 'real world' is its point of origin: its destination is a characterisation of the work members do to sustain a social order in which there are 'suicides,' 'ethnic groups,' 'clear matters of fact,' and the rest of the furniture of everyday life. Scepticism and doubt enter only in so far as for the members they are sanctioned phenomena: the conditions under which members are entitled to display scepticism, the features of the world they are warranted in doubting – these are themselves aspects of practical reasoning, and hence proper matter for the study of social order (Turner, 1974, Introduction, p. ii).

Some of the analyses by ethnomethodologists, e.g. by Cicourel,

Garfinkel, Wieder, etc., lead to interesting conclusions. For example, the exactness of statistics and of organizational and official data are put in doubt from a quite new point of view. It has been traditionally maintained that such data are apt to be spurious because of the 'dark numbers', limited access to information, routine methods of data collecting, purposeful withdrawing or distorting of information, etc. Ethnomethodologists point out that organizations have their own, more or less latent, lives or 'second lives', so that in effect such organizations tend to reshape their image by means of data-collecting procedures, including outright faking. Ethnomethodologists also point out that various organizations give different meanings to the same kinds of events (such as birth, death, mental disease, disease in general, etc.). For example, the meaning of 'death' is quite different for a family, a church and a hospital:

> A hospital can be treated as an arena of accidents and as the place in which death does occur; hospital accidents have their own special character and are seen as more or less significant and memorable and more or less characteristic for the hospital's working, depending on their background settings. Cases of death causing spontaneous talk among hospital staff are those which have occurred in unusual ways, or resulting from errors in diagnosis or therapy, or affect very young patients (Sudnow, 1974, p. 107).

In fact, such remarks are quite pertinent. They remind us how often it is that events felt as different in their respective contexts are interpreted as identical by social science. Thus, such ultimate, existential occurrences like death are treated in the pragmatic-official manner from the standpoint of hospital routines.

Ethnomethodologists emphasize that the collecting and processing of official data is only apparently based on objective and formally standardized techniques. Those data, ethnomethodologists maintain, are also collected on more or less subjective criteria, on an ad hoc basis to satisfy practical purposes at hand, or are based on uncontrolled rumours and off-the-cuff information. Such selection of data fails to provide an objective synthetic image, but it is largely subject to pressures by current values, political tendencies, local styles of government, biased viewpoints, etc. It should be remarked that this idea has been already expressed by sociologists, in particular by those concerned with the sociology of law and criminology; for example, this problem was set in relief by studies of US police and their attitudes to juvenile delinquency (cf. Skolnick, 1966). The next fact emphasized by ethnomethodologists (in particular Garfinkel, 1967) was that organizational files cannot be properly interpreted without additional assumptions tacitly employed as classification principles. Those assumptions can be discovered by studying the more or less precisely codified inner sub-culture of the given institution or organization.

Ethnomethodologists keep emphasizing that a social researcher ought to, as a matter of principle, always question what seems to be obvious. Garfinkel asked his students to look over everyday situations and try to bring out their underlying assumptions by exploring their contexts.

> When a subject, for example, says he had a flat tyre, he is astounded by the question, 'What do you mean you had a flat tyre?' When a woman's husband remarks that he is tired, she asks, 'How are you tired? Physically, mentally or just bored?' To which he replies, 'I don't know, I guess physically, mainly.' And she continues to badger him with like questions until he tells her, finally, to 'drop dead' (Zeitlin, 1973, p. 184).

Apparently, Garfinkel's 'experiments' have never been widely employed as research methods. They were used rather as 'illustrative examples' designed to draw attention to various key points about the basis or orderliness in everyday life. Apparently, Garfinkel had hit upon something he knew to be important but he was unable to formulate what to make of it in terms of further research and analysis. The task of others lay in finding a way of developing from the suggestive material collected in Garfinkel's work a systematic and empirical way of doing research. The above two single examples illustrate the approach which is apt to be employed in other cases in a more systematic and precise manner. It is worthwhile to mention that, in order to make his point stronger, Garfinkel carried out a rather complex and, in fact, controversial experiment to test the assumptions hidden behind beliefs on which opinions and evaluations are grounded. In this experiment twenty-eight students about to begin courses in medicine participated in a three-hour interview in which they answered questions about what they believed to be the right methods of recruitment to medical schools (who should be accepted, how should a good candidate appear in examinations, whom should medical schools avoid, etc.). After that, students heard a recording, presented to them as genuine, of an examination-interview with an applicant for medical studies. In fact, the recording was make-believe; the interviewer and the applicant just played their roles. All twenty-eight students wanted to listen to the recording. The fake candidate was evaluated by listeners on the basis of the interview as an ignorant, unacceptable candidate; the experimenter said that in fact the candidate did very well on the literature exam and that he wrote brilliant essays on Milton and Shakespeare. Subjects who said that the candidate certainly had a lower-class background were told that, in fact, he was the son of a vice-president of a large company. Subjects who emphasized that the candidate would experience difficulties in contacts with people because of his personality traits heard that in fact the candidate was currently one of the most popular doctors in a New York central hospital. After such 'brainwashing', the subjects were again offered the opportunity to listen to the fake interview. The subjects also heard that the candidate had been laudably accepted by the medical school, and that, besides this, he had been recommended by six psychiatrists. The last thing the subjects were told was that in another identical experiment with thirty participants, twenty-eight expressed overall positive opinions about the same candidate and only two felt inclined to be slightly critical. After the second hearing of the interview, twenty-five out of the twenty-eight subjects changed their opinions. When in the end they were told the truth, twenty-two persons felt very happy about it (ten of them expressed their joy violently) and everybody returned to his earlier opinion.

The above experiment is interesting not so much because of its results (the same type of conformism to the massive pressure manufactured as uniform opinion was disclosed long ago in a much more 'elegant' manner in the famous Asch experiment) but because of the effects of its systematic realization of the directive of undermining the apparently strongly established opinions and values. Garfinkel is very much concerned with the problem of vindication of norms and evaluations. According to him, the more important a principle is, the greater are the chances that its acceptance is grounded on avoidance to test it. Similarly, when an individual accepts certain norms, he need not necessarily also accept the underlying values. He may very well just be afraid of forthcoming situations in which he might face the alternative of behaving against these norms (Garfinkel, 1967b). On the whole, these techniques of inquiry intend to reveal the vulnerability of the everyday world to blows caused by attacks on the tacitly accented assumptions. It was noticed that 'the ethnomethodological ''demonstration'' is in effect a land of microconfrontation with a nonviolent resistance to the status quo' (Gouldner, 1973, p. 394).

It should be noted that so-called conversational analysis may be regarded as a branch of ethnomethodology (or possibly as the more elaborated version of it). It has generated some coherent - in contrast to ethnomethodology's main stream - attempts to draw together its findings (Sacks *et al.*, 1974). This approach seeks to elaborate a model which provides both for context-sensitive and general properties of conversational practice. In short, this model looks like a formal model of a basic speech exchange system, i.e. conversations, and it may be suggestive of further research especially in areas which link social relationships with linguistic and psyche processes.

In general, ethnomethodological empirical studies do not seem to bring much new knowledge. They deal, for example, with such topics as the ways in which conversations are ended, the counting of deaths in hospitals, the establishing of principles, the collecting of data not usually revealed in organizations of various types, etc. One study concerned the norms adhered to by drug-addicts in asylums. It was found out that inmates of such institutions have their own special code, with the following basic norms: (1) you must not inform against others; (2) you should not admit to having done illegal things; (3) you should not exploit other inmates; (4) share with others what you have; (5) help others; (6) mind your own business; (7) do not trust the authorities; (8) be loyal to other inmates (Wieder, 1974). There is nothing remarkable about these findings, if we compare them with many studies about the so-called 'second life' and inmate subcultures in correctional institutions, prisons, etc. But such researches are characteristic of ethnomethodology in their focus on language and its uses, social meanings, underlying principles of interaction, latent meanings, etc.

However, not all ethnomethodological studies are language-oriented. For example, one of them is about how people normally move and walk. This quite sophisticated experiment yielded two by no means trivial findings. It turned out, in the first place, that people have certain navigational abilities. Even when they are engaged in conversation or contemplation, they sensitively and deftly avoid clashes with others. In the second place, people walk differently when alone and in company. When two people are walking together, there is a specific link between them reflected in their movements, even if they do not talk to each other (Ryave and Schenkein, 1974).

There is much interest in ethnomethodology, both inside and outside the group of its adherents. However, it cannot be described - at least at the present moment - as a scientific theory. Ethnomethodology does not present any set of statements suggesting any specific hypotheses. It also does not formulate any precise research hypotheses. Still, ethnomethodology can be described as a new research trend, pointing attention, on the one hand, to some new problems and, on the other hand, being a reaction against too dogmatically understood or applied (and often too self-oriented) methods and techniques of inquiry. In the latter

96

respect, ethnomethodology reflects a more general disappointment, streaming from various branches of social research, with the fact that the results of main sociological methods are more or less banal.

Again, if the blueprint of the body of tested hypotheses is to decide if ethnomethodology should be regarded as a possible scientific discipline, the answer will be relatively simple: this type of approach to social problems does not comply with the established criteria in social sciences. However, ethnomethodology must not be rejected: much interesting potential seems to be contained in it. As it was revealed, especially of phenomenology (a more general and not positivistically-oriented version of ethnomethodology), social reality is too subtle, too changeable, too fragile to be adequately described and measured by social sciences' standardized techniques. More subtle measures have to be employed to grasp the real sense of social life. Thus, in some way, the gap which exists between the social world as pictured by literature and that described by traditional sociological knowledge might be, at least to some extent, narrowed by ethnomethodological insight. So, ethnomethodology may, if more developed, serve as a complementary meta-method bridging the existing chasm between the illumination coming from poetic revelation and diagnoses built on systematic and rigorous examination.

Generally speaking, one may regard ethnomethodology as a quite useful additional subsidiary approach to analyse psycho-social behaviour in small groups, in closed institutions and in closed societies, and as an approach which may elucidate several subtle interpersonal interchanges in institutions and organizations which not only perform technical and administrative tasks but generate also, as a by-product of these tasks, a social life of their own. The particular usefulness of ethnomethodology may be visible also in situations in which social or interpersonal pathology is under study. One may wonder to what extent ethnomethodology may be useful in providing answers for classical ethnological studies, especially in situations in which subtle interchanges of communication between the researchers and the 'subjects' may essentially 'colour' accumulating data, being at the same time labelled as results.

Again one may notice that, as in the case of the 'Frankfurt School', ethnomethodology, which emerged rather as an intellectual adventure, could, in consequence, transform itself into a pattern of vicarious scientific perspective with a potential to double-check possible traps of classical sociological methods, or could turn itself into a specific trap: the self-adoration characteristic of scientific pretentiousness and of false self-awareness.

On the whole the above analysis of intricacies of ethnomethodology intends to show that its role in the general process of scientific investigations – if performed *lege artis* – may be of a subsidiary nature. Thus ethnomethodology could play an important complementary role (as a meta-method) in all those instances when other approaches to understand social reality, like structuralism or functionalism, appear to be too inadequate and too crude to penetrate the subtle texture of social reality.

Notes

1 The author of this chapter is grateful to J. M. Atkinson for his helpful criticism and insight made at the draft stage of this chapter.
2 In terms of originality (and additionally because he coined the term 'ethnomethodology') Garfinkel should go first in any such list. Cicourel, although probably more widely read, never really succeeded in gathering a coherently recognizable 'school' around him – unlike Garfinkel, whose students and colleagues include Sacks, Schegloff, Sudnow, Turner and others.

Bibliography

Atkinson, M. (1978), *Discovering Suicide*, London: Macmillan.
Cicourel, A. V. (1964), *Method and Measurement in Sociology*, New York: The Free Press.
Coulter, Jeff (1974), 'The Ethnomethodological Programme in Contemporary Society', *Human Context*, vol. VI, no. 1.
Denzin, N. K. (1969), 'Symbolic Interactionalism and Ethnomethodology: A Proposed Synthesis', *American Sociological Review*, vol. XXXIV, no. 6.
Douglas, J. (ed.) (1970), *Understanding Everyday Life*, Chicago: Aldine Press.
Garfinkel, H. (1967a), 'Some Rules of Correct Decision Making That Jurors Respect' (unpublished).
Garfinkel, H. (1967b), *Studies in Ethnomethodology*, Englewood Cliffs, N.J.: Prentice-Hall.
Gouldner, A. W. (1973), *The Coming Crisis of Western Sociology*, London: Heinemann.
Mullins, N. C. (1973), *Theories and Theory Groups in Contemporary American Society*, New York: Harper & Row.
Ryave, A. L., and Schenkein, J. (1974), 'Notes on the Art of Walking', in R. Turner (ed.), *Ethnomethodology*, Harmonsworth: Penguin.
Sacks, H., Schegloff, E. A., and Jefferson, G. (1974), 'A Simplest Systematics for the Organisation of Turn-Taking in Conversation', *Language*.

Schutz, A. (1963), 'Common Sense and Scientific Interpretation of Human Action', in M. Natanson (ed.), *Philosophy of the Social Sciences*, New York: Random House.

Skolnick, J. (1966), *Justice Without Trial*, New York: Wiley.

Sudnow, D. (1974), 'Counting Death', in R. Turner (ed.), *Ethnomethodology*, Harmondsworth: Penguin.

Turner, R. (ed.) (1974), *Ethnomethodology*, Harmondsworth: Penguin.

Wieder, D. L. (1974), 'Telling the Code', in R. Turner (ed.), *Ethnomethodology*, Harmondsworth: Penguin.

Zeitlin, I. M. (1973), *Rethinking Society*, New York: Appleton-Century-Crofts.

9 Symbolic interactionism
Maria Łoś

Until one can respond to himself as the community responds to him, he does not genuinely belong to the community.

Mead

Symbolic interactionism is not a uniform school centred around a single master or theory. Within this perspective are distinguishable a number of threads represented by several authors, although they are later considerably modified. Among these authors are, first of all, George Herbert Mead, Charles Cooley and William Thomas – American authors whose works at the beginning of the century exerted a great influence on the development of sociology and social psychology.

Mead published little during his life. Only after his death (in 1931) did his pupils and colleagues arrange and publish his works (Mead, 1932, 1934, 1936, 1938). In philosophy, Mead was, like Dewey, an eminent representative of American pragmatism, developed under the influence of the stormy upsurge of science and new conceptions of evolution. Mead rejected mechanistic and individualistic conceptions of man's lot in the world (under the influence of Darwin, among others). He focused his analysis on the processes shaping the personality through social interaction and the symbolic role of language, on the scope of autonomy of the individual in the social world, the sources of innovations and progress, the role of conflict in the process of evolution, the subjective character of history, etc. In his view, scientific method was not only an instrument for understanding the world, but primarily a tool for changing it – a dialectical tool for control of man's environment. The very process of cognition is, according to him, a process of change, since the fact of perception of certain phenomena automatically contributes to their transformation.

However, the most direct influence on the development of the symbolic interactionist school was exerted by Mead's exposition of social psychology (particularly Mead, 1934). He opposed determinist definitions of man as a passive object of the action of his environment and focused his attention on man's activity. Action is the intermediate link between an organism and the environment. It is always an element of interaction which Mead figuratively calls 'the conversation of gestures'. When gestures have the same meaning for the two sides engaged in an interaction, or for two potential sides (within the same social context), they are 'significant gestures' or 'significant symbols' (usually verbal). Such symbols are learned within groups which constitute symbolic territories where interactions and common activities are possible. In such a symbolic community one can place oneself in the place of the other and share his experience. Thus every member of the group acts under the assumption that others understand the meaning of his actions in the proper manner and is also capable of imagining the others' reaction to his behaviour. Group members may, for instance, try out various roles, or imagine different versions of behaviour and make a final choice on the basis of the imagined reactions by others (internalized conversation of gestures). They are thus in a position, on the basis of internalized group symbols, to link the future dimension with current processes of shaping their own attitudes and behaviour. Everyone of us is undoubtedly aware of that type of situation from his own experience. So does fine literature provide numerous vivid descriptions of the kind of internal dialogue in which the hero plays simultaneously the parts of himself and of his imagined partner (numerous examples can be found in the novels by M. Proust).

The human personality is thus shaped within a definite social context and as a result of concrete social interactions. It cannot originate outside the society. It is capable of self-awareness and self-evaluation and may, therefore, simultaneously appear to itself as both subject and object, which is an essential characteristic distinguishing people from other species and man's inner-self from his body. What is more, the self-evaluation is made imaginatively through the eyes of others, owing to previous experience. The personality, hence, always contains an intersubjective element. But man's activity is not totally determined by the group's coded world of symbols, since he himself has to make the ultimate choice.

Mead's contributions in the sphere of the psychology of child development are interesting in this context. According to him, infants do not possess the ability to look at themselves from the outside, through the eyes of others, nor do they have as yet a generalized picture of others. The imagination of others is limited to concrete persons (for example, mother) and is not of a synthetic character. The main instruments for leading children into the world of adult interactions and for teaching them to perceive imaginatively the roles of others are: language, play and games (games are more advanced than play because of the multiplicity of roles, as well as the interpersonal obligatory character of conventional norms and rules). This is why Mead and his followers devote so much attention to the various forms of game-playing.

One must comprehend Mead's dual conception of the personality in order to understand the main principles of his social psychology. He distinguishes two components of the self. One is a reflection of others' expectations and attitudes and it is shaped through the interactions within the group or society. This component of the self ('me') assumes the form of the most general system of attitudes of others (in Mead's terminology this is the 'generalized other'). The second component of the self, the 'I', may be conceived of as 'the individual self', or more boldly – the transcendental self.

According to these conceptions, the 'I' is not subjected directly to any standards which inner-group interactions would make obligatory. It is spontaneous, nonconformist, capable of impulsive reactions, and it often surprises the 'me', the reactions and expectations of which are far more conventional and shaped by the social roles. New ideas, innovative solutions, creative thoughts, rebellious reflexes – everything which stimulates change and contributes eventually to progress is incited by that individual component of the self. In contradistinction to 'I', 'me' stands guard over social integration and harmony, constitutes the principal instrument of social control (in the form of self-control), enables interpersonal communication and the emergence of institutions and rituals. The individual 'I' is directed towards the future, while the social 'me' relates primarily to the retrospective generalized experience.

This complex vision of the self has often been erroneously interpreted and criticized. An example of this may be the discussion by Lichtman (1970, pp. 75–94) who falsely interprets Mead's theory of the personality by attributing to the social self, 'me', a completely dominant role (because of the ungraspable character of the individual 'I' which is not grounded in experience) and on that basis accuses Mead of crude social determinism. He fails to perceive the transcendental character of the 'I', or the feed-back loop between the individual and society. Cronk's polemics with Lichtman seem to be correct when he writes:

While the generalized other is an instrument of social control, it is also a condition of human liberty or, at least, a foundation for the possibility of individual and group liberation from social pressures and structures. The generalized other, internalized in the 'me', is the occasion for the action of the 'I'. Since self and society are poles of a single process, change in one pole will result in change in the other pole (Cronk, 1973, pp. 327-8).

The objection (by Becker, 1968, p. 94) that Mead envisages a conflictless society based on social consensus also seems – at least partly – unfounded. The imputation that the acting mechanism of the 'me' effects the complete uniformization of norms, interests, values, etc., in the given society seems evidently inaccurate, since Mead devotes so much attention to the consequences of internal group conflicts, of the affiliation of individuals to different, often conflicting, groups and classes and to groups of various levels (concrete groups of direct participation and abstract groups of rather symbolic forms of participation), etc. He did not limit the individual's social self to a single form of the 'generalized other' connected with one group, but implied a multiplicity of 'generalized others'. Pioneering propositions in relation to the theory of conflict are even attributed to Mead. For, as Denzin (1969, p. 925) writes: 'By placing emphasis on conflict and on situations which demand new interpretation, Mead anticipated subsequent statements concerning the positive functions of conflict.'

One can agree, however, with the fundamental criticism concerning the failure to consider the objective social structure as a subject of investigation. The image of social reality perceived by people is undoubtedly to a considerable extent purposefully manipulated by ideology, economic pressure and the structure of possibilities. An investigation of the mechanism of its emergence without the simultaneous analysis of the given society's objective social and economic relationships is essentially incomplete.[1] This criticism also pertains to some degree to most of the other representatives of symbolic interactionism, such as Cooley, Blumer, Berger and Luckmann, Becker, Goffman and others.

The above discussion of the fundamental ideas and concepts of George H. Mead's social psychology seemed necessary as an introduction to the further critical analysis of the nature and meaning of that perspective. In this brief presentation the emphasis was laid on those of Mead's ideas which have been later absorbed into symbolic interactionism as the distinctive orientation in social psychology.

Undoubtedly the work of Cooley (1902, 1909) on interactions in primary groups and local communities also influenced significantly the formation of that school. This pertains to his assumption that others exist for us primarily in our imagination and to his conception of the 'looking-glass self'. Although the latter is only one fragment of the 'social self' as defined by Mead, it arose from the same conviction that the individual is able to make its own self an object of observation by means of anticipation or interpretation (on the basis of previous social experience) of others' reactions. The concept of the 'looking-glass self' refers basically to the processes of formation of one's self-image. It seems to have three principal elements: one's guess as to the way others perceive one; one's speculation about the evaluation of one's appearance by others, and, finally, one's tendency to develop in response some sort of self-feeling, such as, for instance, pride or mortification.

That conception plus the previously discussed elements of Mead's theory exerted a great influence on the development of the symbolic interactionism as a distinctive perspective. Its later representatives, among whom certainly Blumer has been most influential (1931, 1957, 1966, 1969), devoted much attention to the problem of the individual's self-lodging in a given social context. How the individual appears to others (Goffman, 1959), how he reveals to them some of his personality traits, how he interprets their reactions to himself, how these interpretations influence his awareness, how he anticipates social interaction and then interprets it, how he manipulates prevailing symbols and how he participates in their creation, what part of his activity is of a routine character and what is the range of his free interpretation and creative initiative – all these problems have been of primary interest to the representatives of this school.

Their work contributed to the development of research in the fields of socialization, social roles, reference groups, social processes within groups, etc. As an example may be cited the work of Shibutani (1955, 1962) which made an essential contribution to the development of the concept of group reference (which will be discussed in later parts of this book). He hypothetically assumes that the choice of a group of reference should be identified with the choice of a 'generalized other' or 'significant other' (both terms are culled from Mead). A reference group thus serves the given person as the matrix of perception of various social situations and of ordering them according to socially given symbols and interpretations. The individual uses the criteria of the reference group to define situations; he also regards the group as a stage where he seeks response and acceptance.

It may be added, in the light of the considerations of other symbolic interactionists, that the process of selecting the individual's frame of reference consists in the search for such a group in which he finds a proper response, in which the process of self-lodging proceeds most favourably. This does not necessarily have to be the most rational choice, from the viewpoint of the individual's objective interests. As Denzin indicated:

If persons return to those quarters and settings where crucial aspects of the self have been lodged, then their actions cease to be directed entirely on either the most rational or most effective grounds . . . persons judge interactions to be satisfactory or unsatisfactory in terms of their success at self-lodging. If valued portions of the self are not lodged, recognized and reciprocated, a dissatisfaction concerning that encounter is likely to be sensed (Denzin, 1969, p. 924).

It may be worth stressing that a distinctive feature of symbolic interactionism – from the viewpoint of the sociology of science – is that it has taken root in American philosophical thought. It is somewhat unusual, considering the fascination of American sociologists with European social philosophy (as in the case of functionalism, phenomenology and marxism, for instance). Symbolic interactionism emerged in a considerable degree as a counter-reaction to the dominant behaviourist approach of modern American social psychology. Its basic methodological directives may be summarized in the following way (see Denzin, 1969):

(1) Investigations of the visible aspects of behaviour must be supplemented by knowledge of its concealed symbolic aspects:
(2) The investigator must acquire the attitude and outlook of the 'investigated' (in studies on deviance, for example, it was a revolutionary novelty when representatives of the trend in question identified themselves with the deviants, tried to comprehend their interactions with others, etc.):
(3) The investigator must try to connect the symbols and meanings assumed by the 'investigated' with the social circles and groups from which those symbols are derived (this is associated, for instance, with emphasis on the question of reference groups):
(4) If the behaviour occurs in a given social situation which may subjectively influence that behaviour, then that situation must be included in the fields of analysis (this pertains also to situations where the investigator conducts interviews, etc.):
(5) The investigator's strategy must make it possible to grasp the dynamic and stabilizing aspects of interaction:
(6) Sensitivity must be a dominant trait of the investigator and of his methods. While some degree of formalization is necessary in the later phases of the investigation, the initial phase should aim at the reconstruction of the concepts and meanings in force without defining them *a priori*. There is no single, fully satisfactory research method. A multiplicity of mutually complementary methods is the best strategy. But, as is known, the methods decidedly preferred by the representatives of the orientation in question are: participating observation,

'sympathetic introspection', analysis of personal documents (letters, diaries) and of records of actual situations.

A few remarks may be in place, in conclusion, on the organizational aspects of symbolic interactionism as a scientific school. The germs of this current and of its rapid development are fully associated with the Chicago school of sociology and the scientific careers of Mead, Cooley (of the University of Michigan but considered to be a member of the Chicago school), Thomas and Znaniecki and then with those of their pupils, the most eminent of whom are: H. Blumer, R. E. L. Faris, Elsworth Faris, W. Burgess and W. C. Reckless. The latter in turn trained such students as L. Cottrel, A. R. Lindesmith, F. Merrill, H. S. Becker, C. Hughes and T. Shibutani. These were under the strong influence of Blumer and are basically identified with symbolic interactionism, although they represent varied interpretations and different degrees of involvement.

Another centre using the terminology of symbolic interactionism is the Iowa school with Manfred Kuhn as scientific leader. However, their research direction basically departs from the methodological principles at the foundation of Mead's conceptions. Contrary to Mead and Blumer, Kuhn postulated unity of research methods in all scientific disciplines. He sought a universal method enabling the anticipation of human behaviour, while Mead and Blumer desired primarily to comprehend it. Kuhn rejected the method of empathic introspection and identification with the objects of investigation by posing the proposition of the operativeness of the personality conception (test TST - 'Who Am I?'). But he almost entirely overlooked the individual aspects of the self - the 'I' (as understood by Mead). He conceived the self as a kind of relatively stable structure of attitudes resulting from the individual's internalization of the role requirements associated with his social position. Hence, he departed from the conception of man's self as a process - so characteristic of symbolic interactionism (see, for instance, Meltzer and Petras, 1970).

Herbert Blumer was the intellectual and organizational leader of the Chicago school from the death of Mead (1931) to 1952, when he transferred to Berkeley (University of California). With his departure came a radical decline in the number of students identified with that school's scientific tradition. Blumer's pupils and co-workers in California include Erving Goffman, Thomas Scheff and John Loffland (see Mullins, 1973, pp. 75–104). But the diminished organizational activity of H. Blumer and the emergence of an active competitor, the phenomenologico-ethnomethodological school of sociology, caused the interactionist school to disperse and weakened its distinctive intellectual influence in sociology. Critics appeared who charged that this orientation failed to apply its methodology to the analysis of macro-social processes and broader social phenomena, neglected the question of social change on a macro-scale, belittled the role of emotion in the interpretation of human behaviour, showed basic ambiguity in its treatment of the determinacy-indeterminacy issue, did not consider subconscious phenomena and, finally, that its concepts and theoretical propositions were very vague and could not be empirically tested. (For a broader critical discussion of symbolic interactionism see Mannis and Meltzer, 1967; Brittan, 1973; Meltzer, Petras and Reynolds, 1975.) Some of those critiques have been directed against both symbolic interactionism and phenomenology, as they share many assumptions and their visions of society and man are basically compatible. Moreover, in many interpretations they merge in a more general, humanistic, sociological orientation (or, simply, way of thinking).

It is certainly true that symbolic interactionism has not developed satisfactorily its methodological foundations. It has managed to discredit the methodology which was unable to transcend the 'behavioural' model of man, the methodology which produced an artificial 'sociological man' which fitted well into the sociological realm which he inhabited. The symbolic interactionists hoped to develop a methodology which would be subordinated to their vision of the self and mind, instead of dictating to them an image of man. They gave many imaginative suggestions and recommendations as to how the sociologists can try to retain their sensitivity and autonomy from the pressures of the positivist methodology. Yet they have not proposed any reliable methods of systematic inquiry.

What are the basic features of man's nature assumed by the symbolic interactionists? Their man is unemotional, co-operative, seeking reciprocal relationships, responsive to the signals of others, overconcerned with his appearance to the others, calculated and somewhat theatrical. He is not fully determined by his primary groups, but they provide the symbolic framework without which he would not be able to develop his social self and capacity to interact symbolically with himself and with others. The structure of the group is not static and complete, it is emerging all the time through the processes of negotiations among the emerging selves. They are not faced with the petrified, stable patterns – so overwhelming that an individual would have to surrender completely to them. The members of society can play games, negotiate their rules, make moves and anticipate, but also influence their consequences; they can also pretend that they are autonomous when they are, in fact, conforming to the pressure of a group or an authority. They can pretend it not only to the others, but also to themselves. But – as suggested by Thomas and Znaniecki – the subjective perceptions of reality, even when inadequate, have real, objective consequences. Thus, the interactionists' man believes in his sovereignty (which is essential from the point of view of his self-esteem) and he believes that he exercises free choice, when he conforms ('it is in my own best interest'), when he is kind to others (the reciprocity rule makes it rational), when he is reasonable ('I could jump out of the window, but I choose not to') and so forth.

The interactionists do not speak of oppression, inequality and exploitation because they are interested in the *make-believe reality* which people construct in their everyday effort to maintain self-respect, to gain approval, to establish successful relationships and to avoid expulsion from the community which feeds their social selves. The social structure is believed to be built of such communities and relationships which socialize and provide audience for the audience-seeking individuals, and which secure an effective self-control mechanism, making excessive, external, formal, social control unnecessary. Such a vision is not so unrealistic and utopian as many critics maintain. Even in the situation of very acute restrictions of freedom and total lack of the individual's influence, as in the case of, for example, contemporary Poland, one witnesses persistent efforts of the people to save their dignity by fostering illusions of personal autonomy, and by emphasizing the significance of successful intimate relationships.

The social self, 'me', may be understood as a product of the individual's active participation in the utopian community life where creative co-operation, egalitarian opportunities and shared definitions of goals prevail. Yet it may also be understood as a negotiated outcome of the accumulated structural, economic and cultural pressures. It is negotiated because it oscillates between micro- and macro-structural definitions, between certain perceptions and counter-perceptions, values and counter-values, temptations towards conformity and nonconformity. Such social self includes awareness that it is possible to sacrifice one's stable, favourable 'looking-glass self', his convenient routines, his safety or his property, in order to manifest his choice of nonconformity or detachment from shared social order. There is a whole range of possible choices and symbolic bargaining transactions even in the situations when one is actually bargaining with oneself because one is the only party likely to consider certain sacrifices in exchange for satisfactions of a different kind. If one protests against, for example, the autocratic exercise of power one confirms one's freedom to neglect the wisdom of the 'me', to bargain with the 'me', to negotiate its acceptance of the foolish but noble act. If someone who is tortured by jealousy spies on the loved woman, he bargains with the respectable 'me', he finds excuses, he negotiates adjustments of the 'me' towards acceptance of the humiliating, yet infatuated, act.

'Me' incorporates moral order, rational outlook and generalized - treasured or feared - reactions of 'significant others'. Therefore, the success of any social system in achieving the conformity and integration of its subjects depends on its efficiency in cultivating appropriate moral criteria of the positive self-image, and in promoting the criteria of rationality which discard any nonconformism as irrational or counterproductive. If the positive self-image and self-esteem constitute such a powerful motive as symbolic interactionists claim, then the criteria which one applies when assessing them, as well as one's anticipation of the criteria used by others, are of crucial importance. They may appeal to the moral, 'natural' order, and/or to the rational ('reasonable') image of man. It seems, for example, that the self-image of contemporary Poles depends on their ability to control themselves in public places, their ability to be realistic and not to believe in the political and economic fiction, but to adjust skilfully to it and to take advantage of it whenever possible, to achieve a higher standard of living or a higher professional standing than their neighbours, to secure a 'better' future for their children and so forth. Such criteria are not imposed by force upon them. Some aspects of these criteria are certainly suggested by the authorities in various ways - direct and indirect - but they result above all from experiencing the pressures which continuously threaten one's dignity. The individual redefinitions of the criteria of the positive self-image are not only moulded by the influences of others upon the individual, they also generate his tendency to make them socially binding once he has assumed them. Such a mechanism brings strong enforcement of those forms of the generalized self-image which maximize the successful process of self-lodging within the system, but avoids too far-reaching redefinitions of the self which would openly threaten its integrity. Such a balanced version of the self-image is additionally supported by the criteria of rationality. The self-image is saved when one can convince oneself that one's protest would not change anything except to bring some negative repercussions for oneself and others; that one's dismissal (or resignation) from a significant post would open the way for someone far more harmful; that encouraging one's children to comprehend conditions of social injustice and repression would aggravate their future problems and unhappiness in the situation when they could not change these conditions anyway.

These are rational neutralizations similar to those described by Sykes and Matza (1957) in their analysis of juvenile gang members' defences. The boys argue that they do not steal – they take the property of those who have so much that they are not able to use it all anyway; they are not violent – they fight in order to protect their friends or their territory (it would be irrational to give in to the enemy when one is able to fight), and so on. The boys learn the neutralization techniques as a part of their roles as members of the gang. These techniques are based on extensions, often unconscious, of the rules that preclude or limit the responsibility for breaking social norms without damaging the self-respect of the breakers. Similar devices to defend their self-images were offered by the interviewed prostitutes (Bryan, 1965). They were stressing vigorously the positive function of their activity which protects the institution of marriage, lessens the probability of rape and sexually motivated murders, provides consolation to the lonely and abandoned, helps to overcome sexual problems and inhibitions, etc. The 'ideology' used by the Party officials in Poland would probably not be so much different. They would take for granted the hopelessness of the geographical location of Poland and her unfortunate, but irrevocable, external political relationships, and would argue that in the circumstances their role consists in lessening the factors of hardship, moderating the conflicts and trying to establish some order in the general chaos. These tasks can be done only by the Party members, since the Party is the only officially recognized authority.

Berger made somewhat similar observations writing about Second World War criminals:

> it is much more likely that the Nazi murderers are sincere in their self-portrayals as having been bureaucrats faced with certain unpleasant exigencies that actually were distasteful to them than to assume that they say this only in order to gain sympathy from their judges (Berger, 1966, p. 127).

The symbolic interactionism school has been criticized, in that it takes for granted the nature and stability of the political and economic structure of the society instead of studying it and seeking to change it. Naturally this substantial omission makes the contribution offered by symbolic interactionism rather one-sided and crippled. However, much can be said in its defence in the light of previous remarks. It seems that many members of the societies which are not undergoing any radical changes treat the social system as given (even when it is strongly disliked) – as the reality which will continue to exist in a similar manner, which is inert and not fully comprehensible, which can be psychologically 'neutralized', but not influenced. The 'common' people try to develop the most suitable solutions to the problems and opportunities the system creates for them, including the development of an optional model of self-image – desirable but realistic, moral but still rational, individual but covering the crucial relationships with others and with the institutions. The studies of the patterns of 'solutions' and self-images in the societies of different structure may be most revealing, not only in the field of face to face relationships, but also in respect of the characteristic features of the different social systems.

One should not, however, overlook those sections of the population which take an actively negative attitude towards prevailing political and economic conditions, and which orientate both their action and their self-images towards the goals of essential macro-structural changes. They should not be considered as irrelevant or atypical, but should be given the same attention as the more passive majority. There is no reason why symbolic interactionists should not try to cover the whole spectrum of the symbolic solutions to the real problems and their definitions. But in order to produce any significant results they would have to recognize the concrete 'objective' features of different economic and political systems, even if they focus their inquiries on the prevailing forms of the 'self' and its symbolic context.

Attempts to trace such a typical shape of the self under various social conditions have been undertaken by several authors. Most prominent among them are Riesman's other-directed man, Adorno's (*et al.*) authoritarian personality, Marcuse's one-dimensional man, Berger's (*et al.*) homeless mind, Goffman's creature, whose most accurate name would be 'nobody' or, perhaps, 'a hypocrite', and Brittan's privatized self (see Riesman, 1966; Adorno *et al.*, 1950; Marcuse, 1968; Berger *et al.*, 1974; Goffman, 1959, 1961; Brittan, 1978). All these authors were trying to establish links between social structure, institutions, class-related family structure, social processes (like, for example, urbanization, bureaucratization, expansion of the mass culture) and the transformation of the self. The ideal types which they constructed have all the advantages and disadvantages of ideal types. They are very general and do not mirror reality, but they draw one's attention to some crucial features and dimensions of the relationship between micro- and macro-social reality.

The conception clearly associated with the interactionists' perspective is Goffman's manipulative individual who skilfully changes and negotiates the masks, in order to fit well into the multiple, anonymous requirements and audiences. It is not at all clear who is the actual manager behind those masks. Is it a genuine self – a 'true' identity – or, perhaps, some sort of 'radar' directing him towards generalized and concrete others who can give him life by validating his temporary identities? It may be that the 'core identity' of Goffman's man consists of those masks which have actually taken root and have been most convincingly confirmed by others.

> The implication here is that if the self is presented, is consistently successful, that is, it is validated by others, the actor will become convinced by his own performance, this interpretation will become or be perceived to be real. . . . the individual who successfully sells himself as an intellectual and is accepted at face value because he has played the game so well will in time begin to be convinced of his own intellectuality. The labels that others attach to his performance are internalised as part of the way he begins to perceive himself. Thus, what starts off as a trading gambit, ends up as value capital for the actor. He now believes in himself intrinsically as an intellectual (Brittan, 1973, pp. 148-9).

Goffman's studies provide a most penetrating insight into the ways in which routine interactions are carried out and routine definitions of situations are produced. But his vision of man seems grossly exaggerated and one-sided. Although impression-management and game-playing are common features of human interactions, they are not the only, and most probably not even the crucial, aspects of social relationships. Similarly, the role theory speaks about a very real aspect of moulding one's self-image, but cannot be sustained as a sole or a fully deterministic explanation.

It is hard to believe that identity is nothing more than a combination of masks or roles, usefully displayed in episodic encounters, or in routine exchanges. One can certainly assume that contemporary members of highly organized societies want to believe that their selves are much more authentic and individualistic. Or, at least, that they should be. Apparently, they do feel frightened that something wrong is happening to their selves, something very similar to the processes described by Goffman, Berger and others. The desperate search for identity in the USA has not been triggered off by interactionists. It has certainly been influenced by some intellectuals and experts, but its expansion has been largely spontaneous and guided by common feelings of 'identity crisis' - of being dissolved in constant efforts to 'please the boss', to be up to all requirements and challenges coming from the sources distributing benefits and not to stay behind in the race. Yet the very ability to reflect upon such a situation means that man's self is not completely exhausted within those masks and roles, even if they take the upper hand in some circumstances.

112

It is not surprising that the explosion of the interest in the hidden and unique features of individuals has taken place primarily in the USA. Many factors have contributed to the fact that the alienation of the self has been more acute there than in many less efficiently organized countries. Among them special roles have been played by the puritan traditions, emphasis on self-discipline and adjustment to the ever-growing administration, efficiency, politeness, 'objective' criteria of success and fluid, noncommittal relationships which would not hamper mobility. The so-called sensitivity training (T-groups) constituted one of many institutionalized attempts to counter the impersonal bureaucracy and dehumanization of social relationships within organizations. The encounter groups (growth groups, etc.) emerged as a more spontaneous measure aiming against the safe shallowness of the conventional forms and phrases, as well as the façade nature of interpersonal contacts in private life.

The dehumanized and desensitized environment is functional from the point of view of formal efficiency. The interactions between the roles are so much more predictable than those between the individuals. The consensual definitions of situations are so much more desired in the organized world subordinated to the supreme tasks. As Goffman suggested, such a common definition of the situation may not involve so much a real agreement as to what exists, but rather an agreement as to whose claims concerning what issues will be temporarily honoured (Goffman, 1959; see also Becker, 1976 – on hierarchy of credibility). Growing opposition against such a state of affairs was in the USA strongly supported by the common feelings of dissatisfaction with the widespread practice of giving one's problems away to the patronizing psychoanalysts. The personal problems had been gradually alienated from their owners and defined as rooted in a remote, unconscious and uncontrollable past. To feel anxiety about one's identity meant that something had been wrong with the way in which one had handled the relationship to one's mother when one was an infant. At the same time, one's identity problems could also be recognized as a sign that one was not fit to continue in the responsible job one held. It is worthwhile noting the institutionalization of this one particular social role – the role of psychoanalyst has had more profound and more far-reaching consequences for the social order in the USA than many other, more conspicuous factors of social structure of that country. However, it was exactly its social functionality and convenient message which caused its success and expansion. The disillusionment with the guidance provided by psychoanalysts, the breakdown of marriages, the middle-class awareness of the social imprisonment of bored housewives and 'square' husbands, together with the general climate of the 1960s brought new – mainly middle-class – energy into the ever-present search for identity. For some it meant a political attack upon the habitually taken for granted world; for others, psychedelic experience of the new aspects of oneself and of the surroundings; yet for others, more deeply rooted in their conventional roles, it meant occasional 'trips' into a different social reality of artificially created, short-lived groups, encounters and meditations. One can postulate that the role of the latter has been as significant and far-reaching as that of the psychoanalyst revelation some years earlier. Is it equally functional to the stable socio-economic system? Certainly it helps to moderate some of the more alarming by-products of the long-term emphasis on efficiency and ritual consensus; it brings new commercial tricks and commodities, new careers for the moral entrepreneurs and human experts, and it also gives new illusions about the possibilities of significant transformations of the private sphere which would bring new meanings to one's whole life. However, while it is fair to suggest that it is 'opium' for some it may also be claimed that it institutes a step towards greater reflexivity and social awareness in the case of some others.

The sensitivity training is focused on the existential 'here and now'. It emphasizes a man detached from the social tradition and his own biography. It is also a man without the future as he does not plan, does not calculate the future effects of his actions, nor does he adjust himself to the noticed shifts in the main currents which are supposed to carry him towards successful accomplishments. Instead, he contemplates his own present time, his emotional and physiological state and his relationships with others. He is liberated from the programme, within which he normally performed some, automatically accepted, tasks; he is removed from the organized routine of his life, surrounded by questions about his present identification, separated from his past and his future.

It seems that such a perspective may help one to achieve distance from the routine, the scheme of one's biography, as well as the external pressures and expectations, and to look at oneself in a more direct way. One may become, at least for the time being, more human – less socially conditioned and programmed. One's rational reasoning and habit of carrying out some instrumental actions appear of little value in situations when only the present moment is important. It seems that people are actually capable of experiencing themselves and others in various ways – and the encounter groups offer them such an alternative opportunity. It is a different experience of time, but also an opportunity of a very rare experience of the world without hierarchy, without institutionalized domination, and so forth. It may stimulate an appreciation of the need for social and political equality and the abolition of economic barriers. Yet the valuable 'counter-experience' does not equip one with any means of changing one's surroundings in order to accommodate one's new awareness and new ability to relate to others. The effects of the group experience are therefore negotiated and neutralized by 'normal' order, where some of the participants feel more frustrated, while others demonstrate rather increased ability to adjust and to make their façades appear more spontaneous and authentic than before (see, for instance, Cooper and Mangham, 1971). Such discrepancy in the effects of the encounter groups' experience on different people is understandable when one realizes that this experience concerns both the 'I' and the 'me'. It may increase the awareness of one's individual self, but it may also provide some support to the 'me' and especially to the sensitivity of the 'looking-glass self'. The latter is due to the enormous stress laid by the encounter movement (and humanistic psychology in general) on the improvement of one's ability to perceive how exactly one is seen by others. One of the main goals of the group experience is to make one's interactions with others more successful. When incorporated into one's 'normal' life this may mean that the movement born from the sincere disapproval of the façade interactions may simply cause the reshaping of them on a more sophisticated level.

In conclusion, symbolic interactionism may be strongly criticized for its methodological underdevelopment and for very selective perceptiveness. However, it seems capable of elucidating the relationship between the structure and culture of the society and the nature of interpersonal and intrapersonal interactions. It may also help to comprehend the shifts in collective efforts to seize, protect or reshape the individual identity and its social expression.

Such a task can be carried out only if it is clearly understood that the selves, the meanings and the interactions cannot be explained apart from the social structure, and that the structure is equally incomprehensible (and inconceivable) apart from them. Moreover, it seems obvious that such a task may be acceptable only if it is assumed that although concern with appearances and self-images is rather common among people, they happen to care for other things as well.

Note

1 See the considerations concerning the impossibility to interpret the marxist concept of 'false consciousness' and the role of ideology on the basis of Mead's theory (Lichtman, 1970, pp. 75-94).

Bibliography

Adorno, T., Frenkel-Brunswik, E., Levinson, D., and Sandford, R. (1950), *The Authoritarian Personality*, New York: Norton.

Becker, H. S. (1968), *The Structure of Evil, An Essay on the Unification of the Science of Man*, New York: George Braziller.

Becker, H. S. (1976), 'Whose Side are We On?', *Social Problems*, vol. 14, no. 3.

Berger, P. L. (1966), *Invitation to Sociology. A Humanistic Perspective*, Harmondsworth: Penguin.

Berger, P. L. and Luckmann, T. (1967), *The Social Construction of Reality*, Garden City, New York: Doubleday.

Berger, P. L., Berger, B. and Kellner, H. (1974) *The Homeless Mind*, Harmondsworth: Penguin.

Blumer, H. (1931) 'Science Without Concepts', *American Journal of Sociology,* vol. 36, January.

Blumer, H. (1957), 'Collective Behaviour', in Joseph B. Gittler (ed.), *Review of Sociology*, New York: Wiley.

Blumer, H. (1966), 'Sociological Implications of the Thought of G. H. Mead', *American Journal of Sociology*, vol. 71, March.

Blumer, H. (1969), *Symbolic Interactionism. Perspective and Method*, Englewood Cliffs, N.J.: Prentice-Hall.

Brittan, A. (1973), *Meanings and Situations*, London: Routledge & Kegan Paul.

Brittan, A. (1978), *The Privatised World*, London: Routledge & Kegan Paul.

Bryan, J. H. (1965), 'Apprenticeship in Prostitution', *Social Problems*, vol. 12.

Cooley, C. H. (1902), *Human Nature and the Social Order*, New York: Scribner's.

Cooley, C. H. (1909), *Social Organization*, New York: Scribner's.

Cooper, C. L., and Mangham, I. L. (1971), *T-Groups. A Survey of Research*, London and New York: Wiley – Interscience.

Cronk, G. F. (1973), 'Symbolic Interactionism. A Left-Meadian Interpretation', *Social Theory and Practice*, vol. 2, no. 3.

Denzin, N. K. (1969), 'Symbolic Interactionism and Ethnomethodology: A Proposed Synthesis', *American Sociological Review*, vol. XXXIV, no. 6.

Goffman, E. (1959), *The Presentation of Self in Everyday Life*, Garden City, New York: Doubleday.

Goffman, E. (1961), *Encounters*, Indianapolis: Bobbs-Merrill.

Lichtman, R. (1970), 'Symbolic Interactionism and Social Reality. Some Marxist Queries', *Berkeley Journal of Sociology*, vol. XV.

Mannis, J. C., and Meltzer, N. (eds) (1967), *Symbolic Interaction. A Reader in Social Psychology*, Boston, Mass.: Allyn & Bacon.

Marcuse, H. (1968), *One-Dimensional Man*, London: Sphere Books.

Mead, G. H. (1928), 'The Psychology of Punitive Justice', *American Journal of Sociology*, vol. 23.

Mead, G. H. (1932), *Philosophy of the Present*, University of Chicago Press.

Mead, G. H. (1934), *Mind, Self and Society*, University of Chicago Press.

Mead, G. H. (1936), *Movements of Thought in the Nineteenth Century*, University of Chicago Press.

Mead, G. H. (1938), *The Philosophy of the Act*, University of Chicago Press.

Meltzer, B. N., and Petras, J. W. (1970), 'The Chicago and Iowa Schools of Symbolic Interactionism', in T. Shibutani (ed.), *Human Nature and Collective Behaviour*, Englewood Cliffs, N.J.: Prentice-Hall.

Meltzer, B. N., Petras, J. W., and Reynolds, L. T. (1975), *Symbolic Interactionism. Genesis, Varieties and Criticism*, London: Routledge & Kegan Paul.

Mullins, N. C. (1973), *Theories and Theory Groups in Contemporary American Sociology*, New York: Harper & Row.

Riesman, D. (with N. Glazer and R. Denney) (1966), *The Lonely Crowd*, London: Yale University Press.

Shaskolsky, L. (1970), 'The Development of Sociological Theory in America. A Sociology of Knowledge Interpretations', in Larry T. Reynolds and Janice M. Reynolds, *The Sociology of Sociology*, New York: David McKay.

Shibutani, T. (1955), 'Reference Groups as Perspectives', *American Journal of Sociology,* vol. 60, May.

Shibutani, T. (1962), 'Reference Groups and Social Control', in A. M. Rose (ed.), *Human Behaviour and Social Processes,* Boston, Mass.: Houghton Mifflin.

Sykes, G. M., and Matza, D. (1957), 'Techniques of neutralization: A Theory of Delinquency', *American Sociological Review,* 22 December.

10 Multi-dimensional sociology
Maria Łoś

It may happen as in human life, that the more an individual is
compelled to defend his own immediate physical existence, the
more will he uphold and identify with the higher values of
civilisation and of humanity, in all their complexity.

Gramsci, 1971

'Multi-dimensional sociology' is a possibility. It does not exist at
present and there have not so far been any conscious attempts to
construct it. In the Introduction to this book some steps leading
to its creation have been suggested.

The overview of the several leading sociological perspectives has
shown – not quite unexpectedly – vagueness, triviality and underdevelopment of many of their epistemological assumptions. Yet,
on the other hand, it has proved that sociology has many
interesting faces and an attempt to develop sociology within the
confines of one selected view would mean a significant restriction
of sociological imagination and perception. Moreover, a synthesis
of the various perspectives in sociology can lead eventually to the
elimination of the divisions between them and destroy the vital
impact of conflict, competition and polemic which they offer.

Multi-dimensional sociology does not aim at curbing pluralism in
sociology, but it seeks to take fuller advantage of it. It seems that
sociology is now mature enough to be able to produce something
more than flat ('one-dimensional'), black-or-white pictures of
society. It is discouraging indeed to watch the endless quarrels as to
whether individuals create society or whether society creates
individuals, whether subjective or objective reality has the upper
hand in social processes, whether face to face relationships or
macro-structural ones are the proper subject of sociology and so
forth. As if one part of the social reality could exist without others!

Another type of controversial ontological issue is related to some
basically incompatible visions of human nature and of the 'iron'
laws of history. It seems that no particular view can claim ultimate
scientific superiority on these matters at present. Although the
polemicists are usually aware of this, they use scientific labels
because they are far more convenient than open appeals to the

political or religious ideologies (or else, individual predilections). The multi-dimensional sociology would be apolitical in the sense that it would not make false claims about the scientific nature of assumptions to which it is the least applicable. It would have to recognize the fact that both human nature and history (or rather, the future) will continue to surprise us. The ontological assumptions intrinsic to each theoretical orientation will have to be kept in mind. The mutual confrontation of the orientations based on different, or even contradictory, assumptions, would show the alternative options for man and society. Each of these options could be popularized, utilized or practically induced by the politically motivated actors. It must be emphasized that their actions are able to influence the actual level of correctness of the theoretically predicted options. A fixed and definite level of correctness is a fiction. The involved actors may clearly influence it. Does this mean that human nature and the laws of history do not exist in the void, waiting patiently for their discovery, but are continuously moulded by both intentional and accidental developments? Obviously, such a view seems rather reasonable. And it is exactly the reason why the battle between various sociological orientations is so dramatic – it is carried on with the awareness that something more than purely scientific issues is at stake. There is the ever-present hope of discovering new ways of management, salvation or reconstruction of the human societies. Of course, one can dismiss this as the dreams of the powerless, dreams which have little chance of attainment. But it is an easy and not fully justified standpoint, which does not change or clarify anything.

A relevant question which may be asked in this context is whether human nature and the development of society are infinitely flexible and fully dependent on the shaping circumstances and forces. It would be reasonable – in view of our present historical knowledge – to assume that there are limits to the social architecture (the one which precludes genetic intervention). Yet those limits are not absolute and fixed for ever. They are related to both external conditions and the stage of development of social consciousness. The most obvious limits are certainly those of time, space, biological needs, technology and so forth. This matter is dealt with in different ways by various sociological orientations.

Certainly *marxism* entails the belief in a programme imprinted in the human history (unfolding of the history). It could, of course, be only a matter of faith which can neither be proved nor even submitted to any empirical test. However, Marx utilized much more systematic observations of the 'empirical' reality when he defined the conditions which have to be fulfilled, in order to trigger the change in the specific context. He avoids extreme one-sidedness by focusing on the dialectical process in which both consciousness and the objective mode of production play their respective, inseparable roles. It has certainly constituted an invaluable contribution to the assessment of the limits of the plasticity of society and history. Marx's method, however, did not provide him with the means of deeper exploration of the area of consciousness, despite its clearly crucial significance for social development. This limitation has had further consequences. He was able to visualize the economic, 'objective', reality after the revolutionary abolition of the capitalist system, but he did not have any clue as to what would happen to the post-revolutionary social consciousness. As a consequence many marxists take convenient refuge in the myth of the limitless impressionability of human beings who, faced with the possibility of a just and 'good' world, would respond in a fully satisfactory way, showing their good and altruistic nature. Clearly, whatever the 'true' nature of man, he will not immediately drop his historically moulded make-up when a new, still unknown and unpredictable, situation emerges. He will probably test the situation very carefully, he will make slow adjustments, but in the meantime he will behave according to the old – often unconscious – aspirations, attitudes, habits and routines. This could certainly provoke the return of the old institutions or the creation of their substitutes. Studying consciousness one does have to take into consideration time. Phenomenology provides, in this respect, invaluable guidance and, indeed, a very useful body of knowledge, proving therefore that processes of social consciousness can be studied systematically.

The practical aims of *phenomenological* and marxist orientations are clearly different, yet not totally incomparable. The first (particularly the existentialist variety) aims at the unmasking of alienating institutions, demystification of manipulation and at the creation of the social conditions for continuous human self-discovery and self-liberation. The real nature, the essence of man, is to be discovered in the course of the conscious demystification processes. For the phenomenologists, the future society has an unknown quality. It will emerge through the dialectical processes of growing self-awareness on the individual and social levels. Objectivization and alienation of consciousness will be constantly checked by the conscious reflection on the real nature of those processes. It would necessitate a collective effort towards full destruction of the societal alienating mechanism opening up the horizon of society beyond the mystified limits and restraints. Naturally, such a stand may be severely criticized – from the practical point of view – for not being concrete enough. The

120

purified and authenticated consciousness of various groups calls for tolerance and free promotion of pluralistic, genuine coexistence. It is a very vague and innocent vision indeed. If taken literally it implies that the process of self-analysis of man's consciousness will eventually eliminate power, domination, inequality and exploitation when their mystified nature is unmasked. The phenomenological approach is not able to provide on its own any valid insight into the 'objective' causes or functions of the given distortions of social perceptions. It has to look for some other sources of inspiration and it usually does (consciously or unconsciously). It seems that many phenomenologists would willingly admit that while they are predominantly interested in the study of subjective perceptions and construction of meanings, it is most likely that these forms of consciousness appear within the framework of particular ideologies, which play a concrete role within the given socio-economic system.

The practical goals of marxists are different. When they are guided by the early works of Marx, they assume *a priori* the quality and potentials of 'true' human nature and they have a ready design of social institutions tailored to fit it. According to this view, the revolutionary consciousness of the working classes will provide them with the right attitude towards the post-revolutionary, new society. It would give them a positive willingness to become immediately fully socialized into this society and to suppress any thought of an alternative design for it. Some more careful predictions would refer to a slightly different process. The spectacular demonstration of the triumph of the 'progressive' forces – the upheaval and the trauma of the revolution and the abolition of the old system – would constitute sufficient brain-washing (or the 'historical lesson') to compel even the unconvinced members of the society to eagerly reject the old prejudices and actively accept the new, superior and just order.

It seems that in the case of the quoted marxist interpretations, the rigid (and, in fact, untestable) assumptions about the real nature of man and, above all, about the dominant role of the material base, have led eventually to the careless disregard for the nature of the temporary, historically conditioned features of man, and of the more or less persistent structure of the individual and collective consciousness.

Phenomenology does not make any clear moral claims about human nature. It penetrates quite successfully the subjective and intersubjective conscious processes, but it certainly overestimates the 'material' power of the subjective intentionality. Thus, though it does not deny the 'objective' forces beyond social perceptions, it does not give sufficient guidance on how to study them.

The above brief discussion of some aspects of marxist and phenomenological theory and practice leads to several observations. The areas where they radically diverge (independently of significant variation within each perspective) are the ontological matters of a very arbitrary and untenable nature. Yet, those matters are of great significance, as they clearly predetermine theoretical and practical priorities (and these different priorities tend to be exaggerated by many). Nevertheless, it may be suggested that some gaps and weaknesses in both approaches could be at least partially remedied by a careful scrutiny of the counterpart's offer on their particular area. True, it may bring some turbulence into the solidly petrified cognitive patterns and the splendid isolation of both perspectives, but it could also force them towards a more precise definition of their assumptions and their methodologies. If they resist such a confrontation, as they have successfully done so far, the need for the construction of a multi-dimensional scheme becomes even more evident.

Structuralism certainly does not have a fully developed ontology. It is based on the belief in hidden structures, due to which one can speak about some organized and meaningful wholes in various spheres of reality. The main task consists in locating the essential relationships between some identifiable elements within the given whole. These objective relationships explain the whole and determine the meanings and roles of its parts and their patterned combinations. The internal structure of the particular parts, linked by the relevant relationships, is of lesser interest. The idea that the relationships, as such, and their structural configurations should be established first and only then can one trace the elements linked by them, is interesting, although not fully convincing. Certainly, one has to have some predefinitions of the relationships (or, at least, some criteria allowing one to define them), when trying to specify them. And so the search is basically directed towards those relationships which one expects to find, or towards those which one defines in advance as important. Therefore the tools provided by structuralism may lead to very different findings when applied by various individuals or epistemological 'schools', although the style and logic of their quest will basically correspond.

It explains the enormous differences between, for instance, structural-functional orientation in sociology and Althusser's structural version of marxism. As far as methodology is concerned, Parsons and Althusser have quite a lot in common. They share the aspiration to construct an all-embracing paradigm, consisting of a set of highly abstract concepts expressing the relationships selected as crucial. They agree that such analytical schemes are not supposed to mirror the social reality, or, even, to correspond to it in any direct way. The role of such schemes is to provide guidance for the scientific inquiries which would lead to the further elucidation of the initial theoretical vision of structure. Such a vision is not, and cannot be, derived from the empirical data or any kind of empirical generalizations. However, although Parsons and Althusser share several basic methodological assumptions, they are clearly orientated towards different points of reference (*status quo* versus potential change). Those are undoubtedly based on their varied ideological commitments and different views on the functions of science (descriptive and explanatory versus material and revolutionary).

The *structural-functional approach* assumes the necessity of taking the system of a whole society as a frame of reference in any sociological inquiries.

> It is always of the greatest importance to specify what the system is which is being used as the object for a sociological analysis, whether or not it is a society, and if not, just how this particular partial social system is located in the society of which it is a part (Parsons, 1951, p. 19).

According to Parsons the major task is to develop the categorization of the structure of social systems and to estimate the modes of structural differentiation within such systems, as well as the range of variability of each structural category. His strategy consists in studying the rules of differentiation of essential elements in order to proceed to the analysis of the ways in which they are integrated with each other in a form of social order. If this is achieved, one can actually 'place' a dynamic process structurally in the social system, and at the same time test its 'functional' relevance within it.

In conclusion, it may be said that the structural-functional school tends to portray society as a whole consisting of various subsystems which contribute to the existence, persistence and development of this whole. They are analytically separate and irreducible to each other, although empirically they appear indissoluble. Their meanings and functions are defined within the context of the whole system, which seems to be well equipped to protect its totality and integration. The consequences of the tensions between various subsystems or deviations of some of them are evaluated from the point of view of the quality of their overall contribution to the entire system which allocates tasks and meanings to its parts. The vision of the system is, in a sense, dialectical – the whole expresses the superior normative orientation which unites and guides the parts towards its fullest realization; the parts, although subordinate, are at the same time indispensable and indeed their contributions and transformations make the integrity of the whole possible. It is, however, clearly this type of structure of dialectic which Althusser would reject as idealist and akin to the Hegelian 'problematic'.

Althusser's *structural marxism* conceives of the social whole as composed of distinct and relatively autonomous, but interrelated, 'instances' linked by the relations of determination. Economy determines other elements only in the last instance, which means above all that it assigns to a particular element (instance) the dominant role within the complex structural whole and it prescribes specific roles for other instances (for example, the nature of the contradictions within the feudal economy decided that the political instance was to play the dominant role). None of those instances is reducible to the economy. According to Althusser, Marx has introduced

> a new conception of the relation between determinant
> instances in the structure-superstructure complex which
> constitutes the essence of any social formation. . . . Marx has
> at least given us the 'two ends of the chain' and has told us to
> find out what goes on between them: on the one hand,
> determination in the last instance by the (economic) mode of
> production; on the other the relative autonomy of the
> superstructure and its specific effectivity (Althusser, 1969,
> p. 111).

Althusser argues that the structure of the marxist dialectic is completely different from that of Hegel. It is different in terms of both the content of the concepts and the understanding of the nature of relationships. He stresses the major importance of the introduction of the concept of social class which can only be understood when analysed through the relations of production.

> The intervention of this new concept and its interconnexion
> with one of the basic concepts of the economic structure
> transforms the essence of the State from top to toe, for the
> latter is no longer above human groups, but at the service of
> the ruling class; it is no longer its mission to consummate
> itself in art, religion and philosophy, but to set them to serve
> the interests of the ruling class, or rather to force them to
> base themselves on ideas and themes which it renders ruling; it
> therefore ceases to be the 'truth of' civil society, to become,
> not the 'truth of' something else, not even of the economy,
> but the means of action and domination of a social class, etc.
> (Althusser, 1969, p. 110).

Marxist dialectic rejects the presupposition of an original simple unity which is never lost throughout the complex dialectic process leading to its pure and universal manifestation. It rather assumes pre-given structural complex unity ruled by the laws of uneven development. The contradictions are not all of the same nature; there is one principal contradiction in any complex unit and a principal aspect in any contradiction. Social structure is thus characterized by the domination-subordination relations between the contradictions. This feature is essential to the complexity itself. Social structure has the unity, but it is articulated in dominance – in the complex, structured relations of domination between contradictions and between their aspects. According to Althusser, only the assumption of the presence of this 'structure in dominance' makes it possible to see real complexity as a unity and to grasp the object of a political practice which aims at transformation of this structure. The 'structure in dominance' articulates and constitutes the condition of the very existence of the given complex whole. It means that the change would necessitate the transformation not only of the principal contradictions, but also the secondary contradictions, and above all the relationships between them.

It is very clear that the different epistemological perspectives and radically different world-outlooks have led Althusser and Parsons towards quite disparate images of social structure. They have also developed completely different tools of analysis, despite initial similarities in their commitments to structuralism.

One can, of course, argue that if the image of society is adequate it may be utilized for the construction of programmes, both of change and of stabilization. Therefore, only one of these basically incompatible visions of society can be true and should be considered as a sound basis for any action. But it is not quite so. Surely, both of those competing visions have had not only theoretical but also practical implications. They have been seeking to imprint some of their features into the reality and to shape social and political practice accordingly. And they might have been quite successful without being true (in a strict, static sense).

It is worth noting that none of these authors formulated any really convincing, valid, criteria for locating either the 'principal contradictions' or the basic 'maintenance mechanisms'. Although they have succeeded in designing very consistent, highly elaborate and systematic visions of social structure which are logically irrefutable, the test of logic does not apply to their basic assumptions. As complete theoretical systems these visions can be defended only from the standpoint of the respective ideological positions of their creators. To refer once again to Althusser, one can say that they use different ideological (or pre-scientific) concepts as the initial material for further scientific elaboration. Obviously, various social groups and various areas of social practice generate different sets of concepts and ideas whose adequacy cannot be tested because of their openly unscientific nature. Therefore, the origins of every social theory are bound to have some initial ideological bias. It would imply that the examination of various theories, as well as competition between them cannot be conducted solely on scientific grounds.

What both the above versions of structuralism appear to have in common is that they produce some abstract and ahistorical images of society which can be either accepted or rejected, but they cannot be utilized as an inspiration or starting-point for further theoretical search. And surely, any synthesis of these two images cannot be even conceived of today. Does this mean that if one rejects Parsons's paradigm one has to discredit all its implications and all the research findings inspired by it? It seems that the primary importance of the socialization mechanisms, the general contexts of shared values and motivational patterns and so forth, can be spotted and analysed in any society which is not undergoing an acute crisis. They may, however, be seen in various ways. They may be linked to the reasonableness of human nature which guarantees co-operation towards order and development of overall value orientation. They may also be seen as manipulated and moulded by the power centres (or general strategies of ruling classes) in order to facilitate achievement of their goals. These two viewpoints may also merge if it is assumed that the specific forms of order are shaped by the interests of the ruling class (or the power elite), but the social need for order is not created by them.

Antonio Gramsci is certainly the most prominent among the scholars who appreciate the reality of value consensus in the otherwise antagonistic social systems. His well known *concept of hegemony* grasps this dimension very imaginatively.

> Undoubtedly the fact of hegemony presupposes that account be taken of the interests and the tendencies of the groups over which hegemony is to be exercised, and that a certain compromise equilibrium should be formed – in other words, that the leading group should make sacrifices of an economic-corporate kind. But there is also no doubt that such sacrifices and such a compromise cannot touch the essential; for though hegemony is ethical-political, it must also be economic, must necessarily be based on the decisive function exercised by the leading group in the decisive nucleus of economic activity (Gramsci, 1971, p. 161).

Gramsci's idea of hegemony was clearly inspired by Machiavelli's teachings addressed to the prince who was instructed 'to make a nice use of the beast and the man' (Machiavelli, 1961, p.

99), to use force and consent, coercion and persuasion. The State cannot be seen as a direct expression of the interests of the dominant group, but instead

> the life of the State is conceived of as a continuous process of formation and superseding of unstable equilibria (on the juridical plane) between the interests of the fundamental group and those of the subordinate groups – equilibria in which the interests of the dominant group prevail, but only up to a certain point, i.e. stopping short of narrowly corporate economic interest (Gramsci, 1971, p. 182).

The superstructure and its various elements can be analysed in this context. The law, education, mass media and so forth are described by Gramsci as instruments used for the smooth creation and maintenance of a type of civilization and citizen which is in harmony with the dominant economic forces, but is also well grounded in the general consciousness and ethical traditions of the given society. The major role in the promotion of this aim is played by the representative ('parliamentary-electoral') political institutions which derive their force from consent. 'Indeed, the attempt is always made to ensure that force will appear to be based on the consent of the majority, expressed by so-called organs of public opinion – newspapers and associations – which therefore in certain situations are artificially manipulated' (Gramsci, 1971, p. 80).

Naturally, this image refers to a basically successful exercise of power where hegemony plays a principal role. Its crises expose immediately what has been successfully hidden: the forces of coercion and enforced order which suddenly appear absolutely vital for the survival and reproduction of the existing economic and political relationships. According to Gramsci, the crisis of hegemony (in other words, the crisis of the State) may develop due to two different types of causes. One is the ruling class's failure 'in some major political undertaking for which it has requested or forcibly extracted, the consent of the broad masses'. The other cause is connected with political activization of masses who 'put forward demands which, taken together, albeit not organically formulated, add up to revolution' (Gramsci, 1971, p. 210). As it is convincingly documented by Stuart Hall *et al.*, in their impressive study of 'Policing the Crisis' (1978), the modern Western democracies are very likely to turn towards 'Law and Order' slogans and practice when political consensus appears to be visibly weakened.

The image of society presented by Gramsci is, of course, consistent with main marxist assumptions about the social structure. It is, however, more balanced in terms of paying much more than lip service to the marxist thesis about the relative autonomy of the superstructure. It provides a sociological insight into the working of a social system and it also shows in a different light the bulk of sociological findings, pointing to the social consensus, co-operation, shared perceptions of the 'natural order' and so on. However, Gramsci's proposal is not always consistent, not quite clear about the actual links between the structure and superstructure or about the mechanisms of change. Gramsci's perspective corresponds with the phenomenological sociology as far as it attempts to explore the process of mystification of people's beliefs and perceptions. They share the suspicion that what the people take for granted and treat as natural may actually constitute an integral part of the oppressive reality imposed upon them. The nature of this imposition and its determinants are naturally perceived in different terms by phenomenologists and by Gramsci. In comparison with other marxist authors, however, he is much less dogmatic, and his thoughts could be interpreted in such a way that the consciousness of the members of the Communist Parties would also be seen as a form of mystification. The hegemony of the Communist Party over its membership may be as real in this case as elsewhere.

It seems that Gramsci's vision corresponds quite closely with some aspects of the socio-political reality of Western democracies (as well as of the Western Communist Parties). However, the utility of various methodological approaches for the purpose of achieving an adequate insight into social reality should be systematically tested in diverse social contexts. It is very likely that the images of society implied by the above sociological orientations correspond – more or less adequately – to the Western societies, being, however, quite alien to the social reality in the so-called Third World, or the 'socialist' countries. Since most of the methodological orientations have been developed and tested in the West (particularly in the USA) it may be instructive to test their applicability to the 'socialist' countries. Once again, Poland can serve as an example of a concrete society belonging to this category. The following will aim at a confrontation of the 'multi-dimensional' society emerging from those theoretical orientations with the Polish society, as it can be apprehended with the assistance of their distinctive methodologies.

In the attempt to examine Poland as a distinctive society, one can start by describing the economic institutions and rules of organization of production, as well as the basic economic relationships and distribution of wealth within that society. This would lead to a predominantly economic diagnosis. If one subsequently describes political institutions and rules of political organization of that society, one will achieve a picture which belongs to the domain of the legal and political sciences. In fact, many Western scholars limit their inquiries into the Soviet or Eastern European reality to these two levels. It leads to the picture of a society which is dry, and dominated by forms without social substance. Even if the description is correct and reaches beyond the official ideological fiction, one is still not able to sense the real society and its change through the presented legal and economic frame. This is not to say that economy, law and political organization of the society are unimportant. They are of enormous significance. But could an unbiased outsider possibly draw any sociological implications merely from their characteristics? Could he develop this formal frame into a real, complex, social structure? Would he know what part of this formal system belongs to the officially propagated fiction, which part is, in fact, being transformed into its opposite and which is actually enforced? To answer this one should analyse the basic economic relations of the studied society. It is also of crucial importance to achieve a grasp of its history and cultural tradition. The international relationships would, of course, be of great importance too.

The analysis of the basic economic relationships in Poland reveals that they are based on the state ownership of the means of production (with the exception of the agricultural area) and on the necessity for the labourers to sell their labour for the means of subsistence. The surplus value is contributing to a considerable degree to the wealth of the political elite, but above all, it is being shifted into the gears of the ideological machinery. The analysis of the structure of the real state budget (if one had access to it) would show the enormous share of expenditure on – besides the external defence sector – the internal security and control, on the state and Party bureaucracy and on propaganda. As far as the political dimension is concerned, one would have to note the one-party rule (which implies that the opposition is outlawed); the lack of democratic elections; the lack of opportunities for any political participation by the working people and, in particular, by the non-Party members; the all-embracing censorship and so forth.

The 'objective' data (if available at all) would provide much more information of this kind. They would be of major importance in locating the basic dimensions of the political and economic structure. But it is very unlikely that the real society – with the historically and geographically located inhabitants – would emerge out of this frame. Having achieved the general insight into the 'objective' aspects of the system, the sociologist may want to know what this 'objective' structure 'does' to the people. What kind of society and what kinds of social consciousness are being produced as a response, adjustment, defence, resistance, as well as original expression of living within the society (which aims at either constituting this society or transcending it).

There are many questions which may be asked, in order to grasp the nature of the basic interpersonal relationships and attitudes. One can utilize one of the theories of social needs, of social interactions and so forth. One can also ask rather naïve, intuitive questions about the 'evident' conditions of social coexistence: for instance, the ability to communicate, to trust, to co-operate, to predict. The phenomenological inquiries into this sphere (especially those by Schutz) may be helpful at this stage.

It is not possible to present here a lengthy analysis of the nature and degree of the presence of those primary conditions of existence of society in the case of contemporary Polish society. Highly sensitive tools of observation and testing should be introduced, in order to reach this hidden and vulnerable area. One may suppose that the factor of communication assumed by the phenomenologists as the basic feature which makes society possible will differ in various social systems. The Polish society is rather homogeneous, as far as ethnic, religious and national features are concerned, therefore one should not expect any basic language barriers (besides those connected with regional differences, differences in education, occupation, etc.). There is, however, a very widespread feeling that there are at least two radically different languages: one, the declaratory language of the official fiction (ideology), used in the public places (mainly for the purpose of survival), and the other, the language used as a means of communication in the very restricted private space. In this sense, the area of communication seems to be limited to the scope of the primary groups (family, friends) and they thus constitute the main domain of social life (according to the criteria of phenomenologists).

Trust may be seen as a factor necessary for the development of any reciprocal relationships and emotional bonds. Even an unsophisticated observer would notice immediately its marked absence in present Polish society. Nevertheless, a more penetrating observation would suggest that perhaps not all relationships are completely devoid of trust. The unusual role and specific nature of friendship would suggest that trust is very highly valued, but that it occurs only in those relationships which have been submitted to long-lasting and many-sided trials. It suggests that the predicted price of a misplaced trust is probably unusually high. Further detailed analysis would bring a much more elaborate insight into the nature of those two (communication and trust), as well as other basic factors of social bonds.

Having completed such an analysis on the very basic, grassroots level, one has to turn back to the blueprint of the political and economic 'objective' institutions and relationships. The observations in the area of basic interpersonal relationships would suggest some questions which could be answered only with the help of thorough knowledge about the 'macro'-organization of the society. But a really thorough knowledge of that sphere can be obtained only with the guidance of the questions generated on the grass-roots level. Only then can a more penetrating analysis of the 'objective' system be undertaken. What are the 'objective' mechanisms which necessitate and guarantee the replacement of the language of communication by the language of declaration in very large areas of societal existence? What sort of mechanisms necessitate and guarantee a growth of fear and mistrust so immense that it destroys almost all social bonds, except the very rare and unique bonds of friendship which become elevated to such exceptional importance? Questions of this sort would facilitate a thorough analysis of the power structure from the top to the bottom. This procedure would make it necessary to study the intermediate levels of social organization – the workplace, the school, the 'cultural participation' and so on. Their implications for the social consciousness would throw further light on the basic features of the studied social structure. Gradually, the basic contradictions will become evident.

Assuming that the Marxist-Althusserian understanding of dialectic is, in the light of the present development of knowledge, more adequate than other structuralist interpretations,[1] an attempt should be made to relate it to the society in question. It seems that such a test would somewhat shake a neat scheme based on the assumption of the determining (in the last instance) force of the economic factor. Naturally, economy (production) constitutes a necessary condition of the very existence of the society. It also contributes to the considerable inequalities within social structure. But its major role ends here. The basic contradiction within the *economy* consists in the fact that workers' efforts contribute to the greater and better-equipped *political* oppression and control (rather than to the growing wealth and economic domination of the ruling class). It seems that the determining force can be found in the contradictions of ideology, which in various ways and to a varying extent determine the nature of political, economic and cultural contradictions and the structure of relationships among them. Sometimes it would assign the actual dominant role to the economy, but it would be an arrangement of a temporary and symbolic nature. It seems that most of the time bureaucracy (including the security forces) plays the dominant role and other 'instances' are subordinated to it. Its basic contradiction consists in the incompatibility of the rational demands of bureaucratic organization and the irrational requirements of the ideology. This major contradiction produces the constant growth of bureaucracy, its ever-growing ambiguity (for instance, widespread double recording of information – fictitious and more realistic items separately), and the intensification of the repressive apparatus within it. The bureaucratized ideology substitutes a fiction for reality. When the contradictions within the fiction are negated, they produce even a grander fiction, which must reinforce itself in ever more inclusive domains. The essential role of the economy consists of its ability to produce sufficient material, military and security bases, to inspire the ideology with the necessary confidence (coercive power).

In the socialist society, the economy is not constructed according to the interests of any group or class of that society; it is constructed according to the ideology and the extra-national political and military pressures. It seems that the role of the economy in the capitalist system is much more real. The 'objective' contradictions of the economic interests can be, more or less, clearly located. The class division – although not so clear-cut as some would maintain – can be spotted. In the socialist system the economy does not really serve anybody in any material sense. It is inefficient and in a constant crisis which cannot be relieved, because there is no remedy which would be acceptable from the ideological point of view. The ideology is satisfied when its demands (for example, the Plan) are fulfilled on paper. Real productivity is of secondary importance. The ideology reduces its inner tensions and contradictions by ideological means. The Communist ideology does not serve the interests of any class distinguished by its relationship to the production. It serves predominantly the interests of the ruling elite, distinguished by its relationship to the ideology (position in the party power structure). The subordinate 'class' (the society at large) is not only forced to sell its labour for wages, but also to give up the human rights connected with other areas of expression and activity. The core of oppression lies above all in that latter fact. It does not mean, of course, that low economic living standards are irrelevant.

The economic hardship is acute and oppressive, but it cannot be seen in the clear-cut perspective of exploitation. The workers realize that their potential is wasted, rather than appropriated by the rulers. They are not given the opportunity to work efficiently and competently. The poor organization of production (for example, constant stoppages of production due to inefficient co-operation between various units of industry), the low standard of technology, the alarming safety risks, and the discrepancy between ideology and reality – all together contribute to widespread work-shyness and alcoholism among the employees.

The phenomenological excursions into the social consciousness would probably discover that large parts of the surrounding reality are treated by the people as absolutely unnatural and unacceptable. On the other hand, many features of this reality appear natural in the sense that they have become predictable, constant elements of the everyday life of the people. When, however, they are given a conscious reflection they are not treated as desirable or necessary parts of social life. The idea of hegemony does not find confirmation here. The consent is of a very different nature than that spoken about by Gramsci. It is spurious, declarative and defensive. The 'class of organizers' assumes that the dominant ideology should find an automatic expression in the people's consciousness. But if it does not, it does not really matter, because of the ban on free expression, which makes social consciousness invisible and atomized. Thus, genuine acceptance of the ideology and its correspondence with the whole range of values and beliefs held by the people are not crucial to the exercise of power by the despotic ruling elite.

Even within the structure of the ruling party the hegemony mechanism is conspicuously absent. A quite opposite development may be noted.

> The bureaucracy is the most dangerously hidebound and conservative force; if it ends up by constituting a compact body, which stands on its own and feels itself independent of the mass of members, the party ends up by becoming anachronist and at moments of acute crisis it is voided of its social content and left as though suspended in mid-air (Gramsci, 1971, p. 211).

Once the analysis of the extent and nature of consensus is completed (which cannot be done in detail here), the requirement to study dissensus – its content and forms of expression – becomes quite evident. In this context the necessity to refer the findings to the 'objective' organization of the society emerges once again.

The above sketchy reflections on the possibility of sociological inquiry into the Polish reality have revealed the crucial importance of the knowledge of the 'objective' structure of this society for the understanding of the 'subjective' social reality. However, it has also been argued that the thorough analysis of the 'objective' side of the picture is practically impossible without some inspiration derived from the inquiries into the 'subjective' aspect. Some further tests of the validity of these conclusions can be provided. It would require a comparative analysis covering various countries belonging to the Eastern socialist bloc. Several of them share similar 'objective' structures and external relationships. A careful analysis of the social consciousness, of the nature of informal relationships, etc., in these various societies could bring very important findings pertaining to studied relationships between the formal and informal structures. One can guess that the similarities would be striking enough to give considerable support to the theses suggested above.

However, one may also predict quite conspicuous differences. They would have to be explained by, among other factors, the history, the cultural and religious tradition, as well as the level of social development and the shape of the social structure prior to the introduction of the 'socialist' system. The discovered differences would call for further research into our specimen case of the Polish society. The areas where these 'subjective' differences are significant should be thus scrutinized in the light of the peculiar historical features and traditions of that society. It may also be expected that some differences would be discovered within the 'objective' structure of the compared societies. Such a discovery would, in turn, necessitate further inquiry aimed at the examination of the possible consequences of these 'objective' differences. Moreover, an attempt should be made to locate the most likely reasons for those differences. One may predict that some of them would, in fact, be causally linked to the differences in the consciousness of the people which could be explained by the uniqueness of the historical and cultural background of various countries. The private ownership of the farms in Poland may serve as a good example of such a situation. In Poland, unlike other socialist countries, all the attempts at collectivization of the agricultural production have failed, because of the firm rejection of the scheme by the peasants. Their individualism and the subjective importance attached to the private ownership of the land and independent farming gave their resistance sufficient strength to resist the official attempts at coercive collectivization. It seems that the peasants' social consciousness indeed played the decisive role in moulding the basic relations of the agricultural production.

The above considerations suggest that starting the study of a society with the analysis of the 'objective' structure and political organization, does not necessarily mean that the researcher decides in advance what is the exact nature of the relationship between the 'objective' and 'subjective' world. Multi-dimensional sociology means, in fact, constant testing of this relationship. It should also be noted that the reference to the *subjective* and *objective* world is treated simply as a distinction between two analytically distinct levels of societal organization: the formalized level organized mainly along the political and economic dimension, and the more intimate level of direct, informal interactions and relationships. This distinction is not based on the positivist faith in the objective existence of the social reality which can reveal itself in the same manner as the natural/physical objects do. It is also sceptical about any imputations that social phenomena can be free of meaning, or that they have fixed, 'objectively' given meanings, determined by their nature and structure.

An important recommendation of the multi-dimensional sociology is that each level of social organization can and should be studied from the perspective of another level. Thus, the level of the formal organization of a society can be studied as an 'objective' structure, in the light of the reliable documents, data and sociological generalizations. But it should also be studied as a 'subjective' structure, as it appears in the consciousness of the people. The divergence, as well as consistency, between the two pictures (or different versions of these pictures) may be subsequently subjected to many-sided scrutiny aiming at a better understanding of the relationships between those two analytic levels of reality in the given social context. A similar operation can be carried out on the informal, subjective level. The nature of inter-actions, negotiations of meaning and formation of the individual selves can be studied in the most immediate manner proposed by symbolic interactionism. However, these processes should also be looked upon from the perspective of the 'objective' organization. The question can be asked, what is the explicit import of the political and economic institutions in question for the scope and nature of the symbolic context in which individuals are operating, and the quality of their relationships with the others? Further inquiry should, of course, be focused on the relationship between the implications of the 'system' in the sphere of interpersonal relationships and the actual nature of this sphere (as it is experienced and negotiated by those directly involved). As was indicated earlier (in Chapter 9, 'Symbolic Interactionism'), this type of inquiry may be orientated towards a search for the 'typical self' within whole societies or social classes and the relationship between it and social structure. The application of this idea into the social reality in Poland is presented in Chapters 16 and 17 on 'Class Ethos' and 'National Ethos' in the second part of this book.

Finally, multi-dimensional sociology should look at the correspondence of various sociological perspectives to the social reality from yet another point of view. In order to better under-stand the ideological dimension in various contemporary sociological traditions, one has to study the social reasons for the development, the success or the failure of the given sociological vision in certain socio-political contexts. The Frankfurt School,

Parsons or Gramsci responded to some concrete conditions in their attempts to construct the most adequate visions of the structure of a society. This link has been lost subsequently, and their theoretical systems started to lead their own, quite eventful lives. Many theories make careers of a clearly extra-scientific nature. They do not have to be true to be actually utilized in practice. But the effects of such a utilization are nevertheless real. The theories are usually concerned with the discovery of the truth, but the 'practice' is interested more in the convincing ideas than the actually true ones. It seems that something new can be learnt from inquiry into the reasons why certain theories gain application and popularity among some groups in certain countries, why they are accepted as convincing by certain practitioners. An educated guess suggests that when the image of society emerging from a theory is rather bleak and frightful, it is likely to feed anarchist movements (for example, Marcuse); when the society is portrayed as bound to change, due to the objective laws of progress it would appeal to the revolutionary forces (for example, Marx); when, finally, the image of society emphasizes the mechanisms of organizational integration and self-regulation, it would most probably appeal to the official organizers and controllers of the society (for example, Parsons and general systems theory; see the interesting analysis of the career of this theory in the Soviet Union, Kelley, 1977).

It seems that the stress on one-dimensional sociology, propagating one 'obligatory' version of the image of society, has not only theoretical but also clear political implications. The domination of sociology by one theoretical orientation would necessarily mean that sociology has become a tool of political strategies of one, selected section of society. Multi-dimensional sociology would not, by definition, be suitable for ideological appropriation by one social group or one type of political system. It would actually pose problems for any group looking for one-sided yet 'convincing' ideas, in order to elevate their political programmes to the status of science. Finally, multi-dimensional sociology should not be expected to solve our moral and ideological dilemmas, but it should help us to see them more clearly.

Note

1   The Parsonian model, for example, seems evidently inapplicable to the Polish Society. Its history, as well as the present situation, calls for a model which would grasp a complex reality of conflict, oppression and domination.

Bibliography

Althusser, L. (1969), *For Marx*, Harmondsworth: Penguin.

Gramsci, A. (1971), *Selections from the Prison Notebooks*, London: Lawrence & Wishart.

Hall, S., Critcher, C., Jefferson, T., Clarke, J. and Roberts, B. (1978), 'Policing the Crisis', London: Macmillan.

Kelley, D. R. (1977), 'Group and Specialist Influence in Soviet Politics: In Search of a Theory', in R. B. Remnek (ed.), *Social Scientists and Policy Making in the U.S.S.R.*, New York and London: Praeger.

Machiavelli, N. (1961), *The Prince*, Harmondsworth: Penguin.

Parsons, T. (1951), *The Social System*, London: Routledge & Kegan Paul.

Part two

Social structure and consciousness (selected concerns)

11 Incipient relative naturalism[1]
Adam Podgórecki

'Why are you crying?' a young siskin asked an older one.
'You now have more conveniences in the cage than in the field.'

'You were born in it,' said the old one, 'so I forgive you. I
was free and now in a cage and that is why I cry.'

Ignacy Krasiński

In the history of the development of social ideas, quite often
philosophy influences sociology (like, for example, positivistic
empirical sociology, materialism-marxism phenomenology-
ethnomethodology, etc.). But the reverse direction is not so dis-
cernible. Nevertheless, it would be difficult to assume that philosophical concepts have a clear validity *per se*. Thus it would not be
easy to defend a position that philosophical notions, due to the very
fact that they are philosophical, possess specific cognitive power
elucidating the reality as it is. Leaving apart the detailed analysis of
the vested meanings which become interjected by various social
processes into the cognitive network of philosophical concepts, it
might be useful to coin a general meta-methodological notion
which might serve as an instrument which makes it possible to look
closer into the social determinants of philosophical notions. A lot
of work was done in order to disclose the economic, political,
social, etc., functions of different types of philosophies, but not
enough attention was paid to the problem of the way in which
abstract concepts (and especially philosophical ones) obtain total
independence from their own origin. That this independence is
doubtful the reasoning based on 'incipient relative naturalism' (a
specific meta-methodological notion) intends to show.

Analyses conducted in the social sciences are particularly
interesting when they reach out to factors not directly perceivable.
Each time one succeeds in penetrating behind the symptoms of
phenomena and disclosing the elements shaping those symptoms,
there is essential progress in the social sciences. When Marx pointed
to the economic factor as constituting the base on which is built up
a corresponding superstructure, he achieved fundamental progress
in science. For it makes it possible to identify elements which
determine others and, in particular, to identify such elements

141

which, if subjected to purposeful and conscious change, will cause changes in related elements. Freud's conceptions, too, though in another, narrower dimension, are constructed according to a scheme making it possible to grasp the correlation between observable elements and elements which transcend and determine them. In Freud's conception, subconscious drives play the role of determining factors. Petrażycki's little known conception which interprets the process of individual and collective life by introducing the empirical 'imperceptible' emotions is also an unusually effective instrument for systematizing and explaining a multiplicity of divergent empirical data, which would remain uncoordinated without applying that conception. Methodological revolution of this kind dictates in the social sciences the postulate of seeking beyond the sphere of available empirical data other data which would be the key to the understanding of the take-off data.

But there are certain epistemological difficulties involved in carrying out the above directive. For it is not easy in the social sciences to transcend the sphere of the analysed known data and to seek their starting-point factors, especially those which would essentially influence the action or shape of the known factors. Moreover, there arises a further difficulty, namely the rather strong tendency to regard the given, known world as the natural world besides which there are no other different worlds. This creates a sort of 'natural' barrier between the world of established empirical data and the world of other data which possibly lie beyond the known data. How, then, can that 'natural' barrier be surmounted? It will undoubtedly be possible to overcome this gnoseological limitation when the very nature of the cognitive limitations is adequately investigated.

Therefore, it might be useful to introduce a new theoretical concept, the concept of *incipient relative naturalism*, in analyses of perceived tendencies to limit the known world to already established data. Some simple examples indicating a certain intuition in connection with the new concept might elucidate its main sense.

Thus, the course of history shows that even in most stabilized and petrified periods of the life of various social systems, there are, as a rule, antagonisms between the older and younger generations. While the older one tends to be more conservative, the younger one is more prone to change, or, in certain situations, to revolutionary moods. Whereas the positive groups of reference for the former come from its own generation and those who have a good understanding of youth are often regarded as shifty hypocrites seeking notoriety, the younger generation often treats its predecessor (which introduced it into social life) as a negative model.

In some historical periods, when changes were particularly sudden or especially conspicuous and induced – for instance, by a technical revolution – teachers and upbringers often became a laughing-stock to their pupils. This is a queer paradox. Pupils begin to orient themselves better on various novelties of daily life, while teachers lose verbal encounters because of their very diffuse specializations. Basically immersed in the routine of certain narrow spheres of the reality and systematically deepening their knowledge in these very limited fields, educators become insensitive to the new phenomena constantly appearing which become compelling because of their newness. By losing their prestige in limited partial spheres which are new to them, teachers lose authority on a general scale, thus also, consequently, in the field of their speciality.

Eminent creators may become epigones in their own lifetime. It is well known that imitators, followers, co-workers, rivals gather around those who create some new ideas. Then they adopt the discoverer's patterns, standards and procedures and utilize his preliminary experience. Not burdened by complicated trial and error procession and the persistent work which led the discoverers to the new ideas, and leaning, so to speak, on the shoulders of the innovators but equipped with fresh ideas and counter-ideas, they begin to question previous ideas, schools, styles of work. Treating original, new discoveries as already objectivized and accepted, these followers and imitators commence to express superiority over their inspirers in concrete individual questions. If inability to reach a compromise bars the way of the original creator to establish some kind of *modus vivendi* with his successor, he may not even necessarily become the epigone of the idea he once initiated, but sometimes a heavy ballast which the objective needs of development of his own idea demand to be eliminated as a current retarding factor.

Abstract painting is for many a controversial question. Some maintain that a composition of colours and shades without content constitutes only a kind of eccentricity of modern painting which has very little, if anything, in common with the tradition of that field of art. Essentially, smudges and smears, a chaos of colours, the impossibility of reading the sense of the picture, the lack of shape and subject, astonishing compositions of form and constructions seem to be only studies, preparatory operations for the main task, namely, composing a picture. Such is the traditional view. But the contemporary world provides modern man with qualitatively different experiences and sensations, unknown to preceding generations. The formal and geometrical strangeness of machines, landscapes seen from an aeroplane in flight, television pictures of the cosmos, shapes of bacteria, atom models, pictures taken through microscopes and telescopes, etc., arouse in contemporary man new sensations in relation to the hitherto cultural tradition. It may, hence, be said, considering the new experiences, that abstract painting is an attempt at a generalized synthesis of these experiences and sensations. The task of such a synthesis is to make it possible for man today to encompass the totality of varied data which had appeared at the beginning to constitute only a disjointed collection without a common denominator.

The situations presented above are expected to stimulate semantic intuition in order to create a basis for the introduction of the new concept defined as *incipient relative naturalism*. This concept should thus be understood as the apprehension of a given stage of development of some process or of its place in the total structure of a given system, which when separated from its genesis inclines to regard that stage or place as an independent, idiopathic element, as a principal matrix of comparison unconnected with systems of reference which determine its other, previous stages of development or other possible aspects of its place in the totality of the given structure. A given state of things is perceived in this sense as completely detached and the system of values associated with it is conceived – like itself – as *naturally* given, as excluded from the sphere of evaluation. According to this conception, individuals, groups or social circles regard certain convictions as self-evident and irrefutable, starting-point data which constitute their frame of reference for the assessment of and critical comparison with all other beliefs. Beliefs of this type have the special character of meta-convictions, of axioms.

It should be noted that the subjective recognition of states (of affairs) remains beyond critical assessment and, as a basic standard for the analysis and evaluation of other, related situations, needs no objective grounding at all. Involved in the conception 'incipient relative naturalism' is the proposition that every social group or each individual has within the store of experience a certain complex of convictions and norms which are regarded as 'natural'. This complex constitutes part of the cultural heritage acquired in the course of socialization by the given group or individual. It is not a matter in this conception of ascertaining whether the complex of convictions and norms is correct and well grounded. It is only a question of establishing that there must be at least a provisional system of convictions and assessments serving as the point of departure in undertaking evaluations at all and in general. The designation of a state of things considered incipient relative naturalism as 'relative' comes from the observer. For the observer assumes that the viewpoint referred to as incipient relative naturalism is that felt naturally in the given conditions. In other

144

conditions, not accessible to the experiencing individuals, the same may be regarded not as natural, but as decidedly different. Whereas the determination of some view as 'natural' means the introjected analysis of the state of feeling of the experiencing individual. Finally, the concept 'incipient' means that what is regarded as natural is also viewed as the starting, basic matrix of all comparisons.

Before analysing the further characteristics of the incipient relative naturalism concept, it is necessary to note views which to some degree approximate the concept in question here. In his time, Scheler introduced to the theory of cognition a conception he defined as 'the natural worldview'. He maintained that there is a constant and 'natural' core in the philosophy of world views for the human species, and he further asserted that a scientific philosophy, as compared with the philosophy of world views, is a monstrous freak which limits philosophy precisely where it should extend its analysis to such questions as the foundation of science, all its potential consequences, its internal contradictions (Scheler, 1960, pp. 82-3). In Scheler's opinion, the natural world view appears when the individual regards the world surrounding him at a given moment as the existing world. According to him, it is also characteristic of the natural world view that the individual confronted with the infinite cosmos has a tendency to select from the human environment only phenomena consonant with human instinct and sensory structure as the permanent framework of his cognitive experiences. Scheler furthermore held that within the natural world view, the individual primarily perceives an object's pure existence and not its essence (Scheler, 1960, pp. 93-6).

Schutz expressed somewhat similar ideas. Analysing the various world views not so much of philosophers as of 'average' people, he concluded that

> The sum-total of these various typifications constitutes a
> frame of reference in terms of which not only the
> sociocultural, but also the physical world has to be
> interpreted, a frame of reference that, in spite of its
> inconsistencies and its inherent opaqueness, is nonetheless
> sufficiently integrated and transparent to be used for solving
> most of the practical problems at hand (Schutz, 1970, p. 119).

The author also distinguishes three kinds of knowledge, or natural world view: those of the expert, of the man in the street and of the well informed citizen:

> The expert's knowledge is restricted to a limited field but
> therein it is clear and distinct. His opinions are based upon

warranted assertions; his judgments are not mere guesswork or loose suppositions.

The man in the street has a working knowledge of many fields which are not necessarily coherent with one another. His is a knowledge of recipes indicating how to bring forth in typical situations typical results by typical means. The recipes indicate procedures which can be trusted even though they are not clearly understood . . . This knowledge in all its vagueness is still *sufficiently* precise for the practical purpose at hand.

The ideal type that we propose to call the well-informed citizen (thus shortening the more correct expression: the citizen who aims at being well informed) stands between the ideal type of the expert and that of the man in the street. . . . To be well informed means to him to arrive at *reasonably founded* opinions in fields which he knows are at least mediately of concern to him although not bearing upon his purpose at hand (Schutz, 1970, pp. 239–40).

Although there is a similar distinction in the Polish literature of three kinds of knowledge within various world views – common knowledge, professional knowledge and systematic knowledge (Podgórecki, 1968, pp. 303–5) – it should be noted that the Scheler and Schutz conceptions relate only indirectly to the concept proposed here: incipient relative naturalism. Although Scheler and Schutz stress the need of analysing the perceiving individual's world view and point to the naturalist traits of some of these world views, they do not create a definite concept and fail to compare the chosen intuitions with corresponding empirical data. Nor do the conceptions of the above authors pay sufficient attention to the starting-points – which we designate by the concept incipient – of individuals or groups holding that kind of world view. Hence, by incipient should be understood the starting-point of individuals or social groups in the world in some respect important to them. Detailed research discloses that individuals like groups in their relation with the external world acquire new experiences successively, in stages, by leaps. Nevertheless, sometimes they have to petrify completely certain types of experiences which remain unchanged during their lives. So a girl or a boy might exist in a grown-up woman or man. The finiteness of the life of the individual and of the social existence of various groups makes impossible the continuous and in every respect open accumulation of experience. Experimentally tested situations are known, where several-hour-old goslings were given wire apparatus in place of their mothers. After the period of induced representation, the young goslings ceased to react to their natural or species mothers and refused to allow the removal of the simulated ones. Essential in this procedure is that the induced reaction to the world takes place in a strictly designated time; the phenomenon in question cannot appear earlier or later. Anthropological research discloses that some 'primitive' people elaborated very complicated ways of inculcating boys with moral habits during their initiation. Upon segregated young boys subjected to the forces of nature and directed dramatic situations are imposed given moral canons in a categorical manner. Patterns thus applied penetrate deeply in the newly moulded psyche in a period particularly propitious for ethical principles. Norms inculcated in that manner are particularly durable. Other sociological research has established that the leaders of fashion in American provincial towns are not married women or those from higher-placed social circles. They are, rather, unmarried young ladies who are especially apt to adopt new fashions and are particularly effective as personal models gladly imitated by others. The readiness to accept certain fashions and the ability to transmit them to others are explainable in this case by the particular situation of unmarried women in the structure of the broader social system.

It may be objected that the above considerations pertain to cases involving some kind of cultural adaptation, of accustoming oneself or (less elegantly) of acculturation. According to that critique, wherever certain addictions or habits of thought are adopted, there results a state of inertia, of opposition to attempts to change them. In this critical understanding, the feeling of starting-point naturalism would be something different from far-reaching familiarity with a given state, way of life, manner of reaction to social reality. For in the case of feeling the naturalism of the inception (starting-point), it is not a matter of acquiring any sort of habit, but the kind which in the given stage of development of the individual, group or social system, or in their particular social situation in the social structure, is adequate in relation to the existing need. It is striking in its veracity which sometimes seems to reflect the very essence of things. It provides answers to troublesome questions which arise during the accumulation of life experience of a new type. Hence the feeling of naturalism is the starting-point of a particular case of habit acquisition which constitutes the complete release of the tension associated with previously unsatisfied needs.

Ascertainment of the incipient naturalism sometimes does not come as a rapid presentiment, but in the course of a slow process. Thus a view which takes shape gradually, imperceptibly, step by step, which from many sides and on varied levels reveals additional ramifications and rationalizations, may be felt as natural at the moment when it coalesces into a synthetic whole. The initial, unnoticed danger of Fascist ideology was not so much the climate of severe public control surrounding the individual and social groups, as the creation of a feeling that there was no alternative and a state of delusion in which it was assumed that the prevailing situation was inviolable and permanent, the affirmation, it seems, of a tradition whipping up consent to the universal conformity of attitudes and behaviour. This social climate, this peculiar public aura, is a side-effect of purposeful intentions and action, and is all the more dangerous because, precisely by arousing the feeling of naturalism the starting-points of a further multiplicity of evaluations, behaviours, attitudes are created, and consolidated by their later being put into practice. Later attempts to eliminate such assessments or attitudes, as in the case of denazification, required not only an ideological struggle to prove the groundlessness, viciousness and injustice of the evaluations and attitudes; it was also necessary to solve the problem, difficult to perceive but of great practical consequence, of eradicating the feeling that those assessments and attitudes were 'natural'.

All resocialization processes, both on a mass scale and in relation to the individual, should consider whether the negative state of affairs having to be changed is felt by those affected to be due to 'the natural course of things' or if it is the consequence of the action of more or less manipulating forces. If diagnosis confirms the first situation, then resocialization activity faces a double task. It not only has to eliminate erroneous and harmful evaluations or attitudes, but also to expose its seemingly natural origin.

The unsolved problem of false consciousness perhaps finds its solution by the application of the content of incipient relative naturalism. Imprinted ideas at a certain stage of development or change, not recognized as dysfunctional, may attain the features of 'naturality' through the persistent process of associations. An attempt to break this feeling of 'naturality' may arouse rationalizations which constitute, as a whole, the false consciousness.

The above considerations suggest the following general hypothesis: those who changed the world view which they once regarded as natural, more easily reject newly adopted world views than do those who consistently cling to their 'natural' world views.·

Note

1 This study is based on the author's previous work entitled 'Relatywny naturalizm startu czyli pojecie wdrukowania' ('Incipient Relative Naturalism, or the Concept of Imprinting (Engraving)'), *Studia Filozoficzne*, no. 5/72, 1971. The concept 'social imprint' has a certain similarity to that of M. Scheler's 'natural worldview' or to A. Schultz's

concept of 'relative naturalism'. But when he formulated his conception, the present author was not aware of these concepts.

Bibliography

Podgórecki, A. (1968), *Perspektywy socjologii stosowanej (The Prospects of Applied Sociology)*, in *Socjotechnika,* Warsaw: Książka i Wiedza.
Scheler, M. (1960), *On the Eternal in Man*, New York: Harper.
Schutz, A. (1970), *On Phenomenology and Social Relations*, University of Chicago Press.

12 The concept of meta-attitudes
Adam Podgórecki

Although the concept of 'attitude' is, in social sciences, a relatively young one (in its fifties), it would be practically impossible – due to the richness of literature in that field – to present an adequate description of the vital achievements in this area. Inquiries conducted in 'small groups', several laboratory experiments, a lot of field studies in anthropology, a massive body of research in the area of the sociology of law, morals and deviance, etc., brought about an incredible amount of attitudinal data of a different kind. Nevertheless, to a large extent these data are incompatible or, even worse, uncomparable. The bulk of them was collected in different cultures or in such diverse social settings that their fruitful comparison now becomes methodologically quite haphazard. So, this enormous quantity of findings is still waiting for a successful synthetic attempt.

In order to make this attempt more viable it seems to be useful to introduce the concept of 'meta-attitudes'. This concept, if accepted, may also be used as an important link between psychology and sociology.

Definitions

There are varied definitions of human attitudes. Znaniecki and Thomas, among the first in this field, thus defined that conception: 'By attitude we designate the process of awareness determining the individual's possible or actual activity in the social world' (Thomas and Znaniecki, 1918–20, p. 27). Other definitions are: 'Attitude = specific mental disposition toward an incoming (or arising) experience, whereby that experience is modified; or a condition of readiness for certain types of activity' (Warren, 1934); 'An attitude is a mental disposition of the human individual to act

150

for or against a definite object' (Droba, 1933); 'An attitude is a mental and neutral state of readiness, organised through experience, exerting a directive or dynamic influence upon the individual's response to all objects and situations with which it is related' (Allport, 1935, quoted after C. W. Allport (in 'Introduction' to Warren and Jahoda, 1976, p. 24). According to the humanist psychologist Rokeach, 'An attitude is a relatively enduring organisation of beliefs around an object or situation predisposing one to respond in some preferential manner' (Rokeach, 1968, p. 450). Another more developed definition reads: 'The attitude of a person towards some object is in general a relatively constant disposition to assess that object and to emotionally react to it as well as the contingent accompanying emotional-evaluative disposition to relatively lasting convictions regarding the nature and properties of the object and behaviour towards it' (Nowak, 1974b, p. 23).

The above definitions apparently have a number of defects. Thus attitudes may be the expression not only of individual consciousness but also of various subconscious or unconscious processes. They do not always pertain to some given object, regardless of all the epitomological difficulties which the concept 'object' introduces directly to the definition of attitude. For example, acceptance of the norms 'do not lie' or 'do not kill' does not make it possible to designate or indicate all the objects or situations in which the above norms may find actual application. Inclusion of mental (and also emotional-motivational or behavioural) elements raises some objections regarding their completeness and distinctiveness. Moreover it accepts not only a doubtful criterion of the partition of psychic phenomena as the basis for defining attitude, but it also entangles attitudes thus defined into otherwise important questions of the adequacy of actual behaviour and the attitudes designating it. The statement that attitude constitutes 'a consistent cognitive organization' does not take into consideration the well known phenomenon of attitude ambivalence; while to incorporate in the definition 'convictions regarding the nature and properties . . . of the object' means to directly include in the very definition of attitude all possible philosophical tracts on the 'nature of things', etc.

The above exemplary definitions of the conception attitude and the reservations regarding them incline us to accept a simple regulating definition, namely, 'A relatively lasting disposition to react in a socially given manner'.

Scope of the problem

The adoption of this kind of definition of attitude as the point of

151

departure for further considerations makes it possible – on the basis of its content – to indicate in advance the range of problems essentially linked with the shaping, persistence and changes of attitudes. The following may be primarily reckoned among these problems: classification of various types of attitudes and their ambivalence, the dissonance and divergencies between them, relations between attitudes and behaviour, the degree of their inner acceptance, analysis of attitudes of a higher order (meta-attitudes) which organize those more elementary ones.

The problem of classification should be treated as a heuristic procedure, ordering in a relatively simple manner numerous kinds of attitudes actually manifested in various empirical situations. Attitudes are thus divisible into the following: (1) erasable and non-erasable; (2) concrete and general (the former pertain to given specific and designated phenomena, the latter to the category of attitudes evoked by given kinds of stimuli); (3) passive and active (respectively: the consumption-oriented, contemplative disposition, and, for example, the creative or aggressive dispositions); (4) the internalized and to be internalized (by internalized attitudes is understood those inculcated in the individual by means of various socializing measures; by non-internalized is meant either attitudes which the individual has not – or not completely – assimilated or those which it voluntarily rejected – de-internalized); (5) consistent or inconsistent (attitudes linked structurally into one harmonious whole – then being close to the idea of meta-attitudes – and those in a relation of ambivalence, dissonance or divergence); (6) open and closed (the first pertains to tolerant, undogmatic attitudes, and the second to the authoritative attitude immersed in dogmas); (7) simple and complex (correspondingly, attitudes displayed without the intervention of modifying situations and attitudes which depend on additional, co-appearing modifiers, such as altruism, refinement, etc. for instance); (8) autotelic and heterotelic (understood respectively as attitudes possessing a value in themselves, not leading to any other values, and those instrumental in realizing extraneous ones); (9) it is also possible to classify attitudes in accordance with the kind of social reality they pertain to. It is thus possible to distinguish legal, political, parental, moral, religious, aesthetic attitudes, etc.; (10) attitudes and meta-attitudes (the latter is understood as attitudes of a higher order which regulate the whole syndrome of several divergent attitudes).

This spectrum of problems evidently calls for an attempt to constitute a basis for formulating various propositions pertaining to the emergence, persistence and change of attitudes.

One may say that the phenomenon of attitudes ambivalence has

152

triggered one of the most theoretically interesting explanatory approaches. Thus, attitudes ambivalence consists of two (or more) simultaneous dispositions to react in a given social manner, despite the fact that the varied dispositions are differently associated with the positive or negative rating of the anticipated effects of activity, and with diverse evaluations of different elements of the situation towards which the attitude had to be manifested or realized. Ambivalent attitudes may pertain not only to different ways of evaluating the effects of reacting in a given manner; they may also pertain to divergencies caused by different, discordant descriptions of given phenomena.

Some theoretical explanations

Attitudes based on discordant convictions are in a state of dissonance 'if overlooking some of them results in one psychologically contradicting another' (Malewski, 1964, p. 95). In arranging the formulations and statements of L. Festinger, Malewski put into an order and presented the following list of propositions in reference to the theory of cognitive dissonance. It is easily observable that all those propositions pertain also to attitudes – with the assumption that the given attitudes are based on the convictions from which they stem. Here is the list of propositions:

1 Generally speaking, cognitive dissonance acts as a punishment – in which connection:
2 Persons experiencing cognitive dissonance attempt to:
(a) eliminate or reduce it and attain harmonious views as well as
(b) to avoid situations and information which might cause or increase dissonance.
3 The greater the punishment effected by cognitive dissonance, the stronger is the desire to eliminate it.
4 The punishment caused by dissonance between different convictions is the greater –
(a) the more important for the given person are the convictions between which there is dissonance, and
(b) the larger is the number and importance of a person's convictions which are in dissonance with the given conviction as compared to the number and importance of convictions in accord with it.
5 Dissonance may be reduced or eliminated by:
(a) adopting additional convictions, for instance, those belittling convictions dissonant with others or which indicate that the dissonance is only seeming; . . .

153

6 Some convictions between which there is dissonance may
   resist change (Malewski, 1964, pp. 95-7).

The relations between convictions as elements inclining (disposing) to lasting reactions in a given social manner may seem relatively clear. Nevertheless, the complicating factor of the perception of one's own status and perceptions regarding statuses of others is so important for the 'social actor' (person who manifests different types of attitudes) that it seems to be worthwhile to analyse briefly possible ramifications of attitude formation from this point of view. In consequence, less clear are the relations between various perceptions of one's social status and the convictions associated with these perceptions. It might be said in this case too that perceptions regarding the coincidence or divergence of the elements of social status – if they are lasting phenomena – will also modify in a relatively constant manner not only their corresponding convictions, but also their associated attitudes. Hence, theory pertaining to divergent status factors may be formulated as complementary theory regarding the changing or modification of attitudes associated with one's social status. Thus, if the elements of his social status perceived by the individual deviate from the expectations of others in respect of those elements, then the individual will tend to modify his attitude in the direction of negating, levelling out or counteracting the divergence. This basic proposition corresponds with that of the theory of status inconsistency. Again, according to Malewski: 'The more a set of status factors represented by a given individual departs from the expectations of people with whom he is in contact, the more is that individual characterized by an inconsistency of status factors' (Malewski, 1963, p. 69). The propositions formulated by Malewski regarding the factors of status inconsistency may be correspondingly converted into propositions pertaining to the shaping and modification of attitudes. Following are the author's detailed propositions:

1 The greater the degree of inconsistency between an
   individual's status factors as perceived by others, the more
   uncertain is his status. This means that others tend to react
   towards him as if he had a lower status than in reality. . . .
2 Inconsistency of status factors perceived also by others is a
   source of punishment and its elimination is a source of
   reward. . . .
3 An individual with a number of inconsistent status factors
   some of which are rated much lower than others, will tend
   to raise the lower rated status factors. . . .
4 An individual with a number of inconsistent status factors

some of which are rated much lower than others and he is not able to raise the lower factors of his status – such an individual will tend to avoid those who react to the lower factors. . . .

5 An individual with a number of inconsistent status factors some of which are rated much lower than others and who is not able to raise the lower factors of his status will tend to reject the system of values justifying that low status and to solidarise with systems opposing them.

6 People whose status is very high and very certain attach least importance to behaviour which would be a conspicuous symbol of high status. . . .

7 In the case where nonconformism with accepted norms brings a reward, people whose status is both very high and very certain do not observe prevailing norms more often than do people of average or less certain status. . . .

8 People whose status is very certain display greater resourcefulness and more daring ideas than those of uncertain status. . . .

9 The more members of a group represent a set of status factors incompatible with the expectations of others, the greater will be the degree of their mutual antipathy (Malewski, 1963, pp. 72–83).

The above propositions are readily applicable to the question of the shaping or modification of attitudes. Thus, proposition 1 indicates when the phenomenon of attitude ambivalence will appear. Propositions 3–5 denote the directions of attitude modifications, propositions 6–7 designate the conditions for adoption of nonconformist attitudes; number 8 provides information on the assumption of innovative attitudes, and number 9 establishes the conditions for the appearance of conflicting attitudes.

When cognitive and status inconsistency 'theories' point out, quite clearly, some substantive elements which play the roles of independent variables, another 'middle range' theory (formulated by P. Cohen) deals mainly with structural conditions which are associated with attitude formation. The main propositions of this theory are: (A) malleability of attitudes varies inversely with (a) the involuntariness of social relationship; (b) the diffuseness of social relationship; (c) the degree of isolation of a social group; (d) the hostility of a group to those outside it; (e) authoritarianism; (B) attitudes are less malleable (a) if they are linked together with other attitudes in a system; (b) if they are learned in highly punitive or threatening situations; (c) if they are linked with powerful 'primordial' aspects and motivations; and (C) malleability of attitudes depends on the type and degree of reinforcement which they receive during the learning process (Cohen in Warren and Jahoda, 1976, pp. 64-5).

It is interesting to notice that the above presented 'theories' point out, at least by implication, as an essential problem in this area, the relation between attitudes and corresponding behaviours. Thus a given behaviour associated (actually or mentally) with a given attitude may be a real behaviour (actually taking place in the empirical world) or only prescribed, normatively designed and imagined (potentially possible) behaviour. Moreover, behaviour may be in accord with the attitude which designates it, may be only partly and seemingly in such accord, or completely discordant. Differences in consonance between attitudes and behaviour are variously manifested in different spheres of life. The discord is great in spheres where people - because of given subcultures, traditions, fixed cognitive dissonances - are inclined to behave hypocritically. Whereas discord is less where behaviour is under strict control (in the small group, for instance), where the peculiar type of authority affiliates one with others and easily solves potential conflicts, where public and private life are not structurally differentiated and clearly separated, etc. This problem is important in the field of moral and legal attitudes and their relationship towards conformist or nonconformist behaviour. Empirical research in this field, despite its theoretical and practical importance, is paradoxically rare. The research findings of J. Kurczewski established some empirical relations between attitudes and behaviour in this sphere of social life. The very cautious conclusions from his research are: 'It is still worthwhile, as it seems, to do research on a small - even on a very small - scale if it will enable the discarding of at least some general propositions (e.g. that a judge is never influenced in his sentence by his personal attitudes' (Kurczewski, 1971, p. 127).

Other research in the same field on the attitude-behaviour relation aimed to verify hypotheses to the effect that behaviour probably depends more on situational factors than on the individual's attitude to the contents of a question. The short summary of this research indicates that:

An analysis of the interrelation between a verbal attitude to the legislation of marijuana and the respondent's attitudes showed a high degree of consonance. Certain limitations introduced to the system of interactions, such as: clarity of answers, perception of more general norms and of attitude of the group of reference had a slight effect on the observed relations (Albrecht *et al.*, 1972, p. 165).

Some practical applications

The beginnings of the research which intended to link attitudes with behaviour caused an essential break in previous theoretical approaches. This pertains to the so-called 'desensitization' (making insensitive) and 'learning by observation'. By making insensitive is understood the creation of a situation in which the investigated individual is placed in a state of complete security (peace of mind) in order to convert into neutral or positive factors. The individual thus gradually acquires a state of tranquillity. Then, while taking constant care that he continues to feel secure, the respondent is put into a symbolic situation which arouses fear or a feeling of danger. If the procedure is effective, then the stimulus which previously aroused fear ceases to act thus. Learning by observation consists in the respondent gradually being put directly into contact with a situation which previously constituted a threat. The individual thus does not make contact with that situation by means of symbols but by personal touch. Two examples may clarify better the difference between these approaches. Both of them illustrate the basic strategy of the making insensitive and learning by observation procedure.

The first one which pertained to overcoming the fear of public appearance, applied the following different therapeutic strategies: rendering insensitive, psychoanalysis, a control 'placebo' situation and by using a normal control group. Under the psychoanalytical treatment individuals characterized by considerable fear of appearing in public were subjected to the traditional procedure: influence by means of deepened interviews. In the case of 'placebo' technique respondents were administered meaningless chemical pseudo-pacifiers. In rendering insensitive, desensitization procedures were used. In the control situation no treatment was administered. The effectiveness of the experiment was assessed on the basis of three criteria: (1) the consideration of rating the respondent's public statements by impartial observers; (2) the respondent's own evaluation of his public speaking ability after he had undergone the necessary 'cure'; and (3) registration of physiological changes caused by behaviour during public appearances (heart beat frequency, etc.). The findings established that the self-evaluations changed in the same manner under the influence of the three applied ways of influence: rendering insensitive, psychotherapy and influence by means of 'placebo'. But it turned out in further follow-up research that only persons who went through the influence of desensitization actually lost their fear in situations in public (Paul, 1965).

The second research, pertaining to learning by observation, was more complicated. A number of persons were selected who for different reasons (experience while hunting in a park, or when buying a new home) were terribly afraid of snakes of various kinds. These persons were subjected to the influence of making them insensitive and of learning by observation. In the latter, they observed from a distance how the snakes' handler touched them, carried them or played with them. When they came near the respondents first touched the snakes very lightly, then took them in their hands, then carried and began to play with them. It turned out, as in the first experiment, that the subjective responses to new attitudes towards fear-causing stimuli (snakes in this case) are similar for both kinds of influence. But only in the case of learning from observation were the new attitudes of a character essential enough to influence behaviour. Thus persons subjected to the technique of this influence experienced considerably less fear later when they came again into contact with the stimuli (snakes) actually and physically (Bandura, 1969, pp. 182-92).

It thus appears that certain techniques can effectively influence and subjectively change, individuals' attitudes. But the effected changes in attitude are not always deep enough to lead to the simultaneous inducement of behaviour consonant with the newly formed attitudes. This is because attitudes may be internalized on various levels, According to S. Mika, there are four levels of internalization. On the first, attitude is external in relation to the given individual, i.e. it is not accepted. Only the pressure of the social environment may incline to behaviour as if the given attitude were accepted. On the second level, relatively weak internal pressure changes accepted attitudes and induces a change in behaviour which is dissonant with the accepted attitude. On the third level, strong pressure must be exerted for the individual to behave in discord with his initially accepted attitude. On the fourth level of attitude internalization the individual autonomously decides to change his attitude – strong pressure is unable to change such types of attitudes (Mika, 1973, pp. 224-5).

According to another conception, attitude-behaviour relations shape up in accordance with three varied schemes: (1) acceptance of an attitude may take the form of a more or less sincere declaration (a pure manifestation of certain values, often an apparent enunciation aimed at satisfying social expectations in connection with the realization of generally acknowledged values). In this case behaviour is expressed differently, while the attitude is in accord with the external expectation of behaviour, though discordant with the behaviour itself. (2) Acceptance of an attitude may be of an inner character. Then, the given attitude, though essentially opted for by the individual, and though it usually leads to prescribed behaviour, may not reveal itself in his behaviour. This is so either because the attitude is not a strong enough motive for the behaviour in question (and in consequence to avoid temptation) or because external pressure or outright compulsion diverts the behaviour in a different direction, a direction dissonant with the accepted values. (3) Acceptance of an attitude may lead to its complete accord with the corresponding behaviour, i.e. may constitute an adequate basis for behaving in accord with the attitude's disposition. (These conceptions were developed by Sufin, 1968, p. 172.)

A comparison of the above conceptions of attitude internalization with that of S. Ossowski easily establishes the former's greater suitability for deducing the relations between attitudes and behaviour. Ossowski distinguishes between 'acknowledged values', implying that they ought to be respected, and 'felt values' (attractive, if limited to positive values; repulsive, in cases of negative values). Despite its appeal to common sense, the differentiation between 'acknowledged values' and 'felt values' does not grasp satisfactorily the various levels and depths of values injected through the socialization process into the psyche of a given individual.

The considerations presented above suggest the following scheme of the overall attitudes structure:

(1) meta-attitudes – as consistent syndromes regulating various elementary attitudes constituting an independent psychic entity;
(2) manifested attitudes – elements of the meta-attitudes as they present themselves in the everyday life of a given individual;
(3) accepted attitudes – elements of meta-attitudes which are regarded as valid guiding signposts for the given individual's behaviour;
(4) attitudes as real motivational forces (elements of meta-attitudes which actually direct the behaviour of individuals).

Meta-attitudes

We have not so far considered what now seems to be the most strategic category of attitudes, namely, the *meta-attitudes*. By meta-attitudes is understood here an attitude of a higher order which sorts and organizes subordinate attitudes of different types into a cohesive whole. The concept of the meta-attitude originally arose in connection with researches on various moral and legal attitudes. It was a matter of finding an answer to the question: why does immoral and illegal behaviour appear in various situations where moral and legal attitudes are accepted and relatively lastingly internalized. The explanatory hypothesis was advanced that there is no direct connection between legal, moral and customary norms and behaviour inducing attitudes; that attitudes of a particular kind, those closely linked with opinion and behaviour or which loosen their mutual ties, constitute an intermediate bond. According to this hypothesis, the distance between legal, moral and customary norms and their corresponding behaviour is not a vacuum. It does seem that this distance is filled with certain personality traits which first were defined as *invisible factors* but later became specified as *meta-attitudes* (Podgórecki, 1974).

In connection with the above mentioned specification of meta-attitudes one may wonder why 'authoritarian' attitudes were not recognized as such (this specification has been done only on the basis of the Polish studies on moral and legal attitudes). Nevertheless, authoritarianism may be regarded as a meta-attitude since it contains a variety of different attitudes. There are, for example, attitudes like: strictness in sexual matters, a tendency to strong condemnation, insistence on seeing everything in categories of 'white' and 'black', a potential identification with the oppressor, strong religious beliefs, etc. It is also easy to observe that the cluster of authoritarian attitudes is quite functional: it strengthens considerably an already given structured establishment. It additionally points out that in this way a given social system designs certain syndromes of attitudes as to support it. The term 'authoritarian personality', although suggestive in this case, in fact only blurs the specificity of this type of meta-attitude taking advantage of its colourful bundle of elementary attitudes.

At least several types of meta-attitudes might – on the basis of these studies – be specified. There are, for instance, *principled attitudes* (the spontaneous acceptance or rejection of certain principles underlying imagined or actual modes of behaviour) and *instrumental attitudes* (the acceptance or rejection of imagined or actual modes of behaviour based on the calculation of the effects of possible variants of activity and evaluation of the effects of the alternatives). Meta-attitude of instrumentation consists of several elementary attitudes. Among them are: an attitude to suspend the spontaneous reaction to the given stimuli, an attitude to calculate possible gains and losses through various behavioural actions, an attitude to behave according to the subjective vision of individual interests, etc. According to research conducted in 1966 on a representative sample of the Polish adult population, the breakdown of these attitudes (on the basis of the most characteristic question correlated with other, and control questions, etc.) is as shown in the accompanying table.

		City N=1601	Country N=1566
Question:	Some people have fixed moral principles to which they adhere regardless of consequences; others are guided by the attainment of intended aims. What do you think?[1]		
Response:			(in percentages)
(1)	One should always behave in accordance with one's principles regardless of consequence (principled attitude).	22.5	22.3
(2)	If faithfulness to principles should bring bad effects, principles should be reconsidered and adjusted to situations (basically instrumental attitude).	39.3	32.8
(3)	It is not good in general to have rigid principles; one should only behave in a way yielding successful results (instrumental attitude).	31.2	31.6
(4)	Hard for me to say	6.7	13.0

Other research, in 1972–3, conducted in Kielce and Warsaw on continuity and change in the cultural tradition of a parents and children population analysed among others the problem defined by the previous study. Some 690 pupils and 1,246 parents were polled in Kielce, and 1,248 pupils and 2,055 parents in Warsaw. Respondents were asked – among other things – a similar, but differently formulated, question, as shown in the accompanying table.

The data from Kielce and Warsaw show the same tendency noted in cross-national research: i.e. a considerably more frequent expression of the instrumental attitude among young people than among older ones.

A summary of basic research (in 1970) on principled and instrumental attitudes suggested the following observations:

(1) The principled attitude rises with age,
(2) The pool of instrumental attitudes rises with the educational level, but respondents with (completed or incompleted) higher education are nevertheless disposed to a compromise position,
(3) Private farmers are more disposed to the principled attitude than are members of other occupational groups,
(4) The principled attitude is associated with living in the country, and the instrumental attitude with living in a big city,

Question: People differ in their views on to what extent their behaviour should be subordinated to general moral principles. Which of the views below conform with your opinions on this question?[2]

	Kielce		Warsaw	
	Parents	Youth	Parents	Youth
		(in percentages)		
Answers:				
(1) A person should have moral principles and never depart from them.	37	11	27	8
(2) A person should have moral principles but may depart from them in an exceptional situation.	28	20	37	25
(3) A person may have definite moral principles but there is nothing wrong in departing from them when required by situations.	14	21	15	22
(4) Behaviour should not be tied in advance to moral principles, but proper behaviour should depend on each situation.	19	48	20	45

(5) The principled attitude is linked more with the lack of an insecurity feeling than with symptoms of insecurity, while the instrumental attitude is associated with a strong feeling of insecurity,

(6) Proper adaptation to life is essentially linked with the principled attitude, while maladjustment is linked with the instrumental attitude.

A comparison of the these findings with those of the 1966 research discloses some interesting data and leads to some modification of earlier formulated generalizations. So, some of the previous hypotheses find additional verification, but others have to be rejected. Among those particularly reinforced by the 1970 research is the hypothesis regarding the relation between age and acceptance of a basic or instrumental attitude (rise in frequency of the basic attitude with age) and the relations associated with subjective-social traits. The instrumental attitude is thus linked in the previous and 1970 research with insecurity and maladjustment. While the principled attitude is associated in both with proper adaptation to life and a security feeling. (The 1970 findings were presented in a study by A. Podgórecki and A. Kojder, 1972.)

Still other meta-attitudes may be distinguished, such as: the *social ethical orientation* (in consideration of the effects and consequences of the roles played and positions occupied in given institutions, organizations or organizational systems) and the *individualistic ethical orientation* (harmony or lack of it with the patterns of social behaviour in small, more or less informal groups). Meta-attitude of social ethical orientation contains several elemental attitudes. There are, among them: an attitude to restrain one's own interests; an attitude to search for ethical consequences which, although hidden behind seemingly neutral legalistic dispositions, are heavily loaded with more consequences; an attitude to take into consideration the benefit of larger (than an individual or his family) social entities, etc.

A summation of the findings of the research quoted above and conducted in 1970 thus far indicates that the individualist ethical orientation is linked with a low educational level, living in the country, unskilled occupation, being a rank and file worker, with no engagement in public activity, but with a strong feeling of insecurity and maladjustment. The social orientation is associated with a higher educational level, living in a big city, occupying a directing position at work, a feeling of security and better social adjustment.

These dry data sketch a relatively clear picture: those in a worse life situation (rank and file workers, low educational level and maladjustment) show a defensive disposition towards the world and their ethical attitude is individualistic. They seem inclined to defend the kind of worldly goods they possess (objectively or in their subjective assessment). They also attempt to bring into play instrumental attitudes in order to increase their resources where they can. Those who display a social orientation in ethics (to judge by their verbal declarations) behave differently. These are well-off (either objectively or in their subjective assessment) and think in the categories of broader social welfare, since - it may be assumed - their own basic needs have already been satisfied (Podgórecki and Kojder, 1972).

Although the proposal to introduce the concept of meta-attitudes to the social sciences comes from empirical studies on moral and legal attitudes one may try to find some similar phenomena also through historic investigations. Indeed one of the unique aspects of Dutch society, generated by the historic conditions of that society, consists of the generally accepted *pattern of 'verzuiling'* (untranslatable concept of agreed-upon peaceful coexistence of different world views - especially religious) (Goudsblom, 1967, p. 32). The Dutch, traditionally being traders, constantly played the role of middleman. This type of generalized social pattern and role had socialized them to be efficient in go-between relationships: to achieve their own objectives without the unnecessary antagonization of the partner (opponent). Thus traders' attitudes of reconciliation reinforced by the tolerance of various religious groups produced, in effect, the specific meta-attitude of *verzuiling*.

Some knowledgeable students of this phenomenon express an opinion that the real source of *verzuiling* stems from the recognition of the impossibility of reconciling the divergent views. But even if the genesis of this notion is a controversial one, the real functioning of this attitude may be employed to explain a peculiar psychological situation which exists in Dutch society: relatively strong moral condemnation of all behaviours which depart from generally accepted social norms (at least stronger than in neighbouring Belgium; van Houtte *et al.*, 1976), and from another point of view the observable tolerance on the behavioural level. The acuteness of this inconsistency (between the strength of condemnation and actual acceptance of possible deviant behaviour) seems to give additional evidence of the functioning of the above mentioned type of meta-attitude. An opposite meta-attitude might be regarded as a *conflict-prone posture* (litigious troubler): a tendency to look constantly for disagreement, opposition and formal challenge.

The concept of *verzuiling* may be useful to explain the apparent paradox which is visible in Dutch society.

This paradoxical concept of *verzuiling* was described essayistically by the *International Herald Tribune* in the following way:

Amsterdam (IHT) - the Dutch are like missionaries, one shrewd British resident here observed. They always want to convert somebody and have an unshakeable conviction they possess the truth.

Yes, and like some missionaries they can also be tolerant of others' faults and harshly critical of their own. Moreover, there is a curious contrast in this nation between nonconformist extravagance and disciplined social behaviour. It is so marked as to be a paradox, though the terms have become somewhat exaggerated in many foreign eyes. Despite a reputation for tolerance, the country is not as liberal as its apologists often suggest. The Dutch have a reputation for being a fun-loving people, but stern moralities and attitudes cramp domestic life. . . .

That paradox again: it is odd how deeply rooted and flourishing the Calvinist strain persists in Dutch society alongside more recent and exotic trends in social attitudes. Whether the latter will eventually take over more traditional values is an open question, but for the moment they seem to have no great difficulty living side by side (Paris, June, p. 56).

Conclusions

The introduction of the conception of 'meta-attitude' may also throw light on the question: why do some people, being deprived of the pressure of religious control, and additionally subjected to the influence of other factors of strong social anomalies, still remain morally irreproachable although surrounded by negative subcultures? The interventions of meta-attitudes may be regarded as providing at least a partial explanation of this phenomenon.

These attitudes, as intermediate invisible factors (in this particular case - principled attitudes) may moreover be treated as independent variables which are responsible for the production of functional defence mechanisms - in many cases sophisticated rationalizations.

The above considerations suggest several implications. Although the critique of ethnomethodology seems to be valid -

> The ethnomethodologists argue that the conventional sociology endows actors with some internalised attitudes and assumes that norms are relatively automatic guides to role playing. But this fails to distinguish between interpretative procedures (deep structures) and norms (surface rules) (Taylor, Walton and Young, 1973, pp. 201-2)

- nevertheless this critique loses its substance when the concept of meta-attitude is introduced. Research on attitudes must be conducted as a multi-level enterprise. Consequently this research and concrete case studies on the shaping, persistence and change of attitudes should apply a co-ordinated combination of different levels of inquiry. For the study of a given attitude may lead to false conclusions if it fails to take into account its counteracting ambivalent dimensions. Thus, for example, the behavioural potential of certain attitudes existing on a given level of its internalization may be inoperative on another level, because even deeply internalized attitudes may lead to dissonance with the content of convictions and assessments of this attitude, if its potential is changed by intervening meta-attitudes. These interrelations must be taken into account if the construction of an adequate theory of attitude formation, persistence and change should be formulated.

Finally, it might be said that manifested attitudes (as they appear in the everyday life of different individuals) are shaped not only by the constant processes of accumulation of personal experiences but also by two additional essential factors. The first one is linked very closely with a given individual and comes from the interplay between various types of his own *self*. The second factor is rooted in the given social environment and is basically shaped, and generated by this type of environment – these are *meta-attitudes*. Thus, it might be said that the everyday attitudes – as they appear in the social interactions of individuals – emerge as a by-product of the perpetual clash of various types of individual selves and various types of meta-attitudes designed as general patterns of life prevailing in the ethos of a given society. In consequence the concept of meta-attitude links individual psychology with sociology in a way which strives to unite knowledge coming from different sources of social sciences. It may be noticed additionally that the specification of this concept discovers the missing link between the sociology of everyday life and the final notion of sociology: if the syndrome of everyday attitudes constitutes a meta-attitude and the syndrome of meta-attitudes constitutes the ethos of a given society, so, finally, the syndrome of ethoses of all types of existing societies constitutes the concept of – *mankind*. And this is what sociology, in the final analysis, is all about.

Notes

1 Source: Podgórecki *et al.*, 1971, p. 56.
2 Source: Nowak, 1974a.

Bibliography

Albrecht, S., De Fleur, M. L., and Wagner, L. C. (1972), 'Attitude-Behaviour Relationship', *Pacific Sociological Review*, April, p. 165.
Allport, G. W. (1935), 'Attitudes', in Murchison C. M. (ed.), *Handbook of Social Psychology*, Worcester, Mass.: Clark University Press.
Bandura, A. (1969), *Principles of Behaviour Modification*, New York: Holt, Rinehart & Winston.
Droba, D. D. (1933), 'The Nature of Attitude', *Journal of Social Psychology*, vol. 4, pp. 444-63.
Goudsblom, J. (1967), *Dutch Society*, New York: Random House.
Houtte, J. van, *et al.* (1976), *Aanvaarding van de rechtsnorm: Houdingen en opinies t.a.v. fiscaliteit en regels in de morele biosfeer (Acceptance of Legal Norms: Views and Opinions Regarding Duties and Rules in the Moral Sphere)*, Antwerp/Utrecht: De Nederlandsche Boekhandel,
Kurczewski, J. (1971), 'The Penal Attitudes Behaviour of Professional Judges', *The Polish Sociological Bulletin*, no. 1, p. 127.

Malewski, A. (1963), 'Stopień rozbieżności czynnikòw statusu i jego nastepstwa' ('Degree of Status Factor Divergence and Its Consequences'), *Studia Socjologiczne,* no. 1(8).

Malewski, A. (1964), *O zastowaniach teorii zachowania (On the Applications of Behavioural Theory),* Warsaw: PWN.

Mika, S. (1973), 'Uwagi o "internalizacji" postaw' ('Some Remarks on Attitude Internalization'), in S. Nowak (ed.), *Teorie Postaw (Attitude Theories),* Warsaw: PWN.

Nowak, S. (ed.) (1974a), 'Ciaglosc i zmiana tradycji kulturowej' ('Continuity and Change in Cultural Tradition'), Warsaw: Department of the Methodology of Sociological Research at Warsaw University Institute of Sociology.

Nowak, S. (1974b), *Teorie Postaw (Attitude Theories),* Warsaw: PWN.

Ossowski, S. (1967), 'Konflikty niewspolmiernych skal wartòsci. Z zagadnien psychologii spolecznej' ('Conflicts Between Incommensurable Scales of Values: Some Problems of Social Psychology'), in *Works* of S. Ossowski, vol. III, Warsaw: PWN.

Paul, G. (1965), *Insight vs. Desensitisation in Psychotherapy,* Stanford University Press.

Podgórecki, A. (1974), 'Prawo i sprawiedliwosc – glowne pojecia i problemy' ('The Law and Justice: Principal Conceptions and Problems'), *Prawo i Zycie,* no. 7/488 and no. 8/489.

Podgórecki, A. and Kojder, A. (1972), 'Ewolucja swiadomości prawnej i postaw moralnych spoleczenstwa polskiego' ('Evolution of the Awareness and Moral Attitudes of Polish Society'), Warsaw: Polish Radio and Television Committee Poll.

Podgórecki, A., Kurczewski, J., Kwaśniewski, J., and Łoś, M. (1971), *Poglady spofeczeństwa polskiego na moralność i prawo (Views of Polish Society on Morality and Law),* Warsaw: Książka i Wiedza.

Rokeach, M. (1968), 'The Nature of Attitudes', *The International Encyclopaedia of Sciences,* vol. I.

Sufin, Z. (1968), *Kultura Pracy (The Culture of Work),* Warsaw.

Taylor, I. T., Walton, P., and Young, J. (1973), *The New Criminology,* Routledge & Kegan Paul, London.

Thomas, W. J. and Znaniecki, F. (1918–20), *The Polish Peasant in Europe and America,* vol. I, Boston, Mass.: Dover.

Warren, H. C. (ed.) (1934), *Dictionary of Psychology,* Boston, Mass.: Houghton Mifflin.

Warren, N., and Jahoda, M. (eds) (1976), *Attitudes,* Harmondsworth: Penguin.

13 Small groups – fiction or reality?

Maria Łoś

According to traditional sociological opinions, immediate social control is exerted over individuals mainly by small groups. It is striking, however, that the content of these opinions has remained unchanged for many years, constituting an unshaken pillar of social-psychological lore. Thus it might be worthwhile to take a critical look at this 'scientific' stereotype, and to see if it matches the real social phenomena, despite the resistance of concepts solidified in their old moulds.

The existence of small groups, the complex processes taking place in them and their significant influence on the beliefs and behaviour of individuals have represented the dogma in social psychology. Moreover, sociology, which continually records essential changes in social macro-structures, does not provide any new analyses, which critically grasp the changes in the basic phenomena that are supposed to make up the so-called micro-structure of society.

Much has been written on small groups from the psycho-sociological perspective. Writers have normally relied upon abstract theoretical analyses, as well as, and above all, laboratory experiments. Knowledge has been piled up, without sufficient questioning of the relevance and import of studies on small groups, and with even less questioning of the existence of such groups. Despite the lack of broader empirical investigations of the subject, it can be supposed that our contemporary civilization has destroyed the basic types of groups in their traditional form, still taken for granted by many social scientists. How far advanced those processes are in many of the modern societies can be evidenced by the anxious attempts at finding new forms of group identification (such as common dwelling by a few families or friends, group marriages, youth communes, or the rapid growth of new religious

168

and meditation groups or of the so-called sensitivity training groups). These movements have emerged, so it seems, from the desire to fill the void brought about by the want of genuine and stable attachment to any permanent social groups. The contemporary speed of life; the small and less stable families; in many countries the prevalence of very small flats which thus limit the social life of families; the extensive geographical and social mobility; the large distances in growing cities; commuting facilities lagging far behind the fast growth of metropolitan areas; fundamental changes in the nature of local communities; the development of mass media and entertainment which act largely as substitutes for face to face human contacts – all these are well known factors handicapping the formation of new groups, whilst the traditional forms of group ties are disrupted and atomized.

The definitions of a 'small group' usually accepted in classical sociological handbooks assume mutual contacts and links among all the members of a group. An oft-quoted example of a typical small group is that of close friends. But most of us know from observation (which is, of course, limited to a definite time and space) that when we talk about the group of friends of Mr and Mrs X, we mean that they invite and meet rather frequently their friends: Mr and Mrs Y, Mr and Mrs Z, Mrs M, Miss B, and Messrs L, N and R. It would follow from the conventional definition of a group that all these persons also regularly meet each other – that the Ys invite, besides the Xs, also the Zs, Mrs M, etc. However, this is frequently not the case. Each of these individuals makes his own friends, not on the principle of group participation and identification, but rather as a result of his individual choice, habits, preferences and circumstances, such as neighbourhood, job contacts, children of similar age, common holidays and so on. These are links which (following the typology proposed by Homans) can be characterized as the open systems of relationships. Unfortunately, the available knowledge about small groups tells us little about the characteristics of such patterns. The sociological concept of a group of friends, or peers, or mates, etc., seems to be clearly out of date. One of its underlying assumptions is that the predominating type of man is the *homo ludens*, for whom it is not work, or study, or the rearing of children which are the main factors determining his contacts with other people, but playing together in a group.

Another type of a collective studied by sociologists is a group of people working together. But certainly not all types of organizations and not all patterns of job segregation provide opportunities for group contacts among workers. Besides, such a group does not often reflect free choices, but it is assigned, restrained and con-

169

trolled by broader institutional patterns, by the hierarchy and specialization of jobs, etc. In such a situation, the small group does not influence an individual by the mechanisms recognized in the studies on relatively isolated groups – for instance, those submitted experimentally to various types of leadership. It influences him by a complex network of circumstances, both formal and coercive as well as informal and personal. In some socio-economic systems or circumstances the link between people working together is based mainly on a plot, or negative integration, to cover the more or less flagrant deviations from the legal and organizational standards. Furthermore, the link among the people working together is often apt to be purely occasional, as if forced by the situation; this is enhanced by extensive labour turnover and movement of workers within the company. Contact necessitated by the job is apt to develop into private, informal friendship within the group working together, but the chances for this to happen are not great, for the eight hours of forced confinement in one place does not often reinforce the readiness to keep company outside.

Perhaps there are chances to find a 'true' small group (i.e. conforming to classical sociological definitions) among the young. But even there, informal links, although laden with strong emotions, are usually much more atomized, differentiated and changing than it is commonly believed. Does that mean that the phenomenon, successfully studied for years by sociologists and social psychologists, is completely absent from contemporary social life? This question certainly involves an appeal for reliable observations and diagnostic research concerning the actual (and not experimentally arranged) relationships among people, but it is also a question about the validity of a theoretical concept which seems more to blur than to reflect the complexity of the social reality. The answer to our question certainly depends both on the definition of a group and on the theoretical and cognitive ends that we have set forth. For the concept of a small group has in fact proved to be very useful in sociology and in social psychology; it has helped to explain a lot of mechanisms shaping human motivation, behaviour and interaction. Could such a cognitively fertile concept have been simply an outcome of the imagination of researchers? Probably not at all. It is not from a scholar's fanciful mind that the 'small group' has emerged, but from a scientific paradigm which has adopted a network of concepts initially based on certain systematic, empirical data. Subsequently, however, they have become divorced from the reality and rearranged into their own universe, able to subsist and develop on their own and demanding more concepts to describe them. The concept of a group and the related concepts, such as norms, roles, positions, the social structure, etc., make up a scheme, through which any human community can be seen as a concrete stable system, or as an analytical whole which may and ought to be expected to manifest certain essential qualities peculiar to all organized wholes. Concepts are thus multiplied. And the changes of their contents and also their labels correspond with the changing theoretical currents in the science about society. This tendency is responsible for the fact (it is, of course, a hypothetical statement) that *the changes in approaches to the nature of small groups have more to do with the development of definite theoretical schools in sociology and in social psychology than with the actual changes of the small groups as essential elements of the social reality in transition.*

The main theoretical models of small groups that can be recorded during the comparatively short history of research in this field can be listed as follows:

(1) *Psychological models*, based on assumptions concerning the development of the human psyche. In this category we can mention the psychoanalytical model (for example, Freud's thesis that the primitive horde survives in every social group and it may potentially reveal itself at any time; Freud, 1955); models emerging from the theory of attitudes (a group as a system of interactions between attitudes) or from the theory of motivation (a group as a sum or resultant of motivations of its members).

(2) *The philosophical model*, based on certain generalizations about the 'cornerstones' of human coexistence, of the origin of human solidarity, of the direction of the development of mankind, etc. An example is the conception deriving the principles of group coexistence from the so-called social contract; the hypothesis by Petrażycki of the supra-genial social adjustment in a group, whereby only such judgments and norms which serve the well-being and survival of the group are fixed and remain as the valid norms; the phenomenological conception by Berger and Luckmann, postulating the processes of hierarchical symbolic institutionalization of the social order, as a result of which the relationship between an individual and a group becomes a dialectical relationship of domination and subordination.

(3) *The mechanical model* - comparing a group to well oiled machinery: each part performs its function, contributing to the smooth working of the whole, without developing or transforming itself and without stepping beyond the accepted scheme of functioning in its interactions. Attempts at developing this scheme were made, for example, by Bales (Parsons, Bales and Shils, 1953, pp. 111-61), who tried to

elaborate a matrix of typical interactions in groups. T. M. Mills writes about this approach: 'Group behaviour is like a game that is played over and over again so many times that one knows both the game and the players well enough to predict what will happen next' (Mills, 1967, p. 12).

(4) *The organic model* – comparing a group to a biological organism which comes through all the states of its development and in which there is an obvious division of roles among the specialized and interdependent parts (Bennis and Shepard, 1956; Mills and Rosenberg, 1970). For instance, the life cycle of learning groups is summarized by Mills in the following way: 'There are five principal periods: (1) the encounter, (2) testing boundaries and modelling roles, (3) negotiating an indigenous normative system, (4) production and (5) separation' (Mills, 1970, p. 70). 'No formulation to my knowledge adequately accommodates group mortality. Some, in fact, would seem to require fundamental modification to make room for processes of dissolution, liquidation, and separation' (p. 69).

(5) *The system model* – developed under the influence of the so-called general systems theory, and also of the structural-functional school in sociology. A group shares many features in common with all other systems. The universal laws of the functioning of social systems, their evolution and their resistance against the disruptive inner forces – formulated, by Parsons (among others) – are valid for both the large societies and the small groups (Parsons, Bales and Shils, 1953; Buckley, 1967, pp. 186–207; Buckley, 1968, pp. 490–513; M. Deutsch, 1953; and others).

(6) *The cybernetical model* is directly related to the system model, but for the concept of the steady state, associated with the assumption that there is a tendency to equifinality in systems, it introduces the concept of the feed-back which facilitates the analysis of the intentionally shaped or modified development processes in systems. This model assumes that the constitutive feature of each organized whole is its communicating capacity; it thus emphasizes the process of circulation and the processing of information in a group. It treats a group as an open system, capable of self-regulation (K. W. Deutsch, 1968, 1970; Buckley, 1967, pp. 120-5).

(7) *The conflict model*, based on the assumption of conflict. It approaches the social processes as the continuous overcoming of incompatible interests, needs and pressures. It implies an image of a group in which conflict prevails over consensus; the tendency towards change is stronger than that towards stability and more phenomena can be explained by compulsion and

172

pressure than by free and unrestrained action (cf. Dahrendorf, 1959: Coser, 1956). Characteristic for this trend in small group sociology are studies of the mechanisms of the emergence of power and domination, of the shaping of coalitions within a group, of the limiting of freedom of small group members in favour of the efficiency of its rivalry with other groups, etc. (e.g. Mills, 1953; Caplow, 1956; Vinacke and Ackoff, 1957).

(8) *The structural-cultural model*, about which Blumer wrote that its conception of a group was based on empirical studies pursued by sociologists and anthropologists focusing on such concepts as 'culture', 'social structure', 'social roles', etc. He points out that observations of historical permanence and continuity of customs, styles of life, etc., of definite groups have influenced the formation of the idea of culture. From this conception are derived the approaches to a social group as a social structure and as a system of social roles. We can agree with Blumer that those concepts have been 'imported' into the field of small group sociology, rather than discovered in the research of human interactions as processes. It appears that not the interactions, but their products have been actually studied by the representatives of this orientation. (We can mention here, by way of example, such scholars as Newcomb, Faris and Sherif. It is also worth emphasizing that Manford Kuhn, usually, but not quite soundly, regarded as a representative of symbolic interactionism, apprehends a group in similar, i.e. behavioural-deterministic, terms.)

(9) *The interactionist model*, in which the processes of individual interaction are put forth as the supreme aspect of group coexistence. At least two varieties of this model can be discerned:

(a) The model defining a group in terms of symbolic interaction, based on the theory of G. H. Mead. 'In my judgment', Blumer wrote, 'the most important feature of human association is that the participants take each other into account' (Blumer, 1969, p. 108). 'Perceiving, defining and judging the other person and his action and organizing oneself in terms of such definitions and judgments constitute a continuing and running process' (p. 109). Each party takes his partner into account, but also considers him as someone by whom, in turn, he is himself taken into account. Blumer called this a process of trans-action, essentially consisting in the mutual adjustment of the activities of all concerned, by definitions and redefinitions of the activities of others.

The prevalence of relatively ordered and stable human group life in face of the fact that such group life is constantly being built up brings to light the controls that enter into the development of a transaction (Blumer, 1969, p. 110).

Situations are interpreted depending on the schemes of definitions adopted by an individual – his definitions incorporate those adopted by others, but are not strictly determined by the latter. An acting individual must either make choices between his own various definitional schemes or produce new definitions. This is feasible owing to the ability of an individual to engage in symbolic interactions with himself, during which confrontations (dialogues) take place between his 'I' and 'me'. As we know, the latter represents, in the conception of Mead, a group (or a local community) which is symbolically included into the imagined and actual interactions of the given person with other individuals, even when the group is physically absent. It is an intuitive model, born from the rejection of the behavioural approach and of the tendency to make concepts measurable and operational.

(b) The model which sorts out a group by the frequency of observed interactions and is supposed to facilitate the study of the regular relationships between the particular elements of behaviour of individuals. Homans (1951, 1961, 1962), who is an eminent theoretician of this trend, distinguishes four elements of behaviour: interactions, sentiments (motivations), activities (actions) and norms. Processes that take place in a group can be reduced to the exchange of certain valuables by its members; the pattern of the exchange determines, in its turn, the status of each individual and the directions of their influences on each others. In this way the structure of the group is formed. Prizes and punishments regulating the behaviour of group members towards each other are direct and immediate. Their distribution is based on the tendency to preserve some definite rules of distributive justice. As distinct from the former model this one relies fully on the behavioural approach. It strives at the precise definitions of concepts and the quantitative appreciation of group processes (the patterns of interaction and exchange). It aims above all to grasp their main regularities, so as to be able to predict the behaviour of particular individuals.

An important problem is the relationship of the models mentioned above and their changes with the processes and transformations taking place in actual small groups in highly developed societies (particularly since most of the discussed conceptions were born in the USA). Are they results of empirical research on small groups and do they reflect any features or processes unique to such groups? Both the *psychological* and *philosophical models* assume as their starting-point some conceptions not directly related to the processes taking place in small groups, and they derive definite conclusions from these conceptions concerning social groups. The

174

models labelled as *mechanical, organic, systematic and cyberne-tical* transport, by way of analogies, some properties of other phenomena on human groups, thereby causing a bias which makes it difficult to notice the properties or processes peculiar to these groups. It seems that the *cybernetical model* differs from the *mechanical* one only in that it compares a group not to any machinery, but to such a refined and vulnerable mechanism as the computer, or the automatic pilot, or radar, etc. Reading some texts that discuss this model, one has an impression that it is not people who construct machines like themselves but that the machines, perfected by independent evolution, are the archetype for humans. Anyway, it seems to be a justified supposition that it was not the changes in real groups, but changes in the world of technology which have influenced the emergence of this model of a social group. The *conflict model* is a consequence of the definite image of society, focused on conflict and domination which are also sought for in small social groups. There is much of a self-fulfilling prophecy in it: when testing a hypothesis on the role of definite factors in a small group context, experiments are so planned as to bring out these factors for easier measurement, and thus the theoretical assumptions about their significance are validated. If we accept the rules of the game as set out by those researchers, the validations based on arrangements devised for research purposes cannot be questioned. If, however, we challenge those rules, such validations and assumptions may be out of touch with reality. The *structural-and-cultural model* has created a group as an indis-pensable framework for phenomena discovered by sociologists and anthropologists in their studies of the most diverse communities. But we may ask whether the concepts, elaborated for the most part in investigations of macro-structures, are not too crude to describe phenomena taking place in micro-structures. It is rather doubtful whether the concept of a role or social position, convenient for statistical descriptions and analyses, shows sufficient flexibility to actually explain the patterns of interactions and other behaviours in small groups. Moreover, such global indicators as the intensity of emotional relations, the significance of the personal impact of the group members on each other, etc., seem to be of little use for the analysis of the real problems of group life. The fact that those concepts have been useful for the study of artificial experimental groups is not sufficient proof of their adequacy to natural groups (if such exist at all). It can be understood that the formal factors resulting from the experimentally programmed distribution of roles, tasks, types of leadership, normative accommodations, etc., play an important part in the shaping of behaviour in laboratory conditions, because experimental groups can hardly develop any 'second life'. Such an inner life of a group, community or society, is basically informal, evolves during long periods and represents a net result of changing and uncontrolled emotions, individual biases, calculations and responses to the changing circumstances, pressures and conflicts. There is no reason to assume that the role of the above mentioned formal factors in natural groups is, in fact, similar. *The interactive model* approaches most nearly the essential current of group life, but - like the other models - it fails to say about the small group anything that is unique to it and that would justify its status as a separate object of study. In fact, it fails even to produce a proof of its existence. Interactions do take place outside the group, too, as is in fact admitted by the adherents of both trends within the interactionist approach. According to symbolic interactionism, the group is necessary for the construction of the complex conception of personality, but, as we know, the physical presence and permanence of a group is not required for the functioning of the 'generalized others' as a guiding force of 'me'. We are offered no grounds to devise a systematic test for the verification of what the symbolic interactionists tell us. However, one has to admit that they help us to understand intuitively the social behaviours of individuals and the complexities of human interaction.

The attempt at constructing an empirical test of this essentially immeasurable conception, taken up by Manford Kuhn, has gone so far away from the original ideas, that there are no reasons to include Kuhn's theory in the symbolic interactionist tradition. The theory of Homans - according to its author's declared intention - does not deal with peculiarities of small groups, but with those rules of human interactions that take place in the so-called open systems as well. Groups are simply a convenient ground for their observation, because of the intensity of contacts, direct rewards and punishments, etc.

It may be concluded that neither of the trends of research on small groups brings convincing proofs of their existence, offers a diagnosis as to their range, possible types, transformation, etc., or provides knowledge relevant *exclusively* to the phenomena in natural small groups.

To analyse critically the concept of the 'social group' it will be convenient to consider the theoretical utility of some narrower concepts, in terms of which the most important types of social groups are defined in sociological literature. Their interpretations and definitions are rather varied. Instead of an unduly extensive terminological survey, we shall present only one variant which seems to be the most commonly accepted and to be better defined than others. According to Cooley and his followers, primary groups are those characterized by the strongest links and the most intensive contacts and interaction. Relationships among their members tend to be close and intimate. Those groups are of fundamental import for the shaping of the social nature of man, his personality, ideals, aspirations and value hierarchies. Primary groups, beside the family which is their classical example, are tight groups of peers, friends, neighbours, etc. By secondary groups are usually meant groups related by common work or by any other mainly formal link, and only eventually by informal ties. Sometimes the term 'secondary group' refers to all groups in which an individual participates without committing himself emotionally as strongly as he does in the case of primary groups and with which he identifies himself only with reference to some limited sphere of his activities.

It appears that the rather ambiguous set of the so-called primary groups can be reinterpreted in a certain way, keeping in mind the scepticism as to the existence of small groups. We can distinguish between 'primary social bonds' and 'basic social bonds'.

Primary bonds are characteristic of childhood, or the period of intensive socialization; they are the 'given' or assigned personal links, as the opportunities of their choice are rather limited. They mainly *shape* and *make dynamic* the physical and social needs, as well as the attitudes of an individual. They include the family or the rearing environment, like a boarding school, peer groups or school-mate groups.

Basic bonds are characteristic of adult life and they are in principle the links of choice, involving a strong identification. They mainly *satisfy* the psychical and social needs of an individual, *fix* his attitudes and stabilize him psychologically (it may be the family founded by the individual, his relatively permanent close friends, sometimes also persons engaged in the realization of the same idea, emotionally committed to the same organization, etc.).

The concept of the *secondary social bond* can be made more precise without reference to the degree of its formalization. All links marked by relatively permanent relationships of an individual with others, which do not involve as strong an identification as the primary and basic links, can be treated as secondary bonds.

Adopting the above distinction, it is worthwhile to analyse the statement, that the primary (or basic) groups exert a particularly strong shaping influence on the pattern of norms and values and on the social personality of an individual. It appears that this statement holds true for the primary bonds (affiliations), but it is not quite sound for the basic bonds. The latter - relying on identification with, and emotional attachment to, other people - often become habitual ties which are certain, accountable, offering safety, permanence and trust. In their case, acceptance is apt to be almost automatic, and appreciation expected. The defects and merits, as well as the range of possible behaviour of the partners, are usually well known. Those links satisfy the basic psychological and social needs of an individual and establish his system of values, warranting it the stability of emotions and outlook. But quite often the social attitudes and aspirations of an individual are more spurred by contacts with persons to whom he is less attached, whose approval is less certain, who do not take him for granted, with whom he may play fair or bluff. In consequence, an individual's behaviour and attitudes are likely to be more strongly stimulated by links which seem to be less important, if they are measured by the frequency and intimacy of contacts and by the emotional commitments. Those links bring about the feeling of distance and anxiety and thus they often tend to be more rewarding in the case of praise, approval or acceptance, than the basic links. It is only a hypothesis, but its test cannot be found in the impressive inventories of propositions concerning the relationships between variables in small groups (e.g. Thibaut and Kelley, 1959; Cartwright and Zander, 1953; Berelson and Steiner, 1964). In fact, we can hardly expect from laboratory experiments that they would cover the various circles of identification, dependence, influence, etc.

It seems that transferring the problems of small groups entirely into the hands of social psychologists has in part led these researchers astray. The rash sociological thesis that it is the small group which is the basic cell of the social structure and the laboratory of social attitudes and norms, has been picked up by social psychologists to justify the isolating of the group as a self-contained entity. It appears that the focus on phenomena taking place within the small group, with the omission of the relations of each member and of the group as a whole with the broader social context, is a methodologically fallacious approach. It has led to the creation of several artificial concepts whose designates are experimentally introduced (like, for example, coherence of statuses, i.e. the coherence of the rank order assigned to individual group members on the ground of various status factors). It has also led to the emergence of sociologically irrelevant research problems, born of research procedures (e.g. the problem of the experiment's influence on the behaviour of the subjects; the influence of the awareness that one is an object of study, etc.). Human relationships seem to be much richer than social psychologists are ready to admit, and they cannot be reduced to the group affiliation, either actual or potential.

The want of both recent and older studies on the genuine phenomena of group participation, membership, identification, etc., dictates great care in the formulation of hypotheses on this subject. However, it seems reasonable to suppose that before the processes of rapid industrialization and urbanization occurred, group participation formed the basis of social life within the traditional local communities. Thus, the concepts put forth by Cooley had reflected actual social phenomena. It can be supposed that the groups had been very tightly connected with certain permanent and respectable institutions, like the family, church, school, numerous clubs and associations, etc. In that time, the groups, being the embodiments of these institutions, used to provide the frames for family life, work and pastimes of people. Under the growing impact of the processes of migration, revolutionary changes in relationships between generations, in attitudes towards things, towards the past and tradition, in the ways of production and consumption, etc., the old sacred institutions have been undergoing gradual transformations. In some social environments they have lost their authority altogether, in others its content has been largely modified. A strong tendency towards individualism and often, too, towards the weakening of affiliations to this kind of institution has emerged particularly among young people. Family bonds have become a matter of individual choice, and have eventually become transformed into the links between individual members of a family. Religious affiliations have ceased, for many, to be a problem of institutional membership in a definite group or community, and they have become a form of individual identification, or struggle, or inner conflict, on the spiritual, intellectual or emotional level. The school has become a mass institution, providing a sort of environment for young people, but - because of the great numbers of students, for example - not determining automatically their participation in a group.

As indicated by many researchers, even gangs or criminal groups, being classical examples of a coherent group, clearly structured and with strong inner links and solidarity, have become atomized, lost much of their firmness, and also relaxed their criteria of selection and admission (this is related to the disruption of the criminal ecological niches, the differentiation of the forms of social deviance under the impact of fast social change, etc.; Yablonsky, 1959; Cameron, 1943). In effect, group participation, focused until recently around definite institutions, lost its essential grounds. The changes in social attitudes brought about by the processes of urbanization, industrialization, etc., manifested in the orientation towards advancement, success, adjustment to the changing world, the raising of the standards of consumption, acquiring of skills, etc., have favoured above all the individualistic motivations and behaviours. It can be supposed that the period of transition has not called forth any new social groups as substitutes of the former ones, which were rejected together with the obsolete institutions, or abandoned as the pace of life and mobility have outstripped them. However, the arguments put forth above (and only by way of examples) indicate that stabilization, which always sets in after rapid changes (and the reaction to it which is always produced particularly among the young generation), brings in the need for new permanent group identifications. They cannot be offered by groups depending for their existence on the sustenance of some stable and respectable institutions, for typical of the contemporary world is the lack of permanence and of the charismatic quality in its changing institutions. Perhaps new kinds of groups are apt to emerge by the development in people of new capacities to create interpersonal bonds, to form new types of psychical contact, new opportunities for intellectual communication, new forms of charismatic initiation into the mysteries of existence, etc. In those directions, it seems, the striving of many people in contemporary developed societies is aimed.

The ultimate thesis of this chapter is not that small social groups do not exist (as might appear to be the main hypothesis after a cursory reading), but that they are undergoing *essential* transformations, metamorphoses and crises and thus the attachment of sociologists to definitions and theories rooted in their traditional forms requires a prompt revision.

Bibliography

Bennis, Warren G., and Shepard, Herbert A. (1956), 'A Theory of Group Development', *Human Relations*, vol. IX, 1956, pp. 415-37.

Berelson, Bernard, and Steiner, Gary A. (1964), *Human Behaviour*, New York: Harcourt, Brace & World.

Blumer, Herbert (1969), *Symbolic Interactionism. Perspective and Method: 'Psychological Import of the Human Group'*, Englewood Cliffs, N.J.: Prentice-Hall, pp. 101-16.

Buckley, Walter (1967), *Sociology and Modern Systems Theory*, Englewood Cliffs, N.J.: Prentice-Hall.

Buckley, Walter (1968), 'Society as a Complex Adaptive System', in Buckley (ed.), *Modern Systems Research for the Behavioural Scientist*, Chicago: Aldine, pp. 490-513.

Cameron, Norman (1943), 'The Paranoid Pseudo-Community', *American Journal of Sociology*, vol. 49, No. 3 (July).

Caplow, Theodore A. (1956), 'A Theory of Coalition in the Triad', *American Sociological Review*, vol. 21, pp. 489-93.

Cartwright, Dorwin, and Zander, Alvin (1953), *Group Dynamics: Research and Theory*, New York: Harper & Row.

Cosser, Lewis (1956), *The Functions of Social Conflict*, Chicago: The Free Press.

Dahrendorf, Ralf (1959), *Class and Class Conflict in Industrial Society*, Stanford University Press.

Deutsch, Karl W. (1968), 'Toward a Cybernetic Model of Man and Society', in Buckley (1968).

Deutsch, Karl W. (1970), 'A Simple Cybernetic Model', in Mills and Rosenberg (1970).

Deutsch, Morton (1953), 'The Effects of Cooperation and Competition upon Group Processes', in Cartwright and Zander (1953).

Freud, Sigmund (1955), 'Group Psychology and the Psychology of the Ego', in *Standard Edition of the Complete Psychological Works of Sigmund Freud*, London: Hogarth Press, vol. 18.

Homans, George C. (1951), *The Human Group*, London: Routledge & Kegan Paul.

Homans, George C. (1961), *Social Behaviour*, London: Routledge & Kegan Paul.

Homans, George C. (1962), *Sentiments and Activities*, London: Routledge & Kegan Paul.

Mills, Theodore M. (1953), 'Power Relations in Three Persons Groups', *American Sociological Review*, vol. 18.

Mills, Theodore M. (1967), *The Sociology of Small Groups*, Englewood Cliffs, N.J.: Prentice-Hall.

Mills, Theodore M. (1970), *Group Transformation, An Analysis of a Learning Group*, Englewood Cliffs, N.J.: Prentice-Hall.

Mills, Theodore M., and Rosenberg, Stan (eds) (1970), *Readings on the Sociology of Small Groups*, Englewood Cliffs, N.J.: Prentice-Hall.

Parsons, Talcott, Bales, Robert F., and Shils, Edward A. (1953), *Working Papers in the Theory of Action*, Chicago: The Free Press.

Thibaut, John W., and Kelley, Harold H. (1959), *The Social Psychology of Groups*, New York: Wiley.

Vinacke, W. E., and Ackoff, A. (1957), 'An Experimental Study of Coalitions in the Triad', *American Sociological Review*, vol. 22, pp. 406-14.

Yablonsky, Lewis (1959), 'The Delinquent Gang as a Near-Group', *Social Problems*, vol. 7 (fall).

14 Theoretical background of reference-group concept and its evolution

Maria Łoś

According to a long established socio-psychological belief, people choose the so-called reference groups which shape their social egos and self-evaluation more strongly than any other groups and influences. But we may ask again, whether the rate of change in contemporary social life might not have importantly influenced the phenomena, formed into a stiff conceptual frame more than thirty years ago. It is thus worthwhile to reconsider the present utility of the concept of a reference group and of its two main types distinguished in the established texts on this subject. If we find that this concept constitutes something more than the relic of the past, then we would be well advised to put forth some tentative hypotheses as to the probable changes in the reference groups' role and ways of influence in the developed, urbanized societies, as this may lead to a modification of their typology accepted in rather obsolete literature.

The concept of a group of reference - like that of a small group - is a rather ambiguous and elusive construct, although its utility for the interpretation of various social and individual phenomena has been many times proved. Turning to the history of the concept, let us be reminded that according to the original conception of Herbert Hyman (1942), a reference group performed the function of a system of comparisons determining an individual's subjective feelings about his position and, in consequence, his self-evaluation. The investigations started by Hyman have been continued above all by Stouffer and his collaborators in their researches on the adjustment processes of American soldiers (1949); the crucial concept introduced by them was that of relative deprivation. Their results were reinterpreted as providing the grounds for an outline of the theory of reference groups by Merton and Rossi (1949). In Polish literature, the most penetrating analysis of the classical distinctions of the types of reference groups and of the hypothesis apprehending the relationships between them and human attitudes, aspirations and behaviours was offered in 1962 by Julia Sowa. Almost at the same time that Hyman developed his conception of the system of comparison, Newcomb (1943), studying the influence of group affiliations on individual attitudes, introduced the concept eventually called by Kelley (1947) a normative group of reference. This direction of studies on reference groups was continued mainly by Sherif (1948) and by other students of the phenomena of group influence upon the individual.

The terminological distinction between groups of normative and comparative references was introduced – sanctioning an earlier conceptual distinction – by Kelley (1947). According to him, groups of the former type are those whose acceptance an individual desires to win or keep. A group of *normative reference* can actively accept or reject an individual; a group of the latter type, i.e. a *comparative reference* group, is altogether passive: its mere existence is what permits an individual to draw his own conclusions. Such analytically distinguished groups can be in actual cases embodied by the same group. Besides, they can either be groups of which an individual is a member, or outer groups (in practice, this is a matter of degree, because of the mainly psychological criteria of belonging to a group). In the latter case, the choice of a reference group may be determined or advised by the group in which one participates, or else be censured by it, or finally the matter can be treated as indifference or as beyond the scope of the participation group's interference. Moreover, reference groups of both types can be either positive or negative. The positive groups of normative reference shape the values, norms and aspirations of an individual according to the prevalent standards, while the influence of the negative reference groups is manifested in the rejection by an individual of their standards and as his conscious intention to accept opposite or essentially different norms. It can be assumed that the positive groups of comparative reference provide the background against which the feeling of an individual's relative deprivation comes into relief (i.e. the distance from others occupying positions which are, in a given respect, higher or more desirable than the individual's own position). On the other hand, the negative groups of normative reference provide the standards of an individual's success, revealing the distance from people on lower levels of the social ladder.

It appears that the processes of comparative and normative reference are woven together and it is impossible to analyse them separately. The process of choice of reference groups is implied by more general individual attitudes, particularly of aspirations.

Those, in turn, are shaped under the influence of an individual's own assessment of his 'objective' situation, as well as of his self-evaluation as confronted with the definite systems of comparative reference. But the latter are not chosen at random. Naturally they themselves are related, among other things, to the individual's attitudes and aspirations. It is difficult to understand the complex processes of social reference of individuals and their role in the shaping of aspirations and of the phenomena of social mobility, if we do not accept these basic assumptions about the existence of multi-level feed-backs among many aspects and phases of the processes here described. It can be supposed that the adopted frames of reference strongly influence human aspirations, but at the same time the definite plans and aspirations of a man concerning various, broader or narrower, domains of his life, largely determine his identification with definite groups (in the sense of adopting their standards both as comparative and normative criteria). However, one often fails to notice that the relationship between aspirations and the direction of group identity can take various forms. The following patterns, among others, are possible:

(1) Aspirations are identical with the participation in a definite group and with the assuming of definite social roles, unique for the given group (e.g. if a boy dreams of becoming a Scout, his dream can only come true if he joins a Scout group).

(2) Aspirations are associated with the choice of a definite group for instrumental reasons, as when participation in the group is expected to facilitate the realization of the aspirations (e.g. participation *in* aristocratic circles would bring Wokulski, a character from the famous Polish novel by B. Prus, *The Doll*, nearer to his beloved lady).

(3) Aspirations determine participation in certain groups as a secondary consequence of the acquired status (e.g. education stimulates identification with those of similar educational level, or migration from the countryside to a city involves participation, in multiple ways, in the urban ways of life as well as identification with the working class).

(4) A concretization of some vague aspirations can be determined by participation in a definite group which offers an insight into the adequacy of such aspirations, their chances of being realized, or the proper ways of embodying them (e.g. a person aspiring to play an active political role may join a party or organization in order to see what exactly he can do and how he can do it, to confront and try out his beliefs and ideals, etc.).

(5) In the end, the attraction and 'appeal' of certain groups is often apt to determine the direction and level of aspirations (e.g. a

fascination with the Bohemian style of life and a desire to belong to this group may determine the aspiration to study art).

Of course, when we refer to the normative reference groups, we mean, besides the aspirations to participate in definite groups, the aspirations associated with definite social roles, values, cultural patterns, ideals, as well as with symbols or outer tokens of belonging or acceptance. People often desire to be perceived by others as members of a given circle (for ambition, prestige, political, conformist reasons, etc.) and this desire is apt to be stronger than the wish for actual participation which might be mitigated by the fear of failing to live up to the standards of that circle. As it seems, the actual frame of reference is then, for the individual, those people whom he wants to believe that he is participating somewhere else. However, the group of simulated belonging may still influence the individual's network of values and aspirations. The conception of *audience (or evaluative) reference groups*, presented below, may help to interpret this situation. However, before its introduction, some additional theoretical comments are necessary.

It seems that without taking into account some assumptions of symbolic interactionism it is impossible to understand the role of reference groups, or to discuss their implications. The conceptions of reflected self by Cooley, the humanistic coefficient by Znaniecki, or social control by Mead, have certainly been adopted by the authors of reference groups theories as obvious and necessary assumptions, permitting the theory of personality to develop as a part of sociology. The main theme of studies and investigations in the field of reference group theory is focused on problems of the shaping of individual self-evaluation, imagined opinions and evaluations by others, identification with 'generalized others' (the term used by Mead, 1934). It is thus a domain of problems largely determined by certain basic assumptions introduced by the Chicago school of symbolic interactionism, ascribing to an individual the ability to pursue a symbolic dialogue with himself, to include into such a dialogue the generalized values, properties, attitudes and evaluations ascribed to others, to become identified with, or to oppose, certain generalized images of others, etc. (for broader interpretations of the normative reference group in terms of symbolic interactionism, see Urry, 1973, pp. 1-26). The neglect of this theoretical tradition in discussions, and particularly in empirical investigations concerning reference groups, not only makes them barren, but also isolates this field of problems, making the concept itself into a 'master key' fitting many empirically discovered situations, but failing to explain them. In the light of the theories mentioned above, it is of course naïve to distinguish mechanically between normative and comparative reference groups as concepts which have little to do with one another (as, for example, Kelley does; see Kelley, 1947). Most important is the process of shaping - by social interactions - of a sort of matrix through which an individual selectively perceives the reality, orders and evaluates it, brings it as an element into his symbolic interactions with himself and takes it as guidance for his behaviour. Shibutani puts forth the following hypothesis, bringing all these themes together:

> the choice of reference groups - conformity to the norms of the group whose perspective is assumed - is a function of one's interpersonal relations; to what extent the culture of a group serves as a matrix for the organization of perceptual experience depends upon one's relationship and personal loyalty to others who share that outlook. Then, when personal relations to others in the group deteriorate, as sometimes happens in a military unit after continual defeat, the norms become less binding and the unit may disintegrate in panic. Similarly, with the transformation of personal relationships between parent and child in late adolescence, the desires and standards of the parents often become less obligatory (Shibutani, 1968, p. 111).

It seems, however, that some analytical distinctions are possible and necessary within such a general perspective. Perhaps it might be useful to expand the classical conception of reference group and to introduce tentative definitions of the so-called generalized others in three aspects:
(1) as the normative system of reference
(2) as the comparative system of reference
(3) as the evaluative system of reference.

The image of generalized others in the normative sense takes care of the internalization or abandonment of definite norms, values, etc., under the influence of particular social milieu. It involves *identification with a definite culture or subculture* and with the social roles implied by it.

Generalized others in the comparative sense allow for the relativization of one's own position as experienced in comparison with another's; thereby a general ego-centred mapping of social distances is made up, determined by seemingly 'objective' standards.

Generalized others in the evaluative sense constitute the 'Audience'; an individual evaluates and perceives them with his eyes and thus *forms his own reflected image.*

A similar conception, although formulated in different terms, was put forth by Rushing (1964) and then by Kemper (1968); the latter gave a different definition of comparative groups, seeing them as broadly conceived patterns providing models for the realization of values drawn from groups of normative reference. He distinguished four types of such comparative reference groups:

(1) the groups which we are apt to consider in order to judge, if we are treated justly by others;
(2) the groups which we consider in order to make sure, if our opinions are sufficiently justified (the role of majority opinion, etc.);
(3) the groups (or individuals) providing us with models of definite social roles and thus making possible the learning of newly assumed roles;
(4) the groups facilitating adjustment (in co-operation) or stimulating intensified efforts (in competition).

Such a modification of the concept of a comparative reference system is justified by the intention of separating the sources of values accepted by an individual from the sources of the patterns of behaviour imitated by him or taken into consideration in evaluating his own opinions, behaviours or achievements. It seems, however, that such a distinction is rather artificial and, in consequence, of limited use.

Returning to the discussion of the third category of reference groups, which is an extension of the traditional typology of such groups, it may be worthwhile to point out the phenomena identified by it and left out in the usual understanding of the concept. The evaluative (or audience) system of reference is the concept including into its scope such phenomena as the pressure of public opinion and of the patterns that should be obeyed in the given circle; the internalized feeling of responsibility to a definite person (or persons) remaining vivid even when it is incompatible with one's own values; the hope for fame which involves one's being oriented to very broad human groups or even to the whole of mankind; institutionalized expectations of a political system, etc. As an example for analysis, let us imagine a young unmarried girl who expects a child and thinks about various aspects of her situation. When she considers the ethical meaning of abortion, her opinion is perhaps largely determined by the normative system of reference adopted by her; when she gives a thought to her material position and job perspectives which are likely to deteriorate, she will probably refer to the comparative system (how the other girls around her are getting on, etc.). When she imagines all the remarks with double meaning, the intimidation and the gossip she will have to suffer, she turns towards the evaluative system of reference; she may not share its norms and values at all, but still she must take them into account as significant for her. An analysis of each of these systems (of its contents, subjective import, relative permanence or dynamism, etc.) and of the degree to which they conflict with each other may permit us to understand the situation in question. If the third kind of reference system was left out of account, our description of the process of interpreting the situation and reaching decisions would be much less adequate.

We may add that what we call the system of reference (in its triple form), when we speak about individuals, can be described as the group ethos when we speak about groups. Various groups (or classes, or strata of society) tend to form certain normative traditions and peculiar styles of life of their own, in response to their 'objective' situation and their own 'subjective' evolution. Maria Ossowska, in her historical studies of the bourgeois and aristocratic ethoses, defined this concept as a style of life approved of by some community or group, a general orientation of its culture and its hierarchy of values (Ossowska, 1969, 1973). A detailed analysis of this phenomenon allows us to distinguish its three aspects which are analogous to those hinted at when we defined an individual's system of reference. The ethos of a group is thus a general system of reference for the group members (or insiders of the subculture), i.e. a specific combination of qualities, values, life styles, directions of participation, etc., constituting *an attractive object for striving and aspiration*, or *a matrix for comparisons* of one's own (or the group's own) qualities or achievements with those visualized by the ethos. The ethos may also provide *a fictitious or real audience* with whose eyes the group members look at themselves critically and attempt to make up for their shortcomings or to attain definite standards to meet the expected judgments.

Similarly, in the case of an individual, the choice of an evaluation system of reference largely determines the way the given individual is perceived by others and what his 'reflected self' is like, so in the case of a group, the choice of a definite image of the 'audience' is apt to determine in great degree the social and subjective status of the group. The analysis by Chałasiński (1946) of the status of the pre-war Polish intelligentsia and the discussions by Ossowska of similar elite groups in other European countries indicate that those groups have enjoyed much stability and real superiority in the social hierarchy owing to their avowed ethos, although it has been based on many illusions.

> Monopolistic claims to culture based on illusions, careful
> avoidance of social degradation, the role played in it by a
> certain demeanour, the importance of good repute,
> conformism, economic idleness or at least the assuming of idle

airs, avoidance of professionalism as degrading, the type of
education fencing off from the 'lower classes' (Ossowska,
1969, p. 293)

- are all qualities indicating how much this ethos used to be
audience directed and how much it relied for the group's survival
on the opinion of others and their ably manipulated perceptions.
This phenomenon is by no means uniquely limited to the privileged
social elite, as is evidenced by the fact that the same can be said
about the ethos of the so-called 'gits' (a slang word connected with
the subculture of juvenile delinquents in Poland) in reformatories
for juveniles; they maintain in the community of inmates a caste
structure, not based on any 'rational', openly defined, criteria; the
privileged caste (the 'gits') skilfully manipulate themselves, with the
aid of magical reinforcements, into being perceived as the actual
elite (Łoś and Anderson, 1976).

The great importance of the audience aspect of reference systems
comes into sharper relief when we analyse large groups than when
we deal with individuals. One may predict that when the group or
society is highly mobile or culturally dynamic, the comparative
aspect of the ethos is likely to come to the fore. It might be
interesting to investigate how the general historical processes isolate
one of the aspects of ethos, giving it a self-sustaining status. There
readily arises a hypothesis to the effect that in many contemporary
societies - complex, essentially open and highly mobile - the role of
normative systems of reference has been much weakened, while the
orientation towards comparative systems has been enhanced. The
urge towards social mobility, the fast pace of life, competition
eliminating the incompetent from the race, cause people to become
more interested in information on the success of others, their
economic standards, or the rate of growth of their prestige, than in
eventual standards of success in terms of achievement of their own
individual goals. If we compare all this to a cycle race, we can say
that people, forgetting about the goal (and the meaning) of the
race, are wholly absorbed with watching how fast the others are
turning the pedals and what is the distance between each man and
the others. It can also be suspected that there is a growing
confusion as to who is the important audience, although without
the audience the whole race is meaningless and unrewarding. But as
the race sweeps by, audiences change swiftly and, in time, they
cease to be concrete and forceful, like the proverbial public opinion
of a small town, they assume instead a form of amorphous,
abstract awareness of the existence of indefinite others, who are
different in various situations and who perceive and judge our
achievements and failures by some unknown and fortuitous
standards.

Perhaps those remarks are not relevant to what is called the youth counter-culture (or rather counter-cultures). It is, usually marked by little normative coherence (or by much confusion as to the values and norms), but its comparative system is - in opposition to the adult culture - of a rather limited significance, because of the weak drive for success and stability within any definite social order. The predominant trait of these subcultures seems to be the orientation towards the audience limited to the subcultural circle, towards 'good vibrations', understanding, approval, acceptance of belonging, etc. Even such an important subcultural value as authenticity demands acknowledgment in that form of the approval of others. However, while the role of the peer audience remains great, a peculiar type of normative reference has risen in some subcultural circles to a special importance. It often takes on the shape of a fictitious individual, group or socio-political system, of an imagined (or imaginatively remodelled) hero, idol, guru, or of a desired, though personally inexperienced form of group coexistence, etc. Introducing the concept of a fictitious reference group, Kubin (1972) pointed to the fascination of various circles of the Polish youth with the models elaborated in Western youth subcultures. In his opinion, we often have to do here with the so-called boomerang effect, caused by the mass media policy of a negative selection of news items about those subcultures, e.g. bringing the ill-famed Manson group to the fore while reporting about the hippie movement; this, in turn, raises interest and a desire to imitate in psychically unstable young people. In effect, information intended to prevent the spreading abroad of definite fashions or movements among the youth, may in fact stimulate the process, contributing additionally to its grave distortions. Very likely, the pathologically warped or extreme forms of these phenomena are picked up by individuals or groups which are the least prepared to develop their own, genuine subcultural contents.

Certainly the fictitious reference groups, or at any rate those unavailable for direct observation, allow for a much more free interpretation of the models and norms provided by them. It is what ought to be remembered (and investigated) when we consider the contemporary societies in which the mobility of the patterns and informations is much greater than the mobility of individuals and groups. It thus may be worthwhile to give some attention, when studying the groups and systems of reference of contemporary people to the fictitious models shaped by mass media, ideologies, counter-ideologies and other factors moulding contemporary imagination. The normative, as well as comparative and evaluative reference systems, can have the fictitious character. In the latter case it can be, for example, a feeling of special responsibility to one's own generation and judging oneself with the eyes of anonymous peers throughout the world.

It seems that recent, rather widespread, repudiation of the 'traditional' perspective in sociology, together with the concepts developed within it, has been a bit too hasty. It might be worthwhile to analyse those old concepts against the background of the theoretical developments which were responsible for their emergence. Perhaps the same theoretical orientations can enable us to adjust the old, petrified, concepts to the changing reality. Perhaps, we shall discover that this task is completely beyond them, but it should be somehow tested. It is also possible that the old concepts may be totally reinterpreted in the light of new theoretical approaches in social sciences.

What seems, however, extremely important, and the most difficult at the same time, is the constant effort to secure the dynamic correspondence among changing reality, sociological concepts and theories. When the evolution of concepts is determined purely by the development of theory they would most likely help to produce or to perpetuate an artificial, fictitious picture of society. When direct contact with the individual phenomena is decisive in shaping the relevant concepts, the picture of society they bring about is eclectic, disintegrated and difficult to grasp as a whole.

First of all, it may be suggested that sociology should not develop separate sets of concepts for the micro-social analysis and macro-social analysis. Its concepts should be capable of dealing with the behaviour and consciousness of people in the whole range of social situations. The same general concept should be capable of accounting for their behaviour as members of their families, work teams or social classes. If their lives are not in fact divided into totally separate spheres of participation, why should the theoretical concepts of social sciences be?

The concept of the 'middle-class subculture', for example, may help us to understand the political role of this class, the family life of its members, the nature of the 'hippie' movement, the middle-class consumer market, etc. This task can be achieved only when the concept refers simultaneously to political, economic and structural dimensions of the given society, as well as to the cognitive, emotional, etc., characteristics of the group in question. It must be dynamic (as the phenomena themselves) and complex (multi-dimensional), and it must refer meaningfully to the other concepts. Finally – and this is particularly difficult – it must be dialectical: it must allow for simultaneous grasping of change and stability, consensus and conflict, freedom and coercion, in the way approximating the actual occurrence of those contradictions in social life.

Reference group concept – like that of the small group, and many others – has been developed within social psychology and has usually been expected to facilitate description and explanation of the people's behaviour within the boundaries of isolated micro-worlds. The complex forces shaping the actual systems of reference accepted by the people as well as their role and place in the changes and stability of the macro-system (by the moulding of particular patterns of participation in culture, work processes, consumption, political reality, class mobility, etc.) have been usually neglected. Perhaps, the concept of group ethos (analysed later in this book) – springing from the above discussion of the usefulness and meaning of the reference group concept – may offer a way to overcome some of those shortcomings.

Bibliography

Chałasiński, Józef (1946), *Społeczna genealogia inteligencji polskiej (Social Genealogy of the Polish Intelligentsia)*, 1st edn, Warsaw: Polski Instytut Socjologiczny.

Hyman, Herbert (1942), 'The Psychology of Status', *Archives of Psychology*, 269.

Hyman, Herbert H., and Singer, Eleanor (1968), *Readings in Reference Group Theory and Research*, New York: The Free Press.

Kelley, Harold H. (1947), 'Two Functions of Reference Groups', in G. E. Swanson, T. M. Newcomb and E. L. Hartley (eds), *Readings in Social Psychology*, New York: Holt, Rinehart & Winston.

Kemper, Theodore D. (1968), 'Reference Groups, Socialization and Achievement', *American Sociological Review*, vol. 33, no. 1, February.

Kubin, Jerzy (1972), 'The Concept of Fictitious Reference Group', presented to the conference 'Youth-Family-Local Community' organized by the Austrian Sociological Association in Vienna.

Łoś, Maria, and Anderson, Palmer (1976), 'The Second Life, A Cross-cultural View of Peer Subcultures in Correctional Institutions in Poland and the United States', *The Polish Sociological Bulletin*, no. 36.

Mead, George H. (1934), *Mind, Self and Society*, University of Chicago Press.

Merton, Robert K., and Rossi, Alice Kitt (1949), 'Contributions to the Theory of Reference Group Behaviour', in R. K. Merton, *Social Theory and Social Structure*, Chicago: The Free Press.

Newcomb, Theodore M. (1943), *Personality and Social Change*, New York: Dryden Press.

Ossowska, Maria (1969), *Socjologia Moralności (Sociology of Morals)*, Warsaw: PWN.

Ossowska, Maria (1973), *Ethos Rycerski i jego Odmiany (Knights' Ethos and its Changes)*, Warsaw: PWN.

Rushing, W. A. (1964), *The Psychiatric Profession*, Chapel Hill: University of North Carolina Press.

Sherif, Mauzafer (1948), *An Outline of Social Psychology*, New York: Harper & Row.

Shibutani, Tamotsu (1968), 'Reference Groups as Perspective', in Hyman and Singer (1968).

Sowa, Julia (1962), 'Teoria grup odniesienia' ('Reference Groups theory'), *Studia Socjologiczne*, no. 7.

Stouffer, Samuel (1949), *The American Soldier – Adjustment During Army Life,* vol. 1, Princeton University Press.

Urry, John (1973), *Reference Groups and the Theory of Revolution*, London and Boston, Mass.: Routledge & Kegan Paul.

15   Tertiary social control
Adam Podgórecki

Primary and secondary social control

It is becoming more and more difficult to explain new social phenomena with the old theoretical concepts. This is why recently accumulated data has generated an urgent need for fresh notions. Thus, the concept of tertiary social control is proposed as a move in this direction.

The distinction between primary and secondary social control is very well known. *Primary control* is defined as the influence exerted by a small group on its members and aimed at making them respect the behaviour prescribed by general norms accepted for a given situation. This elastic and variable form of control functions differently in relation to individual cases. It operates without delay, inexpensively and in a penetrating manner. Anomalies and deviations are spotted instantly and the social valuations of the behaviour involved are labelled at once. Opinions are expressed instantly, and the modes for handling deviant behaviour are well established. This type of social control, characteristic mainly of the family or neighbourly community, is based on common ties shaped over many years of multi-level contacts in various spheres of social life. It is accompanied by the almost total lack of privacy which in any case is the subject of inquisitorial observation by the watchdog community.

Secondary control is bereft of the individualizing traits established in face to face relations. It is characterized by formalism and disinterestedness with an elaborate apparatus of formal supervision including a system of rigid and acknowledged sanctions.

The system of secondary social control may be more or less developed but it is always characterized by the predominance of abstract norms separated from individual cases. It is applied to

194

particular cases through an analysis of their essential traits and their relationship to the system of basic norms. In developing its formal-impersonal apparatus secondary control brings into being the profession of norm creators and their interpreters as well as those charged with enforcing them. The norm-controlling profession contains a number of further specializations consisting primarily of (a) those who identify themselves with the abstract aims of the control system, as well as (b) those who serve as the hired defenders of norm violators; (c) those officially charged with providing some legal aid for people who had 'infringed upon that system' and (d) those who undertake the task of establishing the 'objective' validity of conflicting claims serving as mediators, arbitrators, judges, etc.

It would be interesting to determine to what extent the Weberian model of impersonal bureaucracy is able to grasp the administrative reality, and to what degree, rather, it confused this reality with the desired normative codified projection only postulating certain states of affairs.[1] However, the impersonal model in its acceptable descriptive version, tends at least to characterize the essential traits of secondary social control.

The essence of secondary control is that the mechanisms for solving concrete problems are basically impersonalized through their reference to the legitimized system of norms. The specification and analysis of various cases of possible norms violations, the arbitrary delimitations of the sphere of these violations, as well as the determination of the mode of restoring the equilibrium which has been disrupted, have - all of them - to be based on abstract principles. This is precisely why such an analysis is regarded as impartial and not coloured by tactical biases. Even though this apparatus of control is supposed to consider thoroughly individual motives in a humanistic manner and look into the social situations of the individuals or groups who run into conflict with the system of obligatory norms, the mere construction of this control system does not arise from subjective empathy or moral involvement on the part of norm creators. This is an abstract principle which tends to anticipate all possible cases of law violation, being artificially elastic, even if far-reaching formalism may lead, in some cases, to extreme injustices.

It may be said that while the system of primary control has its human face - in its limited possibilities - the system of secondary control aims to materialize human objectives in an impersonal, formal, pragmatic manner alien - in fact - to true humanism.

Tertiary social control

The reservation must be made at the outset that tertiary social control is not a form of control exercised on the basis of the specific application of any ethical values or, in general, values associated with a given *Weltanschauung*. Tertiary social control is undoubtedly a recurring phenomenon. It should be, therefore, of considerable theoretical interest to establish under what conditions such control is applied, who exercises it, how effective it is, what are the ways of counteracting it, etc. However, the basic subject of the present analysis is to grasp the essential features of tertiary social control as they exist in social reality. It should be noted that although the essence of the 'Watergate affair' may serve here as a spectacular example of this type of social control, nevertheless many situations which appear in so-called socialist systems are perhaps more useful (at least due to the frequency and volume of their occurrence) as illustrations of this type of social phenomenon. So initially it may be stated that the essence of *tertiary social control* consists in the utilization of the existing and established means of secondary social control in order to obtain results different from those which have been regarded as the official goals. It means obtaining results actually defined, in a clandestine manner, by those in a position to master them at a given moment.

Before developing that concept further let us return to the distinction between the essential traits of *primary* and *secondary control*. The former obtains in small groups, which constitute a 'transparent' social structure. Every member of the community is socially necessary to the extent that the basic ties in the group (and the obligations connected with their observance or violation) are evident to all. In this situation, the group is in an effective position to reach all its members by means of pressure, public opinion, ostracism and condemnation.

Secondary control operates in a different situation. The quantitative growth of society, the processes of urbanization, industrialization, professionalization, etc., create a situation where members of social groups are not only unacquainted with each other, but can also avail themselves of convenient screens to hide them from the basic groups which still seek (on the basis of tradition, lasting relations, etc.) to influence the individual by means of primary control. In order to exercise control over a complex society, that is to effect conformist behaviour, social institutions and instruments are created either by means of trial and error experiment, or by rational and purposeful activity, or by political imposition. These situations and organizations, having aims of their own, develop many diverse ways of realizing them. The legitimate legal order, under which they exist, provides them with the general framework of accepted social operations.

At the stage of secondary social control, various institutions are brought into being not only to control the behaviour of isolated individuals and small groups, but also to control other institutions. Such institutions control each other, either for the purpose of establishing an equilibrium of strength or because they are complementary in terms of competence and qualifications. On the highest steps of governmental ladders these institutions incur the task of controlling entire networks of other institutions and organizations.

Such a conglomeration of control institutions can change the process of control into such a formally and factually complicated affair that it would tend to obscure the original aims of the desired control (accepted in a more or less democratic manner). It may also create a situation where the control institutions may lose track of who watches whom, and where institutions originally designed to exercise control would tend to transform their originally subsidiary and ancillary functions into autotetic ones (i.e. valid for themselves only).

What then pulls together these often dissonant, contradictory, uncoordinated control institutions? There is no doubt that a general ideological *Weltanschauung* has the task of providing the framework and coordinating schemes for those control guidances. Although some socio-political ideologies fulfil such a task more or less adequately, nevertheless the modern industrialized societies do not provide sufficient, coherent and efficient standards for the whole evaluation of the function of secondary social control. These types of conditions create a situation in which the various existing elements of social control (i.e. legal constructions, institutions, organizations, etc.) may be utilized by different social groups in a way which usurps their usage or alters their designated tasks. Thus, *tertiary social control* consists of various elements of secondary social control which, being regarded as a means of openly realizing publicly designated aims, are used, in fact, by some networks of individuals to achieve goals defined by themselves.

It is generally assumed that primary and secondary social control subsist in a functional relation with the society in which they operate through the provision of structural patterns for inter-personal relations, resolving conflicts, and so forth, but it is not always the case. There are many situations in which the given type of secondary social control is functional only for a segment of society - often a considerable minority - being clearly dysfunctional for the majority. It may be argued, of course, that this control is functional in a narrow sense; namely, that it gives at least some kind of legitimacy for the entire system. One might assert in that case that the existence of such a system of social control is socially more functional than a total lack of it, since, it might be additionally argued, its absence would replace law and order by normative chaos. Tertiary social control usually operates in more complex social situations where not all social links are easily usable and transparent. Its existence may be established only by a systematic analysis if not by an inquisitorial investigation. Let us use a simplified approximating attempt to examine this problem.

A crude example of a simple form of tertiary social control may be the relation between a private person and an official. Usually because of the existing plethora of legal regulations the official can choose with a considerable degree of discretion those regulations that are convenient for his purposes at a given time. Thus, if the official–private–person relationship happens to be a 'sympathetic' one,[2] the official may then select among many possibilities of existing legal constructions those which are favourable to his client (a positive - from the point of view of a private person - settlement of the matter).

Whereas in the case of a negative attitude towards his clients, the official also has the whole gamut of other possibilities, reducible to the choice of a settlement procedure which has negative effects for the applicant. Another choice may exist, not procedural but substantive legal regulations or constructions may rule out any possibility of a positive settlement (again a negative model of settling the matter for the client).

The official has also other, intermediate possibilities. He may choose a way of settling the matter which is neither positive nor negative, i.e. he may avoid any solution at all. In this case the official may drag out the procedure in such a way that the course of its settlement becomes a problem in itself (the temporizing model of settling the matter). But the multiplicity of legal regulations may lead to the application of a fourth settlement model.

In that model the official, being unaware of a proper scheme for solving the affair (i.e., one which ought to be adopted in the given situation in accordance with the logic of the given legal system), chooses almost at random some formally possible settlement scheme. He may also, due to conservatism, or in order to not undermine the prestige of his position, insist that it is the only valid way to settle the case (the accidental model of settling matters).

Each of these models assumes from a strictly normative point of view a preponderance of irrelevant considerations and events which determine the choice of a scheme for the settlement of concrete matters. None of them tries to establish the basic factor of consideration. None of them tries to find the optimal way of settling matters; that is, the kind of purposeful solution for which existing legal constructions have been designed as the proper means and instruments.

All the situations described above point to the fact that a seemingly rational, impersonal and formalized system of secondary social control, being converted into the system of tertiary social control, functions entirely differently than would be required by the existing principles of secondary social control. This system operates, then, on the basis of intervention of forces which have been able to intercept the elements of secondary social control.

The essential features of social control: primary, secondary and tertiary might be demonstrated as shown in the accompanying table:

Features which characterize social groups with different types of social control	Primary control	Secondary control	Tertiary control
Size of the group	small	small/large	small/large
transparency of social life (social visibility)	high	low	low
'face to face' relations	intense	sparse	sparse/intense
existence of formalized social institutions	no	yes	yes
adequacy between goals of social control and its practice	yes	yes	no

Tertiary social control operates mainly in large social groups. Transparency of life in those groups is low, although it may appear as the abuse of the parental authority or police infiltration of small groups etc., its internal life is socially visible, being easily accessible. Face to face relations which flourish in small groups do appear in the case of tertiary social control in a limited scope; they are restricted to those close clusters of mutually interlinked individuals who possess the knowledge of how to use the formal devices of the secondary control for the benefit of their own interests. Although secondary social control and tertiary social control are characterized by the existence of a formal structure of codes, institutions, organizations, norms, formalized patterns of solving existing or potential conflicts, nevertheless the basic difference between secondary control and the tertiary social control manifests itself in the attitude towards publicly accepted goals. Tertiary social order, then, is characterized by the misuse of the principles of secondary social control.

A more complex form of tertiary social control than the simplified introductory one presented above may be extremely intricate in so far as its social structure and ramifications are concerned. Thus it may be asserted that there exist specific social groups which skilfully and consciously intercept elements of secondary social control within the higher ranks of administration where they occupy strategic positions exerting an essential and crucial influence on the course of governmental or administrative processes.

The emergence of these private bodies which use public institutions may not always be attributed to the selfish desire of some clique. The bureaucratized administrative apparatus especially in the case of state-owned economy becomes so routinized, inelastic, decentralized and powerless that the central organs may see no other way to keep this apparatus functioning than by saturating it with their own ramified 'mafia'. Then strategically located groups, on this or another level, wield power with the governmental apparatus, utilizing the secondary social control by means of collusion, with the ostensible purpose of strengthening the official bureaucratic apparatus, and con-sequently, the system of secondary control. Invisible collusion is, in effect, contrary to the basic principles of the legal system as they are manifested by the normative obligatory hierarchy of norms. Such processes may appear and become intensified when this type of group faces retirement; is involved in an election; undergoes the process of rotation or is exposed to the system of 'the change of guard', etc. They may also become visible when the clique in power, according to incoming and repeated feed-back information, is regarded as not having fulfilled an accepted external or internal mission, thus being challenged by the forces existing in the given socio-political system, or when its prestige and authority is, in fact, reduced only to empty slogans, manipulative rationalizations or just sheer power.

The degree of involvement of individual members of the clique in the illegal activity and the extent of their participation in masking their activities are not of primary interest for the present analysis. It is quite clear that the intensity of these elements may vary. It may be that officials belonging to the highest administrative hierarchy are mixed up in some policy-guiding aspects of the group's activities, that is, not in actions of overt illegal behaviour which could implicate them in the core of the antilegal activities. In other circumstances, the inevitable processes of developing more comprehensive defensive apparatus (cover-up) by the group when it is threatened by the investigational activity of legitimized agents of secondary social control, the whole group, still escalating the cover-up mechanism, might get enmeshed in totally illegal activity.

A brief consideration of what may be called tertiary social control indicates that when traditional forms of social control cease to be effective, specific corrective forms of this control emerge. This correction consists in the hitherto prevailing elements of social control being used by spontaneously emerging groups as determined by their subculture and task orientations.

It may be additionally stated that the traditional modes of control function manifest themselves, in a more or less transparent manner, in social situations of pre-industrial societies. The manner of utilizing various forms of control and their effects is basically socially visible in these societies, whereas complicated social situations in complex industrialized societies, where secondary control mainly operates,[3] become more impenetrable due to the multi-level control system. Traditional social control is usually regarded and socially perceived as efficient for the society as a whole, precisely because of its penetrability.

Tertiary social control is silent about its authentic goals. Being deprived of legitimacy, it functions in 'darkness' because it operates in situations lacking social transparency. It regards itself as a particular kind of self-appointed corrector of the traditional control activity. It is not eager to disclose its principles and aims, and even more – since it is usually divided into several discretionary centres – it shapes them in accordance with their own subcultures. Although these discretionary centres may constitute (or be directed by) a central body, such a body is deprived of the usual legitimacy of the secondary social control.

It may be argued that, contrary to the above discussion, tertiary social order is *totally* determined by religious and political values, but that would be inaccurate. True, religious and political organizations, etc., supervise institutions of secondary social control and try to shape them according to their interests and intentions, but nevertheless the real 'essences' of phenomena of tertiary social control consist of something entirely different. They differ from political and religious control in that they are not fixed or directed from outside. They arise independently as organisms emanating from the elements of secondary social control constructions which are very much contrary to the manifested interests or intentions of political or religious institutions. These elements have interests of their own and one of the conditions for the efficient realization of their own aims is the avoidance of any external ideological control. Hence, the tendency to reduce the phenomenon of tertiary control to the level of ideological or political control would be a simplified and unjustified reduction of an independent autonomous phenomenon to factors which, although in some way associated with it, are decidedly different. Moreover, such a reduction would blur the fact that tertiary social control is, as a rule, a spontaneous organizational or machiavellian diversion from religious, political and other ideological values when they are not approved by the population at large.

Thus tertiary social control brings into the social life elements of seemingly irrational attitudes and behaviours in order to realize aims basically unknown to, and/or not acknowledged by, the broader public by means of manipulation. This kind of control is very much akin to what may be called a 'unity of dirty interests' or better, *'dirty togetherness'*. It means that elements of traditional social control, plucked from ethical emotions, are so saturated with various erosive influences that they lose their character of agents of social control after a certain time and assume various traits of specific 'perverse' loyalty. This loyalty is additionally cemented by family ties, mutual fiddling services, participation in various crimes or in mutually beneficial informal, but not legal, private transactions with the possibility of mutual blackmail in case of violation of the reciprocal code of collaboration – when the behaviour known to the hitherto tested partners is disclosed. All these relationships turn out to establish stronger ties than the impersonal requirements, and in turn might create their own super-structure network which then, as a new independent or social factor, starts to influence the social system in which it prospers. The existence of that superstructure, the fact that it is perceived as such by the public at large and the uncertainty where it is 'located', evokes various social attitudes of a new qualitative category. It also induces the growing conviction that only those public programmes have a chance to be materialized which will not be confronted with counteraction by the superstructure of the 'community of dirty interests'. Then there is a reason to expect that counter-action, or even retaliation, by the agents of that community will extinguish any attempts to pursue socially constructive programmes replacing them by growing conformity.

Various clusters of 'dirty togetherness' when they link themselves (or are perceived by the public as interrelated) into a developed frame or superstructure may have a very important additional effect. They may bond the social system together as a whole.

In order to make this point more clear let us analyse, for a moment, the concept of 'legitimacy'.

It is possible to distinguish, at least, four types of legitimacy:

(a) *Legitimacy which is based on the normative grounds*: according to this type of legitimacy only those regulations and institutions have legal validity which are properly deduced from the legal norms of the higher order. On the top of the hierarchy of all norms exists the ultimate norm (*Kelsenian-Grundnorm*) which is regarded as the final source of normative power;

(b) *Legitimacy which is based on the democratic support of the population*: legitimacy which is normatively valid but nevertheless is rejected as 'unjust', 'reactionary', 'oppressive' by the majority of the population and is regarded, according to this understanding, as devoid of legal authority;

(c) *Legitimacy which takes its validity from the rejection of all other possible options (negative legitimacy)*: a certain type of legal system which does not have the support of the majority of population nor descends from a legally valid constitution may still be regarded as legitimate if all other options (e.g. lack of sovereignty, war, total destruction) are considered even worse alternatives;

(d) *Legitimacy which is based on the existence of the superstructure of 'dirty togetherness'*.

If behind the given legal system (which is rejected by the population at large as unjust, undemocratic, etc.) there operates a complicated infrastructure of mutually interdependent interests then this legal system may become accepted, not on the basis of its own merits, but because it creates a convenient cover-system for the flourishing phenomenon of 'dirty togetherness'. Then each institution, factory and organization serves, independently from its own production tasks, as a formal network which gives a stable frame of reference for an enormous amount of mutual semi-private services, reciprocal arrangements. For example: the acceptance into a medical school of a daughter of a highly placed person in return for the possibility of buying the unaccessible cement for building a house; the privilege of immediately buying a car in exchange for admission to a well-equipped, specialized hospital for an elderly aunt, etc. In this situation the formal legal network, irrespective of its own questionable productive efficiency, becomes a very precious cover-scheme. It is clear that individuals who operate inside this system start to support this legal matrix after a while, not because they accept it (as a system which has a normative validity, or as a system which is supported on the basis of its own inherent virtues), but because they become familiar with it, with the rules of its game, with its 'who's who' background and with its conditions of efficiency hiding like strategies.

On the basis of this analysis one may state generally that tertiary social control may have, under certain conditions, two essential functions: (a) to give to several scattered organizationally skilful groups the possibility of seizing some formal elements of the legal system for their own, publicly, undisclosed benefits; (b) when the dispersed clusters of tertiary social control become linked into a coherent superstructure, then this superstructure furnishes the unaccepted legal system with a unique 'perverse' legitimacy.

Notes

1 The Weberian concept of ideal types seems, in this respect, to be additionally misleading.
2 The citizen makes a sympathetic impression, finds the official in good humour, establishes friendly, extra-official contacts with him, bribes him effectively, profits from the clerk's ambivalence created by his unjustly (even for himself) vicious behaviour towards the former client, etc.
3 As ramified bureaucracy, multiplicity of institutions and organizations, administrative control, courts activities, ombudsmen checks, etc.

16 Class ethos
Maria Łoś

Independently of whether a man is or is not attached to any small groups, he usually belongs to definite broader categories: to socio-cultural strata, classes, ethnic groups, social circles, occupational categories, etc. These are relatively permanent general classifications, although in the swiftly changing contemporary societies they may undergo vast transformations in actual content. It can be supposed that such broad groups are able to evolve their specific types of ethos. This concept, successfully employed in historical analyses, is almost absent from the literature on contemporary societies. In this chapter an attempt will be made to assess the potential significance of the concept of ethos for the fuller understanding of the contemporary social structures. As an example the present Polish society will be utilized for the purpose of analysis.

The historical studies by Maria Ossowska of the bourgeois and chivalrous ethos (1956, 1973) proved the cognitive validity of the concept. Ossowska (1969, 1973) means by an ethos the style of life appraised by a community, its general cultural orientation and its adopted hierarchy of values. The ethos of a group is, above all, manifested in the model of personality which is commonly accepted within the group, and which represents – according to Ossowska's definition – a ficticious or real character who embodies the prevalent aspirations of the members of that particular group.

It is implied by what was said in the chapter on reference groups that we can speak about the ethos, using the language more congenial to contemporary sociology, as a general system of reference, adopted by the given group. An ethos thus appears to be such a combination of the desirable qualities, values, styles of behaviour, directions of participation, etc., which represent an object of striving and aspirations, a matrix for comparing one's own qualities or achievements with those of other groups, as well as a fictitious or real audience with whose eyes one can take a critical look at oneself and for the sake of which one tends to assume – or at least to pretend to assume – certain attitudes. However, the ethos seems to be a more convenient label to cover all these phenomena than the concept of a reference group, because the latter is generally associated with the study of individuals and thus involves a risk of misunderstanding.

Podgórecki (1976) sought to distinguish between three versions of the concept of ethos:

(1) *The 'working' ethos* – internalized, manifested in the actual behaviours of members of the community:

(2) *The normative ethos* – (a) the accepted ideology of one's own group (Ossowska called it the *adopted* ethos);
(b) the ideology or ethics addressed to the given group, prescribed for or imposed on it by certain ideological centres, moralists, etc. (Ossowska called it the *propagated* ethos):

(3) *The instrumental or 'façade' ethos* – manifested outside in order to secure the group's position, to conceal its weaknesses or real intentions or to attain some other ends.

The ethos probably exerts considerable influence upon the choice of reference systems by individuals, their self-identification, affiliations, choices of values and so forth. However, in order to answer the question, whether the phenomenon of ethos exists at all in the contemporary, dynamic society, and whether this concept helps to grasp and explain any interesting facts, it may be advisable to resort to the empirical data which are available pertaining to one selected society.

In Polish sociology there are no empirical investigations aimed directly at a reconstruction of the ethos of any socially important groups or strata. However, if we limit the meaning of ethos to the actual 'life style' of a group and its so-called cultural consumption, we might find some more materials. On the other hand, if we are concerned with the more elusive normative models which serve to shape the broadly conceived aspirations of such groups, we have to look for the studies which are mainly focused on attitudes (including aspirations). Studies of this type have been carried out, but often on such peculiar samples as to make their results useless, at least for our purposes. Still, there are several valuable studies devoted essentially to quite different problems, but which bring answers of respondents belonging to definite, significant social groups, concerning the aim of life, standards of success, ideals, aspirations, social identifications, moral judgments, criteria of choice of friends or a spouse, as well as information about

206

approved behaviours, styles of cultural participation and so on. Certainly, such data must represent mixtures of declarations to please the interviewer, genuine evaluations and aspirations, actually manifested life styles, etc. It is not easy, and is perhaps unnecessary, to disentangle this jumble. If we sort out what evokes repulsion, discontent, mistrust, anxiety and other negative emotions, we obtain an image of what is called the ethos of the group, in other words, the sum of what its members strive for, what they are satisfied with and what they believe to be expected from them. But referring to the typology of Podgórecki, it must be said that the adopted normative ethos of a group may get mixed in such a description with some elements of the instrumental-or-pretended ethos. What should be also stressed is a reluctance of the Polish respondents to answer freely questions on ideology (for some it would, in practice, cover quite a broad range of matters). Moreover, all the research questionnaires have to be submitted to political censorship for acceptance and all the 'touchy' or politically inconvenient questions would be inevitably crossed out (unless the inquiry has been sponsored by one of the Party's own research units, in which case, however, the results would be kept secret).

Below, several ethoses of the selected groups within contemporary Polish society are discussed. The groups whose ethoses have been reconstructed in the light of the available data were chosen by the following criteria: a key role in the socio-economic structure and conspicuity of the group; its probable coherence and culturally distinct character; the existence of at least several studies by different authors from which information could be drawn. To increase the reliability of the synthetically presented forms of the ethos of the selected groups, it was also important that they had been studied by different methods. The main methods of data-collecting used in the studies taken into consideration have been the questionnaire, interview, diaries and participating observation.

A number of significant groups, however, must be eliminated from the final analysis, simply because they have, for various reasons, been neglected by the researchers. The most important omission is certainly the ruling elite. Ultimately an attempt to reconstruct the ethos of the following groups has been made: peasants (with young farmers and young urban migrants treated separately); workers (including young workers as a separate subgroup); white-collar workers, and the intelligentsia (with intellectuals and the young progeny of the educated class treated separately). The sorting out of the younger and older age groups allows one to trace the dynamics of each separate ethos. However, it is the youth which is the privileged subject of studies on aspirations, life styles and hierarchies of values. Consequently, its ethos has been more fully and precisely elaborated. Nevertheless, the youth culture is not treated here as a separate coherent and homogeneous phenomenon. Instead, the different age categories are viewed within the context of the historical development and cultural tradition of the given socio-economic groups or classes. A similar approach has been assumed by the Centre for Contemporary Cultural Studies, University of Birmingham, in its innovative work on class cultures.

Due to the character of the available material, the main features of the presented types of ethos are focused on attitudes towards the family and informal social environment, towards one's own role in society, patterns of participation in mass culture and certain ethical values. Naturally, the overall description of various ethoses presented below is in many ways crippled. Its relative strength consists in the fact that they have been derived from the systematic research data, but it is considerably weakened by the known limits and biases of the positivist methodology and, above all, by external as well as inner censorship mechanisms on the part of both researchers and their respondents.

The ethos of peasants

Contemporary Polish peasants of the middle and older generations

This is a social category with a very intensive historical experience. It includes the pre-war socio-economic relationships in the countryside, the war, the agrarian reform, the forced collectivization and its failure, the struggle for establishment of individual farming in socialism and its actual introduction, the educational advancement of young people and their outflow to the town, the impact of technological progress, the explosion of mass culture and the mass media.

One factor strongly influencing the ethos of contemporary farmers is the feeling of uncertainty over the future of individual farms in the socialist state, and over the constant changes in the official rural policy. The constant changes in official rural policy breed a fear of new attempts at collectivization and an accompanying reluctance to invest and to develop their farms. Another remarkable factor is the inferiority complex of a country dweller in a world dominated by the urban culture and style of life, as well as by the hypertrophy of bureaucracy. Negative experiences - associated, among other things, with contacts with urban white-collar workers and local authorities who manifest their superiority and neglect towards peasants who have to ask them for vital decisions - also play a very important role in the striving to secure for the children the status of urban employees. A certain ambivalence can be seen here, however, in that peasants are still aware that an urban migrant becomes a hired hand who is necessarily subordinated to his superiors in the job, and thus is no longer able to enjoy the freedom of working as a farmer 'on his own'.

The ethos of the contemporary peasant is formed between rather obvious antinomies, the city dictates to him a style of life, but it is at the same time a threat to his traditional moral values and to his self-evaluation as a representative of the countryside; the city offers him a vision of the future (and thus determines his aspirations for the careers of his children), but it also brings anxiety as to the fate of the countryside which is abandoned by the young and deprived of its genuine and continuous cultural tradition and economic dynamism; the social and political system offers the possibility of educating the youth and to advance them socially, but it also brings a sharp conflict between the generations and questions parental authority. It also brings forth acute frustration and disappointment on the part of those youngsters whose aspirations (moulded by the egalitarian ideology and the myth of openness and superiority of the city) could not be satisfied in existing circumstances. The very common employment of peasants in extra jobs outside their farms (peasant-workers) brings them into the sphere of influence of contemporary industrial civilization, but at the same time restricts their opportunities to participate either in the working-class culture, or in their local one.

The countryside has certainly come under the strong influence of the urban culture. The lack of the relevant research data does not permit us to grasp the changes of the ethos of the Polish peasants of the middle generation, or to define fully its current content; only some of its elements can be synthetically covered. Unfortunately, the existing research does not normally focus on the contradictions, nor does it provide any insight into the perceived or desired availability of any forms of socio-political participation. Most of the research provides rather limited information about some more or less homogeneous consumption patterns, cultural preferences and attitudes towards countryside and agriculture. Some insight into the complexity and dramatic contradictory nature of the structural position of this social class is provided by quite an impressive number of memoirs, written by farmers in response to the 'memoirs competitions' - advertised usually by the mass media, but initiated and supervised by the sociologists. Nevertheless, the present attempt at a synthesis of existing data should be treated rather as a help in tracing the blank spots in existing research than as a source of full and adequate information about the studied phenomenon. Let us keep in mind that the causes of the relative poverty and paleness of the contemporary farmers' ethos stem from the limitations of the available sociological expertise and not from the farmers' culture itself.

In the light of the reconstructed ethos, a contemporary Polish farmer is no longer as emotionally attached to the soil as his fore-fathers used to be, and he does not ascribe to it the superior place in his system of values. The soil is valuable not so much in itself, as – in a large measure – because of the income brought by it and the level of life that it can warrant. He believes that safety in life can be protected both by the soil and by a non-farming occupation. He admits his children the right to choose such an occupation, if they are able to acquire the necessary training, and if they can thereby win satisfaction and material stability. An important trait of this ethos is the emotional commitment to the future of one's children and the belief that it is necessary to ensure that the children acquire proper education and occupational training and thus make their future better and less full of hardship than one's own.

According to the research data, a contemporary farmer accepts the processes of professionalization of agriculture, he understands the need for agricultural training and for broadening professional knowledge by reading, listening to the radio, etc. He supports mechanization and the modern methods of intensive farming. He appreciates highly the independent status of a farmer, but he complains about the round the clock routine of farm work and the lack of vacations. He sees the need of leisure to develop his own interests, social contacts and cultural entertainment. He puts much emphasis on the improvement of the home and hygienic con-veniences for the family and is fascinated by the modern household appliances. He is annoyed by the village's cultural isolation and stresses the necessity of the broader contacts with the world by means of the radio, television and press, as well as the desire (very unrealistic indeed) to have his own vehicle to drive him more readily to a town (Jagiello-Łysiowa, 1969; Pawelczyńska, 1966; Mleczko, 1964; Makarczyk, 1964; Miścicki, 1973; and others).

The peasants' ethos is certainly largely differentiated, depending on the region, ethnic composition of the population, distance from industrial and urban centres, etc., but the lack of reliable data does not permit us to grasp these differences.

The ethos of a young peasant

We can speak about the peculiar philosophy of those who remain in the countryside as farmers, either by their own choice, or – more often – by necessity. They tend to exalt, as if on second thought, their situation in life. In diaries of country youth there are many examples of such – as Jagiello-Lysiowa describes it – 'secondary acceptance of one's own occupation, finding merits in it, demonstrating to oneself and others that a farmer can be a fully modern and cultured man, like anyone else' (1969, p. 44). It is thus a group whose peculiar ethos is focused around a collective experience of failure to follow the prescribed path of social mobility, as well as a feeling of inferiority. This phenomenon is noted by many authors, e.g. Makarczyk (1964).

The analysis of diaries of young farmers, as well as questionnaire surveys, allow us to reconstruct the cherished – although highly *idealized* – image of a member of this group. He purports to be an enlightened man, with broad horizons, well informed about the affairs of the contemporary world, with liberal interests by no means limited to farming, well read, eager to make the best of the mass media and cultural institutions, zealously adopting the urban style of life and consumption, keeping pace with the fashions, keen for technical devices and facilities, actively striving to realize his selected objectives, hard working, straightforward, responsible, appreciating a harmonious family life, motivated by love in the choice of his or her marital partner, accepting the egalitarian, partnership type of marriage and the ideal of the small, two-generation pattern of family, living apart from the parents and siblings and enjoying good health (Jagiello-Łysiowa, 1969; Makarczyk, 1964; Łoś, 1972; Weber, 1971, 1965; Chałasiński, 1964; Krawczyk, 1967; Szymański, 1973; *et al.*).

The ethos of a young city migrant

Young people of rural background who strive to find their way in the city, keep away from those who intend, or are compelled, to remain in the countryside. They tend to be guided by, and orientated towards, the ethos which can be very briefly described as follows: a young man who leaves his village for a town must in the first place obtain the education necessary to gain independence in life. His occupational training should secure, above all, a good material standard and stability; besides, it ought to some extent to suit his interests and eventually promise promotion. However, he should rather keep down his aspirations by realistic judgment, considering that he may count on himself only. He must be mature, resourceful and watchful. It is considered to be ridiculous to dream unrealistically about professions with very high social prestige, or about extravagant ones. He should rather avoid occupations involving adventure, risk or extraordinary experiences; they may suit as childish daydreams, but in adult life he ought to seek stability and choose the surest way to raise his social position.

The most important affiliation group for a young city migrant is his own close family, bringing social and emotional security, as well as the feeling of satisfaction. He ought to establish a harmonious family based on partnership, possibly with an urban dweller (this requirement refers above all to a husband for a girl from the countryside), to live a quiet and decent life, enjoy health, avoid broader social commitments, take full advantage of the urban facilities and opportunities (seen in terms of material standards, entertainment and education). He is distinguished by some optimism in his appreciation of the contemporary world (Chałasiński, 1964; Weber, 1965, 1971; Makarczyk, 1964; Łoś, 1972; Miller, 1964; Horoszowska, 1961; Szymański, 1973; Kutyma, 1974; Niezgoda, 1975; Kiciński and Kurczewski, 1975; *et al.*).

The working-class ethos

The ethos of workers of the middle or older generation

The situation of a worker in People's Poland is radically different from what it was before the war; he shares in the general ideological advancement of the whole social class. However, the systemic changes have by no means eliminated from his social role all the conflict-bearing factors. On the contrary, the working-class place in the social structure and in current socio-political processes is full of dramatic contradictions. As J. Waclawek writes,

It is a double role. On the one hand, as a result of the winning of political power and of the nationalization of the means of production, a worker in this country has got his share in the legal and institutional ownership and decision-making. On the other hand, a worker lives on wages and he sells out his labour . . . . In the next place, the working class is the ruling class, but it cannot - if only for technical reasons - exert its power directly, but through selected, more or less stable managerial groups, who take care of the general interests, but also of their own interests as the group or stratum of administrators. . . . It is the role of a hired hand, living on wages. This fact involves a clash with the interests of the state which hires him. This is the content of the long accepted contradiction between the individual interests of a worker (employee) and the overall interests of the state or society (Waclawek, 1974, pp. 118-19).

Naturally, the workers' powers and their participation in decision-making is merely an ideological fiction. We should also note some aspects of the social role of a worker which are the source of conflict between the white- and blue-collar personnel. It is the latter who apparently seem to be much more exposed to the negative effects of poor management or organization. The faulty and inefficient functioning of the economic system of an enterprise – for which, apart from broader political reasons, most often the managerial and executive staff are to blame – strike direct blows at workers whose economic situation depends on the effects of production. This tends to produce grudges, social and political passivity and impaired motivation on the part of the workers.

> Each hindrance encountered by a worker in his job, each case
> of chaos or waste, is an insult to his sense of orderliness and a
> blow at his welfare, his health, and ultimately at his wages. A
> worker is very well aware that so much waste around must
> needs be paid for by himself (Waclawek, 1974, p. 141).

After this extremely brief analysis of some 'objective' features of a worker's situation we shall now reconstruct his 'subjective' ethos from the available sociological evidence.

The ethos of a worker inclines him to put great emphasis on education and permanent training. He ought to strive to do his job well, to find satisfaction in it and be promoted to tasks or positions requiring higher qualifications, or at least not to be ousted from the obtained position by new developments. He should not be too committed to broader socio-political issues, because he sees little opportunity to influence them, but he may be keenly interested in the affairs and achievements of his own team. He cares very much about the respect of others. He appreciates in people such qualities as solidarity, decency and friendliness.

He chooses his marital partner from the same social milieu. His family tends to be rather traditional, with sustained divisions of the male and female functions; in some milieux (e.g. among the coal miners) it is desirable that the wife does not work, so that the household be kept tidy and thrifty, and so that the children or grandchildren can stay at home rather than be sent to a kindergarten. A worker's social entertainments should be centred around family parties and meetings with his friends. He considers it to be proper to spend his leisure mainly at home, resting, watching television, listening to the radio, reading books and newspapers. He is also fond of strolling and going to the cinema. Sometimes he will go out to see some cultural or sporting event. He thinks that one should take advantage of the mass media not only for entertainment, but also for information about recent developments in technology and politics, as well as for general knowledge promoting his individual development.

During the vacations he should go for either group or individual holidays (in passing, this is another example of how actual behaviour differs markedly from the avowed ethos, since there is multiple evidence that less than 20 per cent of blue-collar employees spend their vacations on leisure activities, while the rest take extra paid jobs, or go to their families in the countryside to help on the farm, etc.).

A worker ought to be realistic in his long range plans; he ought to try to save money in order to improve step by step the material and cultural standards of his family. He attaches great importance to the future of his children, their education, to the securing of a good material start for them, etc. He tends to be fairly strict in the domain of traditionally conceived morality.

There are certainly large differences between the ethos of the skilled and unskilled workers, those coming from the countryside and from urban settings, living in large and small industrial centres, employed in modern and traditional enterprises; but these phenomena require further systematic studies. Very important aspects of the working-class ethos are political attitudes, general outlook, etc., but insufficient data preclude a reliable diagnosis (Nowakowa, 1973; Adamski, 1974; Galdzicki, 1967; Mrozek, 1965; Dobrowolska, 1967; Malanowski, 1962, 1965; Tobera, 1972; Zebik-Koralewicz, 1974; Kulpińska, 1969; Jarosińska, 1964; Jarosińska and Kulpińska, 1971; Podgórecki *et al.*, 1971; Szczepański, 1974; Sarapata 1965a, 1965b, 1975; *et al.*).

The ethos of young workers

A young worker must in the first place have adequate occupational qualifications. He is also expected to plan to study at a university or a college of higher education, or at least not to exclude such a possibility. The ethos of a young worker urges him to train and raise his qualifications continually, in order to advance his occupational position and to become better adjusted to the requirements of the progressive technology and organization of work, as well as to develop his personality and participate more fully in the cultural life of the country. Better training also gives him more freedom in the choice of job and the possibility of a change of job. It also wins him respect and authority in his environment. In choosing his occupation he is supposed to be motivated mainly by his interest, rather than by utilitarian considerations, necessity, chance, etc. Still, a high material standard is important for him as a significant index of success in life. His work should be independent and

214

thoughtful, as well as clean and not too hard. He should not be too committed to social issues, or if he is, only within the factory. He should be aware that his achievements in life depend mainly on his own effort.

A man should marry a woman who has a vocational training (but there are certainly large differences in this respect between various milieux), and who also comes from a working-class background. A man or woman from the working class is expected to devote his or her leisure to the family (in many milieux of young workers it includes some help by the husband in household chores, although the division of tasks into male and female ones is still sustained), to learning and cultural entertainments. They should desire to belong to sporting clubs, amateur musical groups, hobby clubs, etc. They ought to be well mannered, and to know how to behave in café and theatre; they should be able to talk on various subjects, and dress according to the current fashions, although avoiding extravagance.

Moreover, the ethos of a young worker implies his rather sober, unemotional attitude to the historical past, the fatherland and patriotism.

It should be added that the ideal of a young worker as a culturally active person, developing his interests and raising his qualifications is highly *unrealistic* and practically conflicting with the ideal of a family man. T. Goban-Klas, referring to a survey of workers in one of the industrial cities (Nowa Huta), describes this situation as follows:

> The birth of a child practically means – not only for the mother, but also for the father – the necessity to withdraw from amateur teams, clubs, sporting activities. It also limits – more strongly than any other single factor – the frequency of theatre- and cinema-going, and also, in some degree, the opportunities for further occupational training. In the domain of attitudes to work and career, the dynamism manifested earlier is transferred to other domains; extra paid jobs are picked more often, straining even more the daily schedules which are already tense. The necessity of taking permanent care of the children is the reason why the family become isolated and its members spend most of their time at home, limiting their social and cultural entertainments to what is available there (Goban-Klas, 1971, p. 140).

(Nowakowa, 1973; Adamski, 1974; Galdzicki, 1967; Malanowski, 1965; Jarosińska, 1964; Kiciński and Kurczewski, 1975; Goban-Klas, 1971; Pomian, 1965; Tulski, 1965; *et al.*)

The white-collar workers' ethos
Aspirations of the clerical (office and administration) personnel are

shaped by the model of an intelligent and cultured man. The aspiration towards this model is associated with a rejection of the social stereotype of a white-collar worker. Ossowska wrote: 'the role of anti-models in social life . . . tends to be underestimated' (1973, p. 14); this idea is certainly applicable to the analysis of the ethos of clerks. White-collar workers do not identify themselves with the occupational role, or with the social position of a clerk – rather, they tend to see it as a negative reference pattern. In fact, the common ethos of this group is rather loose. According to Lutyńska,

> white-collar workers have no social, occupational, or even political ideology of the kind that has been remarkable for the working class, or engineers, or doctors, or the Polish peasants. . . . The lack of an ideology prevents the shaping of a consciousness within this group. The ideology of an occupational group enhances the prestige of the occupation. Clerical employees usually do not have any ideological beliefs of this kind. Only occasionally an institution would produce the local feeling of professional pride (Lutyńska, 1965, p. 147).

Lutyńska tried to obtain spontaneous self-definitions from her white-collar respondents and she observed that 'there is an obvious feeling of harm, or simply feelings of mediocrity, unimportance and disappointment' (1965, p. 179). Most subjects report that they have been compelled to take the clerical kind of job because of hard material conditions, fate, chance or low education. As to their class self-identification, most of the white-collar workers include themselves among the intelligentsia (Lutyńska, 1965, p. 183). Most of them also believe that before the war the social position of a clerk was higher than it is now; they appreciate his present position as a little above a worker, but below a foreman. They often see themselves as people without an occupation, or as socially useless. Here are quotations from a few diaries:

> I haven't been taught . . . to sew, or cut, or to make boots, or to mend an electric iron . . . in a word, I don't know any craft and I am thus sentenced for life, willing or not, to be an office bug (Lutyńska, 1965, pp. 207–8).

> At difficult moments, I thought persistently and bitterly that shoemaking is a craft on its own . . . and that it can earn you a decent living as compared with a man of high school education, who lacks any occupational training (p. 208).

> I keep feeling that the work I do brings no permanent effects, that I'll leave nothing to others behind me (p. 208).

216

There is no use in piling up papers around the office. It does
not give me the slightest satisfaction (p. 209).

It is hardly sufficient to say that the attitudes and aspirations of
clerks are determined mainly by the peculiar negative model
represented by a petty white-collar worker, an office bug, dull and
colourless, useless and half-educated. Seeking for cultural models
characteristic of white-collar workers, Lutyńska arrives at the
conclusion that

> clerks are under the strong influence of the generally
> widespread cultural model, oriented mainly towards
> consumption. It is consumption to which their life style or
> patterns of cultural behaviour seem to be reduced. In fact,
> these patterns are characteristic not only of the Polish society,
> but of many other contemporary industrialized societies.
> White-collar workers are the 'middle' category; there are
> people from various social strata and classes among them; the
> office personnel is a mixture of people with different levels of
> education, family traditions, cultural inheritage. We can thus
> suppose that they constitute the category among which this
> overall consumptive model of culture has most chances to
> become widespread and accepted (Lutyńska, 1965, p. 225).

Among the requirements of this style (identified in many studies)
there are expensive but tasteless home furnishings, holidays spent
in fashionable resorts or abroad (normally in other socialist
countries, as the Western countries are virtually inaccessible) and
showy and superficial cultural consumption.

A remarkable trait of the clerical ethos is the requirement that
the children attain a 'good' profession, one of those that opens the
door to the 'real' milieux of the intelligentsia.

Social differentiation within the discussed category is so great,
and studies on it so few, that its ethos can hardly be described in
more detail. There is a remarkable and essential division between
three groups of the clerical personnel: those employed in industry,
those in administration and those in financial institutions. There is
very little information available about the first category, whilst the
second one is best characterized by the findings of Lutyńska
(above). The third group is called by Lutyńska 'the clerical
aristocracy'. Its style of life is the closest to the style of the
traditional intelligentsia, while the white-collar workers working in
industry tend to live more like workers. It is among the latter group
that there are most persons with a working-class background, while
among the bank employees there are most representatives of the
pre-war intelligentsia. The spouses of bank clerks have, as a rule, at
least high school education, while the bank clerks are high school

217

or university graduates. They take great care about their homes; a telephone (which is rather hard to obtain in Poland) is a prestigious asset.

A study by Kwaśniewski, made on a national sample of bank clerks, indicates that they have a certain feeling of professional pride and solidarity; they are also conscious of their position which is higher than that of the rest of office employees. They call themselves bank employees, economists, etc., rather than clerks. According to Kwaśniewski's study, the qualities most highly appreciated by bank workers are: integrity, reliability, honesty, the feelings of duty and responsibility, diligence and expertise. Statistical data indicate that a part of their ethos may also consist of occupational stability and permanence of institutional attachment. The peculiarities of the banking business have produced the stereotype of a bank employee as a scrupulous person, absolutely disciplined, abiding by the rules and direct guidance and orders from his superiors. According to the research, however, he is apt to be, at least in what he declares, a legal nonconformist who has no use for impractical, idle or obsolete regulations; he also tends to insist on as much autonomy as possible towards what his superiors demand from him. Thus the subjective group ethos of this category of white-collar workers is different from what has been found typical in descriptions of the objective place of the administrative office personnel in the social structure. For example, according to J. Szczepański, they differ from workers by

> their place in society, by their subordinate position in the
> formal hierarchies, requiring from them loyalty and obedient
> performance of what the authorities order them to do,
> because their chances of advancement and the realization of
> their vital aspirations depend on such loyalty (Szczepański,
> 1965, p. 36).

(Lutyńska, 1965; Dyoniziak, 1969; Grzelak, 1965; Janicki, 1968; Gluck and Kwaśniewski, 1974.)

The ethos of the intelligentsia

It is notoriously difficult to say what is the social and cultural stratum known by the name of intelligentsia in contemporary Poland. Chałasiński (1958) maintains that the new Polish intelligentsia, having lost its former elite status and social significance, has failed to evolve new patterns, or to become reintegrated in any new remarkable form; it is loose, disintegrated and unimportant. On the other hand, Szczepański sees the new intelligentsia as a dynamic and socially significant group, although

218

it is differentiated and quite unlike its pre-war state. On his account, the changes in the political and social system and the rapid industrialization have brought about a shift in the proposition of students of science and technology and of the humanities, to the detriment of the latter; in effect, 'among the new intelligentsia there prevails the type of employee who is a technological or managerial expert, thinking in terms of his trade, with a practical and matter of fact attitude to the social life' (Szczepański, 1965, p. 33). Szczepański distinguishes three categories of intelligentsia: the 'creative intelligentsia' (i.e. intellectuals, scientists and artists); experts and professionals (engineers, doctors, lawyers); managers and executives. According to Szczepański, the creative intelligentsia has retained most of the characteristics of the pre-war intellectual elite. As to the experts,

> the young generation of 'experts' has its clear political and social identity and typically matter of fact, sober attitudes. Ideology is no longer for them what it used to be for the revolutionary pre-war intelligentsia . . . this generation thinks in more logical and earthbound terms of each of its professional categories and it has less sympathy for ideological axioms, and more understanding for rational and efficient action (Szczepański, 1965, p. 35).

As to the third category of the intelligentsia – comprising the managers and executives of the social, economic, as well as political concerns, those occupying strategic positions in the state and administration, etc. – it constitutes 'the part of the intelligentsia among which the changes have been the most far-reaching. The new political power had to create its own managerial apparatus, selecting its members by political criteria' (Szczepański, 1965, p. 35; see also Wiatr, 1965).

One conclusion by Szczepański, which is especially important for the present consideration, is the statement that the intensive changes in post-war Poland, causing, among other things, a notable growth in the numbers of intelligentsia (conceived as the sum of the three categories mentioned above), have contributed to the fact that

> the intelligentsia is no longer a coherent stratum with its own social consciousness, and it becomes an aggregate of professional groups, performing their special tasks, whose social position and prestige is defined by the division of labour and by the importance of those tasks for the development of the industrializing society (Szczepański, 1965, pp. 36-7).

However, it seems reasonable to suggest that there is a certain general ethos, accepted and aspired to by at least two of the three above mentioned categories, i.e. by intellectuals and experts. Besides, this ethos is formed under the strong impact of the old traditions of the Polish intelligentsia, although certainly some of its traits are rather loosely related to those traditions. Scant materials do not permit of a more profound and complex analysis of the highbrow ethos in contemporary Poland. The three models of this ethos here reconstructed follow available sources, rather than any logical classification.

The ethos of the intelligentsia of the middle generation

A member of the intelligentsia must be an intelligent man (it is believed by many that this quality is socially or even biologically inherited), educated, trained to a respectable profession (preferably to one of the traditional 'learned' professions). Apart from having sound professional knowledge, he should be informed in matters of music, painting, literature, the arts, politics, etc. He should keep informed about what is new on the cultural market, know the cultural and artistic fashions, but also have his own judgment. He is expected to behave properly wherever he is. He should show respect for other people, even the poor and uneducated. He should be tolerant, tactful, polite, controlled and calm. His social life should be limited to the elite. He should be rather well-off materially. It is important that his home is furnished in 'good' style and with 'good' taste. On holidays he is expected to travel much, if possible abroad. He is allowed to have some interesting, exclusive hobby.

An important element of this ethos is the absolute requirement of higher education for the children and care for their multi-sided development (private lessons in languages, music, etc.). Marriages are limited to the milieu of persons with similar education and social position. Women are, as a rule, occupationally active.

The lack of sufficient evidence prevents a closer description of the differences between the ethoses of the so-called technical and humanistic intelligentsia. But we can distinguish the ethos of the creative intelligentsia as possessing certain peculiar traits, disclosed by research (Tyszka, 1971; Hoser, 1970; Dyoniziak, 1969; Kowalewski, 1962; *et al.*).

The ethos of intellectuals

The creative intelligentsia is a fairly broad category. It seems, however, that the peculiar ethos presented below is held mainly by those artists and scientists who are creative in the literal sense, i.e. oriented in their activity towards artistic or cognitive values. Both Wallis, in his work about the artists (painters, sculptors), and Siciński, in his book about writers, emphasize that members of the teams working for the mass media, or individuals meeting the requirements of mass culture or of political propaganda, do not belong to these creative circles in the strict sense. Their professional roles and their ethos are quite different. Among scientists, the group of those employed in applied research institutes linked to the various branches of the economy and administration stands definitely apart, as their choice of research problems, the scope and timing of research programmes, etc., are controlled by institutional norms, while the cognitive orientation of employees finds little outlet. E. Pelka-Pelińska reports:

> The interviewed scientific workers, whatever their field of science or technology, declare that their activity in the institute should serve the efficiency of economic endeavours, that this aim should govern all types of research, and that the basic, cognition-oriented research must not be pursued in their institutes, unless they have some other justification, such as providing the background for further development effort, or enabling some people to obtain scientific degrees (Pelka-Pelińska, 1973, pp. 134–5).

The same author found out that employees of applied research institutes 'treat their own activity in an institute as a professional activity, i.e., as they put it, requiring appropriate qualifications and bringing them income which is their basic source of support' (1973, p. 135). Apparently, their kind of work and professional identification brings them closer to the position of an expert, who belongs, according to a quoted classification of Szczepański, to a different subcategory of the intelligentsia.

The ethos of a creative intellectual is certainly strongly anti-bourgeois, both in his attitude towards his professional and social function and in his recommended style of life, moral values, etc. A creative person ought to be somewhat alienated, his position and career not very stable; he is sensitive, or even over-sensitive. (Intellectuals and artists tend to be rather touchy, Wallis believes, because of their strong feelings of insecurity brought about by the special character of their work: they are exposed to criticism or – even worse – to neglect; styles and methods in art quickly become obsolete; they live in a close milieu, rife with envy, fears and unfair competition.) Intellectuals cherish the ideal of equal chances and opportunities for everybody, but they are against absolute egalitarianism (e.g. concerning income).

The study of artists by Wallis brings much information about their ethos which, apparently, may be generalized for other creative milieux. For an artist or academic, his work and its products are among the highest values of the civilization; he feels he is heir and continuator of his great predecessors. Creation is a unique process; neither a machine nor another person can be substituted for a creative personality. It is those permanent features of creation which perhaps underlie the essential continuity of the ethos of intellectuals and artists. Comparing the pre-war and post-war milieux of writers, Siciński found out that

> in spite of the great social, political and economic changes in our country, in spite of the phenomenon of 'mass culture' and its growing significance during this period, in spite of the essential shift of the main problem of the development of national culture (from *integration* to *propagation* of culture) – both the social composition of the professional organization of writers and the problems of its members turned out to be conspicuously similar in both periods (even, contrary to expectations, their social background has changed but little) (Siciński, 1971, p. 124).

Moreover, the

> professional problems of a contemporary writer of fine literature – related to the 'mass culture' in ways which are by no means simple or harmonious – often resemble more the problems of a pre-war writer than those of a contemporary expert in the visual arts who can find his place in the mass culture much more smoothly (p. 129).

Generalizing the results of Wallis, we might say that this ethos is permeated by three great myths: the myth of creative freedom; the myth of the handicapped profession; the myth of the great career. Artists tend to form their views and aspirations with reference to extreme situations of the most eminent individuals. One of the most highly appraised values, in spite of its obvious conflict with the ideology of the political and economic programme of the socialist society, is creative freedom, the right to experiment and to express freely one's individuality. Siciński also emphasizes that writers care most vividly about attempts to limit the freedom of creation, to interfere with literature and to treat it as a tool for propaganda. But apart from their emphasis on autonomy, artists often become 'slaves of the opinions of their own professional circle. This is a natural consequence of their ingrained mistrust against "profane" opinions' (Wallis, 1964, p. 135). Critics, too, are counted among the profane crowd and their competence and ethical attitudes tend to be discredited. According to Wallis, the artists gain social independence for the most part by living in big cities and by 'voluntary alienation from as many social links as possible' (p. 135).

The ethos of a creative individual commands him to be true to his impulses against all setbacks. At the same time, however – as is emphasized by Wallis – paid assignments which demand partial or complete subordination to the requirements of the employer are something so common that it is impossible to observe strictly the uncompromising attitude. The awareness of this fact is equally common. A respectable artist simply does not include his hack works in his creative output. But an artist who does nothing but hack work falls into disrepute.

According to Wallis,

> The artists [and there are grounds to believe that the other creative professionals, too] feel their profession to be handicapped not only in economic, but also in social and moral terms. In particular, they feel bitterly about the discrepancy between the posthumous fame of many artists and their own loneliness during lifetime, and between the value of their works and the little use that is made of them anyway (1964, p. 137).

The myth of a great career is associated with the hope for posthumous fame, as well as with the hope for immediate popularity and respect, welfare, national and international success.

The studied ethos obliges a creative individual to be a true patriot. His patriotism can be manifested in at least two ways: first, by producing eminent works, bringing worldwide fame to his country and multiplying its cultural assets, and second, by the impact of his art on the consciousness of his compatriots and on the nature of social relationships which are thereby elevated to a more sublime level. This is what Wallis writes about the contemporary patriotic mission of the visual arts:

> Since the visual arts have given up their political and national didactic bent in favour of the mass media, wall posters and monumental sculpture, they have automatically ceased to take direct part in the political struggle. The national merits of the works of painting and sculpture have shifted to their artistic and moral functions. At the same time, an end has been put to the model of an artist who used to associate his endeavour with the national or social-and-political mission (1964, p. 140).

Here are some of the more earthbound aspects of the ethos of an artist and intellectual: by his social contacts he is tied predominantly to persons belonging to the creative milieux. Social entertainment is one of his chief forms of leisure (it often involves discussions, inaugurating evenings of exhibitions, or similar events which are, of course, of some significance to the creative process itself). The other activities which are welcome include tourism in its rather exclusive forms, as well as theatre, concerts and elitist sports (for example, skiing). A creative individual is not expected to pursue a hobby, to listen to the radio or watch television. Furthermore, he should not be too much absorbed by family life. (Wallis, 1964; Siciński, 1971; Pelka-Pelińska, 1973; Szczepański, 1962.)

The ethos of the young generation of the intelligentsia

For a young highbrow, it is obvious and natural that he has the right to choose freely his occupation, his job, his manner of dressing and types of leisure activities, his style of life, as well as the person with whom he would form a permanent or temporary link. He thinks of himself as an adult, but in practice he frequently refuses to bear the consequences of adulthood since he accepts financial support from his parents.

His school career commonly follows the typical pattern of a liberal high school, and then university studies. His own decision is in principle limited to the choice of the type of studies, with the necessity of entering an academic institution usually being taken for granted.

His outlook is by no means coherent and unambiguous; he draws freely from such sources as religion, philosophy, ideology. He is suspicious of all institutional forms of belief. He is irritated by the Polish cult of history and the national past; he is interested mainly in the present and – to some extent – in the future. But he is not indifferent to the cause of the fatherland as a superior, symbolic whole, and he is ready, if necessary, to make the highest sacrifice for it. He is reluctant to take part in what is called 'social labour' (organized unpaid effort in favour of the community or factory, which has clear political significance). He does not aspire to play any significant political role, or to win influence on the course of social affairs under the present socio-political conditions. He supports political liberalism and he has a negative attitude to the limitations of freedom and human rights. He despises hypocrisy, routine and ideological opportunism.

He disapproves of narrow specialization, but appreciates versatile knowledge and abilities allowing one to contribute in a creative and original way to the nation's cultural heritage by artistic, scientific or intellectual achievements (mainly in order to leave something permanent behind). He is impressed by humanistic education, even if for practical reasons, or because of the type of his own abilities, he chooses some technical line.

He lays stress on the training and expression of his own personality and on the development of his individual, unique image. He attaches great importance to the definition of his 'place' in society and in the world and to the feeling of being useful, important, original and so forth.

He is sensitive, capable of friendship and romantic love, but he would manifest it to the deserving few only, while he keeps these qualities well hidden from adults and persons outside his circle. His pattern of reference, and at the same time his social territory to which he devotes the maximum amount of his care and effort, is *the narrow circle of trusted friends*. His satisfaction with life is largely determined by his ability to win the real friendship of this narrow circle, and in the first place by a happy family life in a marriage based on deep, mutual love and understanding. His life must not be dull and common; it should be far from petty bourgeois stability and offer him satisfaction, as well as manifold and rich experiences, but mainly of the private, individualistic type. He does not relate his role in life or his aspirations to the broader social process (Nowak, 1965, 1974; Kiciński and Kurczewski, 1975; Trawińska, 1965; Dyoniziak, 1965a, 1965b; Olszewska-Dyoniziak, 1965; Weber, 1971; *et al.*).

The above analyses reveal the essential difficulties that are raised by attempts at reconstructing a group ethos. Some of them result from the limitations of the materials available for analysis, others from the complex character of the studied phenomena and their dynamics.[1]

The outlined types of ethos often refer to secondary or superficial features, while essential ones are left out of account. The blame is to be put on the selection of problems covered by the available studies. Another possible charge is that the analyses of the various types of group ethos fail almost entirely to deal with their underlying social and cultural traditions. They fail to elucidate which of the studied aspects of ethos are manifestations of continuity and which ones reflect change. This is certainly a very important problem, requiring separate extensive elaboration. Another important matter, also left out of account, is the comparison of the particular elements of the discussed types of ethos with the available data on the actual behaviour of members of the respective groups. It cannot be doubted that some of the ethos traits are ideals, recognized but hardly realized in practice, while others can be rather commonly found among the actual behaviours of people (without, of course, losing their normative character).

Still another warning against an oversimplified reading of the above considerations seems to be appropriate. The concept of ethos suggests that we are dealing with stable groups in which positions are socially inherited. But in contemporary Polish society, with its great social mobility, we certainly observe the continuous feeding of particular groups with newcomers (this phenomenon assumes the most massive scale in the case of the migration of young people from the countryside to the urban working class). There have been studies dealing with the cross-influences between the ethoses of the background and arrival groups, involving the abandoning of some personality models and acceptance of new ones – but this problem, too, would require a separate extensive elucidation.

Does the presented material suggest that the concept of ethos can be really useful in studies of a contemporary society? Apparently it does. In spite of much mobility and the dynamic changes of such a society, there are definite cultural milieux in it which have their unique character. However – due to the flexible and changing nature of those groups – the concept of ethos seen as an elite, exclusive and rigid phenomenon is no longer fully adequate and must therefore be updated.

The contemporary types of ethos in Poland are essentially different from those stemming from social conditions in which

> Social identification was easy not only owing to the widespread knowledge of genealogies within a caste community, but . . . owing to the ease of communication by means of the code of behaviour, demeanour, acquaintances, and even language, e.g. the idiosyncratic parlour dialect. The content of a style of life consisted in peculiar behaviour, props and cultural patterns – intelligible and semantically clear only to those initiated by careful socialization. They were derivatives of definite choices of the supreme values and of the subtly evaluating ethos. The symbolic power of the niceties of expression demonstrated abysmal distances, supporting the aloofness of the social elites and corroborating their self-ascribed superiority – sometimes mystified, but still beyond the reach of others (Tyszka, 1971, pp. 100–1).

The contemporary types of ethos in Poland are much more dynamic and they are based on aspirations to the change ethos of each group by its social advancement. Education is expected to be an instrument allowing for a transition from the reach of the ethos of the lower strata to the hierarchically higher circles; it also allows for the modifications of each group ethos. However, the availability of education is still not fully egalitarian and, in spite of the large social mobility from one generation to the next, the access to an ethos continues to be inherited due to differential socialization in various cultural and social strata. It seems that the ethos of the intelligentsia essentially differs from the other ethoses in that it does not insist on its own advancement either in the cultural structure of society, since the intelligentsia is its peak, or in the political structure, as it is governed by very different rules from those peculiar to this ethos. It may be as a result of this that the most conspicuous characteristic of the young generation is its perfectionist attitude, limited to the realm of individual values, oriented at the shaping of one's own personality and individuality and the realization of one's own unique opportunities and abilities by means of social affiliation restricted to the small universe of trusted friends and family. It is only by cultivating its refinement in the spiritual domain and by closing up its sphere of affiliations that this group can retain its endangered exclusivity and its traditionally high position in Polish society.

Poll surveys are certainly a rather limited source of knowledge about group ethos. The concept of ethos can by no means be reduced simply to the sum of attitudes of particular members of a studied group; additional methods should be developed to apprehend cultural orientation of *groups* rather than individuals.

But apart from those significant methodological difficulties, the above analyses allow us to see ethos as an important but often underestimated factor which shapes effectively the attitudes and social position of people. In the contemporary, changing society, it is most probably apt to be a *dynamic and flexible ethos, shaped in some measure under the influence of the mass media, without clear boundaries, not supported by symbolic ceremonies or rituals, but still, in some degree, institutionalized.*

The concept of a group ethos is closely associated with another sociological concept, namely with subculture. The difference between the two concepts consists mainly in the fact that the ethos simply comprises the characteristic traits of the ethics and style of life of a definite group or stratum, while the features covered by the concept of subculture are conceived as relative to the features of some broader, general culture. It is only against such a general background that it makes sense at all to study phenomena defined in terms of a subculture. Another distinction between the two concepts seems to consist in the fact that the ethos is essentially *normative*, while the subculture covers, besides the values, recommended patterns and norms, also the mechanisms of their transfer, the system of human communication, behaviour of people, the material environment as developed by them, etc. Other aspects of the relationship between these two concepts will be discussed later.

It was probably because of the above mentioned relativization of the concept of subculture to the higher-order system of culture that the most attractive subcultures for study have turned out to be those whose normative content was defined as most remote from the standards promoted by 'society at large'. In practice, a frequent criterion by which subcultures are distinguished is the fact that a certain group has adopted norms incompatible with, or at least labelled as deviating from, the 'common' social norms.

Sociological interpretations of subcultures can be classified as essentially belonging to two – complementary – theoretical trends: they are either interaction analyses or structural-functional explanations. The former trend assumes that people who have more frequent mutual contacts, either because of their objective social situation (geographical proximity; similarity of status; common problems, etc.), or because of its subjective definition, develop certain common features, or norms, as well as cultural mechanisms, so that, as a result, the group gradually becomes unique in some respects and thus markedly different from other groups and from broader society (cf., for example, Hollingshead, 1939; Wallace, 1965; Irwin, 1970; Sutherland, 1937). Such subculture is transmitted through the processes of learning and socialization. The reinterpretation of this conception in the light of symbolic interactionism brought some modifications in the perception of deviant subculture. They were supposed to constitute the outcome of a series of individual and collective adjustments to the stereotypes imposed upon them.

The structural-functional approach assumes that subcultures represent a response to certain problems of individuals or of social groups (categories) who unite in a common search for the most convenient solutions to those problems by the means available to them (A. Cohen, 1955, 1970; Cloward and Ohlin, 1960). The solution has been later increasingly interpreted in ideological rather than purely practical terms. It is clear, for example, in Phil Cohen's analysis of the working-class youth subculture in England. According to him: 'The latent function of subculture is this – to express and resolve, albeit "magically", the contradictions which remain hidden or unresolved in the parent culture' (P. Cohen, 1972).

The ideological interpretation of the subculture brings this concept closer to the above characterized concepts of ethos. It may, thus, be useful to draw some distinction between them.

Ethos covers general aspirations and various kinds of normative responses to the structural position of the group, its history, its tradition, its perceived fate or unique mission. In order to grasp the relevant dimensions of an ethos and its dynamics one has to analyse in a historical perspective the following aspects:

(1) objective position of the social class (or other group) in question (its relationship to the organization of the economy of the given society, its relationship to the political organization, its human rights, its access to adequate information, the political, ethnic, religious or other factors which may divide or integrate it, and so forth);

(2) class consciousness (the collective perception and evaluation of the structural position), and, finally,

(3) symbolic and normative arrangements, strategies, codes, aspirations and censures developed most probably in response to the pressures, contradictions, limitations, opportunities and promises presented by the structural situation and collectively digested, reinterpreted, neutralized or exaggerated in a form of class consciousness.

This final outcome (the third of the above aspects) may be treated as a proper ethos, but its understanding is impossible without a penetrating insight into the whole dialectical process, the elements of which are mentioned above.

The somewhat abstract notion of ethos may be translated on the lower level of abstraction into the variety of *subcultures* which develop within the scope of a particular ethos but in interaction with and under the influence of other ethoses and their collisions. The concept of subculture applies to the concrete cases of cultural responses to the symbolic requirements of the ethos as well as to the conditions and contradictions which generate and sustain it. The analysis and description of the culture may concentrate much more on the details than those of the ethos. One can predict the occurrence of some, more or less homogeneous, behavioural patterns, customs, symbols, rituals, meanings ascribed to material objects, etc., within the territory of one subculture. However, the elaborate ethnographic as well as phenomenological studies have to be conducted within the larger framework of the network of class ethoses as well as the historically grasped economic and political relationships which shape them, being at the same time weakened, modified or consolidated by them.

The current studies on subcultures often refer to the more or less taken for granted existence of the dominant culture which frames, programmes, neutralizes or provokes specific forms of subcultural adjustments, resistance or counter-reactions. It has often been identified as the historically formed culture (or cultures) of the dominant class(es), the ruling elite ideology with all its cultural implications, the middle-class mediocre creed and so forth. It seems, however, that such a general concept cannot be very helpful in the attempts to explain better the complex reality of ethoses and subcultures of any concrete society. At least, it does not apply in any meaningful way to the case analysed in this chapter, namely, Polish society.

Focusing attention again on that society, we may postulate that there is some sort of 'core' culture moulded through the centuries by the structural factors, historical events (constant struggle for independence and national integrity), by the unique, historically conditioned mission of art, creativity or individual genius in the processes of existence, resistence and struggles of that society, by the intelligentsia in their traditional leading role, by the popular religious devotion, etc.

We may also speak about the current overwhelming presence of the ruling party doctrine, façade ideology, propaganda vocabulary and self-perpetuating fiction. But these have never been able to evolve into a culture genuinely shared and cultivated by any group of people, nor have these ever been treated by any group as a natural source of values, principles or standards. Therefore, it can hardly be seen as a 'dominant culture'. More convincing in this context, perhaps, would be a concept of 'dominant lack of culture' as the ruling elite seems to aim at the destruction of any authentic cultural unity as well as any cultural potential of the nation. Naturally, its centralized administration is able to produce a glossy substitute for culture divorced from reality and from what is perceived as reality by all the members of society (including the 'rulers'). There is much truth in the statement that

> the essence of the system prevailing here lies not so much in its cruelty, as the liberal stereotype would have it, not in its exploitation as the leftist stereotype would wish it, not in the extermination of national and religious values, as the rightist stereotype proclaims. Its essence is a lie which permeates every sphere of our life. . . . According to those who rule the country, an ideal culture should present itself as one huge, monolithic facade, adorned by a multitude of all kinds of embellishments, giving an overwhelming impression of wealth and strength – but containing nothing behind its front (Barańczak, 1977).

The official anti-culture stand is fully understandable if we believe that a genuine cultural development would have to correspond somehow with the 'objective' reality – the overall infrastructure of the society and its external relationships (a belief fully consistent with the theoretical assumptions on which the doctrine itself is based). Naturally, such a development could be very discouraging and, indeed, threatening to the managers of the repressive system. In such a context it would be rather misleading to talk about the counter-culture in Poland, because there is no culture to oppose in the first place. One can, however, argue that there exists the underground stream of culture which expresses opposition to the official hostility against culture as such. It reflects the existing objective relationships of that society as well as the opposition against them, it lets off the otherwise constrained political imagination and defends the nation's historical tradition and cultural heritage.

Thus, any serious attempt to investigate ethoses and cultures in present-day Poland has to include in the analysis the variety of barriers to any cultural responses bearing some real relationship to the economic and political reality as well as to any symbolic links with the past or imaginary projections of the future. It has also to take into consideration the 'dominant' stream of the subterranean culture.

Once again one becomes aware of the inapplicability of the Western sociological concepts in diverse political contexts. Modern sociology has to accommodate the fact that the majority of the world's population is not ruled by the cultural 'hegemony' of the dominating classes but, rather, by cultural repression and by steady attempts at the cultural sterilization of the subordinated masses. The lack of interest of many marxists (and indeed of Marx himself) in the complex domain of culture has led to the exclusion of one of the essential social practices of any society from most of the radically-oriented analyses.

Only culture (i.e. the real culture – that which corresponds to the objective reality of human existence) can give the self-confidence, the strength of resistance and the drive towards liberation to those subjected to the repression, exploitation, misinformation, etc. The existence of real culture is the necessary condition for the development of social consciousness and for formation of any organized movement. When the destruction of culture is being successfully carried out, the integrity of individuals is easily broken. They have to rely ever more on their own perceptions and judgments while their vision is drastically restricted by the limits of their particular social placement, as well as by the barriers to the free flow of information. At the same time, the soundness of their judgment and senses is constantly called into question by the pressures of the massive propaganda and constant confrontation with the 'façade' reality.

Note

1 It should be remembered that most of the data refer to the late 1960s and early 1970s and are thus somewhat obsolete. This is due to the prolonged periods of their processing (due mainly to the extremely limited access to data-processing equipment) and by the delay in publication, amounting to about five years from the research to the publication of its results.

Bibliography

Adamski, W. (1974), 'Postawy spoleczno – zawodowe mlodzieży pracujacej' ('Social Attitudes of Working Youth'), *Studia Socjologiczne*, no. 53.

Barańczak, S. (1977), 'Poland's Unofficial Crusade: Publish and be Free', *The Times*, 23 December.

Chałasiński, J. (1958), *Przeszlość i Przyszlość Inteligencji Polskiej (The Past and the Future of the Polish Intelligentsia)*, Warsaw: L.S.W.

Chałasiński, J. (1964), *Mlode Pokolenie Wsi Polski Ludowej (The Young Generation of Poland)*, Warsaw: Ludowa Spóldzielnia Wydawnicza.

Cloward, R. A., and Ohlin, L. E. (1960), *Delinquency and Opportunity*, Chicago: The Free Press.

Cohen, A. (1955), *Delinquent Boys*, Chicago: The Free Press.

Cohen, A. (1970), 'A General Theory of Subculture', in D. O. Arnold (ed.), *Subcultures*, Berkeley, Calif.: Glendessary Press.

Cohen, P. (1972), 'Sub-Cultural Conflict and Working Class Community', *Working Papers in Cultural Studies*, no. 2, spring, CCCS, University of Birmingham.

Dobrowolska, D. (1967), 'Z zagadnień kultury robotniczej' ('Problems of the Working Class Culture'), *Studia Socjologiczne*, no. 26.

Dyoniziak, R. (1965a), *Mlodzież Epoki Przemian (The Youth of Changing Times)*, Warsaw: Nasza Ksiegarnia.

Dyoniziak, R. (1965b), *Mlodzieżowa Podkultura (Youth Subculture)*, Warsaw: Wiedza Powszechna.

Dyoniziak, R. (1969), *Zróżnicowanie Kulturowe Spoleczności Wielkomiejskiej (Cultural Differentiation of the City)*, Warsaw: PWE.

Galdzicki, Z. (1967), *Pracownicy Przedsiebiorstwa Elektronicznego (The Employees of the Electronic Industry)*, Wroclaw: Ossolineum.

Gluck, L. and Kwaśniewski, J. (1974), 'Postawy Pracowników Bankowych' (I, II7 ('The Attitudes of Bank Employees'), *Bank i Kredyt* nos. 8 and 9.

Goban-Klas, T. (1971), *Mlodzi Robotnicy Nowej Huty jako odbiorcy i wspóltórcy kultury (Young Workers of Nowa Huta as recipients and co-creators of culture)*, Wroclaw: Ossolineum.

Grzelak, A. (1965), 'Kadra Urzędnicza FM na tle innych grup zawodowych' ('Clerical Staff in FM in Comparison with Other Groups'), in M. Hirszowicz (ed.), *Czlowiek w Organizacji Przemslowej (Man in the Industrial Organization)*, Warsaw: PWN, pp. 215–42.

Hollingshead, A. (1939), 'Behaviour Systems as a Field for Research', *American Sociological Review*, vol. 4, December.

Horoszowska, B. (1961), 'Zyczenia Zawodowe Mlodzieży szkolnej', ('Vocational Aspirations of the School Children'), in *Jak Pracuje Czlowiek (How does a Man Work?)* Warsaw: Książka i Wiedza.

Hoser, J. (1970), *Zawód i Praca Inżyniera (Engineer's Profession and Work)*, Wroclaw: Ossolineum.

Irwin, J. (1970), 'Deviant Behaviour as a Subcultural Phenomenon', in D. O. Arnold (ed.), *Subcultures*, Berkeley, Calif.: Glendessary Press.

Jagiello-Łysiowa, E. (1969), *Zawód Rolnika w Swiadomości Spolecznej Dwóch Pokoleń Wsi (Farmers' Vocation in the Social Consciousness of Two Generations)*, Warsaw: Książka i Wiedza.

Janicki, J. (1968), *Urzednicy Przemyslowi w Strukturze Spolecznej Polski Ludowej (The Place of the Industrial Clerical Staff in the Social Structure of Poland)*, Warsaw: Książka i Wiedza.

Jarosińska, M. (1964), *Adaptacja Mlodzieży Wiejskiej do Klasy Robotniczej (Adaptation of the Young Rural Emigrants to the Working Class)*, Wroclaw: Ossolineum.

Jarosińska, M., and Kulpińska, J. (1971), 'Proces Gromadzenia Spolecznych Doświadczeń Zalóg Robotniczych' ('Process of Accumulation of the Social Experience by Workers'), *Studia Socjologiczne*, no. 43.

Kiciński, K., and Kurczewski, J. (1975), *Poglądy Etyczne Mlodego Pokolenia Polaków (Moral Opinions of the Young Generation in Poland)*, Warsaw: OBOP i SR.

Kloskowska, A. (1964), *Kultura Masowa (Mass Culture)*, Warsaw: PWN.

Kowalewski, Z. (1962), *Chemicy w PRL, (Chemists in Poland)*, Wroclaw: Ossolineum.

Krawczyk, M. (1967), *Z Badań nad Spoleczno - Moralną Postawą Mlodziezy Wiejskiej (Studies on the Social Attitude of the Rural Youth)*, Warsaw: PZWS.

Kulpińska, J. (1969), *Aktywność Spoleczna Pracowników Przedsiębiorstwa Przemyslowego (Social Activity of the Employees in Industry)*, Wroclaw: Ossolineum.

Kutyma, M. (1974), *Progi Zyciowego Sukcesu (Limits of Success)*, Warsaw and Wroclaw: PWN.

Łoś, M. (1972), *Aspiracje a Srodowisko (Aspirations and Environment)*, Warsaw: PWN.

Lutyńska, K. (1965), *Pozycja Spoleczna Urzędników w PRL (Social Status of the Clerks in Poland)*, Wroclaw: Ossolineum.

Makarczyk, W. (1964), *Czynniki Stabilizacji w Zawodzie Rolnika i Motywy Migracji do Miast (Determinants of Farmers' Stabilization and Motives of Migration to the City)*, Wroclaw: Ossolineum.

Malanowski, J. (1962), *Robotnicy WFM (Workers at WFM)*, Wroclaw: Ossolineum.

Malanowski, J. (1965), 'Stosunek Mlodych Robotników do Zawodu i Nauki' ('Young Workers' Attitudes Towards Work and Education'), in Dyoniziak (1965a).

Miller, R. (1964), *U Progu Mlodości (Entering Adolescence)*, Warsaw: Nasza Ksiegarnia.

Miścicki, W. (1973), *Zróżnicowanie Spoleczne a Orientacja ku Wartościom (Social Stratification and Attitudes)*, Wroclaw: Ossolineum.

Mleczko, F. W. (1964), *Z Badań nad Aktywnością Zawodową i Spoleczną Chlopów (Studies on Social and Vocational Activity of Peasants)*, Wroclaw: Ossolineum.

Mrozek, W. (1965), *Rodzina Górnicza (Miner's Family)*, Katowice: Wydlawnictwo Sląskie.

Niezgoda, M. (1975), *Spoleczne Determinanty Wyboru Zawodu (Social Determinants of the Vocational Choice)*, Wroclaw: Ossolineum.

Nowak, S. (1965), *Studenci Warszawy (Warsaw Students)*, Warsaw: Ministerstwo Szkolnictwa Wyższego.

Nowak, S. (1974), *Ciaglość i Zmiana w Tradycji Kulturowej (Continuity and Change in Cultural Tradition)*, Warsaw: Universytet Warszawski, Instytut Socjologii.

Nowakowa, I. (1973), *Robotnicy w Uprzemyslawiajacym sie Mieście (Workers in the Town under Industrialization)*, Warsaw: Książka i Wiedza.

Olszewska-Dyoniziak, B. (1965), 'Epoka Wspólczesna w Ocenach Mlodziezy Licealnej' ('Contemporary Times in the Opinions of Youth'), in Dyoniziak (1965a).

Ossowska, M. (1956), *Moralność Mieszczańska (Bourgeois Morality)*, Lódź: Ossolineum.

Ossowska, M. (1969), *Socjologia Moralności (Sociology of Morals)*, Warsaw: PWN (English Edition: *Social Determinants of Moral Ideas*, Routledge & Kegan Paul and University of Pennsylvania, 1971).

Ossowska, M. (1973), *Ethos Rycerski i jego Odmiany (Knights' Ethos and its Changes)*, Warsaw: PWN.

Pawelczyńska, A. (1966), *Dynamika Przemian Kulturowych na Wsi (Cultural Change in the Rural Areas)*, Warsaw: PWN.

Pelka-Pelińska, E. (1973), *Pracownicy Naukowi Instytutów Badawczych (Employees of the Research Institutes)*, Warsaw: PWN.

Podgórecki, A. (1976), 'Concept of Morals', paper presented at the conference devoted to the work of Professor M. Ossowska, Polish Sociological Association, Warsaw.

Podgórecki, A., Kurczewski, J., Kwaśniewski, J., and Łoś, M. (1971), *Poglady Spoleczeństwa Polskiego na Moralność, i Prawo (Polish Public Opinion on Morality and Law)*, Warsaw: Książka i Wiedza.

Pomian, G. (1965), 'Problemy Kwalifikacji Robotników w Zakladzie Przemyslowym' ('Problems of Workers' Training in Industrial Enterprise'), in M. Hirszowicz (ed.), *Czlowiek w Organizacji Przemyslowej (Man in the Industrial Organization)*, Warsaw: PWN, pp. 79–106.

Sarapata, A. (1965a) *Przemiany Spoleczne w PL (Social Changes in Poland)*, Warsaw: PWN.

Sarapata, A. (1965b), *Studia nad Uwarstwieniem i Ruchliwością Spoleczną w Polsce (Studies on Stratification and Social Mobility in Poland)*, Warsaw: PWN.

Sarapata, A. (1975), 'Z Badań nad Hierarchia Prestiżu Zajeć w Polsce' ('Studies on the Hierarchy of Prestige in Poland'), *Studia Socjologiczne*, no. 56.

Siciński, A. (1971), *Literaci Polscy (Polish Writers)*, Wroclaw: Ossolineum.

Sutherland, E. H. (1937), *The Professional Thief*, University of Chicago Press.

Sutherland, E., and Cressey, D. (1960), *Principles of Criminology*, New York: Lippincott.

Szczepański, J. (1962), 'Mitologizacja Intelektualistów' ('Myth of Intellectuals'), *Studia Socjologiczne*, no. 6.

Szczepański, J. (1965), 'Zmiany w Structurze Klasowej Spoleczeństwa Polskiego' ('Changes in the Class Structure in Poland'), in Sarapata (1965a).

Szczepański, J. (1974), *Narodziny Socjalistycznej Klasy Robotniczej (Birth of the Socialist Working Class)*, Warsaw: Instytut Wydawniczy CRZZ.

Szymański, M. J. (1973), *Środowiskowe Uwarunkowania Selekcji Szkolnej (Social Determinants of Dropping Out from School)*, Warsaw: PWN.

Tobera, P. (1972), *Zróżnicowanie Spoleczne Pracowników Przemyslu (Social Differentiation of the Industrial Employees)*, Warsaw: PWN.

Trawińska, M. (1965), 'Aspiracje i Zyczenia Zawodowe Mlodzieży Szkól Srednich' ('Aspirations and Vocational Choices Among the High School Youth'), in Dyoniziak (1965a).

Tulski, J. (1965), 'Aspiracje i Wzory Zawodowe Mlodych Robotników' ('Vocational Aspirations of the Young Workers'), in Hirszowicz (ed.), *Czlowiek w Organizacji Przemyslowej (Man in the Industrial Organization)*, Warsaw: PWN, pp. 137–69.

Tyszka, A. (1971), *Uczestnictwo w Kulturze (Cultural Participation)*, Warsaw: PWN.

Waclawek, J. (1974), 'Z Problematyki Grup Spolecznych w Zakladzie Przemyslowym' ('Social Groups in Industrial Enterprise'), in Szczepański (1974).

Wallace, S. E. (1965), *Skid Row as a Way of Life*, New York: Harper.

Wallis, A. (1964), *Artyści-Plastycy (Artists)*, Warsaw: PWN.

Weber, B. (1965), *Nad Pamiętnikami Mlodzieży Wiejskiej (Studying Memoirs of the Rural Youth)*, Warsaw: Iskry.

Weber, B. (1971), *Mlodzież a Wspólczesne Wzory Wychowawcze (Youth and Contemporary Educational Patterns)*, Warsaw: ZMW.

Wiatr, J. (1965), 'Inteligencja w PL' ('Intelligentsia in Poland'), in Sarapata (1965a).

Zebik-Koralewicz, J. (1974), *System Wartości a Struktura Spoleczna (Value Systems and Social Structure)*, Wroclaw: Ossolineum.

17 National ethos
Adam Podgórecki

Essential features

It is possible to analyse not only the ethos of various segments of the given society, but it is also interesting to attempt to present a synthetic picture of the ethos of the whole society. In the context of this book the ethos of the Polish society may be regarded as a 'natural' example.

In investigating and analysing problems relating to the ethos of a society or nation, at least three approaches are possible. The phenomenologically-essayistic approach attempts to penetrate deeply into the so-called spirit of a nation or society; by specific insights it aims to reveal its characteristic features and essence. This kind of approach is usually the most attractive but, by its very nature, may produce – by jumping onto the wrong track – a false picture. The method most often used in analysing the national character of a society is the *historical method*.[1] This method consists of collecting various facts and historical data which are subsequently used for generalizations derived from this material. One suspects, though, that the methodological procedure for preparing this type of historical generalizations is basically mis-leading: *a priori* accepted political opinions, ideological values, and subjective factors generate a certain – usually unexplicated – disposition, according to which historical data and facts are later collected as convenient illustrations.

But another approach is also possible. *Anthropological and sociological methods provide* – at the present stage of the development of the social sciences – more reliable empirical data on the basis of which one may attempt to construct an initial global synthesis of the given society or nation. The latter approach has the advantage over the others of being based on data collected in a systematical and inductive way. However, it does have a certain weakness – generalizations based on these data often far exceed

236

their legitimate scope. The following reconstruction of the ethos of Poles is not free from this limitation.

There are already several studies dealing with the basic attitudes of the Polish population. For example, we can mention research into the moral and legal attitudes of society; also five national surveys carried out between 1962 and 1970 (Podgórecki, 1964; Podgórecki, 1966; Podgórecki, Kurczewski, Kwaśniewski and Łoś, 1971) into the ethics of young people (Kiciński and Kurczewski, 1975). It is worthwhile to remember that the above mentioned studies took into consideration representative samples of the whole society and were systematically repeated during more than one decade (1952-75). Although they were directed towards the same research targets, they still dealt with one (crucial) aspect of the whole spectrum of attitudes characteristic of Polish society. This pertains to the above mentioned limitation for the following generalizations. All this research allows us to suggest the following classification of attitudes:[2] (1) 'declared' and 'accepted' attitudes, and (2) meta-attitudes. Declared and accepted attitudes are brought together in one group, above all, because these attitudes are usually manifested externally, more or less openly, in accordance with the content of the values to which they relate. Meta-attitudes, on the other hand, are attitudes of higher order. They exist outside 'ordinary', 'everyday' attitudes and they structure the latter into the syndromes and systems which together constitute a complex whole. Declared attitudes should be understood as those attitudes which are manifested as signs to inform others what opinion one holds concerning a given situation. 'Declared' attitudes are generally those attitudes which are instilled into individuals as the result of various educational measures, socialization processes, idealistic appeals, etc. Nevertheless, declared attitudes are not always identical with 'accepted' attitudes. Various historical situations have taught the members of Polish society to find numerous ways of concealing any possible divergence of declared and accepted attitudes. Accepted attitudes are not always those which are declared externally, and they do not always constitute the basis of actual behaviour. They are often 'suspended' under pressure of some kind of *ad hoc* need or intensive pressures. Limiting ourselves, for the moment, to the attempt to characterize (on the basis of existing research) the declared and accepted attitudes of Polish society, we can distinguish at least three basic categories: acceptance of ascribed status, severity (especially rigour in relation to others); and 'trans-individual individualism'. This heuristic and subsidiary classification is regarded as a step to a further elaboration of essential attitudinal features of Polish society.

Acceptance of ascribed status is the attitude connected with the acceptance of ascribed, rather than achieved, social position. As was said, from the historical point of view, the life style and values of gentry culture have dominated the Poles' mentality. Belonging or not belonging to the gentry-landowning circle of culture (despite a more intensive mobility in Poland than in other European countries) was decisive for the whole disposition and fundamental life goals of the majority of Poles. In the course of historical change, the status ascribed to the world of the gentry became transformed into that ascribed to the world of the intelligentsia. Again, however, it should be remembered that the ethos of the Polish intelligentsia was clearly formed in the shape of the norms of the previously dominant gentry ethos. As several recent studies, not described here, indicate, the prestige accorded to various occupations in Poland was until recently linked with the social structure formed along traditional principles. But it could be easily documented that recently we were able to see the emergence of prestige according to various occupations, based not on traditional principles but on the principle of individual achievement. The distance which an individual traverses between his starting-point and what he achieves is becoming important; thus new social strata are creating their own criteria of success.

In relation to moral norms and attitudes towards the law, Polish society is *rigorous* (Jasiński, 1973). This rigour is manifest, above all, in relation to others (this seems to be a characteristic of human nature in general). This rigour does not remain, however, only at the level of the expression. Research shows that the sanctions of the Polish legal system are applied in social life in a manner matching these general attitudes. This tendency towards social punitiveness can be explained in a number of ways. One may suppose that it is the expression of a certain kind of ambivalence regarding the law. On the one hand, it may express respect for the law (this is linked to the demand for its widespread application); on the other, it may reflect the fact that the law is not adequately applied and followed, (consequently there are demands for the curbing of the law through the utilization of its own sanctions). One may also suppose that social punitiveness constitutes the expression of certain elements of accumulated social frustration. (It should be noted for comparison, that Finnish society - precisely on the basis of historical frustrations similar to the Polish ones - also demands, and applies, the sanctions of criminal law on a large scale.) This problem is nevertheless an extremely complex one. All in all, one may state that when social rigour produces its expected results, then it may constitute a basis for the extension of respect for the law. In general, legal rigour seems to be more socially functional when the law is to a greater degree just and fair on the basis of accepted social values.

By *trans-individual individualism* we mean the tendency for individuals to expound their 'egos' to the external boundaries of elementary primary groups. The attitude which appears here is a specific, extended individualism. Quite precise studies indicate that at the forefront of the values respected by the contemporary Polish population is the welfare of their own children and marital success (quite often understood as mutual defence union). Acceptance by others and one's good health are also highly placed (Kocowski, 1975). The situations in which the children in Polish families are coming to be treated as idols symbolizing the closeness of the small group are characterized by the kind of emotional humanism specific to the world of values confined within the framework of narrow communities. In situations of uncertainty related to external threat, this internal asylum is treated as both a heterotelic and an autotelic value: autotelic because of the rewards which it directly provides, and heterotelic because of the possibility of cutting oneself off from disturbing external events.

It is well known that the Polish ethos is characterized by *individualism* in its everyday, organizational and imaginative versions, as well as by a tendency to cultivate friendship ties. Yet it is not always recognized that the focus towards friendship in Poland is an expression of the tendency to associate with equal individuals. Associating with someone on the basis of choice, of making one's own decisions – often marked by *Bruderschaft* – is itself a manifestation of *sui generis* - elitism. This equality holds for those in the same status category, although not automatically. A voluntary act of internal acceptance is necessary if the potential informal possibilities are to be transformed into more concrete, if still informal, ties. These mutual ties constitute the unusually strong and vital fabric of the inner life of Polish society. In this context, it should be noted that only scant attempts were made to link problems of social structure with social values. On the basis of research carried out in 1969, J. Koralewicz-Zębik states that a basic uniformity in the hierarchies of values held by various socio-occupational categories has appeared; they are quite similar in the case of four general values investigated: (1) education, (2) income, (3) cultural consumption, (4) managerial position. Also the hierarchy of specific values displays a far-reaching similarity (Koralewicz-Zębik, 1974, pp. 242, 245). Before approaching the kernel of these considerations it should be noted that unfortunately most of the survey studies are only able to grasp the attitudes of these types. As we noted above, declared and accepted attitudes should be distinguished from meta-attitudes.

Three basic kinds of meta-attitudes can be identified: fiddling attitudes oriented towards survival; instrumental attitudes; and attitudes of 'spectacular principledness' as characteristic for the Polish ethos. These meta-attitudes do not find direct expression in behaviour. They influence, however, other attitudes. Attitudes of this kind operate as hidden factors which exist outside the sphere of perceived opinions and values and which determine how the latter are manifested externally. (Meta-attitudes thus can be defined as a kind of disposition towards a stable reaction in any socially defined way which does not manifest itself externally, but structures from inside externally expressed motivations. Meta-attitudes are hidden and petrified attitudes. The definition and description of specific attitudes which can be observed externally may sometimes lead to false conclusions, just as such symptoms as rapid breathing, rapid pulse rate and heavy perspiration may signify either joy or fear. When a given syndrome of attitudes which manifest themselves externally appears to be relatively stable, we can assume that behind these manifested attitudes lies some kind of deeper attitude which has formed the socially visible attitudes into a coherent unity.)

The most important of these attitudes is *the fiddling attitude of survival*. This meta-attitude, which constantly intervenes in the individual and collective life of the Poles, is incredibly flexible. It aims to accumulate material possessions in order to have security (either psychological or material) in the face of the fluctuations of uncertain events. The attitude of survival in the particular versions worked out by the Poles has an autotelic attitude (value for itself). Even the tendency to acquire relationships (that enlarges the association of equals) is teleologically subordinated to ensuring conditions for survival. Envy is not 'envy for its own sake' but a negative regulator generated by the attitude of survival which in an anticipatory way peeps into and undermines the skills and strategies of others, in order not to give them the possibility of threatening one's own options.[3]

By *spectacular principledness* we mean the attitude which not only approves a given norm or value for its own sake, irrespectively of the circumstances, but which also celebrates certain norms or values because they are considered sacred and symbolically significant. The clear tendency of the Poles is to accord particular respect to everything connected with the fatherland, political independence, the suffering of the nation throughout its history (martyrology), their organic scepticism regarding everyday systematic work, the apotheosis of such historical events as the 'defence of Vienna', the Polish participation in 'the air battle of England', or the 'charge at Samosierra', the tendency to be the Messiah of 'the world of the spirit', and also the celebration of even

240

the least important minor social, religious and state holidays and so forth. Ordinary, common-sense, everyday principledness is alien to this attitude. There are data which suggest that the attitude of spectacular principledness has been maintained in Polish society through traditional attachment to religion. Data from 1964 show that about 86 per cent of the urban and 90.01 per cent of the rural population define themselves as believers (Podgórecki, 1966, pp. 197-204). Subsequent research carried out in 1966 (both studies based on a representative sample of the adult population) shows that 72.5 per cent of the urban and 82.8 per cent of the rural population claim to be believers. On the other hand, research carried out in 1971 dealing with what might be called the middle-level intelligentsia (young people undergoing occupational training in institutions of further education, teachers and local government employees - a total of 1,115 people) shows that 64.8 per cent of those investigated defined themselves as believers. Women claim a religious world view more often than men do; a lower level of education is more frequently associated with declared religious faith; rural more often than urban respondents define themselves as religious; this is also true of older people. This kind of residue of religious belief may support attitudes of spectacular principledness. It may also constitute the basis for the approval of status traditionally ascribed by the previously existing social structure. Thus, religious attitude may constitute a kind of link between the attitude of spectacular principledness and the traditional attitude of acceptance of ascribed status.

In order to present more adequately the essential features of the attitude of spectacular principledness, it should be noticed that in Polish society the value of gesture is more important than the value of relevant behaviour which is supposed to solve the given task. To be more specific – in this culture, an attempt to do something which has the form of a spectacular gesture, a form which undertakes in an impressive way the given problem, is valued higher than a pragmatic, logistic, practical or economic solution of it. In this culture, the social position of a given person is not determined by its real potential (qualifications or possibilities), but is established by the social show which a given person delivers when approaching the problem. Symbolic values certainly overtake real ones. Informal evaluations are more significant than the tangible, socially and officially recognized effects of the acts and tasks in question. Legends and myths become the most crucial factors. The subjective aura of an intended social action and the capacity to transmit it into a social performance visible for the relevant audience seems to be more important than the consequences of the actual action.

Another meta-attitude common among Poles is *instrumentality*.

Just as the principled attitude accepts or rejects certain norms for their own sake, the instrumental attitude is selective and calculating. On the basis of the subjective calculation of profit and loss it accepts those norms which appear to be convenient for the attainment of desired goals and rejects all others. It would be a fundamental mistake to think that this attitude – as a rule – is socially destructive. It may form the basis for carrying out various tasks going beyond one's individual interest. Research shows that the present younger generation in Poland is characterized by this attitude to a greater extent than the previous generation. Of course, we can discern various kinds of instrumental attitudes: in the sphere of financial activities, in sex life, in personal relationships, in political options, in institutional arrangements, etc. These different kinds of instrumental attitudes may appear isolated from each other in certain patterns, or they may constitute a whole instrumental personality.

It is easy to notice that instrumental attitude may be regarded as a *sui generis* consequence of the fiddling-survival attitude. It should also be recorded that this attitude is contradictory to all those attitudes which stress the principled approach to interhuman relationships. So, although instrumentality, in this way, has some roots in the Polish national character (even if fiddling was directed mainly against governance imposed by foreign powers which occupied Poland through more than 100 years – it certainly is a calculative, teleological live perspective; even if spectacular principledness stresses mainly the attachment to sacred public norms – it nevertheless gives a certain type of suspense in the cases of the real, everyday breach of the law), nothing else but 'socialism' carried on instrumental attitudes to their full flowering. The fight of contradictory hierarchies of values, the constant tendency to suppress the traditional attachments to institutions and organizations generated by the Polish society through its history, the everyday lessons of inefficiency based on the departure from norms otherwise regarded as healthy and valid, the erosion of the trust among close friends, even among the members of the family, the distribution of rewards for political flexibility caused by changeable ideological programmes – all these elements introduce, wave after wave, the new floods of instrumental attitudes.

The essence of the matter

It might be said that one of the underlying assumptions of the analysis of the Polish ethos is the general thesis that the main, proper and not hypostatic subject of sociological inquiry is – the society taken as a whole. If this indeed is the case, then the question

242

immediately arises: what is the content and scope of society which should be taken as a whole? The proposed answer: the type of society which is able to generate common meta-attitudes.

Although research on the Polish social structure is scattered and fragmentary, it shows clearly that this structure is going through fundamental changes. These transformations consist, on the one hand, of the tendency towards a flattening of this society's social structure through an increase in its homogeneity (the decomposition of the classes and strata of the pre-'socialist' social structure), and, on the other hand, of the emergence of new, unplanned heterogeneous strata based on the secondary distribution of incomes which are derived from additional sources of income and from the instrumental use of position affording access to social rewards on the basis of privilege. These kinds of processes give rise not only to planned social recomposition, in accordance with the ideological measures undertaken to implement the principle of egalitarianism, but also to a recomposition which is contrary to the expectations of the planners. Apart from the distinction between functional (consistent with expectations) and dysfunctional (giving rise to unexpected, negative side-effects) recomposition, we should also distinguish between spontaneous recomposition processes and those which are directed. One of the crucial problems concerning social structure which has not been sufficiently investigated is the distance between 'functional' and 'dysfunctional' changes and the extent to which processes of social structure have so far ignored the question of psycho-social pathology, particularly institutional pathology – namely the special type of social schizophrenia.

Yet somewhat paradoxically, the two-fold dualism of the processes taking place in the heart of the existing social structure has its equivalent in the life style of the present-day Poles (*sui generis* social schizophrenia which is, by the way, kept 'under control' by the most excessive vodka-alcoholism in the world). Nevertheless this 'schizophrenic' ethos of Polish society is strengthened by the ambivalence which is created on the one hand by the respect for authority which comes from pragmatic and practical sources (if a given government does possess full legal and factual power, one would be well advised to comply with its regulations) and on the other hand from intuitive and informal factors (in Polish society the so-called informed public – the intelligentsia – plays an especially important social role). These latter factors constantly check and reinterpret all regulations issued by the government – informal opinions comment on all essential public issues. A member of Polish society is – according to this pattern – all the time under an official pressure of, and under the control of an invisible force which, in sum, give him contradictory guidance. It is not difficult to see that these two sets of factors (official and informal) do not always support each other. This being so, those who possess the power – among other things – are not eager to reveal that the basis of their very existence is not always supported by the public. And this is precisely why those who occupy official positions curtail studies which dig into this area. As a result, blank spots emerge. In consequence a synthetic picture of the society is *a priori* crippled. The historical experience of Polish society and the systematic and pragmatic lessons of 'socialist' construction (and destruction) have created a complex situation in relation to the system of socially disclosed attitudes. On the one hand, we can observe the intensity of patriotic slogans, the acceptance (to what extent is it real?) of socialism, traditional legal and moral attitudes satiated with a substantial dose of punitiveness; on the other we have the formation of certain meta-attitudes which are difficult to discern by the traditional research methods. As has been stated earlier, these meta-attitudes, which constitute the basic axes structuring the attitudes which are manifested externally, can be reduced to three basic ones: the fiddling attitude of survival, instrumentality and spectacular principledness. These attitudes emerge as crucial factors which not only delimit the scope and the hierarchy of actual and motivational social values, but, moreover, as an active cluster influence directly the composition of the macro-structure of Polish society.

The assertion that the ethos of the Poles, formed by their own tradition and the specific characteristics of this nation, constitutes an outcome of its past history, would be merely banal if it were not for the fact that the modern structure and stratification of Polish society seems to be the result of these historically-created characteristics, to some extent maintained and finally drastically changed by the force of imposition of 'socialist' – personality patterns. These patterns influence – are present at least – the essential elements of social stratification. To be more concrete and support the thesis presented above with historic and economic perspective: the specific sort of underdevelopment of Polish society (historical lack of a developed middle class) shifted the accents of social development towards the ethos of higher social classes, thus giving them almost direct access to the process of designing basic patterns of life for the 'lower social strata'. Consequently, it is possible to say that in the historical composition of the structure of Polish society, the economic motivation did not have enough momentum for its full development. This, in effect, created a situation in which patterns of social behaviour became more influential than external conditions. If these generalizations are correct, then Polish society gives an illustration for a case which contradicts the most vital marxist theses; it presents a situation in which the 'superstructure' is more influential than its own 'base'. Without any doubt this is sociologically a very interesting case and as such deserves quite scrupulous consideration.

Anyway, the explanatory potential of the idea presented above seems – in the case of Polish society – still not to be exhausted. So, the very concept of the socio-political structure of this society may be apparently elucidated better through the shift (and its effects) of instrumentally-oriented members of this society towards positions of power, than the existing economic differentiations. Again, the visible inefficiency of social and legal institutions may be explained more by the concept of trans-individual 'individualism' (with the phenomenon of 'dirty togetherness' as its consequence), than by the lack of proper 'socialization' of the new intelligentsia or its backward social origin. Also the informal but inefficient use of the vast sector of public property and administration is probably more strongly supported by the attitudes of fiddling-survival than by the questionable rationality of the central management. For fiddling-survival attitudes seem to be more responsible for the 'miraculous' transformation of the existing institutions and organizations into a 'hidden second life system' which lies behind them (developed private arrangements – how to use the capacities of the official system). When official institutions and organizations give shelter to 'second life activities' – then practically all have vested interests to keep the formal system going.

In general one may say that Polish society has a tendency to generate a special type of attitude which seems to be in accordance with the general conditions of this society, and that these attitudes, when generated, work for their own unity, the protection or identity of its members and defence or adjustment towards the spreading social schizophrenia. Apparently, on the grounds of repeated historical, collective experiences, these attitudes have been singled out and selected as the most appropriate to the general situation of social life in Poland. Another problem is to what extent these more or less unconscious selection processes have been misguided.

In consequence, meta-attitudes such as fiddling-survival, instrumentalism and spectacular principledness strive for specific and unique historical conditions of the life of Polish society. Although these attitudes seem to operate quite efficiently and smoothly – as a result, several invisible, internal conflicts may constantly grow. It is not necessary to repeat that the emergence of these attitudes is connected with rapid and extreme changes in social and economic conditions which characterize Polish society not only recently but also in the past: partitions of the country, changes of political and social systems, losses of the population, migrations, etc. Growing instrumentalism of attitudes (especially among the younger generations) seems to be connected directly with the modernization of present-day life (changes in technical environment; rapidly increasing expectations on the one hand and, on the other, the scarcity of attractive and possible social actions; constant shifts in the basic social and economic conditions which determine perspectives of success or social adjustment; general rationalization of individual and social decision-making processes, and the inability to implement them, etc.). Thus, trans-individual individualism seems to be in accordance with the peculiar ambivalence of a Pole; he is quite ready to retreat into the shell which is constantly waiting for him (his family and a cluster of friends) – and he is always ready to sacrifice himself for the fatherland or engage himself in actions which are guided by the spirit of social service. The same goes for spectacular principledness. Those attitudes may be regarded as a response to the historical and social conditions of the country.

Notes

1   This method is in this particular case important since Polish society, historically speaking, shaped its main 'life styles' on the basis of social patterns generated by the medieval Polish gentry.
2   Compare the more developed classification in Chapter 12: 'The Concept of Meta-Attitudes'.
3   Perhaps an anecdote will be a better indication of the meaning of the meta-attitude oriented towards survival. An American millionaire of Polish origin once told this writer how he had achieved his remarkable success. He was the owner of several helicopter factories and he maintained that his helicopters were better than any others because they were tested by Polish pilots. The latter, equipped with this incredible drive for survival, were psychologically able to withstand tests and individual strain which other nationalities were not able to withstand. Thus, in his opinion, this national characteristic which he had used in evaluating the technical potential of his products in connection with American technology had built his impressive success and wealth.

Bibliography

Chałasiński, J. (1946), *Społeczna genealogia inteligencji polskiej (Social Genealogy of the Polish Intelligentsia)*, Warsaw: Polski Instytut Socjologiezny.
Jasiński, J. (1973), 'Punitywność systemów prawnych' (Punitiveness of Legal Systems')' *Studia Prawnicze (Legal Studies)*, no. 35.

Kiciński, K., and Kurczewski, J. (1975), 'Postawy młodego pokolenia wobec wartości społeczynych i indywidualnych' ('Younger Generations' Attitudes Towards Individual and Social Values'), unpublished manuscript.

Kocowski, T. (1975), 'Potrzeby a wartości' ('Needs and Values'), *Odra*, no. 3, 1977.

Koralewicz-Zębik, J. (1974), *System wartości a struktura społeczna (System of Values and Social Structure)*, Wroclaw: Ossolineum.

Podgórecki, A. (1964), *Zjawiska prawne w opinii publicznej (Public opinion on legal phenomena)*, Warsaw: Wydawnictwo prawowe.

Podgórecki, A. (1966), *Prestiz Prawa (Prestige of the Law)*, Warsaw, Książka i Wiedza.

Podgórecki, A., Kurczewski, J., Kwaśniewski, J. and Łoś, M. (1971), *Poglądy społeczeństwa polskiego na moralność i prawo (Views of Polish Society on Morality and Law)*, Warsaw: Książka i Wiedza.

18 Restrictive and anarchic deviance
Maria Łoś

The sociological definitions of deviance, as well as the numerous theories concerning its causes, show great variety. Quite often, however, they simply emphasize different aspects of the same phenomena without denying the existence, or even importance of other aspects. The basis for competition between various theories is rather vague, as they rarely demarcate clearly the boundaries of the phenomena they claim to explain adequately.

More traditional approaches to crime and deviance usually utilize legal definitions of the field and concentrate on the causes and factors conducive to the behaviour defined as criminal or illegal in general (in other words, the behaviour indicated by the norms of civil and administrative law besides those of the penal law). The supporters of the human rights perspective argue that criminology should focus on the violation of these basic, 'obvious' rights and needs of individuals. The sociologists of deviance who focus on the so-called labelling processes, which study the inter-personal and intrapersonal interactions as the main aspect of the processes leading to deviance or amplifying it. The marxist inter-pretations vary considerably. In one version, law and crime are analysed as resulting from the economic relationships of the society. In another version, law and crime contribute to the existence and persistence of the economic structure and facilitate exploitation. According to still another interpretation, crime is not a proper subject of the marxist theory, as it does not bear any direct relation to the phenomena encompassed by the marxist 'problematic'.

It may be noted that the contemporary literature on crime and deviance rarely refers to the fault or malevolence of the offenders, focusing instead on the external and internal factors and forces pushing them towards such behaviour (whatever its definition).

The nature of those factors has been described differently by various authors. They have been portrayed as connected with the biological constitution of the offenders, with various kinds of deprivation (for example, of maternal love), with rapid social change (for example, disorganization theory, cultural lag theory), with some features of the social structure (for example, anomy theory, differential opportunities theory), with subcultural pressures and differential associations, with the impact of mass media, with the stigmatization and general punitiveness of social control, as well as with the privileged and uncontrolled social position ('crimes of the powerful') and so forth.

The consequences of deviant behaviour are seen in terms of the damage and danger to individuals and society, in terms of its functionality for social integration, in terms of its functionality for the existing economic structure and political domination, or in terms of its progressive and liberating potential.

Apart from the concern with the causes and consequences of deviant behaviour, there is also the problem of the nature of the behaviour which is defined as deviant. One may suggest that the 'healthy' behaviour (act) is one which is chosen among several possibilities and undertaken with the free will and awareness of the broader consequences and the responsibilities involved. Therefore the behaviour which does not meet these criteria may be treated, at least in extreme cases, as deviant. Such behaviour is alienated from the actor and does not express his potentialities as an individual, and as a member of a social whole. The relationship between the individual and the social control is, in this context, of crucial importance. Deviant behaviour may be seen as related to the inadequate nature of this relationship. And, indeed, the situations which have been specified by many authors as the main causes of deviance are usually viewed as significant departures from the necessary minimum of social control, leading to situations of 'over-control' or 'under-control'. Of course, the notion of the necessary minimum of social control is not a very precise one, and - as in the case of many other sociological concepts - its meaning can be grasped only with reference to the subjective perspective ('humanistic coefficient') as well as with reference to the socio-political structure and the level of its legitimacy. The belief that man, as a social being, has to accept some rules securing a basic order and a peaceful coexistence within a group is rather generally shared by contemporary people. The perceived scope of those necessary rules varies greatly and must always be related to the opinions of particular individuals, groups or communities, as well as to the 'objective' conditions of the given society. The roots of this widespread conviction, that some level of social control is needed, have been quite well characterized in the works of phenomenologists.

> We would contend here that both perspectives - the liberation myth of the 'left' and the nostalgia of the 'right' for an intact world - fail to do justice to the anthropological and indeed the ethical dimensions of the problem. It seems clear to us that the unrestrained enthusiasm for total liberation of the self from the 'repression' of institutions fails to take account of certain fundamental requirements of man, notably those of order - that institutional order of society without which both collectivities and individuals must descend into dehumanising chaos (Berger, Berger and Kellner, 1974, pp. 87–8).

One can distinguish two basic types of departure from the perceived 'necessary minimum' of social control: the considerable intensity of social control and its acute deficiency. The situations of the first type may be called *restrictive deviant situations* and those of the second type *anarchic deviant situations*. These two types of deviant situations are often closely intermingled in the sense that liberal social control over some groups or individuals tends to be related to oppressive control over others. The permissiveness of the social control may strengthen the position of the group subjected to it and reinforce its ability to control the others. It may be further argued that the intensification of social control over some groups automatically creates more possibilities of infringements and conflicts, justifying in a sense subsequent increases of the scope and punitiveness of the control measures.

Restrictive deviant situations occur where a person, group, society or social category is deprived (subjectively or objectively) of the possibilities of any meaningful choice, or where these possibilities are extremely limited. Their behaviour is not autonomous, but determined to a considerable degree by such factors as:

(1) domination of force (on a macro-social level, for instance, Fascism, terror, Mafia; or on an individual scale, for instance, physical pressure or violence, blackmail and so forth);

(2) fully one-sided indoctrination or ideological manipulation (brain-washing, techniques of operant conditioning and so forth);

(3) economic pressure and discrimination;

(4) pressure of public opinion which deprives an individual or a group of the possibilities of controlling their private lives (for instance, in the case of homosexuals);

(5) pressure of institutionalized factors of social control (for example, the justice system) based often on the deterministic

forecast and imputation of deviant or criminal roles;
(6) addictions which considerably hinder the possibility of controlling one's life (for example, alcoholism, drug-addiction, gambling);
(7) inborn or acquired features of appearance, state of health, intellectual development and so forth, which drastically limit the choices of action, the scope of participation in social life and the level of attainable achievements (the social definition of these features has often a much more restrictive character than the features themselves).

It seems, in fact, that the criminologists and sociologists of deviance refer usually to one or more of the above situations when they attempt to locate the main factors conducive to deviance. Due to their clear link with deviance those situations are often considered by the criminologists as deviant themselves. Given the fact that they are often analysed much more thoroughly than the vague category of deviance or deviant behaviour, one has an impression that these very situations and mechanisms, rather than the deviant behaviour, constitute the proper subject-matter of the deviance theory. If this is the case, one can speak about the deviant behaviour only in conjunction with these deviant background forces. It may then be useful to distinguish several types of the most obvious deviant situations:

Reactive deviant situations occur when social reaction transforms authentic, consciously chosen behaviour into forced and defensive behaviour, deprived of its original sense; or when social reaction enforces, provokes and generalizes, through punishment and stereotyped expectations, behaviour which was accidental, desperate or meant to be performed only once. Hence, the resulting behaviour is unauthentic in the sense that an individual or a group were deprived of choice and determined by their environment (labelling theory):

Economic deviant situations occur when economic pressure and/or specific economic relationships restrict the possibilities of choice to such an extent that the behaviour of the individuals or groups is practically determined by them (economic deviant situations have been studied by the functionalists exploring the poverty subculture or lower-class criminality, as well as by Engels, Bonger and others):

Political deviant situations occur when individuals, groups or whole societies are totally deprived of any political participation and access to information on the political processes (theories of alienation, of totalitarian control, as well as of political crime or collective protests):

Cognitive deviant situations occur when the behaviour cannot be consciously chosen because one's socialization or indoctrination has completely programmed one's actions and one's perception of choice (this type of deviant situation has been accounted for in the differential association theory, behavioural theory, the marxist conception of the false consciousness and so forth).

All the above types of deviant situations belong to a more general category of restrictive deviant situations. The anarchic deviant situations constitute a polar opposite to them.

Anarchic deviant situations occur when individuals or groups achieve (subjectively or objectively) a much greater liberty than their neighbours in choosing their actions or their relationships with others. 'Anomia of success' analysed by Durkheim and Merton, offensive nationalism, criminality of the powerful are but a few examples of the deviant situations of this type. The somewhat obsolete theory of social disorganization also referred to an anarchic situation of the widespread breakdown of social control under certain social and economic conditions. Moreover, the notion of charisma can be useful in characterizing some types of anarchic deviant situations. Often great liberty granted to an individual by his social environment is due to the assumption that he possesses some special, nearly 'super-human' qualities. Similarly, restricting the liberty of others is often linked to the attribution of a 'subhuman' character to them (Katz, 1972; Znaniecki, 1974).

The anarchic situations may be external and independent of the will of the individuals or groups concerned, but they may also be created or simulated by them. They may, for instance, reject the restrictions of the stable world and attempt to realize the ideals of freedom, spontaneousness and self-determination. They may try to achieve it through a broader social movement or charismatic leadership, but often their attempts are much more esoteric and confined to the isolated communities or other enclaves of anarchy (for example, the ideology of hippies). In still other cases, limited control over some individuals, groups or organizations results from their place in the legal or illegal power structure and their ability to inhibit or manipulate the controlling mechanism (the Watergate affair, crimes of the powerful, Mafia and organized crime in general, may serve as selected examples of such a situation).

In sum, the anarchic deviant situations are characterized by considerable scope of uncontrolled possibilities, by the attribution of omnipotence, supernatural powers or charisma, or by privileged access to political power and economic resources.

Dynamic relationship between restrictive and anarchic deviant situations

The basic dimensions of the above distinction between restrictive and anarchic deviant situations are related predominantly to inequality of access to the power, information and economic resources, inequality in the scope and nature of subordination to social control and inequality in personal abilities and socially defined qualities. The analytically defined situations of anarchy and restrictiveness are not occurring in the real life separately; they seem to be interlinked in various ways in different social contexts. Especially interesting for the sociologists may be the peculiar type of situations characterized by the extreme intensity of both restrictive and anarchic aspects at the same time. It appears even more interesting if one appreciates the fact that both restrictiveness and anarchy are prone to escalate. Several examples may illustrate this tendency.

The conventional crime is very often caused by situations of a restrictive nature. The most common reaction to it is punishment, isolation, restrictions of choice of behaviour, stigmatization, imputation of a criminal role and so forth. All these factors may mean further aggravation of restrictiveness; they are also quite likely to amplify criminal or deviant behaviour, thus provoking intensification of the restrictive reaction. However, these dynamic processes lead often to the simultaneous creation of artificial spheres of anarchy and liberty of choice by the persons or groups involved. The extreme example of such a development can be found in the penal institutions, where one witnesses massive accumulation of deprivation and restrictiveness preceding the conviction and following it. On the other hand, however, in such closed total institutions some substitutes for social opportunities and power are usually constructed, and some self-appointed individuals or groups tend to monopolize them. They are likely to terrorize and exploit the others, and to succeed in developing – effective even if magical or purely symbolic – ways of exercising their authority and enforcing the inequality. In the situation where real, socially shared, possibilities of choice and promotion are practically absent, the 'privileged' groups create a world of fictitious opportunities, relationships, social distances and degradation rituals, in order to lift themselves to the top of this artificial hierarchy of 'underdogs' (see Łoś and Anderson, 1976).

One can assume that the more restrictive the general situation of a given group, the more desperate and vigorous the efforts to create symbolically certain zones of anarchy within it (for instance, escapism into the world of fantasy, invention of powerful myths,

253

special esoteric use of language or encouragement of violence and disorder). If such efforts are subsequently met by new forms of restrictiveness (e.g. some forms of punishment are administered) they may be further intensified. The accumulation of restrictiveness is thus likely to produce escalation of anarchy, even if it is camouflaged, or hidden, within the 'underdog' world.

It seems that the increase of the role of language constitutes one of the common by-products of the restrictive group situations. Both restrictive and anarchic uses of language tend to be enhanced under the restrictive conditions. Special phraseology, esoteric codes of communication, magic meanings ascribed to some words or phrases, may produce the appearance of might and superiority. Language is thus utilized as a mainly defensive measure, and it serves as a medium by which some people are symbolically subordinated to the others in a generally restrictive social context. Certainly, those who happen to be subordinated can also divide themselves into subgroups, which would be able to generate their own schemes of communication and domination according to the same general rule. A man suspected of a crime, for instance, is confronted with the justice system which uses its own specific language, not fully intelligible to him. The representatives of that system communicate with each other, interpret his motives, pronounce a decision and so forth in a language which is quite foreign to his world of meanings. They immediately gain some superiority over him because within that system their language, and not his, is really valid. If he is later confined in an institution he would find himself in a community which is sharply divided according to certain verbal criteria. It has been established by Polish inquiries into the prison and correctional subcultures, that there exists a clear-cut division of the inmates into two basic groups, one of which has a full monopoly over the special prison argot, magic rituals and courses, definitions of meanings, flow of information and so on (see Łoś and Anderson, 1976). If our inmate is symbolically degraded to the lower-class status, and he receives an appropriate derogatory label, he is exposed to enormous pressure of cumulative restrictiveness and deprivation of any meaningful interactions and communication with others. If he is qualified as a member of the higher inmate class, the restrictiveness of the prison situation is partially balanced by the anarchic subculture. However, negation of the restrictions coming from outside leads usually to some peculiar forms of auto-restrictiveness among inmates (submission to the rigid codes of behaviour and language, rituals and so on). The pressures resulting from this kind of restrictiveness are at least partially neutralized when they are transformed into a very acute form of coercion and repression of those who are defined as being inferior on the ladder. Similarly, the psychiatric inmates, or indeed the subjects of the totalitarian states, faced with purposeful language barriers between them and the staff (or the rulers) develop some defence mechanisms of this type.

It seems that most of the communities or societies which are exposed to a very restrictive control (for example, societies under occupation or communities experiencing extreme poverty) develop some kind of 'second life', directed symbolically against the overwhelming restrictiveness. This 'second life' is prone to create within its limits some new spheres of restriction and anarchy located according to some strict rules and secured by special use of language. One can also assume that the more acute and painful the restrictive situation of a given group or society, the more severe and wayward are the restrictions and repression directed against its selected, 'inferior' subsection. Such a subgroup may be accused by the rest of the oppressed of being weak or too conciliatory, of being likely to inform or even to commit treason, or, perhaps, of being too aggressive and provocative and so forth. In fact, they are often selected as scapegoats or failures simply because their lowered status may help others to maintain their self-esteem and sense of dignity.

It is worth noting that when the spheres of restrictiveness are relatively isolated from each other, hierarchically arranged and reinforced by some symbolic measures, it is actually very difficult for the subjects of the restrictive control to grasp the hidden mechanisms of the manipulated accumulation of restrictiveness. They are prone to perceive only the most immediate sources and forms of restrictions. The inmates oppressed by their peers may easily confine all their hatred and fear within the limits of the common 'underdog' subculture. On the other hand, however, when the general, political or economic situation of a society or a group is not legitimized and is perceived as basically oppressive, the above assumption may not be confirmed. In such circumstances the anonymous and external political system would be blamed for all restrictive situations and constraints occurring within its borders (even on the informal, interpersonal level). This tendency would probably persist even if the system spends much of its energy attempting to reinterpret officially various restrictive situations and reactions to them, in terms of personal failures or anarchy. Such verbal manipulation, however, may have some impact upon those groups and individuals who are officially expected to administer some restrictive measures to the others. They are likely to accept the theory that those restrictions are directed against groups or individuals who are particularly unruly and anarchic. This is facilitated by the fact that anarchy constitutes a frequent by-product of the defensive reaction against restrictiveness.

The exploration into the processes of accumulation of the restrictive aspects of social situations and anarchic reactions against them, accompanied by the downward transmission of restrictiveness, may help us to understand better many aspects of modern societies. Various bureaucratic organizations, for example, can be analysed in terms of the ongoing processes of imposition and transmission of restrictions and development of spheres of anarchy, varying greatly according to the position within the hierarchical structure. Naturally, it necessitates a careful analysis of the inequalities within such a structure, and in its relationships with the broader social context. The organization of the police force, for example, may be described as a very restrictive environment for its members in terms of the peculiar indoctrination and training, as well as the authoritarian rule of formal obedience to superiors. On the other hand, it is also a very anarchic situation indeed, since it gives the policemen considerable power of discretion in relation to those who are subjected to their control and services. The members of the police force tend, in fact, to develop a peculiar ideology which allows them to see themselves as servants appointed by society, socially indispensable and benevolent, yet at the same time justify their often very repressive and domineering behaviour towards others.

Modern life in the cities is also full of those contradictory, restrictive and anarchic pressures and situations. It frees people from some forms of traditional, restrictive control, offers more diverse opportunities and patterns of behaviour and so forth. Yet at the same time it restricts them by numerous regulations, pressures of technology and of the mass media, density of population, unification and commercialization of consumption and so on. Certainly, along with the replacement of the old inequalities by the new ones, appropriate changes in the restrictive and anarchic aspects of social control may be expected to follow. These problems are well reflected in the situation of the young generation in modern societies. These young people are granted verbally a very privileged status and considerable freedom, but in reality they are separated from the rest of society and denied any meaningful participation in the social life, as well as any concrete role to perform. Therefore, their feeling of having a special mission to fulfil - which is generally encouraged by the society - is, in reality, confronted with a somewhat minimalistic requirement to adjust to the existing restrictions, and to take advantage of the anarchic options.

The above conceptions of the restrictive and anarchic aspects of

256

social organization and control covers, in fact, a variety of factors and mechanisms which have already been mentioned in different theoretical contexts as conducive to deviance. It seems to help to group them into two distinctive categories, which make it possible to see more clearly their interplay and mutual relationships on various levels of the social system and its contradictions. It also shifts our attention from the deviant behaviour to the contradictions and inequalities of the social context within which all kinds of behaviour acquire certain social meanings.

Bibliography

Berger, P. L., Berger, B., and Kellner, H. (1974), *The Homeless Mind*, Harmondsworth: Penguin.

Katz, J. (1972), 'Deviance, Charisma, and Rule-Defined Behaviour', *Social Problems*, vol. 20, no. 2, fall.

Loś, M., and Anderson, P. (1976), 'The "Second Life": a Cross-Cultural View of Peer Subcultures in Correctional Institutions in Poland and the United States', *Polish Sociological Bulletin*, no. 4.

Znaniecki, F.(1974), Ludzie Teraźniejsi a Cywilizacja Przyszłości (Contemporary People and Future Civilisation), Warsaw: PWN.

19 Dehumanization
Adam Podgórecki

The social relations prevailing among chimpanzees very often recall human behaviour. Perhaps more often than we would like to admit.

Jane van Lawick Goodall

Traditional positivistic sociology avoids certain themes, regarding them as taboo. Among such – until recently – was a whole group of problems of evaluation. For it has been considered that certain spheres of the world of values lie beyond the scientifically legitimized circle constituted by the description and the explanation. But, since it was impossible to ignore completely questions of evaluation, it was postulated – by this sociological approach – as a direct methodological requirement to disclose them openly – wherever it could be done. But even then ethics remained outside the scope of sociological interest.

Nor has traditional sociology occupied itself extensively with fields conventionally belonging to criminology or social pathology. Although the subject-matter of social disorganization and anomie has been one of the central theoretical axes of some sociological analyses and although such questions as conformism, rebellion, withdrawal, counter-culture, etc., have been quite extensively considered, still, they did not affect too much the basic questions, namely, the ones of the analysis of description and evaluation.

On the whole the question of assessment and values has been treated by traditional sociology – if dealt with at all – as the sphere of possible dependent variables. It has hence investigated which social, psycho-social, personality factors shape given attitudes, convictions or evaluations. Whereas the problem of to what degree values or systems of values constitute independent causes in relation to various social phenomena has been, in general, underestimated in traditional sociology. This situation generated one of the most important – although mainly of an ideological character – arguments of the heavy criticism which is presently directed against positivistic sociology. The same reason contributes to the present popularity of marxism.

258

The above explains at least to some degree why the theme of dehumanization has not been tackled by the social sciences in a proper scientific manner. To add to the confusion, the concept 'dehumanization' is closely associated with other, similar concepts: deindividualization, depersonalization, alienation, violence, even terrorism and cruelty, etc. Without at present going into a more detailed semantic analysis, let us denote dehumanization preliminarily as the situation in which an individual, group or society is denied traditionally acknowledged human attributes. Such an understanding of dehumanization points out (at least indirectly) another concept systematically omitted by sociology – the notion of mankind.

Dehumanization has been treated as a convenient instrumental rationalization of cruelty of various types. We may accept A. Mitscherlich's definition of cruelty which deliberately effects someone's suffering and thus satisfies the actor's own needs (Mitscherlich, 1973). Illustrating his definition the author points out that genocide has often not been the result of spontaneous action. He thus writes:

> Premeditation of this kind belongs to the well established tradition of paranoiac systems. In the case of Himmler it was a matter of ridding humanity of cunning sub-humans (dehumanised human beings). Himmler thus declared: 'The majority of you have experienced what is felt when a hundred human corpses lie in a heap, or five hundred, or a thousand. To go through that – except for cases of breakdown and human weakness – and remain honest makes us hard. This is a glorious page in our history which was never written before and will never be written again' (Himmler on the occasion of the selection of group leaders at Poznan, 4 October 1943, cited by Mitscherlich, 1973, pp. 18-19.)

Cruelty thus denoted is defined in psychoanalytic terms.

> The two kinds of cruelty we would like to distinguish may be defined as: cruelty oriented to pleasure and cruelty oriented to accomplishing a task. Cruelty oriented to pleasure results from an earlier reversal of experience pertaining to the libido; cruelty oriented to task-accomplishment is aggressive, asexual, destructive.

And further:

> It is highly probable that in the process of fulfilling a task a destructive pleasure (akin to a sadistic pleasure) appears in connection with the cruelty caused. But this is an aggressive

pleasure which goes hand in hand with an assumption of superiority and – according to H. Kohut – with the experience of the 'splendid ego' (Mitscherlich, 1973, p. 21).

The above psychoanalytic analysis, although it to some extent notes the essential characteristic of the subject at issue, overlooks the exceedingly important question of the social foundation of dehumanization. Although ancient and modern history provides numerous examples of collective and individual attitudes associated with cruelty, there has been relatively little scientific research on and analysis of the question. The reluctance of investigators to occupy themselves with the traditionally neutral and cold-blooded question of various situations of human depersonalization is undoubtedly due to ethical objections of various kinds. This is why, surprisingly, the few systematic researches conducted in this sphere are worthy of closer attention.

One experiment which aimed to establish whether or not evil deeds derive from 'human nature' or are due to specific characteristics of a given social system and the special fabric of social roles, is the so-called Zimbardo Experiment (Haney, Banks and Zimbardo, 1972).

Zimbardo and his associates conducted an experiment at Stanford University in 1972 which consisted of creating a make-believe prison. The prison applied all possible theatrical accessories to lend it an air of reality. Seventy-five people responded to a newspaper advertisement. Of these twenty-two young people were selected who had previously no experience whatever of the administration of justice. This group was divided at random into two sub-groups: guards and prisoners. Those selected as the prisoners were officially arrested according to the standard police procedure, while those 'nominated' as the guards were provided with such symbols of authority as whistles and clubs. Neither guards nor prisoners received any special instructions on how to fulfil their new roles unknown to them from direct experience. But physical force was prohibited and this prohibition was one of the very few norms set as principles of the experiment. The artificial prison was to function for two weeks during which concealed microphones, hidden television cameras and other electronic equipment were to gather data on the behaviour of guards and prisoners.

It turned out that the guards and prisoners at once split themselves into two very strictly separated populations. The former, who initially carried out three ten-minute regulation roll calls a day, later changed them into elaborate affairs of several hours. Some 90 per cent of the recorded prisoners' conversations pertained to the bad prison conditions, their treatment by the guards and possible self-defence tactics. They also solicited legal aid through the chaplain and their families. Although among themselves the guards used their own names, they addressed the prisoners in an impersonal manner, generally using only their numbers. The guards, as a rule, behaved towards the prisoners in a degrading manner.

When the experiment was finished one of the simulated guards stated: 'Looking back, I am surprised how little I felt for them [the prisoners]. . . .'
And another: '. . . prisoners did not regard it as an experiment. For them the situation was real and they fought to preserve their identity. But we always knew how to show them who is the boss.' Still another guard declared: 'It is fun to have power; power may be a great pleasure.' And a prisoner declared:

> 'I realise only now (when everything is over) that, regardless of what I thought then, my behaviour at the prison got out of control. Although I had good relations with other prisoners I functioned in the prison as an isolated person preoccupied with his own affairs, rather as a rational than a co-operating individual' (Haney *et al.*, 1972, pp. 31-2).

The experiment as a whole clearly showed that the guards as well as the prisoners rushed into their assigned roles to such a degree that they almost immediately lost the feeling of the experiment's artificial character. Furthermore, the experiment, contrary to the original intention, was completed in six days instead of the planned two weeks because of the prisoners' violently growing dissatisfaction, depression, attempts to escape, etc.

Zimbardo's experiment is interesting inasmuch as it shows clearly that the situation in closed institutions such as prisons is neither the complete result of (1) the 'oppressor's mentality' or (2) of the negative selection, including auto pre-selection, or of (3) the negative prisoners' subculture. For the experiment established that the source of 'bad behaviour' is not 'bad people', but that certain specific features of institutions, certain types of social organizations, elements of their inherent structure and some internal unique processes induce decidedly negative social behaviour.

The so-called Milgram Experiment went even further. Conducted in 1960 at Yale University, the experiment basically pertained to 160 men (altogether about 1,000 were investigated) between 20 and 50 years of age, employed at various occupations. Its essence was to establish the conditions influencing the manner of carrying out the experimentor's orders by the investigated individuals. The drastic nature of the experiment consisted in the fact that punishment (only seeming punishment of persons co-operating with the experimentor for deliberate mistakes in memorizing various sentences) was to be applied in the shape of administering a number of electric shocks - from 0 to 450 volts. The subjects of the experiment, 'naïve subjects', had to resolve the following conflict: either obey the experimentor's orders and administer electric shocks up to the limit of a clear danger to the victim's health or life, or refuse to carry out the orders. It should be noted that in order to impress with the genuineness of the experiment and thus better mislead the 'naïve subject' (he who had to push the button), those receiving electric shocks of 120 volts began to cry out, with 180 volts the victims screamed that they could not stand the pain, in the case of 270 volts the response was a yell of extreme desperation, and finally with 315 volts – a violent scream followed by silence, with some uncoordinated sounds at continuing the electric shocks. (This kind of simulation was practised in the most essential version of the experiment.) When the 'naïve subjects' heard no audible reactions to the administered electric shocks, 66 per cent of them carried out the experimentor's order and gave the maximum, up to 450 volts. When they did hear the voices of the victims (played on a tape recorder), fewer, 40 per cent, gave the maximum.

The above investigation was repeated in Bridgeport, with the institution conducting the same experiment without enjoying university prestige. In this control (supplementary) investigation 48 per cent of the 'naïve subjects' applied the maximum shocks. Forty psychiatrists from one of the best medical schools were also examined. The psychiatrists anticipated (when asked how the 'naïve subjects' will behave, in accordance with their own professional knowledge) that the majority would not apply electric shocks stronger than 150 volts, that about 4 per cent would administer 300 volts and that 0.1 per cent would administer the maximum (Milgram, 1965). In Polish sample research (conducted on eighty-two students by the author of this text), 31 per cent stated that a quarter of 'naïve subjects' would apply the maximum shocks, 36 per cent considered that a half would so so, and 31 per cent were of the opinion that three-quarters of 'naïve subjects' would apply the minimum (the rest had no opinion). In consequence, one may ask rhetorically: do Polish sociology students (taking advantage of their social and political experience) have more 'common sense' than American psychiatrists? Or is this profession so corroded by its own myths and mystifying notions that its departure from everyday reason is even so far reaching?

Milgram attempted to interpret the astonishing findings of his experiment in various ways. He stated that a situation where the naïve subject does not see or hear his victims leads to different results for such situations (different from the case when someone's voice is heard, and more so when someone's presence is observed) lack elements of empathy. The cruelty of the 'naïve subjects' may also be explained, in his opinion, by the appearance of mechanisms restricting their field of cognition or also of its negation (the respondents turned their backs on their victims; they were so much absorbed in their task that they seemed not to notice their victims' behaviour, etc.). Another factor which may make people more cruel to others is the relation between them: the 'naïve subject' is not the partner of his victim, but the executor of his superior's will. He primarily identifies himself with the source of the orders he receives, i.e. the experimentor, and he tries to create a division, a gulf, between them and the victims. Where the victim is not directly visible and all the more when he cannot be heard there is a break, in Milgram's opinion, in the phenomenological unity of action. The act is severed from its consequences. Finally, the 'naïve subject' recognizes and reassures in the course of the experiment his acquired dispositions, including the disposition to aggressive behaviour. The fact that Milgram has had several troubles as a consequence of the ethical evaluation of his experiment does not belong directly to the matter of this analysis (being significant as a possible reaction of the psychiatric profession).

The above cited experiments clearly reveal that social conditions or institutional requirements (demands) may lead average, ordinary people to situations where they lose (sometimes completely) respect for others and even deliberately treat them in an object-like manner.

The importance of social dehumanizing conditioning becomes more evident if the role of other factors is considered which may have an influence on determining interpersonal relations. It thus turns out that various elemental catastrophes (caused by nature and not man-manufactured events) in times of peace do not carry any potential seeds of destruction or aggressive behaviour, but are on the contrary triggers of spontaneous co-operative behaviour.

A summary of various researches on people's reactions and behaviour in such non-war situations as floods, serious explosions, storms, for instance, leads to the following conclusions (the hypotheses cited below derive from the work of Berelson and Steiner):

The response of people to a peacetime disaster, such as a tornado or a flood or a large explosion, typically takes the following form:
(a) People who have previously experienced a disaster tend to respond appropriately to an advance warning: people who

have not had such experience tend to respond to the warning by seeking other cues that allow them, in effect, to disregard the warning. Just as there is a tendency to underplay the likelihood of the event's occurring at all, so there is a tendency to underestimate its destructiveness afterwards. Many people tend to deny or disbelieve information that danger is near at hand. They seize on any vagueness, ambiguity, or incompatibility in the warning message enabling them to interpret the situation optimistically. They search for more information that will confirm, deny, or clarify the warning message, and often they continue to interpret signs of danger as signs of familiar, normal events until it is too late to take effective precautions.

(b) There is very little panic during and immediately after the disaster.

The notion that people typically 'panic', become 'hysterical', or 'go to pieces' in the presence of danger is not supported by disaster research findings. . . . Although some cases of individual or small-group panic have occurred in disasters, its frequency and significance in disasters have been grossly exaggerated. It is a rare response rather than a typical one.

Usually there is much more traffic *to* the scene of a disaster than *from* it.

(c) An informal but effective and highly solidary social organisation arises soon after the disaster to deal with the consequences, even in isolated communities, and the leadership is more likely to come from those with most at stake in the community – heads of families, for instance, rather than single men. At this time the normal social distinctions are sharply lessened, but gradually reappear with the passage of time. Only later do conflicts arise over alleged inequities in handling the consequences.

The widespread sharing of danger, loss and deprivation produces an intimate, primary group solidarity among the survivors, which overcomes social isolation and provides a channel for intimate communication and expression and a major source of physical and emotional support and reassurance. . . . The social disorganisation that occurs in disaster is essentially a social disorganisation of secondary group life. . . . Except momentarily, it does not disorganise primary group life. On the contrary, this is strengthened, and this in turn constitutes the nucleus out of which the society can once again reconstitute itself and develop a new complexity of organisation.

(d) The first reaction is typically concern for the safety of one's family and other intimates and then for the larger community – even on the part of those with community responsibilities, who often feel caught in this cross-pressured situation. In general, there is less feeling of self-interest and more concern for the community than exists in normal times.

The net results of most disasters is a dramatic increase in social solidarity among the affected populace during the emergency and immediate postemergency periods. The sharing of a common threat to survival and the common suffering engendered by the disaster tend to produce a breakdown of social distinctions and a great outpouring of love, generosity and altruism. During the first days and weeks following a major community-wide disaster, people tend to act toward one another spontaneously, sympathetically, and sentimentally, on the basis of common human needs rather than in terms of pre-disaster differences in social and economic status.

(e) Most people experiencing a severe disaster soon suffer some kind of emotional or physical upset – nausea, diarrhoea, 'nerves', or the like – that continues to some degree for days or even weeks. But such transitory reactions do not incapacitate most of the sufferers from responding realistically to the event and its aftermath; moreover, they rarely arrive at chronic states of severe mental disturbance.

(f) The further people are from the scene of disaster, the less accurate their information about it and the less their concern for the victims.

(g) For the victims themselves, the disaster remains for years the major event in their lives (Berelson and Steiner, 1964, pp. 623–4).

Thus the brief overview of the social consequences of various catastrophes indicates that sudden and destructive occurrences coming from the outside (from the forces of 'nature') may generally be regarded as an integrative factor for the society concerned. So, it may be said that in general social bonds become rather consolidated by means of very many systematically accumulated interactions.

They may also crystallize and consolidate on the basis of some 'sporadic event'. If the sporadic event is of the character of a situation of an exceptional vitality to the existence of an entire community, to which it pertains, then the resulting physical and technical disorganization may give rise to social bonds of a new type, i.e. social ties flowing from this particular experience.

Thus, if it turns out that the quest for the sources of cruelty or aggressiveness (hence of dehumanization) in the analysis of various neutral catastrophes confronting social groups or communities is not cognitively fruitful enough, it may then be considered whether aggressiveness and cruelty are not latent in so-called 'human nature'. But then, of course, the question, 'What is human nature?' appears as a complicated one.

Leaving this perplexed question aside, let us consider the problem of dehumanization from another perspective. Various empirical data relative to the shaping of primitive societies indicate that sociology may inadequately conceive its task by limiting itself exclusively to the analysis of values and human behaviour. This is because research on different types of animals (which seem not to be 'cruel' without a biological necessity) – and especially on the higher mammals (mainly chimpanzees) – reveals far-reaching similarities between the social behaviour of humans and of these animals. These researches had the objective of presenting a synthesis of various studies devoted to aggressive behaviour in social contacts among the higher mammals in their natural habitat, in a semi-natural environment and in laboratory experiments. They lead – in consequence – to the following conclusions:

> There is one clear result of previous research on various species of mammals not belonging to the group of the highest. This result is in accord with the findings of research on the highest group of mammalian animals. It thus turns out that there is a long heritage among vertebrate animals of aggressive behaviour which is manifested when a crowd of alien individuals meet in the presence of valuable objects. There are also data regarding human behaviour in primitive society. And these data reinforce the observation of the evolution of human behaviour in cities that that tendency still persists – and is in some ways strengthened even today. The neuro-chemical, physiological and pathological aspects of the crowding together of alien individuals and their aggressive interactions are becoming the subject of research of late. In contemporary society conflicts between various groups are often very destructive and differ considerably in content. There are nevertheless certain common traits in antagonisms of that type which may be suitable to explain certain relations between society, stress and aggressive behaviour (Hamburg, 1971, p. 217).

While the proposition that human individuals (and some animals) tend to behave aggressively when they find themselves in a strange crowd, facing the problem of division of unoccupied objects may be rendered as a very interesting general and synthetic result of many studies, the proposition still does not explain sufficiently human cruelty and other phenomena associated with dehumanization. It may be assumed that various environmental or biological determinants may influence aggressive behaviour. Nevertheless, the most essential factors leading to structuralized aggression are of a strictly social character. This is because the dehumanization phenomenon appears in numerous social contexts: in labour alienation, wars and social disturbances, in anomalous situations connected with large urban and industrial agglomerations, etc. The question hence arises: which specific factor in each case leads to dehumanization?

It seems probable that dehumanization always appears mainly as the consequence of the rationalization of certain attitudes. These rationalizations flourish when a given social system leads to the situation of a breakdown of traditional elements of social control and the conflicts arising from the lag of aspired values behind the ability to attain them are resolved not by means of informal interpersonal arrangements, but are, on the contrary, worsened by antagonistic systems of ideologies. Dehumanization is hence an instrumentally useful consequence of rationalization of aggressive behaviour caused by the philosophy of specific social systems. It spontaneously serves these systems and strengthens them on the principle of the feed-back.

Dehumanization may thus assume various forms. It may, for instance, be an expression of certain traditional ideologies which regard certain categories of people as 'lower' beings (or of a lower race). That point of view may assume the form of a 'neutral' philosophy when a given society is based on elements of caste or a class system. Dehumanization may also take the shape of a certain seemingly rational ideology which uses various pseudo-factual arguments in an attempt to justify irrational principles. These principles are generally to the effect that people of certain traits constitute a lower category of human beings, or, in some extreme cases, are completely deprived of human traits.

In the modern world dehumanization at times assumes a masked form. This consists of treating individuals, groups or even entire societies purely as objects in technical or organizational activity, although they are attributed human traits on the abstract level. Paradoxical situations may arise in highly developed social systems: agencies designed to eliminate social differences and introduce elements of social justice may in practice lead to contrary results.

It is well known that the general effect of formal education in America is a humanising one. A number of researchers have shown the relation between educational level and such traits as autonomy, resilience, tolerance, feeling of identity or ability to self-expression. The schools have nevertheless been correctly accused of not having done everything to realise genuine humanism and even of activity (and encouragement) calculated to dehumanise their pupils. One-fourth of American young people are drop-outs before the 12th class. Many pupils show symptoms of mental disturbance, lapse into states of apathy, self-accusation, often open destructiveness and desperation. Our study of the process which led to that detrimental state of affairs leads to the proposition that schools where the teachers themselves lack humanist attitudes will show a higher percentage of failures by pupils (Sanford and Comstock, 1971, pp. 333-4).

The above considerations undertook a task to support the proposition that a system of assessment and values, in short a given ideology, itself the result of the functioning of given social relations, may have far-reaching social consequences and act as a specific independent variable. The concept 'dehumanization' is treated here as the result of the functioning of rationalization of various destructive attitudes. The reservoir of these rationalizations may be regarded as an accumulation of techniques of 'negative socialization'.

In sum – dehumanization appears when spontaneous aggressiveness, envy, hostility, etc., are 'enriched' by the elements of rational, planned and organized patterns of social activity.

But how – among conflicting ideologies – may one distinguish this particular one which rightly (not leading to dehumanization) selects the real humanistic values? To answer this basic question it seems advisable to trespass the limits of positivistic sociology. Therefore, it would be necessary to enter the realm of essential human values through the understanding of the concept of global ethics.

If the above analysis is correct, then the main cause of dehumanization appears to be an ideological commitment of a special type. Neither the consequences of natural disasters nor possible background of humanity seem to be comparable with the consequences of an 'idealistic viewpoint'. It is quite well known that 'idealistic' images of the world of this type are generated mainly by intellectuals.

It might be possible to assume a relationship between the choice and study of these subjects and involvement in socio-political crimes. Of the terrorists that the group had investigated as many as three-fifths of them had been students, most of them reading sociology, political science, psychology or education. A third of the fathers of terrorists active in the Federal Republic of Germany had completed their studies at university. The terrorists came for the most part from the upper or upper middle classes. In most of the cases studied, something was lacking in the home background (report from the Conference on European Crime Prevention, *The Times*, 13 April 1978).

If indeed intellectuals alienate themselves so far from those commitments of the intelligentsia which are expressed by the global ethics, then the perverse power of the intellect may appear as the most destructive factor of the integrity of mankind.

Bibliography

Berelson, B. and Steiner, C. (1964), *Human Behavior*, New York: Harcourt Brace & World.

Hamburg, D. (1971), 'Crowding, Stranger Contact and Aggressive Behaviour', *Society, Stress and Disease*, vol. 1 (ed. Lannart Levi), Oxford University Press, pp. 209-18.

Haney, C., Banks, C. and Zimbardo, P. (1972), 'Interpersonal Dynamics in a Simulated Prison' (mimeographed).

Milgram, S. (1965), 'Some Conditions of Obedience and Disobedience to Authority', *Human Relations*, vol. 18, no. 1, pp. 57-76.

Mitscherlich, A. (1973), 'Two Kinds of Cruelty' (multigraphed), Stanford, Calif.

Sanford, N., and Comstock, C. (1971), *Sanctions for Evil*, San Francisco: Jossey Bass.

Zimbardo, P., Ebbesen, E. and Maslach, C. (1977), *Influencing Attitudes and Changing Behavior*, Reading, Mass.: Addison-Wesley.

Part three

Sociology and practice

20 Definition and scope of sociotechnics

Adam Podgórecki

> As a sociologist and philosophical optimist, I like to believe
> that sooner or later the solution of all important human
> problems will be entrusted to humanist scholars, while
> sociologists will undertake the task of establishing how the
> innovations of specialists in various spheres of culture
> (including the natural and technical sciences) may be utilized
> for the welfare of humanity by groups of social practitioners.
>
> Florian Znaniecki

Introduction

Sociotechnics (social engineering) may be defined as the theory of
efficient social action or, more concretely, as applied social science,
the task of which is to inform the potential practitioner in what
manner to seek effective ways and means to realize intended social
aims, provided there is a given accepted system of values as well as
a usable set of verified propositions describing and explaining
human behaviour.

The works of such scholars as L. Petrażycki, R. Pound, G.
Myrdal, K. Popper, H. Zetterberg, P. Lazarsfeld and others should
be acknowledged as essential contributions to shaping modern
social engineering (sociotechnics). The propositions of Zetterberg
may serve as the starting-point of sociotechnics, as now understood:

1 There is a body of seasoned sociological knowledge,
  summarized as principles of theoretical sociology, which is
  superior to our common-sense notions about society.
2 Social practitioners are not consciously and systematically
  using this body of knowledge in their professional
  activities.
3 There is, however, a general formula or schema that can be
  used to make theoretical knowledge help practitioners in
  solving social problems (Zetterberg, 1962, p. 22).

The subject-matter he thus synthetically formulated was then
followed up by many, including Zetterberg himself. In 1970,
Lazarsfeld and Reitz proposed a certain model summarizing the
possible relations between theoreticians in the sphere of social
science and so-called decision-makers (persons or institutions

empowered to make decisions). This model is reducible to the simple formula: P-R-D (problem-research-decision). This otherwise interesting conception seems to be limited by the fact that while trying to describe in objective terms existing and possible expert-decision-maker relations, it does not basically go beyond that enchanted circle (Lazarsfeld and Reitz, 1970, pp. 7 ff).

Though valuable, this kind of approach is inadequate for regarding sociotechnics as a fully formed discipline in the field of the social sciences.

Sociotechnics, as developed in Poland first of all by the activity of the Social Engineering Section of the Polish Sociological Association, occupied itself with three basic spheres of analysis of the social reality: (1) methodology of the practical social sciences, (2) the problem of the application of social science in practice, and (3) analysis of the processes of macro-decision-making. This understanding of social engineering was later, in principle, taken over by the Research Committee on Sociotechnics of the International Sociological Association. As a result of activities of this Research Committee, the following works appeared: Schmidt (1975), Cherns (1976), and Podgórecki (1975b).

Theoretical versus practical social sciences

The differences between theoretical sociological sciences and the practical social science (but analysed from a theoretical point of view) consist not only in the varied concepts and subject-matter which they elaborate and analyse. The fact that sociotechnics embraces the question of rational social change is associated also with the varied methodological principles of the above two types of sciences. Consonant with the general methodological principles of the practical social sciences, social engineering has its distinct methodology which may be summarized as follows.

Paradigm of purposeful procedure

Sociotechnical methodology - as it is specified in the general methodology of social sciences - is composed of a number of mutually conditioning stages. The *first stage* consists in fixing the hierarchical order of social priorities and ideological values appropriate to the means and ends of sociotechnical activity.[1] In the *second stage* a diagnosis (preliminary or final) is made of the social situation constituting the given social problem. The *third stage*, evaluation of the situation which was the subject of the diagnosis, has to provide an answer to the question: whether the acknowledged values and existing situation dictate efforts aimed at

274

changing the situation, or if the costs of such change would not be greater than toleration of the existing liability. If the answer is positive and change is recommended, then preventive, planned or reforming procedures of social change may be applied. The *fourth stage* of activity consists in considering available theoretical hypotheses resting on previous investigation or on research conducted for the purpose of solving the given concrete practical problem. Those hypotheses are then chosen which are the most convenient foundations for the projected strategy. This choice is based on a prognosis of the consequences of different configurations of the hypotheses variously integrated.

In the *fifth stage* a plan of action is prepared on the basis of the accumulated knowledge. This stage is often defined as one of social planning. But methodologically justified social planning is possible only on the basis of previous analysis. Drawing up the plan requires additional anticipation of particulars, of variables, reduced to the technical level, i.e. a detailed analysis of the conditions for substantiating the provisions of the plan. That mental extrapolation, that anticipation and investigation of all eventual verifiable effects on the proposed activity, constitutes the *sixth stage* of practical procedure. In the *seventh stage*, after the introduction of the given social change, an integral evaluation is made of the procedure applied: investigation of the sphere and range of intended and unintended negative effects and side-effects inducing additional processes of spontaneous social change, etc. At this stage an integral assessment is also made of the social changes introduced. The entire circle of methodological canons of the various practical sciences thus opens and closes with values and assessments (Podgórecki, 1962, 1975a).

Practical application

The above presented *goal attainment paradigm of the practical social sciences* constitutes a certain ideal matrix which should be utilized in all purposeful strategies engaging means and ends in fields of social practice. The extent of digression from that paradigm may be regarded as an indication of the distance of the concrete goal-attainment strategy from the ideal pattern, on the one hand, and how close the former is to what may be called 'social quackery', on the other.

Quite often competent and potential social engineers (due to their inferior social position) are, almost forcibly, pushed into the situation of 'social quackery'. This happens because a peculiar relation usually exists between a sponsor (agency which hires experts to solve problems which it directly or indirectly faces) and the client (social engineer). This relation might be easily compared to the situation of an eighteenth-century physician whose duty it was to help his patient without any delay – and without touching his body – on the basis of data provided by the person who was under 'treatment', but who also had power over his healer.

The second field of special interest to sociotechnics is that of the application of social science in practice. The problems involved, namely, to what degree the attainments of social science are utilized to transform social life, are exceedingly intricate, for they depend on (1) the type of social system, (2) the degree of development of the social sciences in the given system, (3) the shape of institutions developing and disseminating knowledge, (4) the degree of preparation of the society and its directing centres to absorb the attainments of social science, (5) the training in various types of transmitting roles capable of conveying complicated results of scientific research to concrete spheres of practical life, etc.

Generally speaking, allowing for certain modifications in some countries, the state of application of social science in practice may be summarized as follows: (1) The potential inherent in sociological knowledge thus far accumulated is not fully utilized: (2) One of the principal ways to put that potential to use is to shape a general humanist-sociological culture: (3) The development of sociological theory is not an adequate condition for the diffusion and grafting of the attainments of sociological knowledge: (4) The most effective way of making unvulgarized sociological knowledge widely accessible to practitioners is to make many-sided analyses of cases of the successful penetration in practice of the findings of social research. Such penetration (after the necessary description and classification) should be analysed from the point of view of in what spheres they are in a position to further develop the goal-attainment paradigm of the social sciences: (5) Professional practice and procedures of collective resourcefulness shaped by it should not be belittled, but their general rules should be systematized: (6) One should not stimulate unrealistic appetites or multiply the boomerang effects caused by disseminating essayistic delusions and futurologistic witchcraft, thus clipping the wings of the young in prestige social sciences (Kubin and Podgórecki, 1973, pp. 46-7): (7) The sociotechnical approach should be accompanied by the global analysis of the given society in which sociotechnical action is envisaged. Only the comprehensive, empirically grounded picture of the given society promises the possibility of placing the problem at hand in its proper place – this type of approach sometimes counteracts the dangers of diminishing and aggrandizing in evaluating the problem under consideration.

The processes of decision-making on a macro-social scale are the third basic domain of sociotechnical interest. An analysis of these processes should consider not only the specifics of micro-decision-making conditioning, but also the above mentioned broader social context in which they transpire. Although that context, with varied political, economic, traditionalist, anthropological, etc., conditions, creates various styles of decision-making, these styles manifest themselves as objectivized products of social activity associated with the preparation and execution of specific social decisions. There are, moreover, various patterns of decision-making developed in the course of economic, administrative or political activity. So do the spheres of their social effectiveness and acceptability differ in varied social and anthropological contexts? For impersonal models of decision-making, which are so characteristic of the ideal bureaucratic pattern, lose their value in the sphere of undertaking some essential political decisions, and are restricted to an insignificant degree on the lower levels of administrative and industrial activity, or lose their momentum when transplanted to a different culture. The classification and analysis of coded knowledge pertaining to this type of decision-making pattern may also be interpreted in the canons dictated by the goal attainment paradigm of the practical social sciences.

The above outlined subject-matter and reflections based on its analysis at once suggest the question: What should be done in concrete social situations where there is a need for rational change? A precise answer requires consideration of additional problems. One of them is: If the social engineer is to occupy himself with purposeful and rational social change, then what means of social influence exist in general, and how may they be used to effect rational change? R. Merton distinguishes seven forms of goal-attaining exertion of influence: (1) compulsion; (2) a superior-inferior relationship in which the behaviour of the latter is distinguished by recommendation or order without the threat of force; (3) manipulation, in which the available mechanisms of influence are used without the straightforward revealing of the aim; (4) putting matters clearly, with indication of alternative directions of activity; (5) presenting a pattern to be imitated, except that the influence-exerting person or institution is not aware that it represents and provides a certain pattern; (6) rendering advice and guidance; (7) an interchange in which one of the parties deliberately alters a situation in such a manner as to induce (by that activity) a given behaviour in the other party (Merton, 1967, p. 419).

Fields of sociotechnical actions

The multiplicity of various manners of exerting social influence may be expressed in a simpler scheme. A certain misunderstanding with reference to the possible benefits of social engineering seems to be due to the confusion of measures in the sphere of opinion and attitude and procedures in the realm of material conditioning. It is thus claimed that the spheres of sociotechnical influence are basically the subjective substrata of individuals - their opinions, assessments, views, attitudes - and that change in these elements is change in a limited sphere, for it does not alter the so-called realities. This kind of objection overlooks the fact that various real situations flow precisely from given opinions, aspirations and attitudes; and furthermore, that sociotechnics also proposes directives on how to effect material transformations, in the sphere of economic behaviour, for instance. It is thus possible to classify the various spheres of socio-technical activity as (1) persuasion (where it is attempted to effect change by various means of conviction); (2) manipulation (where it is attempted to change the views of others against their will or without their knowledge); and (3) facilitative (where some real social or factual situation is created which indirectly or directly influences people's attitudes or views).

An example of persuasive influence may be an investigation aiming to reduce the hiatus between situation and decision. The Kodak Corporation at first made considerable profits from the sale of small film cameras, but soon the negatives began to turn out rather poorly. The enthusiasts of this kind of photographic equipment, after spending considerable sums, in a short time stopped making films. An investigation disclosed that film amateurs feel a strong urge to show their films to their families and friends, who soon, however, had their fill of that kind of activity. The investigation resulted in a recommendation to the enthusiasts to organize clubs and make amateur films. In these clubs they could screen their films in their circle and from time to time show them to families and friends. The effectiveness of that recommendation was not verified because of the outbreak of war (Lazarsfeld and Reitz, 1970, p. 23).

An example of manipulative procedure may be the situation in Germany during the Second World War. In the concluding phase of the war Germany's rulers decided to evacuate the population of one of the major cities to the provinces. It turned out that the fear of aerial bombardment was not a sufficient inducement to realize an administrative decision of this kind. So the people were told that the persistent bombing created a severe shortage of food. Hunger was a stronger motivation than the fear of bombing. And stocks of food were located in that connection in the provincial centres, where they wanted to direct people. This procedure was considerably effective (Lazarsfeld and Reitz, 1970, p. 23).

278

Some sceptics in their criticism of social engineering evaluate a manipulation of their own. They equate sociotechnics with manipulation and then condemn manipulation, consequently rejecting social engineering. This type of argumentation is not only biased, but additionally it overlooks the problem of possibly justifiable action which might be directed towards the dangerous enemies of mankind. (What, then, is worse: to give them leeway or to neutralize them by manipulation?).

The recommendation based on Coleman's research may serve as an example of the facilitating method. The Congress of the USA turned to sociologists for needed research on the unequal educational opportunities of the racial and national minorities. One of Coleman's essential determinations (he investigated that question for a Congressional Committee) was that if there are no specially significant differences in other factors, then it turns out that black students' attainments are considerably higher, if the classes they attend include also white pupils, a majority of whom are of middle-class origin. The facilitative recommendation flowing from that research was to establish the proper proportion of white and black pupils by means of their appropriate distribution (mainly by busing them) and thus create for the latter improved educational opportunities (Coleman *et al.*, 1966).

Sociotechnical models

The above means of sociotechnical influence may be used in different proportions in various sociotechnical models. For three basic sociotechnical approaches may be distinguished: the classical, clinical, and experimental-interventive.

The *classical conception* consists in arranging and synthesizing various general regularities in the field of sociology and related sciences in order to fashion them into appropriate directives. The preparation of a general recipe in the shape of a set of varied directives constitutes a kind of translation of general and particular descriptive propositions into the language of utilitarian evaluation, i.e. into recommendations for action. Adherents of that conception of social engineering are not too much concerned whether that set of directives is used in practice or not.

The *clinical conception* of sociotechnics, chiefly advocated by A. Gouldner (Gouldner and Miller, 1965), is interested not only in propounding sets of practical directives, but also considers it its task to co-operate in its way with those whom the directives concern in order to gain the acceptance and realization of the directives by means of explanation or persuasion. In this conception the evaluation is considered not only to designate proposed social changes, but is also designed to prepare sponsors of these eventual changes to understand fully their own goals and also – in case of their resistance – to give them the ability to overcome this resistance. This conception of sociotechnics counteracts its rather well established pattern described by the parable: sponsors (like drunkards) do not use the light of their lantern (experts) to find the proper path, but use their pillow to protect themselves when they fall down.

The *experimental-interventive conception* of social engineering regards it as its task not only to formulate recipes of practical activity, not only to exert the necessary influence on the 'client' whom the research concerns to accept and realize the recommendations. It considers it its task also to intervene in relation to various social groups, institutions, organizations, etc., to indicate the need for sociotechnical activity, the profit and loss involved, and what basic evaluations will be made in that activity. This type of conception of social engineering, being not passive, should be supplied with the elaboration of the set of values which the sponsor might include in his possible plans of action. Sometimes not only values should be specified but also those social strata should be singled out which might protect or trigger plans of action regarded as socially optimal.

Different kinds of sociotechnical knowledge

Those three models may in various ways be supported by a plethora of diagnostic knowledge; therefore it is possible to distinguish different types of knowledge: common, professional and systematic knowledge.

Common knowledge is knowledge current in daily life; it is full of contrary opinions, generalizations constructed on the basis of the analysis of individual cases, fragmentary observations, evaluations pertaining to imprecisely designated classes of behaviour. But it would be incorrect to ignore it entirely, despite its shortcomings. For many reasons common views may be the product of numerous unconscious, systematic verifications consisting of the continuous adjustment of general conclusions to various observations made in changing situations. Nevertheless, knowledge of this type often fails to provide the possibility of intersubjective understanding, since it refers to varied, often discordant spheres of personal and social experience. It may also provide rationalizations for differing standpoints.

Professional knowledge constitutes generalized information acquired by some professional circle. The various professions differ essentially in their spheres of knowledge, but they show a considerable degree of homogeneity to the outside world. Within the framework of professional knowledge, the stock of knowledge and skills at the disposal of the individual is at all times subject to correction by individuals belonging to a similar professional category. But irrespective of its undoubted values, professional knowledge has a number of limitations. The most important of these is the professional deviation (also in professional sociological knowledge) which consists in the fact that virtually every profession shapes its particular point of view and that point of view tends to become dominant in the *Weltanschauung* of an individual affected by it in a given professional group, and compels a given personality to one-sidedly conceive the complex structures of analysed phenomena.

That is why systematic knowledge is the best foundation for practical activity. But it is not easily attained, due to several reasons. For example: (1) the expert application of systematic research techniques is more or less artificial or subsidiary cases retards the moment when the research findings, after proper analysis, may be generalized, from the time the need for the research arose; (2) the more precise the technique, the greater is the time-lag between the diagnosis of the given situation and the moment when it is necessary to undertake decisions to change that situation; (3) these time-lags may also cause the generalizations obtained by systematic research to become inadequate because of the very passage of time. These possible defects in the application of research techniques increase, in the case of systematic knowledge, the area of error. Systematic knowledge possesses values, however, which common and professional knowledge lack. It is basically verifiably intersubjective and quite often enables us to obtain a consensus of varied opinions.

Sociotechnical strategies

Different kinds of sociotechnical knowledge may lead to varied types of sociotechnical recommendations based on them. The principle of the scapegoat may be an example of the perverse wisdom flowing from analyses based on common knowledge. It is often said cynically: 'It is necessary to find a scapegoat and even to pick one in advance.' According to this principle, when undertaking some activity one should reckon with the possibility of various, including negative, effects. Then, in order to dissociate the author of the activity from the possible negative effects, it is advisable to find a victim to be made responsible for them. This principle may also be applied when the action undertaken completely or partly fails, for it is evidently convenient then to shift responsibility to some individual or group.

Directives flowing from knowledge acquired in professional-political activity may pertain to winning elections. The undecided voter is a political category which is likely to change views under the influence of the mass media. The directive of luring vacillating elements, rather helpful in election campaign strategy, is based on the hypothesis which proclaims that people who are little interested in some question have no decided opinion on matters pertaining to that question and may thus easily change their minds. The meaning of such directives is made clearer by the following authentic example. Two competing groups, one small but homogeneous, the other large but heterogeneous, fought for the position of leader of the community to which both belonged. The homogeneous group controlled about 30 per cent of the votes and supported its candidate A; the heterogeneous group, representing about 60 per cent of the votes, supported candidate B. The small group concentrated its very intensive propaganda campaign on the vacillating group of 10 per cent of the voters (the campaign was based on the technique of personal persuasion). Besides, the small homogeneous group nominated a third candidate, C, who was very popular in the large group. The election results showed (with some simplification) the following distribution of votes: candidate B (of the heterogeneous group) and candidate C received 30 per cent each. The homogeneous group netted 40 per cent and won the election. Candidate A became the leader of the community. This was made possible by the adroit application of two sociotechnical rules: (1) a smaller group (on the basis of the hypothesis described above) may impose its values on a large heterogeneous group if it causes it to split by internal dissension; (2) the second rule pertains to luring the vacillating elements.

Sociotechnical recommendations may also be obtained directly from the analysis of sociological propositions (they might be relatively easily obtained in the area of small group research studies) verified experimentally. Research of this type thus shows, for example, that the opinions of other children exert a greater influence on changing children's views than do the opinions of adults. Younger children are more subject to the influence of older ones than vice versa. In relations between age mates, children from better situated families wield greater influence. Finally, acquaintances exert greater influence than do strangers. A certain sociotechnical rule flows from those determinations: to influence children - which may be done through known or unknown other children or adults - it is more effective to do so through children of an older age group with whom they are acquainted and whose social position (or that of their parents) is considered higher.

It may be concluded on the basis of the above that sociotechnics (social engineering), generally speaking, disposes of various models of activity, types of dependable knowledge and varied means of influence. It may be asserted in a very general sense that most desirable would be the sociotechnical experimental-interventive model (which makes it possible to act also when no official agency initiates social policy designed to solve a given social problem) based on systematic knowledge (providing the possibility of inter-subjective verification) and on persuasive and facilitating activity (thus excluding the possibility of manipulative influence which leads to the realization of aims not accepted by the influenced subject and creates an atmosphere for violating the principle of self-actualization).

T. Kocowski distinguishes two levels of sociotechnical influence:

Sociotechnics of the first order creates a system of incentives which incline people to given behaviour. In this case, sociotechnical procedure consists in issuing orders, regulations, legal acts, injunctions, prohibitions, etc., or in establishing attractive conditions for the purpose, for instance, to affect a flow of personnel to given posts or to given regions. *Sociotechnics of the second order* induces desirable motivations or moulds desirable personal traits. The end goal of influence may be the same here as in the first case, for it is a matter of evoking given behaviour, such, for instance, as getting people to work more productively, to protect public property, etc. But the method is different. Social engineering acts here not directly as a legal norm, but by means of internalization of such norms in the individual's personality structure. The merit of sociotechnics of the second order is obvious. It is more useful to endow people with such traits as honesty, respect for the law, conscientiousness, than to rely on an elaborate system of administration and control to keep guard over the individual's proper behaviour (T. Kocowski, 1972).

J. Gočkowski notes a particularly important question. For it is an exceptionally significant consideration that various sociotechnical recommendations or strategies may be applied in social life and lead to the realization of desired social effects (and only those effects) if special conditions are met in the structure of the social fabric on which the recommendations or strategies act:

Sociotechnical directives and methods are triply conditioned culturally. The level of knowledge which the social engineer

disposes of in the given conditions, of course, is the first of
three determinants. The intentions and ideological tendencies
as well as the interests and political strategies of the
institutions to which the social engineers belong and on whose
behalf they work – that is the second determinant. The moral
norms and evaluations obligatory in these engineers' circles,
the manner and means of the play and conflict of forces in
the given society and in which the sociotechnicians are
involved or may be involved should be regarded as the third
determinant (Gočkowski, 1973, p. 85).

The general question of course arises of how to develop
sociotechnics of this type. Some answer this question by
implication. They maintain that the stormy development of the
technical sciences somehow, on the basis of spontaneous development, creates various verified systematic possibilities to make
'sociotechnical reductions' of considerable practical value. A.
Etzioni states: 'An idea to the effect that a technical discovery may
be used to reduce costs and injustices connected with the solution
of social problems is an attractive one.' And further:

In order to obtain provisional answers to that question we
undertook a review of existing research which assesses the
advantage of technological short-cuts pertaining to six social
problems. These are as follows: the use of methadon to
control narcotic behavior; the use of contraceptive instruments
(IUD) to control births; teaching aid by the use of television;
the use of antabus in curing alcoholics; the control of firearms
in the struggle to reduce crime and instruments for breath
analysis in the control of road traffic. These technological
interventions may be regarded as short-cuts, since they serve
either to replace manpower (substituting the teacher by a
television broadcast, for instance), or because they reduce the
need of costly personnel (such as, for example, the use of
methadon to influence narcomaniacs on heroin in order to
reduce the need for therapeutists, social workers, guardians,
etc.).

And finally:

The above review of various alternative means which may
contribute to the solution of social problems suggests that
there are more effective ones than the traditional techniques
which may aid a larger part of the population concerned and
that they are cheaper (Etzioni and Remp, 1971, pp. 1-3 and
31).

284

Of course, the importance of 'socio-technological' reductions and their possible advantages in accomplishing rational social change cannot be ignored. It is nevertheless impossible to sit back and passively wait for technical inventions that may be used to erase social pathology or to introduce constructive social change. This is why the answer to the fundamental question, namely, how to develop sociotechnics able to provide dependable directives for macro-social action, is neither simple nor definitive. The most proper way seems to be to successively develop a goal-attaining social paradigm, which, used in their concrete application as matrix patterns, would indicate the stages of practical activity which are omitted, posed defectively, not elaborated and requiring supplementation, etc. The desirable way hence seems to be that of the systematic elaboration of the procedural canons of goal-attaining activity.

Some have complained that social engineering may be dangerous (like the surgeon's knife which does not perform a life-giving operation but kills), when used by the wrong people. As a matter of fact, the sociotechnician is not only obliged to develop his discipline, but also to take care, as a person – hence as a citizen, an ethical individual, a political person – the social engineering does not fall into the hands of people who may use it improperly.

Additional clarifications

After these considerations, it might be useful to recall the important statement of one of the founders of social engineering, Karl Popper:

> I wish to outline another approach to social engineering, namely, that of piecemeal engineering. It is an approach which I think to be methodologically sound. The politician who adopts this method may or may not have a blueprint of society before his mind, he may or may not hope that mankind will one day realize an ideal state, and achieve happiness and perfection on earth. But he will be aware that perfection, if at all attainable, is far distant, and that every generation of men, and therefore also the living, have a claim; perhaps not so much a claim to be made happy, for there are no institutional means of making a man happy, but a claim not to be made unhappy, where it can be avoided. They have a claim to be given all possible help, if they suffer. The piecemeal engineer will, accordingly, adopt the method of searching for, and fighting against, the greatest and most urgent evils of society, rather than searching for, and fighting

for, its greatest ultimate good. . . . This difference is far from being merely verbal. In fact, it is most important. . . . The existence of social evils, that is to say, of social conditions under which many men are suffering, can be comparatively well established. Those who suffer can judge for themselves, and the others can hardly deny that they would not like to change places. It is infinitely more difficult to reason about an ideal society. Social life is so complicated that few men, or none at all, could judge a blueprint for social engineering on the grand scale; whether it be practicable; whether it would result in a real improvement; what kind of suffering it may involve; and what may be the means for its realization. As opposed to this, blueprints for piecemeal engineering are comparatively simple. They are blueprints for single institutions, for health and unemployed insurance, for instance, or arbitration courts, or anti-depression budgeting, . . . or educational reform. If they go wrong, the damage is not very great, and a re-adjustment not very difficult. They are less risky, and for this very reason less controversial. But if it is easier to reach a reasonable agreement about existing evils and the means of combating them than it is about an ideal good and the means of its realization, then there is also more hope that by using the piecemeal method we may get over the very greatest practical difficulty of all reasonable political reform, namely, the use of reason, instead of passion and violence, in executing the programme. . . . As opposed to that the Utopian attempt to realize an ideal state, using a blueprint of society as a whole, is one which demands a strong centralized rule of a few, and which therefore is likely to lead to a dictatorship (Popper, 1962, pp. 158-9).

The sense of polarization of these two opposite approaches, as they are presented by Popper, is quite pervasive; but in the light of recent developments in the social sciences (and especially in the practical social sciences), this conclusion should be accordingly changed. This is because this type of reasoning, which is based on polarization, overlooks the third essential possibility. One might distinguish (1) micro-social engineering, (2) mezzo-social engineering, and (3) macro-social engineering. Basically, macro-social engineering overlaps with Popperian utopian social engineering, and his piecemeal sociotechnics with mezzo-social engineering. Still, he omits micro-social engineering, an omission which should be corrected – particularly if one takes into consideration the accumulation of knowledge which stems from research in social psychology in the area of small group studies.

Additionally, studies in the sphere of economy and sociology of social stratification analyse the area of mezzo-social engineering, thus limiting the scope of 'hazardous' endeavours undertaken by utopian sociotechnics.

One issue which was analysed previously needs some further comment. In connection with the possible uses of sociotechnics it should be stressed again that three basic types of sociotechnical models have been specified above. They are classical, clinical, and experimental-interventive conceptions. But additionally it should be noted that these models may operate in various ways in different social settings. All of them might be utilized to strengthen the existing establishment; they also can take this establishment as the target of its more or less elaborated design of the planned change. As far as the latter possibility is concerned it appears that the use of a classical conception of sociotechnics or a clinical one exists only as an abstract theoretical potentiality. This is because those specialists who are capable of furnishing the recommendations based on diagnostic recognition usually belong to the category of hired experts. And since experts do not have their own 'constituency', they – as a rule – are put into action by the organizational and financial potentialities of their sponsors. This type of relationship, in principle, ties them with loyalties which are defined by the latter ones. Therefore experimental-interventive sociotechnics appears as an exceptionally important element of social life. If this type of sociotechnics is able to find some social and organizational backing, it will be able to play an important role as a promoter of this type of social change which is not designed according to the expectations, wishes, needs, pressure or orders of those who actually possess the power, but by the social stratum which is looking impartially, reasonably, with devotion and without self-interest, for general social justice. Intelligentsia, as it was generated in Poland and later in Russia, plays this role more or less effectively. This social stratum – defined by I. Berlin as 'a group of thinkers . . . opposed to an oppressive and irrational regime . . . committed to rational thought . . . in . . . dedication to . . . civil and personal freedom, personal integrity and the pursuit of the truth no matter what the consequences' – may give this backing and play this role. This is how the recommendation of an action is finally connected with its normative vision.

Note

1 It should be mentioned that the hierarchical order of priorities might be sometimes based on one essential and fundamental value-premise, but

usually this order is structured by the specific balance between different values. Additionally, during the course of the purposeful procedure this hierarchy might be recomposed, according to an already accented meta-type of requirements (on the stage of constructing the hierarchy, analytical reasoning might be stressed while on the stage of the diagnosis, proper use of inductive techniques might be accentuated, etc.).

Bibliography

Cherns, A. B. (ed.) (1976), *Sociotechnics*, London: Malaby Press.

Coleman, J. S., *et al.* (1966), *Equality of Educational Opportunity*, Washington, D.C.: US Government Printing Office.

Etzioni, A., and Remp, R. (1971), 'Technological "Short-cuts" to Social Change', New York: Center for Policy Research (unpublished).

Gočkowski, J. (1973), 'Normy i oceny moralne a dyrektywy i metody socjotechniki' ('Moral Norms and Evaluations and Sociotechnical Directives'), *Etyka*, no. 12.

Gouldner, A. and Miller, S. M. (1965), *Applied Sociology: Opportunities and Problems*, New York: Free Press.

Ikle, F. C., Bureau of Applied Social Research, New York (unpublished).

Kocówski, T. (1972), 'Taktyka i strategia sterowania motywaci ludzkiej w skali masowej' ('Tactics and Strategy of Steering Human Motivation on a Mass Scale'), in A. Podgórecki (ed.), *Socjotechnika, Style dzialania (Social Engineering, Styles of Activity)*, Książka i Wiedza: Warsaw:

Kubin, J. and Podgórecki, A. (eds) (1973), *Stosowanie nauk spolecznych w praktyce (Application of Social Science in Practice)*, Wroclaw: Ossolineum.

Lazarsfeld, P., and Reitz, J. (1970), 'Toward a Theory of Applied Sociology', Bureau of Applied Social Research, New York (unpublished).

Lazarsfeld, P., Sewell, W., and Wilenski, H. (1967), *The Uses of Sociology*, New York: Basic Books.

Merton, R. (1967), *Social Theory and Social Structure*, Chicago: The Free Press.

Myrdal, G., Sterner, R., and Rose, A. (1944), *An American Dilemma*, New York: McGraw Hill.

Petrażycki, L. (1893), *Die Lehre von Einkommen*, Berlin.

Podgórecki, A. (1962), *Charakterystyka nauk praktycznych (Characteristics of the Practical Sciences)*, Warsaw: PWN.

Podgórecki, A. (1966), *Zasady sociotechniki (The Principles of Sociotechnics)*, Warsaw: Wiedza Powszechna.

Podgórecki, A. (ed.) (1968), *Socjotechnika, praktyczne zastosowania socjologii (Social Engineering, The Practical Application of Sociology)*, Warsaw: Książka i Wiedza.

Podgórecki, A. (ed.) (1970), *Sociotechnika: jak oddzialywać skutecznie (Sociotechnics: How to Influence Effectively)*, Warsaw: Książka i Wiedza.

Podgórecki, A. (ed.) (1974), *Sociotechnika, funkcjonalnośc i dysfunkcjonalność Instytucji (Social Engineering: Functionalism and Dysfuntionalism of Institutions)*, Warsaw: Książka i Wiedza.

Podgórecki, A. (1975a), *Practical Social Sciences*, London: Routledge & Kegan Paul.

Podgórecki, A. (ed.) (1975b), 'Sociotechnics', *Current Sociology*, vol. XXIII, no. 1.

Popper, Karl (1962), *The Open Society and Its Enemies*, London: Routledge & Kegan Paul.

Pound, R. (1942), *Social Control Through Law*.

Schmidt, J. K. H. W. (ed.) (1975), *Planvolle Steuerung Gesellschaftlichen Handels – Grundlegende Beiträge zur Gesellschaftstechnik und Gesellschaftsarchitektur*, Opladen: Westdeutscher Verlag.

Zetterberg, H. (1962), *Social Theory and Social Practice*, The Bedminster Press.

21 Applied social sciences and values
Maria Łoś

Social engineering (sociotechnics), according to Adam Podgórecki, systematizes knowledge in order to shape given social situations in a desired direction, on the basis of acknowledged values. However, in many spheres of social life this conscious, purposeful influence on people's behaviour and attitudes is in a certain sense veiled and reluctantly revealed, while in others it tends to be much more open. The degree of openness as to goals and values has, of course, a significant impact upon the nature and quality of the applied research undertaken. A relative clarity as to the main aims and priorities in the domain of economics, for instance (economic growth, efficiency, etc.), has been conducive to the systematic and cumulative development of applied knowledge. Criminology, with its, until recently, rather clear vision of what should be aimed at (combating crime, reforming criminals) was able to produce a great bulk of applied studies with quite openly formulated practical implications. On the other hand, the sociology of leisure has never claimed that the aims it should deal with are obvious and given, and consequently, it has never been successful in providing scientific recipes of how to pass spare time in a satisfying and rewarding way.

The era of scepticism in social science reflecting, and, perhaps, precipitating, some more general, 'counter-cultural' and 'counter-establishmental' movements, has succeeded in shaking the taken for granted assumptions, even of those applied disciplines which pertain to previously well defined areas, like, for instance, economy and criminality. One of the main dilemmas of 'sceptical' sociology has been an inability to bridge a concern for the 'people in the streets' with a reluctance to intervene and impose any values upon them. The sceptical sociologists recognized some, even acute, need for action, but they have never managed to develop any satisfying model of applied social sciences capable of guiding it.

290

'Radical' sociology rejects the feasibility and/or desirability of any piecemeal changes, and places its faith instead in revolutionary upheaval. In such an approach social science is expected to become a vital part of pre-revolutionary and revolutionary social praxis. But, in spite of continuous efforts to interpret this postulate in more meaningful and methodologically consistent ways – its followers have so far failed to provide any clear and comprehensible basis for the proposed reorientation in sociological inquiry.

The positivists' concern for the objective nature of sociology has contributed greatly to the tendency to ignore its normative aspects. However, the claim of some 'sceptical' or 'radical' researchers that sociology is inevitably synonymous with (or subordinated to) ideology has equally contributed to a somewhat nonchalant attitude towards the question of the values and aims permeating the sociological enterprise. It seems that the radical students tend to accept some 'obvious' normative imperatives just as carelessly as their strongly criticized 'functionalist' colleagues. And the first, like the latter, are much more keen to criticize their counterpart's false moral and political involvement than to analyse and elicit their own normative stand and its far-reaching social consequences.

Applied research involves values in various – direct and indirect – ways. While some orientations within the field of applied research are rather insensitive to this problem, the others seem to be strongly concerned with it. As a result, some of them attempt to minimize – or at least consciously clarify – the scope of the influence of personal or group values as well as the ideological preferences of the researchers upon the outcome of the applied research in social sciences. It may be worthwhile to discuss some of these attempts. However, one should not forget also that, as mentioned before, a contrary tendency has been recently receiving much support in the 'west'. It is connected with replacing the social sciences by ideology – which relieves the followers of such an orientation of a more precise definition of the role of social science and of possible sources of values.

One may distinguish four basic approaches in applied social science research which tend to clarify the place and role of values in more or less conscious and effective ways. These already well established and institutionalized orientations are:
(1) goal-attainment orientation,
(2) system orientation,
(3) crisis orientation,
(4) action orientation.
(1) *The goal-attainment model* is oriented towards the scientific

search for the most effective ways of achieving goals which are formulated by external, unscientific means. The social scientist is perceived as free to accept or reject the offer, but if he accepts it then he must detach himself emotionally from the goals or values related to the proposed changes, and focus on the most rational ways of bringing them about. In respect of this orientation, a vast – mostly American – literature has been produced. It deals, among other things, with various aspects of the relationships between decision-makers or research-sponsors and social scientists. In addition, a number of critiques of this approach have been voiced and published, making it unnecessary to repeat them here (see, for instance, Baritz, 1970; Bennis *et al.*, 1969; Gouldner, 1962; Horowitz, 1963, 1967).

(2) For *the system orientation* the specific aims of individual social programmes are not of primary importance. Instead, this approach aims to attain such properties of a given social system (e.g. organization, society), which enable the smooth achievement of various goals without disturbing the fulfilment of that system's other indispensable functions. These functions or basic needs are believed to be made manifest by general systems theory. Such an orientation in evaluative research emphasizes the fact that success or failure in bringing about a particular aim (the basic criterion in the goal-attainment model) often depends on purely accidental, situational factors. The approach stresses, instead, the complexity of the process of social change. Above all, its followers would argue that the goal-attainment model overlooks the significance of the fact that attainment of intended change in a strictly delimited sphere depends on and influences social processes within a considerably broader system (constituting a web of functions and interests of many subsystems).

Many authors have been fascinated by the system model, especially by its key concept 'optimization' (of solutions, decisions, allocation of resources, distribution of means, etc.). It seems, however, that the magic optimization has distracted attention from the basic questions: the sense and the role of the given institutions or programmes of change; the sources of the criteria for optimization procedure, and the role of public opinion or simply the scope of democratic participation in decision-making. The complicated, computerized optimization – which brings into relief the multi-aspected and multi-functional character of the given system – is usually circumscribed by that system in the sense that it utilizes criteria flowing primarily from its principal 'needs': of survival, continuation, adaptation, co-operation, etc. Thus, the system experts do not enter into the question of the sense of that system – a question which must be formulated in a humanist language rather than in mathematical, formal terms.

The system model which tries to avoid a direct involvement of moral or ideological values may be criticized for having a static conception of reality, and a naïve faith in the equilibrium mechanisms and apologia of the *status quo*. Furthermore, the optimization procedure placed in the hands of a socially isolated small minority (groups of experts) – and being basically unintelligible to those whom the planned policy concerns – has created considerable opposition in many countries.

It is worthwhile noting that evaluative research on programmes of change based on the system model tend to use the optimization criteria of the authors of the programme. They, thus, accept automatically the interest groups and the values the experts regarded as basic in their frames of reference.

For many critics of the system model, the participation of broader social circles in important decisions, choice and policy assessments is of crucial importance. But, while accepting this postulate, we must be aware of the danger of superficiality and distortion. Justification of a social policy by appealing to general welfare or generally shared values is often an expression of hypocrisy and a disguised authoritarian manner of dealing with social problems. On the other hand, awareness of the conflicts inherent in social policy-making may arm the population with the criteria to assess various policies and/or demand some alternative solutions. I will deal with this question in detail later.

(3) *The crisis orientation* in social science applied research looks for the justification of its involvement in policy-making in the extraordinary features of the situation, requiring quick intervention. The followers of this orientation often argue that in a situation of overt crisis or obvious, acute conflict some action will be taken anyway. According to them, society is not able to bear such a burden for a long time. So they maintain that in such a case it is better to propose some rational, enlightened, research-based solutions of the problem, instead of giving way to blind, strictly administrative – often repressive – action.

A very broad range of phenomena have been defined as crisis situations: crime, riots, inefficient economy or class exploitation are but a few examples. It seems, however, that the features of the situation which legitimize experts' intervention, actually handicap the effectiveness of their proposals and the predictability of the outcome. Crisis situations simply cannot be dealt with in a strictly scientific way. As a result, the orientation is subject to various, often aggressively stated, criticisms from both sides – ideological as well as rational ('goal-oriented').

On the other hand, it seems that quite often a crisis is both blown up and exaggerated (consciously or unconsciously) by social scientists. It gives 'legitimacy' to their definitions of the requirements of social practice, and justifies their call for action on behalf of the 'victims' of the crisis. 'Crisis' thus becomes a magic word which suggests that anything is better than the *status quo*, and that only inaction requires some justification (and should be condemned anyway). Action is self-justified and indispensable; it is the only way out of crisis. Such an approach takes for granted the existence of crisis and its undesirability. This kind of exaggerated crisis orientation has been demonstrated by both conservative and radical social scientists (for example, in the law and order campaign or in some anti-welfare state attacks).

(4) *The action orientation* consists of an effort to enable the 'ordinary' people to make their own choices and decisions. It aims mainly at broadening the range of available choices, stimulating participation in social and community life, encouraging feelings of responsibility concerning ongoing social developments and policy-making. The most successful and interesting examples of action research are offered by the Scandinavian (mostly Norwegian) experience. In this model the social scientist becomes an intermediary between the 'ordinary' people and the governmental agencies. He does not, however, rely on public opinion surveys to estimate the social needs and preferences. A distinctive feature of action research is an attempt to experimentally introduce, or facilitate in some other ways, various possibilities of needs satisfaction and participation, leaving the final choice and evaluation to the people. The reactions and demands of the population in question are the best guide for making appropriate adjustments and undertaking further negotiations with the decision-making bodies on behalf of the interested population.

Action research may give a very good insight into the conflicting interests of various sections of society. It facilitates the negotiations and bargaining processes between them, usually taking the part of the weaker, underprivileged party, assuming that the stronger party is better equipped to protect its interests.

Quite often, this approach is assumed by those who define themselves as radical social scientists:

For the radical researcher, the point about attempting to remain faithful to the researched population is that he has already taken sides; in the sense that he is concerned to feed back his results, not to the powerful, but to those most immediately and directly affected by the inequalities he is researching.

. . . purposes are to reveal the ways in which the constant

flux of social conflict and the taken-for-granted repression of ordinary men in such conflicts can be transcended, not in terms of the further accumulation of descriptions of repression, but only in terms of an adequate radical politics. In large part, therefore, the success of the research is to be judged not in terms of static description but in terms of the ability of the researcher to feed back the research work into a form of practice with the population with whom he is working (Taylor, Walton and Young, 1975, pp. 26-7).

But only a few of those radical intellectuals are so clearly aware of action research's shortcomings and inherent, insoluble dilemmas, as its fervent defender and critic, Thomas Mathiesen. He speaks with a deep concern about the dangers of this kind of research, while he stresses that

dilemmas through which you cannot maintain a short-term and a long-term objective, but where you must make a choice between the two and exclude one, may quickly reduce the actionist to silence, or at least strongly limit his freedom of speech and action. If the actionist chooses the 'reformist side', any reference to something radical or 'revolutionary' is later picked up by powerful adversaries as something illegitimate and inadmissible. If he chooses the 'revolutionary side', it suddenly becomes 'illicit' for him to adopt changes which are near at hand, pressing and wanted, and he is separated from those he wishes to work for (Mathiesen, 1974, p. 33).

So far, four different models of applied research have been discussed. They are well established and have produced a large literature. Less visible, but patiently breaking through, are three other orientations:
(5) conflict-awareness orientation,
(6) negation orientation,
(7) abolition orientation.
(5) *The conflict-awareness orientation* in applied social sciences would attempt to reveal existing conflicts and create an awareness of conflicts of interests as the basis for realistic negotiation. It would also attempt to determine those spheres in which conflict will remain unresolved after the introduction of proposed action (change). In addition it would aim at the prediction of new conflicts which may arise in the course of introducing change and its aftermath.

An expert's solidarity with a given group – a factor mitigating against the impartiality of the research – may in fact facilitate the success of research oriented towards increasing conflict-awareness.

It seems possible to achieve such a division of roles in the research team (or such broad co-operation and communication
among the interested groups) that the successive stages of the research are confronted with the interests of all parties concerned with
the planned change. In one version of such a research approach,
individual members of the team would represent various interest
groups (at least in a given respect), and they would remain in close
contact with them. They would be expected to sound out the
opinions, problems, fears and preferences of the given group and
to work out a hypothetical model of change - corresponding most
closely to the expectations and aspirations of the given group. They
would also present those aspects of change which evoke the group's
strongest resistance as well as the areas of acceptable compromise,
etc. They could transmit to the groups in question information
about the needs and expectations of other groups and help them to
work out less 'egocentric' solutions. Moreover, they could facilitate
communication among groups having different interests. This may
lead eventually towards the establishment of more lasting channels
of immediate communication and encounter among them, basically
detached from the research situation or any task-oriented activity
at all.

The working meeting at Annapolis in the USA (Hammer, 1963)
may serve as an example of an experiment which brought together
groups with traditional conflicts of interests. Although it was not
capable of disclosing the deep roots of the conflict, it was an
attempt to make a first step in this direction. According to the
published report, prison personnel, inmates, jurists (lawyers,
prosecutors, judges), police officers and representatives of other
groups and communities conferred together for nine days. These
meetings were a combination of lectures, discussions and
psychodrama, in which participants played their true roles or
exchanged roles. The audience controlled the course of the psycho-
dramas and intervened when the stage began to lose its realism.
Scenes presenting police intervention, interrogations, prison life,
etc., were for many participants their first contact with the true
attitudes of persons associated with the administration of justice in
a different manner from themselves. Prison scenes aroused
particular interest. A new prisoner appeared before the audience
(policemen, judges, etc.); the whole process was unfolded of the
prisoner's initiation, his shake-down, the theft of his possessions,
terrorization by other prisoners, and the helplessness of the prison
staff, etc. The picture was supplemented by visits to prisons (the
first for the majority of participating lawyers and even policemen).
In addition, some individuals decided to assume the role of new
prisoners in order to understand better, by experiencing it, the

shocking reality of that situation. Imprisoned with all the appearances of authenticity, these pseudo-prisoners unanimously stressed that they lived through the greatest shock they had ever experienced. The way they were treated by the prison personnel and other prisoners was totally incongruous with what they had imagined. Yet the work of these people – judges, policemen, Department of Justice consultants, etc. – is somewhat absurd if it is not based on knowledge of the nature of basic conflicts and tensions and the manner of their resolution in reality. This is especially so, since it is they who decide such matters in the course of their official duties.

The participation of the representatives of various groups, or at least of the 'expert-advocates', in applied research and in so-called evaluative research should contribute to:

(a) more equal representation of interests;

(b) more accurate estimation of the profit and loss for all sides, and making the groups' expectations more realistic and, perhaps, less egocentric;

(c) revealing the main points (as well as causes) of the conflicts of interests;

(d) making possible communication among various groups, eventually leading to greater efforts by the groups in defining and clarifying their interests, needs, fears, prejudices, feelings of hostility, etc.;

(e) widening the awareness of individual, often isolated, groups of the interests and expectations of other groups which may be incongruent with their interests – thus extending awareness of the conflict of interests and values in spheres where such conflict actually exists;

(f) weakening the hegemony of apparent consensus which legitimizes social inequality and exploitation.

Such a development may constitute a step towards the process of giving conflicts back to the people, giving them a chance of becoming familiar with their nature and letting them decide whether they prefer to live with them, to settle them by compromise or to drift towards some more radical solutions. As Christie (1976) pointed out recently, by letting experts handle people's conflicts for them, modern societies destroy or denaturalize a very important aspect of social relationships. If the people are given back power to define conflicts and to search collectively for ways in which they want to deal with them, this could reshape their consciousness in more profound and genuine ways than any other means of increasing social participation. They would have to face problems in all their complexity and to learn to cope with them. They would also have to bear the responsibility for handling them, but, at the same time, they would be pushed nearer a full comprehension of the real nature of injustice, and, possibly, disclosure of those conflicts which are made invisible by well meaning experts. Above all else, however, they would probably come to perceive that the claim for a conflictless society is a deceptive utopia.

(6) Another model – contrasting with the usual procedure in applied research, based on prognosis and continuation – is *the negation model* (counter-system model). This model consists in the analytical negation, or a search for logical alternatives to the prevailing state of affairs (see Sjoberg and Cain, 1971, p. 224). Its adherents maintain that its importance lies in the fact that it provides external standards and categories for the investigation of a given social order. It also helps to determine the scale of possible alternatives.

It differs markedly from those perspectives which regard the existing structure as the basis of prognosis and planning. Such a perspective contributes usually to continuation and stabilization, setting in motion a mechanism of self-fulfulling prophecies which consolidate the prevailing direction of development (see Sjoberg and Cain, 1971, p. 22). Those involved in applied research have tended to treat values such as effectiveness, productiveness, rationality, reduction of crime, elimination of conflicts, prolongation of life, etc., as unproblematic. It may, therefore, be a useful exercise to imagine the consequences of adopting contrary values. At the least it can provide a broader foundation for conscious choices and less restrained solutions.

Examples of such an approach, inspired by the counter-cultural movements, can be found in the literature. The works of Illich, who provides counter-models for education or health systems, are an example of this orientation. His ability to draw conclusions from the daring negation of the sacred institutions, such as the school, has had a great influence upon contemporary social imagination (Illich, 1973). Similarly, the anti-psychiatric movement has proved that values and institutions conveniently taken for granted can be logically and socially negated.

Naturally, there is a danger of naïvety in the negation perspective and, indeed, the actual examples are easy to find. Particularly, we should be aware that the negation of one stereotype may often lead to the establishment of another one. For instance, some sociologists of deviance who had rejected the image of the criminogenic lower classes adopted the counter-idea of criminal higher classes. Sure enough a change of perspective was very refreshing, but in its crude form it must be accused of neglecting the complexity of social conflicts and their historical context.

(7) *Abolition orientation* constitutes a radical combination of the action model with the negation approach. It is oriented towards 'negative' reforms (Mathiesen, 1974), which aim at the abolition or removal of some parts of social institutions which the system in general is more or less dependent on. These 'negative' reforms are expected to lead to more basic structural changes of the system confronted with permanent social counter-pressure.

Thus the abolition model promotes the idea of permanent action aiming at abolition of the petrified and corrupted in order to give room to the new, spontaneous and unknown. This new relationship between 'theory' and 'action' is characterized by Mathiesen in the following way:

> Continually new organizing presupposes a continual everpresent process of totalizing: a process through which the small individual case is placed within continually wider context of causal relationships, which then in turn is attacked. This presupposed a continual oscillation between action and theory: a continually new understanding of action in the light of theory, a revision of theory in the light of this, a re-evaluation of the action in this light, and so on. The stress on abolition is here turned against your own activity, but through its relationship with the environment, also against the environment, and it may thereby become the basis of a more persistent counter-organizing. A part of the struggle itself is to abolish the boundary between theory and action (Mathiesen, 1974, p. 201).

It is a modest approach as it does not pretend to possess accurate knowledge of what is good and desirable. But it is, also, quite daring in its claim to be able to judge and decide what is basically wrong and condemnable. Finally, it is a very optimistic approach as it assumes that the abolition of the wrong will not be followed by emergence of the worst. And, being a fruit of a recent experience of the Scandinavian professionals, it takes for granted the very possibility of counter-organizing, thus concentrating mainly on the limits of its effectiveness.

One may suspect that the more socially obvious and urgent the need for abolition of the basic pillars of a system the greater this system's capacity to ban any attempt at counter-organizing. Counter-organizing aims at the abolition of false images, ideas and institutions, which give apparent legitimacy to a system. It thus unveils whatever the system veils (Mathiesen, 1974, p. 208; see also the analysis of the unmasking function of sociology by Podgórecki, 1968, and of the intervention model of sociotechnics, Podgórecki, 1975). And, as Mathiesen rightly pointed out, 'there is a connection between "truth" and "freedom"' (Mathiesen, 1974, p. 209), as the counterforces must be 'liberated' in order to perform this function.

Counter-organizing constitutes a natural force preventing the perpetuation of socially unacceptable institutions and relationships; it is vital and inevitable for any living system. It is precisely when this manifestation of the life of a system is frustrated that we witness the most bitter form of social action, which may be described as *resistance movement* or silent opposition.

Conclusions

Let us re-emphasize the distinctive features of the six orientations in the applied social sciences presented above.

The *goal-attainment* model is of a strictly technical character. It does not claim that the values and goals of social change may be established scientifically. The ways and strategies of bringing about the change most efficiently can, however, be derived from systematic knowledge, and the applied research should focus solely on them.

The cybernetic, *system* model is of similar character, although it assumes that aims are not arbitrarily formulated by the research sponsors, but they may be derived objectively from certain more general systems' dispositions.

The *crisis* model refers to the common-sense definitions of the emergency situations and the need for action. It is oriented basically towards a relief or neutralization of the crisis.

The *action-research* model aims at encouraging, facilitating and broadening the possible choices of participation and needs satisfaction of various social groups. The experts act to some extent as the spokesmen for the weaker groups, trying to articulate and defend their interests.

The *conflict-awareness* model, based on the assumption of the existence of conflicting interests of various subgroups, tends to reveal existing conflicts, increase social recognition of the needs and interests of others which are conflicting with one's own, and facilitate communication and negotiations between the groups.

The *negation* model is based on adequate knowledge of the *status quo* and taken for granted rules of social order and attempts to broaden the social imagination and possible perspectives of change by designing alternative solutions based on counter-values.

The *abolition* model aims at unmasking the covert mechanisms of the system and attacking the strategic institutions supporting the system. It requires the totalization of the researcher's perspective by constant evaluation of global, far-reaching consequences of various parts of a social system as a whole. The abolition orientation is intended as a constant challenge to well meaning reformers and managers of control institutions. It also plays the role of a counter-force to the more traditional applied research undertakings, particularly those implied by the first four models described above. It may – together with the negation and conflict models – lead to a sharp polarization of the professional 'community'. But it may also be able to demonstrate that intellectuals can play an important political role in alliance with the powerless, and not only as the advisors or mascots of the 'rulers'.

The aim of this chapter was not to decide which orientation constitutes the best approach of all. They all have some faults and some strong points. And, more importantly, it is impossible to evaluate them without making some further value commitments.

Technically speaking, it may be assumed that the negation model provides a useful methodological tool for applied and evaluative research. The conflict model may bring important features of reality and representativeness to the discussions about social change. The action research model encourages involvement of the expert in community life as well as in decision-making bodies, so helping to break some of the barriers between decision-makers and communities. The crisis model teaches us how difficult it is to deal with irrational situations (or situations labelled as irrational) using 'rational' strategies. It also proves once again how difficult it is to deal with a crisis in some limited area without touching some more basic problems of the broader context. The abolition model offers some help with this problem. The goal-attainment model may enable the investigation of the interrelations between given means and ends, but it has to be viewed through the prospects opened by the other models. The system model may be helpful in testing various strategies for guiding large organizations. However, without the elements of the conflict and negation model it may easily contribute to their sterile stabilization and perpetuation as well as to actually covering up and freezing existing conflicts.

If we now take aside the gross ideological and methodological differences between the various approaches and try to describe the place of values (or value systems) in practice-oriented social science research, we may assume that they may appear, among other possibilities, as
(1) determinants of the basic paradigm through which the social reality is viewed, the research methods selected and the research findings organized (interpreted);
(2) determinants of the desired socio-political solutions and goals;
(3) determinants of the direction of social (or class) solidarity of the researchers;
(4) preconditions of the proposed strategy of implementation of

social change (for instance, when the values held by the given population are perceived as facilitators of the process of change);

(5) the subject of change (when, for example, the proposed policy aims at particular changes in social consciousness and value systems);

(6) evaluative criteria of a research-based policy (in so-called evaluative research).

Finally, we should note that various approaches may be found in works of both 'conservative' and 'radical' social scientists. Those labels seem not to have much to do with the methodological orientation of their research projects. Their attitudes towards the role of values in research enterprise do not actually differentiate them. Probably, the values themselves differ greatly, but this would be much easier to find out if they spoke more openly about them.

Bibliography

Baritz, L. (1970), 'The Servants of Power', in J. D. Douglas (ed.), *The Impact of Sociology*, New York: Appleton.

Bennis, W. G., Benne, K. D., and Chin, R. (1969), *The Planning of Change*, New York: Holt, Rinehart, pp. 359-425, 470-96.

Christie, N. (1976), 'Conflicts as Property', Foundation Lecture to mark the opening of the Centre for Criminological Studies, Sheffield.

Gouldner, A. W. (1962), 'Anti-Minotaur: The Myth of a Value-Free Sociology', *Social Problems*, vol. 9, no. 3, winter.

Hammer, R. (1963), 'Role Playing: A Judge is a Con, a Con is a Judge', in R. Buckhout (ed.), *Toward Social Change*, New York: Harper & Row.

Horowitz, I. L. (1963), 'Sociology for Sale', *Studies on the Left*, vol. 3, summer.

Horowitz, I. L. (1967), *The Rise and Fall of Project Camelot. Studies in the Relationship Between Social Science and Practical Politics*, Cambridge, Mass.: M.I.T.

Illich, I. (1973), *Deschooling Society*, Harmondsworth: Penguin.

Mathiesen, T. (1974), *The Politics of Abolition*, Oslo: Martin Robertson (Law in Society Series).

Podgórecki, A. (1968), 'Five Functions of Sociology', *Polish Sociological Bulletin*, no. 1.

Podgórecki, A. (1975), *Practical Social Sciences*, London and Boston, Mass.: Routledge & Kegan Paul.

Sjoberg, G., and Cain, L. D. (1971), 'Countersystem Models and the Analysis of Social Systems', in Herman Turk and Richard L. Simpson (eds), *Institutions and Social Exchange*, Indianapolis, Ind., and New York: Bobbs-Merrill.

Taylor, I., Walton, P., and Young, J. (1975), *Critical Criminology*, London and Boston, Mass.: Routledge & Kegan Paul.

22 Procreation of social values: 'Intelligentsia of all countries unite'[1]

Adam Podgórecki

Much has been written about values, strategies and ideologies of the different social strata. The involvement – active and passive – of different classes in economic and political social struggle and change is, therefore, well documented, where diagnoses are interwoven with action designs.

For the working classes, a slogan was coined: 'Proletariats of All Countries Unite'; or, 'Workers of the World Unite'. Certain agents act as spokesmen for the group's interests. Some are party members, and some workers at large. Others are self-appointed intellectuals who do not belong to the working class, but intend to represent it. Their interests are either immediate, intermediate or long-term – or a combination. Hierarchies of values, styles of life, aspirations, ways to achieve the success of the middle class are quite sharply disclosed.

Codes of honour and conduct of the nobility have, to a lesser degree, been described and analysed. But the essential threads of this behaviour can be traced through the history of mankind (e.g. Ossowska, 1973; Elias, 1969). Its manifestation in arts and literature underlines the allure of courage and dignity.

Today, the bourgeoisie's implicit and explicit concepts and values are sometimes treated like environmental factors – air, water, a native language or personal milieu – and regarded as such; it has its bearing on social sciences, owing to the social origin of their adherents.

It can be claimed, generally, that attention focuses on each social stratum as it emerges in time; when it finally gains economic and political momentum. These shifts contribute effectually to the accumulated knowledge of an individual social stratum, but also of other social strata concerned.

Nevertheless, careful analysis of this collected mass of material reveals a significant segment of social structure in contemporary societies which is still relatively uncharted. *Intelligentsia*, therefore, may be defined as 'terra incognita' on the map in the modern social atlas.[2]

What, then, are the primary features of this newly identified social group?

In his striking examination of this subject, A. Gella appears justified in his claim that 'the term "Intelligentsia" is used today in almost all industrially developed as well as developing countries to designate groups and strata of educated but un-appropriated people' (Gella, 1976, p. 9). He also tabulates seven basic groups to which the designation 'Intelligentsia' might be applied. Whether the list is sufficiently complete or correct is open to question: it is imperative, however, that it be quoted:

1 The historical 'classical' intelligentsia of Russia and Poland which developed during the nineteenth century and survived in Russia until the Bolshevik Revolution and in Poland until the communist unheavals of 1945.
2 The social groups during the interwar period in Hungary and Czechoslovakia which were called or treated themselves as the intelligentsia.
3 A part of the better-educated and humanistically oriented middle class of the West which together with professional intellectuals have been termed by some sociologists 'the intelligentsia'.
4 The amorphous agglomerate of social groups in the socialist countries which gained the name of the 'working intelli- gentsia'.
5 The educated strata in new African and Asian nations which compete with the native bourgeoisie for national leadership.
6 The incipient groups of dissident and in part revolutionary intelligentsia which, during approximately the last 20 years, have begun to appear within the affluent societies.
7 The small groups of dissidents in the Soviet Union, and only certain morally and intellectually independent groups in Poland and Czechoslovakia whose social role and place in the social structure resemble very closely the old 'classical' intelligentsia of the nineteenth century (Gella, 1976, p. 23).

The various participators in this social group share a common denominator: their function is (and has been) complementary to other social strata; their role is subsidiary – and, in some cases, bordering on servile. Traditionally they have been considered the reservoir of brains and talent necessary for the solution of ubiquitous urgent social problems. In fulfilling its task, the intelligentsia[3] assumes the image of an 'instrumental puppet' or a 'buffer social group', operating on the margins of social life – often becoming defenceless scapegoats. In the event of failure, the blame is theirs.[4]

The main character of the intelligentsia has been so effectively established through social history that its members accept these imperatives, and recognize their mandate: dedicated service, and satisfactory solution of problems confronting – and created by – other social groups. This awarness, however, has not led them to redefine accepted obligations in a format more beneficial to their own specific interests.

How does it happen that a group so devoted to the needs of others – especially the bourgeoisie, who may offer financial reward; or the working class, lacking the *savoir-faire* for self-expression – is unable to define or defend interests of its own? Several factors, reinforcing each other, are responsible:

(1) Systematic conditioning (*sui generis* socialization of the whole group itself) incurs this attitude.
(2) Fragmentation of loyalties and obligations to others provides no one denominator for common and personally identified interests.
(3) Institutions serviced by the intelligentsia are ordered in turn to fulfil the needs of others; this, in itself, redirects their attention to other spheres of development.
(4) Quite often the intelligentsia lacks the capacity or power to reject 'false consciousness' by which it might have been captured.

With these factors in mind, a picture of the intelligentsia emerges, and the following definition is applicable: a group of people who challenge the social and political establishment with proposals for change which appear both optional and realistic, and policies to implement them.

In different social systems, the intelligentsia's function varies. It may be diagnostic, evaluative, that of a judge, spiritual or socio-technical.

Primarily, the diagnostic function is closely associated with their traditional role, stemming from medieval times. Individuals, social groups and entire societies continually face changing social situations, with the task of recognizing and countering the problems that accompany them. Recognition requires definition and explanation of these events, with some agent to label them, condense them and present their essence in concise cognitive notions. With analysis, a network of complicated human interrelations is unravelled, and clearly mirrored by simplistic diagnosis.[5] The more this is enriched by explanation, the better the diagnosis fulfils its purpose. Often, as a response to social expectations, not just one diagnosis materializes; others accompany it, triggering off a spate of cognitive (and emotional) competition. In the wake of ensuing epistemological clashes, one of them may emerge which is – in comparison with the others – the most comprehensive, adequate and appealing, and therefore a final victor worthy of acceptance.

Such diagnoses are expected – unofficially, at least – from the intelligentsia. With their intellectual capacities, its members are favourably pre-disposed to create this sort of *Weltanschauung*. Experts when hired for this work represent a ramified branch of the intelligentsia, and act on the dictates of a sponsor. Volunteer experts – if they emerge at all – are not inhibited by any such commission and their diagnoses may, therefore, be further reaching and more illuminating.

Their disseminated conclusions are generally both descriptive and evaluative: a combination of identification and normative commitments. Seldom – if ever – is a diagnosis purely descriptive. In scientific methodology, this represents an unfortunate mix of elements in differing orders. It is, however, greatly appreciated by members of the society to which it applies, because they welcome value assessments as well as knowledge, and the former are more closely linked with human behaviour. Evaluative diagnosis and approach is also important in formulative *Weltanschauung*, and global acceptance (or rejection) of the given problem rests upon it.

The gap, in modern societies, between the behaviour of social actors and its effects often arises as a result of the sophisticated structure of institutional and organizational links which are in themselves remote, and the evaluative function of the intelligentsia quickly increases. Indeed, considerable intellectual recognition is at times a prerequisite for the syntheses of diverse elements in a single (yet highly ramified) picture. Each spectre is comprised of many elements in complex human interrelations, and plain common sense cannot encompass the array of potentially fragmented outcomes and by-products. In the traditional narrow confines of family life or neighbourly contact, the feed-back of social actions was immediate, its voice and impact clear.

Presently, there emerged – in several nebulous cases – a group of established authorities or informal leaders recognized as a corporate body,[6] who were eager to project their own theories and truths. As individual judges waned, the conglomerate of inter-linked professional specialists materialized, with an institutionally accredited right to evaluation.

Intelligentsia members who enjoy key positions with the sophisticated apparatus of mass media use these channels not only for the dissemination of information: they impress their own message on it. By this process of infiltration – in beliefs commonly supposed to be those of agencies sponsoring preferences of a given establishment – they are able to reinforce their own set of values. These values are salutary, not only as moral pointers to society generally, but for the guidance of individuals (or groups) who may lack instruction in behaviour.

Until recently, the intelligentsia concentrated its energies on instrumental solutions to social disharmony, and cultivation of beneficial social interaction. Its additional concern today is problem assessment. To achieve this goal, it may formulate, amongst other images:

(1) *Hatred targets* Changeable ideas or personalities who, for a given period of time, are subjects of attack and collective rejection. (This rejection helps define more properly the boundaries of one's loyalty and preference.)
(2) *Martyr images* Images of unsuccessful leaders who, notwithstanding possession of all imaginable virtues, are destroyed by a dominant stratum or adverse circumstances.
(3) *Perversely nobilitating coat of arms* Means by which the ill equipped can enter the realm of virtue. (Through myths, legends, mystical allusion, unrealistic or fabricated images.)

Members of the intelligentsia quite often use these and other sleight-of-hand social devices as conjuring tricks, to procure various social bonds.

Closely associated with this particular (evaluative) function is another: that of proclaiming ultimate judgments. Some of the intelligentsia volunteer in a specialist judicial capacity, relating to specific current social problems. Out of this arises a further network. Its existence owes nothing to reflected public glory or prestigious figures – rather to the beneficial collective experience of the whole social system and its human components (sometimes it includes poets or writers, priests, certain categories of ideologist). A number of factors prompt this action:

(1) To gain – or increase – social prominence.
(2) Moral abhorrence of specific events or situations.
(3) The theory that appeals to public opinion (and its possible mobilization) can effect a positive desire for social change.

These aspirations to the office of judgment naturally abound in fields where the gap in values between a ruling establishment and informal intelligentsia circles is wide. In Poland, during the absence of independence, the function of proclaiming judgment (when it was generated) was reserved mainly for poets and writers. They felt almost obliged to express the profound moral, societal and national sentiments. In some cases, they appeared to be the personification of these sacred values.[7]

Those who rose to higher echelons of social prominence could, if they chose, assume the role of 'governors of souls'. In the wake of a monarchy which fell into disrepute by helping to accomplish partition of the Polish state, they found themselves hailed as uncrowned kings.

Amongst present dissenters, the same tendency prevails. It is interesting to observe, however, that some of them – the more astute manipulators – are taking advantage of this situation by using this new game to obliterate their previous errors, evil actions and even crimes, in order to regain social dignity. To achieve this, they sometimes implicate others: novices in a game whose rules they have yet to learn. Now, as a result, a new problem arises. How far can these self-appointed exponents of the values basic to informal public opinion be trusted – when, in instantly changeable social situations, only their paramount desire for social prominence remains constant?

It is also worth recording that some governors of souls often add a corollary to the essential tract of their statements in the form of associated prediction. Individuals and society as a whole (especially its elite circle) like to know what the future holds in store, and welcome supposedly informed prognoses.

Consequently some representatives of the intelligentsia assume the role of prophet, elaborating manufactured myths with a purported recipe for survival. Because these prophecies span a wide spectrum of potential inevitables, some are bound to materialize. The visionaries are then singled out for accolade, with the endorsement of social, political and religious approval.

In time, social tasks may divide. Key figures appear in the intelligentsia, but not as prophet-leaders bent on successfully materializing myths and ideals. This reflects an inherent co-ordination conflict between the principled and instrumental attitudes of intelligentisia. According to these assumptions, the leading group of intelligentsia may undergo several transformations, of which the following is the most typical:

When small groups, organizations, institutions, etc. face an inherent conflict questioning the basic assumptions of the principal ideas which underlie their structure, then several processes emerge. Growing challenges manifest themselves, first through scattered and strident moral accusations, generated by different sources and emotionally loaded, attacking the basic assumptions of the existing order. These accusations are initially often narrow-minded, too hasty, one-sided, based on ignorance, lacking alternatives and loaded with high moral principle. The logical inconsistency of these objections raises the problem of cognitive synthesis. The next, oncoming generation of challengers, taking into account the emotional and risky involvement of their predecessors, invest a new, mainly logical, line of offence. This platform (instrumental and pragmatic from the point of view of the newly emerged group of cognitive innovators) introduces some order into the scattered seeds of the challenging movement of ethical innovators. Then a sharp conflict emerges between often highly involved, usually altruistic but inconsistent or even illogical moral innovators, and pragmatic and instrumental dogmatic leaders. Practitioners who are methodologically immature have a natural tendency to associate themselves with the ethically pure moral innovators, and despise pragmatic and orderly continuators. But this is a sociotechnical trap. The reasonable social engineer takes these conflicting elements equally into consideration: he utilizes as parts of his strategic synthesis the junction of moral forces of ethical leaders and the cognitive innovation of those who seek to capitalize on the social change which the moralists promote (Podgórecki, 1976, p. 33).

These psychological characteristics of the intelligentsia's leaders are not unique, nor are their pragmatic and instrumental attitudes peculiar. These are apparent in the leaders of other strata and social situations. Administrative, managerial and leadership qualifications are sometimes directly attributable to professional ability. Any quasi-sociotechnical forte in the intelligentsia owes its origin to everyday patterns of behaviour, and is not a model art cultivated by the science of administration. These traits reflect the essentially spiritual mode of the intelligentsia, whose motives are activated by altruism, and the desire to create a socially beneficial environment for others. In societies under internal and/or external stress, or where the administrators' action falls far short of its citizens' expectations, it may well be possible that the effects of the intelligentsia's active benevolence are – in sum total – considerably greater than those resulting from the inaugural conception and implementation by organs of rational managerial science.

This phenomenon must be examined in its relative social context. Nevertheless, stratification inside intelligentsia should be taken into more detailed examination. In some societies – Poland, for example – a clear distinction is apparent even to the man in the street. Some echelons of so-called intelligentsia are labelled as the 'one quarter' or 'patchthread' element: this subcategory of intelligentsia, motivated by snobbish pretensions, aspires to social domains beyond their accustomed station.

In societies where the intelligentsia has a specific role, its primary activities, generally speaking, are:
(1) Education.
(2) Global approach to social problems:
    (a) moral,
    (b) rational,
    (c) missionary.
(3) Sociable life.

On average, the intelligentsia are superior in education. For them, knowledge has an autotelic (*per se*) value independent of instrumental potential,[8] and should be the focus of attention in day to day life. This generalized attitude – probably a meta-attitude – has an important impact on numerous aspects of social activity: professional occupation, social engagements, leisure, the choice of friends and life partners, etc.

The essential value of education is transmitted by the intelligentsia, within their member circle, from one generation to the next as an almost natural imperative. (This habit is similarly found in the traditional *modus vivendi* of Jewish communities in the Diaspora.) In all its implications – cult of expertise, practice based on recognition, the resolving power of knowledge, etc. – the merit of education is the basic tenet in the intelligentsia creed.

Owing to their expertise potential, members of the intelligentsia are usually hired by other social forces: in only a few societies do they act on their own initiative. In a way, they are like prostitutes. Supposedly without 'pleasures' of their own, they provide them for buyers. As an agency, in principle, this specific social stratum becomes the spokesman for the affairs of others, and articulates them. Taking this a stage further, it assumes – as a catalyst – the role of intermediary caretaker for divergent social groups. Lacking personal vested interests, it more eagerly undertakes the onerous task of finding a platform on which outside conflicts can be compromised and resolved. A notable disparity should be pointed out here: traditionally the Polish and Russian intelligentsia have been driven by missionary motivation, whereas the Western version of it played (and still, as a rule, play) mainly the role of 'hired experts'.

If the above mentioned primaries – education, social entertainment and a global approach to social problems – have real autotelic value and are genuinely inherent in the character of the intelligentsia, this stratum (structurally similar, socially varied) has a common ground for assimilation in differing societies:
(1) Exchanging news and experience.
(2) Helping to soften oppression in one or another system – by unmasking the oppressors or hidden miscreants.

310

(3) Offering each other support and refuge (to lick the wounds of battle).

(4) Expounding comprehensive diagnoses of both sound and weak elements in different social systems - thereby affording better options and solutions to common social problems.

(5) Defining the path towards a meta-societal system which would embrace the fundamentals of the best social action, and avoid the pitfalls of the worst.

These missionary attitudes - at least in the Polish and Russian intelligentsia - may 'altruistically' prevent partisan leanings.

As champion of education and rationalization, the intelligentsia is seen to be an even more willing advocate at the bar of moral issues. If we accept that a new model of ethics is emerging, the intelligentsia, as the most perceptive social stratum, is a 'natural' for promoting an all-encompassing moral concept.

Unfettered by and being alert to socially-orientated ethics, the intelligentsia - more than any other stratum - has the ability to recognize the essence of global ethics, and to implement its demands. (There is a discussion of global ethics in the next chapter.)

Owing to its genuine, inherent ethical and sociotechnical attitudes, the intelligentsia can provide with relative ease those tested social patterns of behaviour which have been recognized as functional in the solution of problems found within small social groups (micro-social engineering). Also, through the accumulated and varying professional experience of its representatives, it has access to proven remedies for ailments on the mezzanine level (ministries of justice, social services, health and educational direc- tion, etc.). These inductive generics and tested approaches could, within the intelligentsia framework, be expanded and rationalized generally in order to tackle macro-social problems. And if this is successful, politicians may be out of work.

Material possessions and power have never been natural rewards for the intelligentsia. Traditionally they have been satisfied with the benefits of social intercourse; these rate high on the value chart in their stratum, and are not without merit. Power is at the mercy of whimsy, and material assets can vanish overnight - but the pleasures of friendship, loyal camaraderie and mutual entertain- ment are all relatively stable in comparison. In the process of its generation, the intelligentsia was able to amass 'goods' of a more vital and lasting nature.

In the difficult task of creating a unified mundane society, many problems remain unsolved; especially that of potential 'false consciousness' in the intelligentsia. If - again, like a prostitute - the intelligentsia gains its main rewards through services provided (and rendering at the same time its own resources), can it recognize, estimate and evaluate its own genuine pleasures and recompense? Putting this rhetorical, perverse question another way – what basic norms (apart from those mentioned before) could the intelligentsia stipulate as central values for unified mankind? And can it overcome its failure, inherent until now, to resolve the constant dissonance of loyalties?

The answer to these questions lies in the essential features of the intelligentsia – education, global approach to problems and social entertainment. Cultivation of these characteristics may lead to recognition – and consequent rejection – of accumulated elements of 'false consciousness'. Alternatively, if developed by *maieutic* technique, the birth of genuine and authentic values of those who are *positive deviants* may result. The analogy in the latter projection sees the intelligentsia in the role of midwife for creative pain of positive deviance, i.e. with nonconformists and courageous innovators demolishing obsolete residua of existing social systems and – usually through simultaneous self-destruction – pointing the way to positive reconstitution.

This concept embodies both weak and strong features. Of these, the most vulnerable is that if the intelligentsia is not accepted as the steam generator for the 'locomotive' of history (as the working class 'used' to be – and still 'is', according to some), then it should not be regarded as a mainspring in historical development. Nor would it have instrumental power as both a political weapon and a tool for politically viable construction. The most salient feature lies in cautious identification of those social groups and their processes which aid and inspire cultivation of mankind's most human elements. They are sources of informed opinion on ethical and political actions and consequences. Their beliefs are not coloured by avarice. Perception enables them to illuminate the virtues of positive deviants. Who – if not the intelligentsia – is well enough equipped to rescue mankind from totalitarianism (in all its faces), internal alienation and fragmentation, or to avert the horror of nuclear disaster and the total annihilation of our habitat? And also: who is able – if not the intelligentsia – to stop the steady progress of *social nihilism*, and to propose values of *a new order*?

Notes

1 The original text was presented as a paper at the Netherlands Institute for Advanced Study in the Humanities and Social Sciences, Wassenaar, 19 April 1977. I subsequently utilized some elements of the discussion in preparing the present version of this chapter. I would like to acknow-

ledge especially the remarks of Dr R. Gerson, Dr R. Kahn and Dr G. Goodman. It should also be noted that this chapter was published in the Polish (quarterly) magazine, *Oficyna Poetów*, no. 1 (78), 1978, in London. Subsequent correspondence based on this publication between Dr I. Berlin and myself is attached as an appendix.

2　In a classic, but now forgotten book on this subject, Blaha proposed the following definition of this social phenomenon:

> Intelligentsia can be best characterized in terms of its social function, the function of spiritualization. Society cannot exist without a spiritual atmosphere, without spiritual ties and the spiritual values of truth, beauty, good, order, peace, consolation, etc. Through this function intelligentsia creates for society the following necessary essentials of self-preservation: the spiritual integration of all special groups, the same spiritual atmosphere and spiritual values for all. It ranges itself round the cultural spiritualization principles, which links society vertically. Intelligentsia is further a non-class and non-vocational social category. We find it at all levels of income, in all social groups centred upon the realm of economic and political activity,
> namely in the upper social strata; and besides this it has a place of its own in the upper stratum of social space, apart from all state- and class-groupings. It, therefore, represents through its function a factor unifying and integrating all component parts of society (Blaha, 1937, p. 380).

3　The intelligentsia's function varies according to its social background. In Poland, for example, the long established values of Polish society – independence, freedom, tolerance, equality, religious devotion – are championed: its concepts, therefore, are traditionally-orientated, with a focus on the past. But in emerging African countries, the new intelligentsia acts as a prophet for the future.

4　An additional version of intelligentsia can be termed 'compradore intelligentsia', in the role of an intermediary – or buffer – between an imposing political or social stratum and others in opposition. Here, the dominant group (with power, legal and educational systems, and information sources all at its disposal) uses the 'compradore intelligentsia' as a 'stooge', influencing a target community through these representatives. 'Compradore intelligentsia' may be wooed by promises of social promotion and associated rewards, may succumb to bribery or intimidation, or may fall prey to the influence of 'false consciousness', or illusory identification.

5　A distinction must be drawn between intelligentsia and 'intellectuals'. The former observes interaction of standards, interests and behaviour in a society, but until now lacked its own ideology. The latter are attributed with creation of enduring cultural values – as writers, poets, composers, artists, scientists, etc. One interpretation of their relationship is that all intellectuals are, *ipso facto*, members of the intelligentsia, whereas not all intelligentsia are intellectuals (viz. students, dissidents). Another classifies intellectuals as 'literati' (not specifically men of letters, but the learned class as a whole), and intelligentsia as a subcategory of the literati, motivated by its positive independence and moral responsibilities.

6   This suggests a sort of 'cultural jet-set' who, as figures of public interest, enjoy prominence in the mass media (while 'pure' intellectuals remain 'backroom boys'). They include television personalities, film stars, fashion designers, some literati - and anyone whose news value centres on personal character.

7   Thus Isaiah Berlin (*Russian Thinkers*, London: The Hogarth Press, 1978) is not only incorrect when he attributes (verbatim: p. 116) the invention of the term 'intelligentsia' (which is, in itself, a minor problem) to Russians, but he is also wrong when he assigns the emergence and self-recognition of this social stratum to Russian society. Due to the uniqueness of Polish history - the long period of lack of independence when society, rejecting foreign authorities, was looking for its own governance - it was indeed a Polish 'invention' (later adopted by those who are described as 'Russian Thinkers'). So, does the 'Matthew effect' also operate here?

8   Essential elements of the code of integrity which governs intelligentsia engaged in comparative socio-political diagnoses are:

(1) Data interpretation is not influenced by opportunistic motives.

(2) Relevant data is never suppressed or omitted.

(3) Data responsible for informed knowledge (on which judgments are based) is always accessible for inspection.

(4) Proposed social actions are necessarily qualified by considered judgment.

Bibliography

Blaha, I. A. (1937), *Sociologie Inteligence*, Prague: Orbis.

Elias, N. (1969), *Die Hoefische Gesellschaft (Society of Nobles)*, Lufterhand.

Gella, A. (1976), 'An Introduction to the Sociology of Intelligentsia', in A. Gella (ed.), *The Intelligentsia and the Intellectuals*, London: Sage.

Ossowska, M. (1973), *Ethos Rycerski i jego Odmiany (Knights' Ethos and its Changes)*, Warsaw: PWN.

Podgórecki, A. (1976), 'Social Technology and Decision Making', in A. Cherns (ed.), *Sociotechnics*, London: Malaby Press.

Appendix

Correspondence between Sir Isaiah Berlin and Professor Adam Podgórecki, on the derivation and concept of the word 'intelligentsia'.

28 March 1978

Dear Professor Podgórecki,

Thank you for sending me a copy of *Oficyna Poetów* with your article on the intelligentsia, which I read with great interest and attention, and in particular, of course, the note in which you refer to my attribution of the intelligentsia - both the word and the reality which it denotes - to nineteenth century Russia. You may well be right, and, in consequence, I may be mistaken; but I am not clear about why you think this. I think that my concept of the intelligentsia is perhaps somewhat different to that which you indicate in your article. The sense in which it refers to writers, artists, thinkers, academics, intellectuals of various kinds, critics of society, etc. is far wider than the group to which I wish to refer. In your sense of the word, it goes back to the French *philosophes* in the eighteenth century, to the German *Aufklärer*, perhaps to the *libertins* sceptics in France in the seventeenth century, perhaps even to the humanists of the Renaissance. I wish to speak of something much more specific and narrow: a self-conscious group of thinkers who see themselves as directly opposed to an oppressive and irrational regime, united not only by opposition to it, but by a commitment to rational thought, social and intellectual progress, a belief in, and a deep respect for, the methods of the natural sciences, dedication to such values as civil and personal freedom, personal integrity and the pursuit of truth no matter what the consequences - and therefore opposition to the established government, established churches, to tradition, prescription, reliance upon uncriticized intuitions, and irrationality of every kind. In this sense, to take the English alone, neither Dickens nor Carlyle nor Ruskin can be regarded as members of an intelligentsia - besides which, in England the very notion of the intelligentsia is thin and unconvincing, inasmuch as there has not been a modern powerful clerical establishment to be attacked, nor an arbitrary government, at any rate in the nineteenth century. In Russia, neither Gogol nor Dostoevsky nor Tolstoy nor even Chekhov would have thought of themselves as members of the intelligentsia - Tolstoy is very hostile to it, the same applies to the nationalist school of Russian composers and painters - but the term, in my sense, does apply to countless doctors, schoolmasters, agricultural experts, economists, etc., who regarded themselves as disciples of this central oppositional Fronde, on which they looked as leading in the war against obscurantism, despotism, bureaucratic rule, philistinism, etc. I do not know if the Poles used this word before the Russians - I should be much interested to know whether they did - I had always assumed that

315

it was first used by someone in Russia in the 1860s, whether by Boborykin (to whom it is usually attributed) or someone before him. I do not believe, for example, that a Polish poet like Mickiewicz would have identified himself with a group of this type, any more than would his contemporaries Silvio Pellico, Byron, Pushkin or the Decembrist poets – they may have fought against despotism, but they were not committed to idealisation of the natural sciences and scientists, nor to a faith in material progress. The major values of the eighteenth century Enlightenment certainly formed a *sine qua non* of the Russian intelligentsia in the sense in which I wish to speak of them. My 'intelligentsia' had a powerful sense of internal loyalties, in terms of which they could regard men like Katkov, at times even Turgenev, as traitors or backsliders, *and* Slavophiles, however intelligent, intellectual, pure-hearted, brilliant, influential, would not be regarded as members of this movement.

If it is not a Russian phenomenon or a Russian word, I should like to be corrected.

Yours sincerely,

Isaiah Berlin

12th April 1978

Dear Sir Isaiah,

Thank you for your interesting letter of March 28th.

I will try to present my views in the following manner: (A) the origin of the term 'intelligentsia'; (B) the emergence of the social stratum labelled 'intelligentsia'.

A I think that A. Gella is correct when he says:
The origin of the term 'intelligentsia' has been attributed to the three nations: Russia, Germany and Poland. Some historians assume that it was coined by Peter Boborykin, a Russian author, in 1860. This is, however, a misconception, as was noted by Wactas Lednicki, who showed that the term was used in Russian literature by V. G. Belinsky in 1846. But he also knew that the term was used approximately at the same time in Poland and wrote that 'Russia and Poland were the birthplace of this class, and their languages created the term "intelligentsia" . . .' (Lednicki 1967:40). Alan Pollard also questioned the opinion that Boborykin was the inventor of this term (Pollard 1964). Richard Pipes has noted that 'the German word "Intelligenze" was used as early as 1849 to describe the same phenomenon as "intelligentsia", namely a group distinguished from the rest of society by its education and "progressive" attitude' (Pipes 1971). The same year, but six months earlier, I pointed out that the term 'was first used in Polish literature by Karol Libelt in 1844 . . . (Gella 1971:4).

316

I still maintain my claim that this term was born first in Poland
- persuaded in part by linguistic considerations: (1) the term was
taken into modern languages from Latin, which had an
incomparably stronger influence on the Poles than on the
Russians; (2) the suffic 'cja' in the Polish word 'inteligencja' is
closer to the Latin 'intelligentsia' than the Russian 'tsia'; (3) the
suffic 'cja' (tsia in English spelling) is common in Polish but much
less frequently encountered in Russian. (A. Gella (ed.), 1976, *The
Intelligentsia and the Intellectuals, Theory, Method and Case
Study*, Sage Publications Ltd, London.)

I may add that although it was J. Chałasiński who, after the
Second World War, originally revived the Polish studies on the
intelligentsia, the most illuminating ideas in this area came from
the practically unknown works of A. Zajaczkowski (*Główne
Elementy Kultury Szlacheckiej w Polsce*, Ossolineum, Wroclaw,
1961).

B Wherever the origin of this term comes from, the problem of the
emergence of the intelligentsia as a social stratum is the crucial
one. I willingly concede that the Renaissance thinkers prepared the
atmosphere for the creation of this social stratum. (In Poland we
have a parallel group of this kind of intellectuals who, though not
sufficiently known outside the country, still deserve more
recognition as a feature in the European intellectual spectrum, for
example: A. F. Modrzejewski [1503-1572]. See A. Podgórecki,
Law and Society, 1974, Routledge & Kegan Paul, London, pp.
52-65.) Later, toward the end of the eighteenth century a group of
intellectuals (again parallel to the French Encyclopaedists) was
established in Poland around the Committee of National
Education (the first department of education in Europe). Those
predecessors of the intelligentsia still cannot be regarded as an
independent social stratum. Apparently the final one strategic
element which induced the materialisation of it was the loss of
independence of the Polish state and society (final partition
between Austria, Prussia and Russia in 1795). This historic blow
created a call for an enlightened group of informal (since the
formal had been eliminated) social and political leaders who would
be able to lead the national fight against constant political and
cultural oppression. Subsequent deprivation of the Polish
population, and especially of the Polish nobility, of their
existential roots by means of waves of deportations, extensive
confiscation of estates and expulsions directed mainly - but not
exclusively - against the Polish gentry did, in effect, enforce
patriotic attitudes in this population with additional feelings of
material harm, status imbalance, etc. In consequence, not only the
partitions of the Polish state of 1772, 1793, 1795, but also the
risings of its population in 1830, 1846 and 1863, through their
traumatic, nationwide effects, generated and crystallised the new
social stratum - the intelligentsia. A new social entity was born and

moulded by these processes into an opposition to the oppressive and irrational regimes. Although this antagonism was from the beginning mainly political, geared to the recovery of independence, in due course it became directed also against social and economic injustice. It still remains an open question in which way the Russians, who have this remarkable ability to push everything to extremes, adopted the messianic, missionary, service-oriented posture of the Polish intelligentsia and applied it in dealing with problems of their own society. Also interesting is how they obtained 'world visibility' as dedicated, unconditional fighters for social freedom, or to what extent the ex-post influence of the ideology of the Soviet Revolution merely labelled them in such a way. But even if the shift of emphasis from the problems of national independence to the problems of national dissent, from the Moloch of the established economic and political regime may eventually be attributed to 'Russian Thinkers' (incidentally, an excellent book!), nevertheless, this change in emphasis is only of secondary importance. The primary one is the intellectual quest for social justice, pursued, if necessary, even at the expense of individual liberty and integrity. And this feature, characteristic of the Polish intelligentsia, is congruent with your definition of this term: '. . . a group of thinkers . . . opposed to an oppressive and irrational regime . . . committed to rational thought . . . in . . . dedication to . . . civil and personal freedom, personal integrity and the pursuit of truth no matter what the consequences . . .'.

Sincerely yours,

Adam Podgórecki

23 Global ethics[1]
Adam Podgórecki

Traditional ethics

In an interesting recent work by Maria Ossowska, a Polish professor of sociology, an attempt was made to find an adequate definition of morality. She did not succeed, but as the fortunate by-product of her endeavours there emerged the creation of a new branch of sociology or, rather, a special subdivision of it – the sociology of morals. Detailed considerations of findings coming from the sociology and anthropology of morals increased scepticism of discovering a unique and consistent definition or morality. M. Ossowska concluded finally that all attempts to find such a definition were and would continue to be unsuccessful. She added:

> All these attempts at a definition of morality did not lead, of course, to a definition, but formulated necessary conditions which had to be fulfilled by a value judgment in order to make it moral. Whoever accepts this condition will be compelled to agree that moral judgments are extremely rare, since few people who formulate value judgments ask themselves whether they would be willing to generalize their opinion in any of the quoted interpretations. Thus moral valuations would be reduced to rare occasions in which we should probably hesitate over whether our criterion is the criterion of being a right judgment or of being a moral one (Ossowska, 1971, p. 181).

She therefore finally decided to propose her own approach to studies on morality ('Ethics is supposed to be found in books, while morality is to be found in life'). These studies should be used, according to her, on the different models of styles of life which appear in various societies and various subcultures. Thus her notion of morality is based mainly on the concepts of the 'style of life' or on 'ethos' – notions which encompass also several relevant insights derived from anthropology and keen observations on everyday life.

By accepting this concern as a starting-point, it is possible to distinguish at least three stages in the development of morality as a generally accepted pattern of life in a given society. These stages differ not only in being created by different social processes, but also in having different applications of the basic notion of 'neighbour' or 'fellow creature'.

The poet and priest, J. Twardowski, in his sermons which are concerned with morality and addressed to children, began by asking several rhetorical questions. For example: 'Whom do you regard as your neighbour?' The children answered: 'Theresa, Marie, Catherine, Jimmie', and so on. Twardowski then asked again: 'Do you regard uncles and aunts, and all the in-laws of your parents as neighbours and fellow creatures?' After some hesitation, the children answered: 'Yes.' The priest then asked: 'And would you regard a dog or a cat as a fellow creature?' The children answered in a unanimous voice: 'No.' Twardowski then made the question more complicated by asking several subquestions; he asked if the children would help a dog or a cat if it needed their help, or if they would feed a dog or a cat. He asked, too, if they would do the same things for the cat or the dog if the animals' needs were the same as the needs of Marie or Theresa. Finally, the children agreed that they would treat a dog or a cat as a neighbour. The sermons of Twardowski give a vivid example of a process of enlargement of the meaning of the term 'neighbour'.

Possibly, at the beginning, all those people who belonged to the close family circle (based on the group which was linked by blood) were regarded as neighbours. This circle was eventually enlarged by the inclusion of people who were friends, who lived near each other and who were connected by legal relationships. This process of enlargement took place in the group which regarded itself as a separate entity. All members of this were treated and labelled as 'we'; all people who did not belong to this group were treated and labelled as 'they'. Nevertheless, these processes were not stable. When the frontiers of families or tribes were broken down, and when the nation was formed, then those people who were treated yesterday as 'they' might reappear today as 'we'. On this level of development – as the by-product of these processes – some sort of abstract idea of an unknown person such as the neighbour emerged, or was generated. But it created only an extreme case on the possible scale of normative demand. This still did not create a moral working standard for everyday behaviour. (We are not concerned here with the extremes of possible normative demands, for we are dealing with the patterns of behaviour which were accepted as the everyday norm for the treatment of other ordinary people.)

Taking the notion of the neighbour or fellow creature as the starting-point, it will probably be more convenient to distinguish the three stages of the development of moral styles of life. These stages are as follows: individually-oriented ethics, socially-oriented ethics and global ethics.

Individually-oriented ethics might be regarded as a body and conjunction of norms regulating the social behaviour of people; they have as their main target the guidance of everyday behaviour in small groups. The dominating norms are those connected with the informal behaviour of the group. In this context, the fellow creature is a person whom we know personally, or whom we can potentially or easily come to know as a person. Generally speaking, individual ethics condemn thieves, murderers, forgers, people who commit adultery, people who give false evidence and so on. Thus we can say that generally – if we accept the point of view of indivi- dually-oriented ethics – we condemn people who harm other people in the narrow scope of the relationships between them in 'face-to- face' situations. This type of behaviour usually produces direct personal and emotional reaction. In addition, we can say more generally that this type of behaviour results from principal attitudes, by which is meant direct and spontaneous acceptance or negation of a given norm which governs real or imagined behaviour. The range of possible life and social situations in small groups is, generally speaking, well codified and petrified. Typical situations are recognized and defined and described in standard ways. These typical situations also have as their counterpart norms which give recommendations for behaviour. The margin for possible aberration is therefore rather narrow, especially in a stable social system. It is for this reason that norms which correspond to the basic social situation have a *principled character*. They correspond to the approval, and especially the emotional approval or disapproval, of that behaviour. From a strictly pragmatic point of view, this type of social structure is enormously economic. Let us summarize the logistics of the pattern or paradigm which is behind it.

The given social situation generates an emotion, and this emotion – as a result of previous socialization – corresponds to a given norm. A given norm gives a prescription for behaviour. Consequently, behaviour of small groups is generally ritualized and is treated as strictly normative. If small groups or elements of these small groups (which means members of them) encounter a new social situation, then they might have to go beyond the boundaries which have been existentially settled by their own recognition. Thereupon the first tendency of those groups, or members of groups, is to react according to the patterns which have been generated earlier by their own social experience. Later, when these groups, or members of the groups – after several adjustments of their behaviour – finally recognize that the existing patterns are not adequate or, even worse, are highly inadequate, they will begin to generate new patterns. This is done in order to overcome those which are suitable only for small groups.

Summing up what we have said earlier, individually-oriented ethics have been generated to deal with those basic conflicts which small groups encounter. The ethics of the Decalogue are ethics of this type. They safeguard small groups (and their members) against theft, murder and other crimes. It is clear that they are a device to assist the constant interactions within small groups, although they are not necessarily suitable for the interactions which occur within larger groups. This point becomes stronger when we take into consideration the fact that social processes also produce patterns of behaviour which are applicable for a larger society, and that small groups as generators of those patterns of behaviour basically consist of family and neighbourhood associations.

Among those processes which systematically destroy the bonds which exist inside small groups, one can distinguish the following: tendencies which are directed at depersonalizing the individuality of people, to degrade their personalities to the level of exchange-able objects; technological changes which are faster than the adjustment-mechanisms at the disposal of small groups; the systematic impact of mass media – a Moloch which sometimes shouts, and sometimes quietly persuades people to change their behaviour and attitudes; more or less formalized methods of social control; the influence of large organizations which create imper-sonal relationships; and all those persuasive techniques which change yesterday's crimes into today's virtues. All these processes, and others, thus lead – especially in times of rapid social change – to the replacement of various principal attitudes by instrumental ones. Instrumental attitudes are those which are dependent on calculating the various possible results of behaviour and on the subjective evaluation of these options. Empirical research has shown that distinctions between principal and instrumental attitudes occur in social reality. Empirical research which is cited here also shows that individual orientation in ethics generated in Poland in the 1960s is characterized by the following features: it is linked with relatively low education, with symptoms of insecurity (which are measured by lack of trust of other people), with a limited ability to cope with daily living (based on subjective personal evaluation), and with a relatively weak sense of social mission (Podgórecki *et al.*, 1971 and pp. 160–2 in this book).

The individually-oriented ethics mentioned above and the principled attitudes which characterize this type of ethics should be carefully distinguished from socially-oriented ethics. Before the main feature of this type of ethics is recalled, it is advisable to set out the results of research begun in 1954 (which were published in 1970). People who are manipulative and less persuadable gain in situations where they can avoid complicated emotional problems, they are less conformist as far as social pressure is concerned, are preferred as partners in normal relationships, and are identified as leaders (Christie and Geis, 1970). This social psychological research supports to a certain extent the concepts discussed above; it shows that some individuals are characterized by instrumental attitudes in certain segments of or throughout their whole life.

Instrumentalism and pragmatism which lead to reification of the relationships between people (and which in addition increase anomie and alienation among them) contributed much to the creation of the ethics of social orientation. The most important element of ethics of this type is not the evaluation of the personal features of a given individual (his or her 'internal moral face'), but the evaluation of social effects which are generated as a consequence of playing a given social role, or accepting a given social position. The Polish research mentioned above gives some evidence of correlations between people subscribing to this type of ethics and having relatively high education, a relatively high position at work, a lack of insecurity symptoms, a better ability to cope with daily living and a higher involvement in social activities.

It is possible to say that individually-oriented ethics are oriented towards grievances which occur in small groups, but socially-oriented ethics are generated as a reaction against situations in which an individual faces losses which result from apparently anonymous, neutral and impartial organizations or social institutions. Quite often, those who govern organizations of this type are pleasant people (they can even have highly sophisticated aesthetic taste, and apparently impressive humanitarian backgrounds); they may be very sensitive about the psychological reactions of those whom they meet in direct personal contacts – yet at the same time they may be monsters and criminals. They may be monsters in the sense of creating enormous harm through the long-term consequences of their administrative actions. Although this may not be directly visible, it may accumulate until its enormity makes it evident to all. The world of organizations and institutions creates many situations in which these ethical relationships occur. Application of the standards of individually-oriented ethics to this type of situation is highly complicated. In such a situation a person who possesses institutionalized power might not harm anybody directly or intentionally. Indeed, he quite often does not know of the existence of a group of people who are affected by his (or her) actions, and might never even learn about the harm done to people as a result of this administrative and apparently purely instrumental behaviour. Ethics which accept social orientation thus do not treat as a necessary condition of ethical relations the link of direct personal interaction. They do not treat direct personal inter-relations which occur between individuals as being especially important, nor are they mainly concerned with the ethical effects of the instrumental actions of a person in a given role or position who influences the existential situations of others.

It is clear, therefore, that to understand socially-oriented ethics, links must be established between the original impulse of the action, and an intellectual diagnosis must analyse the chain of events which it triggers off, and their final consequences. It is even possible to say that the ability to grasp such a sequence (and its meaning) constitutes the essential features of the ethics of social orientation. Yet the eventual harm which is or is going to be created by the complicated chain of the organizational interactions or administrative measures must still finally be singled out and evaluated by norms belonging to individually-oriented ethics – in other words, by the norms which regulate situations described in the Decalogue.

The institutions and organizations of modern man's daily work have now become his 'second home', and thus recognition of the standards which are accepted by socially-oriented ethics and the application of them are gradually becoming a more and more important problem. Kafkaesque loss inside the bureaucratic machinery is nothing but a forlorn ethical cry for help in situations where individually-oriented ethics cannot be applied, for it is impossible to apply ethics of this type to the anonymous agents representing a given class of bosses, and officials of amorphic and formalistically unified entities. Thus Kafkaesque appeal is an additional call to build canons of socially-oriented ethics. It is a call which highlights the 'limbo' created by explanations given by agents of administration or bureaucracy, explanations which point to efficiency as their main goal. It is also a demand to make the agencies of administration and bureaucracy open and responsible to the 'people', or to those members of society for whom these agencies are designed to work.

Global ethics

In the modern world the growth of different social and political systems, economic entities and states leads to a conglomeration of different institutions and organizations operating outside the control of the people. These conglomerates will soon adopt such proportions that it will be almost impossible to distinguish the basic bonds and affiliations existing between people. This type of world creates additional situations in which the effects of the activities of different organizations and institutions might merge, or contradict themselves and counteract each other, yet multiply themselves at the same time. In this situation the very establishment of a basic moral matrix becomes, for a given person or for a given social group, a task that it is almost impossible to fulfil. So, as an antithesis to this situation, the new notion of global ethics emerges. This type of ethics might serve as a basic standard offering the possibility of piecing together the fragmentized elements of different ethical orientations.

Global ethics can be described as a further enlargement of the notion of the neighbour or fellow creature. In this context, it is not only the physical enemy who becomes a potential neighbour and fellow creature, but also an abstract enemy in the form of the unknown administrator who, with the power of his own *imperium*, could attack people without their having the slightest knowledge that he is doing so. So, the question which arises is: If an enemy might also be regarded as a neighbour or a fellow creature, then is it not possible to regard as a neighbour or fellow creature any other living – but not human – creature? Going back to the idea of St Francis of Assisi (who was able to speak with the birds and treat them as fellow creatures and neighbours) should we not also treat as our neighbour the vicious virus which is visible only on an electronic microscope? If global ethics should encompass the whole scope of living creatures – including tigers and viruses – and not only human beings, then some of the worst enemies of mankind could be treated as neighbours and fellow creatures according to these ethics. Is it not a paradox? How might it be solved? Before attempting a solution, let us recall again the main premises of global ethics. They assert, on the basis of the togetherness of all living creatures, that the earth is the common home for different states, nations, societies and social systems. Global ethics attempt to embrace not only the whole range of existing systems and relations between these systems, but also the relationship of each system to its natural habitat and, consequently, the relation of the whole of mankind towards all the remaining living creatures.

It might be said that global ethics are a response to and conscious criticism of the existing or potential shortcomings of individually- and socially-oriented ethics, and have come about as a consequence of several social processes which are now becoming increasingly visible. These are the population explosion, the energy crisis, diminishing natural resources and the subsequent destruction of the biological environment and, most recently, the destruction of the natural environment. Thus, the features which brought to light essential elements of global ethics are problems which were until recently regarded as purely technical, economic, demographic or biological. In general, the goals of traditional ethics (taking traditional ethics as both individually- and socially-oriented ethics) are the task of harmonizing relations amongst people, the preservation of the dignity of the individual and the evaluation of canons of social justice. (This last goal is the special task of ethics which is socially oriented.) Global ethics are thus concerned with the creation and protection of the lives of all living creatures. It is clear that this type of morality was expressed earlier by some Buddhist sects, and that St Francis of Assisi, when he eventually treated the sparrow as his brother, was subscribing to similar ideas. Without doubt, they were early predecessors. For this reason, it is necessary to recognize bright normative sparks (which eventually become ritualized) that anticipate future ideas that emerge later as real motivations for models of everyday behaviour. Proclaiming the affinity of all living creatures, global ethics embrace the whole of mankind. By this we mean the collection of those creatures that are connected by consciousness, tradition, the ability to foresee coming events, and the ability to invent instruments; and that these creatures are, furthermore, linked by the ability to take care not only of themselves, but also of all other 'neighbourly' creatures.

In this way global ethics become a synthesis of the new trends which have been generated by all previous types of ethics. They overcome the shortcomings of earlier ethics: the egoism and negative attitudes towards those who are regarded as 'others' which is found in individually-oriented ethics, and the possibility of creating harmful devices which are only apparently morally neutral, as well as the lack of a criterion other than expediency for establishing the highest principles of morals, which characterize socially-oriented ethics. Now, when the world becomes 'larger' and, according to the well known precept, a 'small village' – and even a corner of a village is everywhere visible in the mirrors of the mass media – there is the chance of annihilation of not only the whole of mankind but also of all life on earth (including also all tigers and viruses) through accidental nuclear catastrophe. The responsibility for guarding against such a catastrophe, for alleviating the hunger which affects half of mankind, for reducing

326

flood damage, for preventing a more acute energy crisis or such future crises as the final destruction threatening several different types of animals, or the mass destruction of the world and all that is in it - these problems compel people to undertake the task of a global settlement of the problems of the whole of mankind (and other living creatures). Thus, global ethics emerge as a newly created feeling of responsibility which is expanded to encompass the whole living world, thereby providing the general guidelines for all rational and just behaviour of which we are aware.

It is necessary to emphasize that the global ethics do not eliminate several essential recommendations of traditional ethics. Neither are they able to answer all possible ethical problems. But these ethics provide the most general values which give the highest guidance to divergent values of traditional ethics.

So, the essence of global ethics is not only that it enlarges the scope of the notion of neighbour or fellow creatures, and in consequence embraces all living creatures through this notion, but also that it begins to treat the globe as a frame of reference for all relevant ethical standards. According to this understanding, the globe is seen not only as the source of natural resources but also appears as that which unifies everything that lives, and provides the environment for that life. It is the unique and unifying entity.

This type of understanding of global ethics has far-reaching consequences, not only for the individual, but also for states and nations. According to the premises of these ethics (in contrast to traditional ethics) a nation should be concerned not only to guide its own affairs by moral principle, but should also have the right to regard affairs which occur in other nations or states as morally relevant. A given nation should, then, take into consideration events everywhere, and it also has a duty or responsibility to be aware that normatively relevant events which take place somewhere else are essentially linked with its own fate. Thus, the given nation is not only responsible for the moral order which exists in its own society, but is additionally responsible for the moral order which exists in all other societies and not only those which are neighbours linked by physical frontiers. It is linked to all by moral frontiers, frontiers established by the unity of all living creatures.

The above considerations attempt to describe different social processes which give rise to the different versions of ethics that are recognized by people. It is not intended that these considerations should suggest any norms, values or directives about how people should live. Thus the essential question remains open: Is it possible on the basis of the above trends to present a conclusion which lays down what is right and just? It is possible to say with some caution that the dangerous tiger or virus should - according to the above considerations – be treated as a potential neighbour or fellow creature, contrary to our usual practice towards them, their evaluation should be determined by their own behaviour: it should not be assumed *a priori*. If a tiger becomes dangerous, then it is necessary to try to control its aggression, and if a virus no longer exists in a harmless fashion, then it will be necessary to neutralize it.

The most general norm which emerges from traditional ethics is a norm which says you should not harm your neighbour or fellow creature. This is the negative version of this basic norm, although it has also a positive version which says that you should behave towards your fellow creature in the same manner as you expect him (or her) to behave towards you. Tsy-Kung asked his Master: 'Is the rule valid throughout one's life?' The Master answered: 'Is not the principle of reciprocity that you should not do to others what you do not wish to have done to you?' (*Confucian Dialogues*, Chapter 15, Part 23). This positive version is sometimes called the Golden Rule, and sometimes the rule of love of one's neighbour or brother. It has at least two limitations. The first is due to a narrow understanding of the notion of neighbour or fellow creature, and thus an inability to see the consequences of attitudes or actions which are generated not in a direct person to person relationship, but by a spuriously anonymous, formalized actor-agent; and this seems to be quite often the prevalent pattern now. Ethics of social orientations overcome this shortcoming but do not give the required guidance on how to deal with the world of institutions and organizations which affect people by operating through non-public manifested values, or values of a relative character. Global ethics, as has been shown, formulate a general directive which is intended to put all these moral intuitions into one unity. The unified version of global ethics says that the highest morality for all living creatures is represented by the altruism of all the heirs of this particular planet. Of course, it can be argued that in fact these ethics are egoistic: for if we imagine creatures coming from a different planet, global ethics do not dictate how creatures from this – our own – planet should behave if the creatures from the other planet were creatures of a different order. It is not an easy task to answer such speculative questions: everything would depend on what type of creatures these strangers were. Global ethics would suggest, however, that at the beginning they should be – our guests on this planet – treated as potential fellow creatures and neighbours. As in the case of viruses and tigers, their possible behaviour should be examined and then action should be undertaken according to their own behaviour. Anyway, if such creatures should appear, which is dubious, they would probably be intelligent creatures, so the bridge created by intelligence could create a chance of some mutual understanding and might make possible the avoidance of action which would be mutually destructive.

It is worthwhile demonstrating that the notion of global ethics has many possible implications, some of which might now be spelt out.

One of them is an essential question: Who is going to articulate the merging, still fragmentary or even conflicting intuitions, demands and normative requirements of global ethics, and who would consequently have the capacity to piece them together in a consistent manner? If this task is to be accomplished by the so-called intelligentsia, then its representative (also among the intellectuals) should obtain a new and different status to make the task possible.

Another problem is the role of the various organizations and institutions (like the one-time League of Nations, the United Nations, UNESCO, different blocs of states, various multi-national corporations, etc.). They might provide an important link between a given individual (or social group) and the universe of mankind, or they might divert an individual (or social group) by 'false consciousness', pressing them instrumentally, limiting their possible and socially recognized opinions, etc., towards interests designated by given (quite often 'selfish', if not 'pathological') pressure groups. But if some people start now to promulgate the idea that 'all intelligentsia should unite', then the independent power of knowledge and competence will emerge as enormously important factors of social life. This is because socially-oriented ethics, and especially global ethics, show that the principled attitudes which are the main guardians and the main vehicles of the ethics which operate on the individualistic level and in small groups are insufficient as normative 'compasses' in the more complicated work of institutions and organizations. It is necessary to have an intellectual recognition of the many possible formal interactions and legal chains which link together the enormous structure of different formal and semi-formal bodies. The interaction between and the management of these bodies creates an enormous number of social consequences which are ethically relevant. In order to give a final evaluation of the effects of these interactions, it is necessary to have an intellectual understanding of the complicated world of interrelated formal organizational and institutional or bureaucratic entities. The new community of the intelligentsia which is just in the process of creation would have the best chance of recognizing and defining the various social, political and economic situations, and of applying given ethical standards to these situations. Taking these considerations into account, it might be said that the role of the intelligentsia should increase in the future world and that the results of their work should be regarded as blueprints not only for recognizing the ethical problems in many social situations but also for providing guidance for most general desirable behaviour.

But this gives rise to the final question: Who is to control the intelligentsia and who is to warn the community of living creatures of the wrong direction towards which some versions of ethics might possibly sometimes drift?

To answer that, one may turn to global ethics. The uniqueness of it may be, in sum, reduced to three essential statements: (1) the notion of fraternity is enlarged; not only human beings are regarded as brothers and fellows – all living creatures are embraced by this concept; (2) the principle of unity of all living creatures is declared, this fraternity affects not only its members but also the environment in which they live and which they affect; (3) global ethical orientation provides a guide when the previous ones are not sufficient or when they are in conflict.

Note

1 The author is grateful to Dr Sandra Burman for her deep and useful comments made in connection with the draft of this chapter.

Bibliography

Christie, R., and Geis, F. L. (1970), *Studies in Machiavellianism*, New York: Academic Press.

Ossowska, M. (1971), *Social Determinants of Moral Ideas*, London and Philadelphia: Routledge & Kegan Paul and University of Pennsylvania Press.

Podgórecki, A., Kurczewski, J., Kwaśniewski, J., and Łoś, M. (1971), *Poglady społeczénstwa polskiego na moralność i prawo (Views of Polish Society on Morality and Law)*, Warsaw: Książka i Wiedza.

Epilogue
Adam Podgórecki and Maria Łoś

The main ideas of this book have been oriented towards the task of making sociology more responsive to the vital theoretical questions and to the main social problems which wait for satisfactory answers and solutions. In order to achieve that, several new notions have been introduced into sociological thinking. Let us briefly restate them in an appropriate order.

The proposal to understand sociology as a multi-dimensional discipline conveys, at least, two major messages.

The first is a statement that the limitation of sociology to just one selected theoretical perspective is basically wrong. Such an approach would not only deny the cognitive potential inherent in (and accumulated by) other sociological orientations but it would also promote a one-sided sociological world view.

The second one develops a point of view according to which each sociological theory has its epistemological roots in certain philosophical traditions and frameworks.

Both of these points of view have several important implications.

Taking into consideration the above premises, it is thus possible to claim that multi-dimensional sociology might stimulate development of a theory of a higher order leading to a more comprehensive and adequate synthesis. This seemingly attractive possibility is, at the present moment, rejected by the authors. Although such a possibility is recognized, the bases for this type of synthesis seem rather questionable: when it is difficult (if possible at all) to reconcile contradictory philosophical world views, why should one expect that similar tasks will appear more feasible at the level of their implications? Another understanding of the main aim of multi-dimensional sociology - the one intended by the present authors (to the extent to which they agree with each other) - is the development of a complex methodological and conceptual framework which would permit one to analyse social issues from different perspectives, and thus to grasp more comprehensively the variety of faces of social reality. It is not possible to see in the darkness a complicated sculpture unless it is illuminated from different angles at the same time. But when the light comes from one angle only, then the emerging vision would lack entirely the intriguing complexity of the whole. As a result this vision impoverishes the picture of the reality. It only isolates one dimension of it, thus giving the illusion of its pre-eminence. The proposed idea of multi-dimensional sociology is closely connected with the authors' belief that sociology should not focus on abstract, unidentified social systems. Only real, concrete social systems exist actually in social reality! Abstract social bodies appear merely as 'heuristic' beings – and they can (and should) only be studied as such!

The overview of several theoretical approaches in sociology presented above has not only attempted to summarize the essential features of various modern perspectives within this discipline, but also to examine in which way these approaches might be useful for the better understanding of social phenomena. Consequently an effort has been made to establish to what extent these approaches may be regarded as theories – understood as an interlinked set of concepts and hypotheses, or as methodological orientations understood as a set of methods united by a common epistemology, or just as a new way of looking at social reality.

The authors of this book also hold an opinion that several traditional and basic sociological notions should be, in the light of recent analyses, and empirical findings, redefined. In some pressing instances, the authors came to the belief that instead of carrying on the process of redefining already existing concepts, it would be more proper to elaborate some new ones. This belief was upheld despite the shared conviction that it is reasonable not to multiply new conceptual entities without obvious necessity. New proposed concepts tried to bridge the 'subjective' and 'objective' versions of social reality. This was due to the idea that both these versions of social reality are inseparable and influence each other differently in various social settings. It has been assumed that neither of them can justifiably be seen as a primary and determining force within all social contexts.

The development of the idea of sociotechnics is intended to contribute to the further examination of the gap between abstract theory and concrete but unreliable practice. According to this idea it is viable to utilize several achievements of the social sciences to open up the possibilities for certain social changes. Yet, the problem of social values regarded as guiding forces for these changes cannot be avoided in this context. This very issue has been discussed from various angles. Subsequently a controversial proposal has been developed, aimed at the location of social strata, as well as an appropriate moral framework which might be critical from the point of view of the development of sociotechnical perspective. It has been suggested that in certain countries the morally and socially conscious 'intelligentsia' and in the others 'informed and involved working masses' may be regarded as the social generator of these ideas. In this context the concept of the global ethics tries, among other things, to place these social strata into a more general integrative scheme.

Both the authors are fully aware that their way of thinking is deeply rooted in and conditioned by their social background and that they have been struggling throughout the book to combine their unique East European experience with the academically elaborated Western rhetoric.

Subject index

Routledge Social Science Series

Routledge & Kegan Paul   London and Boston

68–74 Carter Lane   London EC4V 5EL
9 Park Street   Boston   Mass 02108

Contents

*Authors wishing to submit manuscripts for any series in
this catalogue should send them to the Social Science Editor,
Routledge & Kegan Paul Ltd, 68–74 Carter Lane,
London EC4V 5EL*

●*Books so marked are available in paperback*
All books are in Metric Demy 8vo format (216 × 138mm approx.)

International Library of Sociology

General Editor   John Rex

GENERAL SOCIOLOGY

Barnsley, J. H. The Social Reality of Ethics. *464 pp.*
Belshaw, Cyril. The Conditions of Social Performance. *An Exploratory Theory. 144 pp.*
Brown, Robert. Explanation in Social Science. *208 pp.*
Rules and Laws in Sociology. *192 pp.*
Bruford, W. H. Chekhov and His Russia. *A Sociological Study. 244 pp.*
Cain, Maureen E. Society and the Policeman's Role. *326 pp.*
Gibson, Quentin. The Logic of Social Enquiry. *240 pp.*
Glucksmann, M. Structuralist Analysis in Contemporary Social Thought. *212 pp.*
Gurvitch, Georges. Sociology of Law. *Preface by Roscoe Pound. 264 pp.*
Hodge, H. A. Wilhelm Dilthey. *An Introduction. 184 pp.*
Homans, George C. Sentiments and Activities. *336 pp.*
Johnson, Harry M. Sociology: *a Systematic Introduction. Foreword by Robert K. Merton. 710 pp.*
Mannheim, Karl. Essays on Sociology and Social Psychology. *Edited by Paul Keckskemeti. With Editorial Note by Adolph Lowe. 344 pp.*
Systematic Sociology: *An Introduction to the Study of Society. Edited by J. S. Erös and Professor W. A. C. Stewart. 220 pp.*
Martindale, Don. The Nature and Types of Sociological Theory. *292 pp.*
Maus, Heinz. A Short History of Sociology. *234 pp.*
Mey, Harald. Field-Theory. *A Study of its Application in the Social Sciences. 352 pp.*
Myrdal, Gunnar. Value in Social Theory: *A Collection of Essays on Methodology. Edited by Paul Streeten. 332 pp.*
Ogburn, William F., and **Nimkoff, Meyer F.** A Handbook of Sociology. *Preface by Karl Mannheim. 656 pp. 46 figures. 35 tables.*
Parsons, Talcott, and **Smelser, Neil J.** Economy and Society: *A Study in the Integration of Economic and Social Theory. 362 pp.*
Rex, John. Key Problems of Sociological Theory. *220 pp.*
Discovering Sociology. *278 pp.*
Sociology and the Demystification of the Modern World. *282 pp.*
Rex, John (Ed.) Approaches to Sociology. *Contributions by Peter Abell, Frank Bechhofer, Basil Bernstein, Ronald Fletcher, David Frisby, Miriam Glucksmann, Peter Lassman, Herminio Martins, John Rex, Roland Robertson, John Westergaard and Jock Young. 302 pp.*
Rigby, A. Alternative Realities. *352 pp.*
Roche, M. Phenomenology, Language and the Social Sciences. *374 pp.*
Sahay, A. Sociological Analysis. *220 pp.*
Urry, John. Reference Groups and the Theory of Revolution. *244 pp.*
Weinberg, E. Development of Sociology in the Soviet Union. *173 pp.*

FOREIGN CLASSICS OF SOCIOLOGY

●**Durkheim, Emile.** Suicide. *A Study in Sociology. Edited and with an Introduction by George Simpson. 404 pp.*
   Professional Ethics and Civic Morals. *Translated by Cornelia Brookfield. 288 pp.*
●**Gerth, H. H.,** and **Mills, C. Wright.** From Max Weber: *Essays in Sociology. 502 pp.*
●**Tönnies, Ferdinand.** Community and Association. (*Gemeinschaft und Gesellschaft.) Translated and Supplemented by Charles P. Loomis. Foreword by Pitirim A. Sorokin. 334 pp.*

SOCIAL STRUCTURE

Andreski, Stanislav. Military Organization and Society. *Foreword by Professor A. R. Radcliffe-Brown. 226 pp. 1 folder.*
Coontz, Sydney H. Population Theories and the Economic Interpretation. *202 pp.*
Coser, Lewis. The Functions of Social Conflict. *204 pp.*
Dickie-Clark, H. F. Marginal Situation: *A Sociological Study of a Coloured Group. 240 pp. 11 tables.*
Glaser, Barney, and **Strauss, Anselm L.** Status Passage. *A Formal Theory. 208 pp.*
Glass, D. V. (Ed.) Social Mobility in Britain. *Contributions by J. Berent, T. Bottomore, R. C. Chambers, J. Floud, D. V. Glass, J. R. Hall, H. T. Himmelweit, R. K. Kelsall, F. M. Martin, C. A. Moser, R. Mukherjee, and W. Ziegel. 420 pp.*
Jones, Garth N. Planned Organizational Change: *An Exploratory Study Using an Empirical Approach. 268 pp.*
Kelsall, R. K. Higher Civil Servants in Britain: *From 1870 to the Present Day. 268 pp. 31 tables.*
König, René. The Community. *232 pp. Illustrated.*
●**Lawton, Denis.** Social Class, Language and Education. *192 pp.*
McLeish, John. The Theory of Social Change: *Four Views Considered. 128 pp.*
Marsh, David C. The Changing Social Structure of England and Wales, 1871-1961. *288 pp.*
Mouzelis, Nicos. Organization and Bureaucracy. *An Analysis of Modern Theories. 240 pp.*
Mulkay, M. J. Functionalism, Exchange and Theoretical Strategy. *272 pp.*
Ossowski, Stanislaw. Class Structure in the Social Consciousness. *210 pp.*
Podgórecki, Adam. Law and Society. *About 300 pp.*

SOCIOLOGY AND POLITICS

Acton, T. A. Gypsy Politics and Social Change. *316 pp.*
Hechter, Michael. Internal Colonialism. *The Celtic Fringe in British National Development, 1536–1966. About 350 pp.*
Hertz, Frederick. Nationality in History and Politics: *A Psychology and Sociology of National Sentiment and Nationalism. 432 pp.*

Kornhauser, William. The Politics of Mass Society. *272 pp. 20 tables.*

Laidler, Harry W. History of Socialism. *Social-Economic Movements: An Historical and Comparative Survey of Socialism, Communism, Co-operation, Utopianism; and other Systems of Reform and Reconstruction. 992 pp.*

Lasswell, H. D. Analysis of Political Behaviour. *324 pp.*

Mannheim, Karl. Freedom, Power and Democratic Planning. *Edited by Hans Gerth and Ernest K. Bramstedt. 424 pp.*

Mansur, Fatma. Process of Independence. *Foreword by A. H. Hanson. 208 pp.*

Martin, David A. Pacifism: *an Historical and Sociological Study. 262 pp.*

Myrdal, Gunnar. The Political Element in the Development of Economic Theory. *Translated from the German by Paul Streeten. 282 pp.*

Wootton, Graham. Workers, Unions and the State. *188 pp.*

FOREIGN AFFAIRS: THEIR SOCIAL, POLITICAL AND ECONOMIC FOUNDATIONS

Mayer, J. P. Political Thought in France from the Revolution to the Fifth Republic. *164 pp.*

CRIMINOLOGY

Ancel, Marc. Social Defence: *A Modern Approach to Criminal Problems. Foreword by Leon Radzinowicz. 240 pp.*

Cain, Maureen E. Society and the Policeman's Role. *326 pp.*

Cloward, Richard A., and **Ohlin, Lloyd E.** Delinquency and Opportunity: *A Theory of Delinquent Gangs. 248 pp.*

Downes, David M. The Delinquent Solution. *A Study in Subcultural Theory. 296 pp.*

Dunlop, A. B., and **McCabe, S.** Young Men in Detention Centres. *192 pp.*

Friedlander, Kate. The Psycho-Analytical Approach to Juvenile Delinquency: *Theory, Case Studies, Treatment. 320 pp.*

Glueck, Sheldon, and **Eleanor.** Family Environment and Delinquency. *With the statistical assistance of Rose W. Kneznek. 340 pp.*

Lopez-Rey, Manuel. Crime. *An Analytical Appraisal. 288 pp.*

Mannheim, Hermann. Comparative Criminology: *a Text Book. Two volumes. 442 pp. and 380 pp.*

Morris, Terence. The Criminal Area: *A Study in Social Ecology. Foreword by Hermann Mannheim. 232 pp. 25 tables. 4 maps.*

Rock, Paul. Making People Pay. *338 pp.*

● **Taylor, Ian, Walton, Paul,** and **Young, Jock.** The New Criminology. *For a Social Theory of Deviance. 325 pp.*

SOCIAL PSYCHOLOGY

Bagley, Christopher. The Social Psychology of the Epileptic Child. *320 pp.*

Barbu, Zevedei. Problems of Historical Psychology. *248 pp.*

Blackburn, Julian. Psychology and the Social Pattern. *184 pp.*

●**Brittan, Arthur.** Meanings and Situations. *224 pp.*
Carroll, J. Break-Out from the Crystal Palace. *200 pp.*
●**Fleming, C. M.** Adolescence: Its Social Psychology. *With an Introduction to recent findings from the fields of Anthropology, Physiology, Medicine, Psychometrics and Sociometry. 288 pp.*
● The Social Psychology of Education: *An Introduction and Guide to Its Study. 136 pp.*
Homans, George C. The Human Group. *Foreword by Bernard DeVoto. Introduction by Robert K. Merton. 526 pp.*
● Social Behaviour: *its Elementary Forms. 416 pp.*
●**Klein, Josephine.** The Study of Groups. *226 pp. 31 figures. 5 tables.*
Linton, Ralph. The Cultural Background of Personality. *132 pp.*
●**Mayo, Elton.** The Social Problems of an Industrial Civilization. *With an appendix on the Political Problem. 180 pp.*
Ottaway, A. K. C. Learning Through Group Experience. *176 pp.*
Ridder, J. C. de. The Personality of the Urban African in South Africa. *A Thermatic Apperception Test Study. 196 pp. 12 plates.*
●**Rose, Arnold M.** (Ed.) Human Behaviour and Social Processes: *an Interactionist Approach. Contributions by Arnold M. Rose, Ralph H. Turner, Anselm Strauss, Everett C. Hughes, E. Franklin Frazier, Howard S. Becker, et al. 696 pp.*
Smelser, Neil J. Theory of Collective Behaviour. *448 pp.*
Stephenson, Geoffrey M. The Development of Conscience. *128 pp.*
Young, Kimball. Handbook of Social Psychology. *658 pp. 16 figures. 10 tables.*

SOCIOLOGY OF THE FAMILY

Banks, J. A. Prosperity and Parenthood: *A Study of Family Planning among The Victorian Middle Classes. 262 pp.*
Bell, Colin R. Middle Class Families: *Social and Geographical Mobility. 224 pp.*
Burton, Lindy. Vulnerable Children. *272 pp.*
Gavron, Hannah. The Captive Wife: *Conflicts of Household Mothers. 190 pp.*
George, Victor, and **Wilding, Paul.** Motherless Families. *220 pp.*
Klein, Josephine. Samples from English Cultures.
   1. Three Preliminary Studies and Aspects of Adult Life in England. *447 pp.*
   2. Child-Rearing Practices and Index. *247 pp.*
Klein, Viola. Britain's Married Women Workers. *180 pp.*
   The Feminine Character. *History of an Ideology. 244 pp.*
McWhinnie, Alexina M. Adopted Children. *How They Grow Up. 304 pp.*
● **Myrdal, Alva,** and **Klein, Viola.** Women's Two Roles: *Home and Work. 238 pp. 27 tables.*
Parsons, Talcott, and **Bales, Robert F.** Family: Socialization and Inter-action Process. *In collaboration with James Olds, Morris Zelditch and Philip E. Slater. 456 pp. 50 figures and tables.*

SOCIAL SERVICES

Bastide, Roger. The Sociology of Mental Disorder. *Translated from the French by Jean McNeil. 260 pp.*

Carlebach, Julius. Caring For Children in Trouble. *266 pp.*

Forder, R. A. (Ed.) Penelope Hall's Social Services of England and Wales. *352 pp.*

George, Victor. Foster Care. *Theory and Practice. 234 pp.*
Social Security: *Beveridge and After. 258 pp.*

George, V., and **Wilding, P.** Motherless Families. *248 pp.*

●**Goetschius, George W.** Working with Community Groups. *256 pp.*

Goetschius, George W., and **Tash, Joan.** Working with Unattached Youth. *416 pp.*

Hall, M. P., and **Howes, I. V.** The Church in Social Work. *A Study of Moral Welfare Work undertaken by the Church of England. 320 pp.*

Heywood, Jean S. Children in Care: *the Development of the Service for the Deprived Child. 264 pp.*

Hoenig, J., and **Hamilton, Marian W.** The De-Segregation of the Mentally Ill. *284 pp.*

Jones, Kathleen. Mental Health and Social Policy, 1845-1959. *264 pp.*

King, Roy D., Raynes, Norma V., and **Tizard, Jack.** Patterns of Residential Care. *356 pp.*

Leigh, John. Young People and Leisure. *256 pp.*

Morris, Mary. Voluntary Work and the Welfare State. *300 pp.*

Morris, Pauline. Put Away: *A Sociological Study of Institutions for the Mentally Retarded. 364 pp.*

Nokes, P. L. The Professional Task in Welfare Practice. *152 pp.*

Timms, Noel. Psychiatric Social Work in Great Britain (1939-1962). *280 pp.*

● Social Casework: *Principles and Practice. 256 pp.*

Young, A. F. Social Services in British Industry. *272 pp.*

Young, A. F., and **Ashton, E. T.** British Social Work in the Nineteenth Century. *288 pp.*

SOCIOLOGY OF EDUCATION

Banks, Olive. Parity and Prestige in English Secondary Education: a Study in Educational Sociology. *272 pp.*

Bentwich, Joseph. Education in Israel. *224 pp. 8 pp. plates.*

●**Blyth, W. A. L.** English Primary Education. *A Sociological Description.*
1. Schools. *232 pp.*
2. Background. *168 pp.*

Collier, K. G. The Social Purposes of Education: *Personal and Social Values in Education. 268 pp.*

Dale, R. R., and **Griffith, S.** Down Stream: *Failure in the Grammar School. 108 pp.*

Dore, R. P. Education in Tokugawa Japan. *356 pp. 9 pp. plates.*

Evans, K. M. Sociometry and Education. *158 pp.*

●**Ford, Julienne.** Social Class and the Comprehensive School. *192 pp.*

Foster, P. J. Education and Social Change in Ghana. *336 pp. 3 maps.*

Fraser, W. R. Education and Society in Modern France. *150 pp.*

Grace, Gerald R. Role Conflict and the Teacher. *About 200 pp.*

Hans, Nicholas. New Trends in Education in the Eighteenth Century. *278 pp. 19 tables.*

● Comparative Education: *A Study of Educational Factors and Traditions. 360 pp.*

Hargreaves, David. Interpersonal Relations and Education. *432 pp.*

● Social Relations in a Secondary School. *240 pp.*

Holmes, Brian. Problems in Education. *A Comparative Approach. 336 pp.*

King, Ronald. Values and Involvement in a Grammar School. *164 pp.* School Organization and Pupil Involvement. *A Study of Secondary Schools.*

●**Mannheim, Karl,** and **Stewart, W. A. C.** An Introduction to the Sociology of Education. *206 pp.*

Morris, Raymond N. The Sixth Form and College Entrance. *231 pp.*

●**Musgrove, F.** Youth and the Social Order. *176 pp.*

●**Ottaway, A. K. C.** Education and Society: An Introduction to the Sociology of Education. *With an Introduction by W. O. Lester Smith. 212 pp.*

Peers, Robert. Adult Education: *A Comparative Study. 398 pp.*

Pritchard, D. G. Education and the Handicapped: *1760 to 1960. 258 pp.*

Richardson, Helen. Adolescent Girls in Approved Schools. *308 pp.*

Stratta, Erica. The Education of Borstal Boys. *A Study of their Educational Experiences prior to, and during, Borstal Training. 256 pp.*

Taylor, P. H., Reid, W. A., and **Holley, B. J.** The English Sixth Form. *A Case Study in Curriculum Research. 200 pp.*

SOCIOLOGY OF CULTURE

Eppel, E. M., and **M.** Adolescents and Morality: *A Study of some Moral Values and Dilemmas of Working Adolescents in the Context of a changing Climate of Opinion. Foreword by W. J. H. Sprott. 268 pp. 39 tables.*

●**Fromm, Erich.** The Fear of Freedom. *286 pp.*

● The Sane Society. *400 pp.*

Mannheim, Karl. Essays on the Sociology of Culture. *Edited by Ernst Mannheim in co-operation with Paul Kecskemeti. Editorial Note by Adolph Lowe. 280 pp.*

Weber, Alfred. Farewell to European History: *or The Conquest of Nihilism. Translated from the German by R. F. C. Hull. 224 pp.*

SOCIOLOGY OF RELIGION

Argyle, Michael and **Beit-Hallahmi, Benjamin.** The Social Psychology of Religion. *About 256 pp.*

Nelson, G. K. Spiritualism and Society. *313 pp.*

Stark, Werner. The Sociology of Religion. *A Study of Christendom.*
Volume I. *Established Religion. 248 pp.*
Volume II. *Sectarian Religion. 368 pp.*
Volume III. *The Universal Church. 464 pp.*
Volume IV. *Types of Religious Man. 352 pp.*
Volume V. *Types of Religious Culture. 464 pp.*

Turner, B. S. Weber and Islam. *216 pp.*

Watt, W. Montgomery. Islam and the Integration of Society. *320 pp.*

SOCIOLOGY OF ART AND LITERATURE

Jarvie, Ian C. Towards a Sociology of the Cinema. *A Comparative Essay on the Structure and Functioning of a Major Entertainment Industry. 405 pp.*

Rust, Frances S. Dance in Society. *An Analysis of the Relationships between the Social Dance and Society in England from the Middle Ages to the Present Day. 256 pp. 8 pp. of plates.*

Schücking, L. L. The Sociology of Literary Taste. *112 pp.*

Wolff, Janet. Hermeneutic Philosophy and the Sociology of Art. *About 200 pp.*

SOCIOLOGY OF KNOWLEDGE

Diesing, P. Patterns of Discovery in the Social Sciences. *262 pp.*

●**Douglas, J. D.** (Ed.) Understanding Everyday Life. *370 pp.*

●**Hamilton, P.** Knowledge and Social Structure. *174 pp.*

Jarvie, I. C. Concepts and Society. *232 pp.*

Mannheim, Karl. Essays on the Sociology of Knowledge. *Edited by Paul Kecskemeti. Editorial Note by Adolph Lowe. 353 pp.*

Remmling, Gunter W. (Ed.) Towards the Sociology of Knowledge. *Origin and Development of a Sociological Thought Style. 463 pp.*

Stark, Werner. The Sociology of Knowledge: *An Essay in Aid of a Deeper Understanding of the History of Ideas. 384 pp.*

URBAN SOCIOLOGY

Ashworth, William. The Genesis of Modern British Town Planning: *A Study in Economic and Social History of the Nineteenth and Twentieth Centuries. 288 pp.*

Cullingworth, J. B. Housing Needs and Planning Policy: *A Restatement of the Problems of Housing Need and 'Overspill' in England and Wales. 232 pp. 44 tables. 8 maps.*

Dickinson, Robert E. City and Region: *A Geographical Interpretation* *608 pp. 125 figures.*

The West European City: *A Geographical Interpretation. 600 pp. 129 maps. 29 plates.*

● The City Region in Western Europe. *320 pp. Maps.*

Humphreys, Alexander J. New Dubliners: *Urbanization and the Irish Family. Foreword by George C. Homans. 304 pp.*

Jackson, Brian. Working Class Community: *Some General Notions raised by a Series of Studies in Northern England. 192 pp.*

Jennings, Hilda. Societies in the Making: *a Study of Development and Re-development within a County Borough. Foreword by D. A. Clark. 286 pp.*

●**Mann, P. H.** An Approach to Urban Sociology. *240 pp.*

Morris, R. N., and **Mogey, J.** The Sociology of Housing. *Studies at Berinsfield. 232 pp. 4 pp. plates.*

Rosser, C., and **Harris, C.** The Family and Social Change. *A Study of Family and Kinship in a South Wales Town. 352 pp. 8 maps.*

RURAL SOCIOLOGY

Chambers, R. J. H. Settlement Schemes in Tropical Africa: *A Selective Study. 268 pp.*

Haswell, M. R. The Economics of Development in Village India. *120 pp.*

Littlejohn, James. Westrigg: *the Sociology of a Cheviot Parish. 172 pp. 5 figures.*

Mayer, Adrian C. Peasants in the Pacific. *A Study of Fiji Indian Rural Society. 248 pp. 20 plates.*

Williams, W. M. The Sociology of an English Village: *Gosforth. 272 pp. 12 figures. 13 tables.*

SOCIOLOGY OF INDUSTRY AND DISTRIBUTION

Anderson, Nels. Work and Leisure. *280 pp.*

●**Blau, Peter M.,** and **Scott, W. Richard.** Formal Organizations: *a Comparative approach. Introduction and Additional Bibliography by J. H. Smith. 326 pp.*

Eldridge, J. E. T. Industrial Disputes. *Essays in the Sociology of Industrial Relations. 288 pp.*

Hetzler, Stanley. Applied Measures for Promoting Technological Growth. *352 pp.*

Technological Growth and Social Change. *Achieving Modernization. 269 pp.*

Hollowell, Peter G. The Lorry Driver. *272 pp.*

Jefferys, Margot, *with the assistance of Winifred Moss.* Mobility in the Labour Market: *Employment Changes in Battersea and Dagenham. Preface by Barbara Wootton. 186 pp. 51 tables.*

Millerson, Geoffrey. The Qualifying Associations: *a Study in Professionalization. 320 pp.*

Smelser, Neil J. Social Change in the Industrial Revolution: *An Application of Theory to the Lancashire Cotton Industry, 1770-1840. 468 pp. 12 figures. 14 tables.*

Williams, Gertrude. Recruitment to Skilled Trades. *240 pp.*

Young, A. F. Industrial Injuries Insurance: *an Examination of British Policy. 192 pp.*

DOCUMENTARY

Schlesinger, Rudolf (Ed.) Changing Attitudes in Soviet Russia.
2. The Nationalities Problem and Soviet Administration. *Selected Readings on the Development of Soviet Nationalities Policies. Introduced by the editor. Translated by W. W. Gottlieb. 324 pp.*

ANTHROPOLOGY

Ammar, Hamed. Growing up in an Egyptian Village: *Silwa, Province of Aswan. 336 pp.*

Brandel-Syrier, Mia. Reeftown Elite. *A Study of Social Mobility in a Modern African Community on the Reef. 376 pp.*

Crook, David, and **Isabel.** Revolution in a Chinese Village: *Ten Mile Inn. 230 pp. 8 plates. 1 map.*

Dickie-Clark, H. F. The Marginal Situation. *A Sociological Study of a Coloured Group. 236 pp.*

Dube, S. C. Indian Village. *Foreword by Morris Edward Opler. 276 pp. 4 plates.*
India's Changing Villages: *Human Factors in Community Development. 260 pp. 8 plates. 1 map.*

Firth, Raymond. Malay Fishermen. *Their Peasant Economy. 420 pp. 17 pp. plates.*

Firth, R., Hubert, J., and **Forge, A.** Families and their Relatives. *Kinship in a Middle-Class Sector of London: An Anthropological Study. 456 pp.*

Gulliver, P. H. Social Control in an African Society: *a Study of the Arusha, Agricultural Masai of Northern Tanganyika. 320 pp. 8 plates. 10 figures.*
Family Herds. *288 pp.*

Ishwaran, K. Shivapur. *A South Indian Village. 216 pp.*
Tradition and Economy in Village India: *An Interactionist Approach. Foreword by Conrad Arensburg. 176 pp.*

Jarvie, Ian C. The Revolution in Anthropology. *268 pp.*

Jarvie, Ian C., and **Agassi, Joseph.** Hong Kong. *A Society in Transition. 396 pp. Illustrated with plates and maps.*

Little, Kenneth L. Mende of Sierra Leone. *308 pp. and folder.*
Negroes in Britain. *With a New Introduction and Contemporary Study by Leonard Bloom. 320 pp.*

Lowie, Robert H. Social Organization. *494 pp.*
Mayer, Adrian C. Caste and Kinship in Central India: *A Village and its Region. 328 pp. 16 plates. 15 figures. 16 tables.*
Peasants in the Pacific. *A Study of Fiji Indian Rural Society. 248 pp.*
Smith, Raymond T. The Negro Family in British Guiana: *Family Structure and Social Status in the Villages. With a Foreword by Meyer Fortes. 314 pp. 8 plates. 1 figure. 4 maps.*

SOCIOLOGY AND PHILOSOPHY

Barnsley, John H. The Social Reality of Ethics. *A Comparative Analysis of Moral Codes. 448 pp.*
Diesing, Paul. Patterns of Discovery in the Social Sciences. *362 pp.*
●**Douglas, Jack D.** (Ed.) Understanding Everyday Life. *Toward the Reconstruction of Sociological Knowledge. Contributions by Alan F. Blum. Aaron W. Cicourel, Norman K. Denzin, Jack D. Douglas, John Heeren, Peter McHugh, Peter K. Manning, Melvin Power, Matthew Speier, Roy Turner, D. Lawrence Wieder, Thomas P. Wilson and Don H. Zimmerman. 370 pp.*
Jarvie, Ian C. Concepts and Society. *216 pp.*
Pelz, Werner. The Scope of Understanding in Sociology. *Towards a more radical reorientation in the social humanistic sciences. 283 pp.*
Roche, Maurice. Phenomenology, Language and the Social Sciences. *371 pp.*
Sahay, Arun. Sociological Analysis. *212 pp.*
Sklair, Leslie. The Sociology of Progress. *320 pp.*

International Library of Anthropology

General Editor   Adam Kuper

Brown, Paula. The Chimbu. *A Study of Change in the New Guinea Highlands. 151 pp.*
Lloyd, P. C. Power and Independence. *Urban Africans' Perception of Social Inequality. 264 pp.*
Pettigrew, Joyce. Robber Noblemen. *A Study of the Political System of the Sikh Jats. 284 pp.*
Van Den Berghe, Pierre L. Power and Privilege at an African University. *278 pp.*

International Library of Social Policy

General Editor   Kathleen Jones

Bayley, M. Mental Handicap and Community Care. *426 pp.*
Butler, J. R. Family Doctors and Public Policy. *208 pp.*
Holman, Robert. Trading in Children. *A Study of Private Fostering. 355 pp.*

Jones, Kathleen. History of the Mental Health Service. *428 pp.*

Thomas, J. E. The English Prison Officer since 1850: *A Study in Conflict. 258 pp.*

Woodward, J. To Do the Sick No Harm. *A Study of the British Voluntary Hospital System to 1875. About 220 pp.*

International Library of Welfare and Philosophy

General Editors   Noel Timms and David Watson

● **Plant, Raymond.** Community and Ideology. *104 pp.*

Primary Socialization, Language and Education

General Editor   Basil Bernstein

Bernstein, Basil. Class, Codes and Control. *2 volumes.*
 1. *Theoretical Studies Towards a Sociology of Language. 254 pp.*
 2. *Applied Studies Towards a Sociology of Language. About 400 pp.*
Brandis, W., and **Bernstein, B.** Selection and Control. *176 pp.*
Brandis, Walter, and **Henderson, Dorothy.** Social Class, Language and Communication. *288 pp.*
Cook-Gumperz, Jenny. Social Control and Socialization. *A Study of Class Differences in the Language of Maternal Control. 290 pp.*
● **Gahagan, D. M.,** and **G. A.** Talk Reform. *Exploration in Language for Infant School Children. 160 pp.*
Robinson, W. P., and **Rackstraw, Susan D. A.** A Question of Answers. *2 volumes. 192 pp. and 180 pp.*
Turner, Geoffrey J., and **Mohan, Bernard A.** A Linguistic Description and Computer Programme for Children's Speech. *208 pp.*

Reports of the Institute of Community Studies

Cartwright, Ann. Human Relations and Hospital Care. *272 pp.*
● Parents and Family Planning Services. *306 pp.*
 Patients and their Doctors. *A Study of General Practice. 304 pp.*
● **Jackson, Brian.** Streaming: *an Education System in Miniature. 168 pp.*
Jackson, Brian, and **Marsden, Dennis.** Education and the Working Class: *Some General Themes raised by a Study of 88 Working-class Children in a Northern Industrial City. 268 pp. 2 folders.*
Marris, Peter. The Experience of Higher Education. *232 pp. 27 tables.*
 Loss and Change. *192 pp.*

Marris, Peter, and **Rein, Martin.** Dilemmas of Social Reform. *Poverty and Community Action in the United States. 256 pp.*

Marris, Peter, and **Somerset, Anthony.** African Businessmen. *A Study of Entrepreneurship and Development in Kenya. 256 pp.*

Mills, Richard. Young Outsiders: *a Study in Alternative Communities. 216 pp.*

Runciman, W. G. Relative Deprivation and Social Justice. *A Study of Attitudes to Social Inequality in Twentieth-Century England. 352 pp.*

Willmott, Peter. Adolescent Boys in East London. *230 pp.*

Willmott, Peter, and **Young, Michael.** Family and Class in a London Suburb. *202 pp. 47 tables.*

Young, Michael. Innovation and Research in Education. *192 pp.*

● **Young, Michael,** and **McGeeney, Patrick.** Learning Begins at Home. *A Study of a Junior School and its Parents. 128 pp.*

Young, Michael, and **Willmott, Peter.** Family and Kinship in East London. *Foreword by Richard M. Titmuss. 252 pp. 39 tables.*
The Symmetrical Family. *410 pp.*

Reports of the Institute for Social Studies in Medical Care

Cartwright, Ann, Hockey, Lisbeth, and **Anderson, John L.** Life Before Death. *310 pp.*

Dunnell, Karen, and **Cartwright, Ann.** Medicine Takers, Prescribers and Hoarders. *190 pp.*

Medicine, Illness and Society

General Editor W. M. Williams

Robinson, David. The Process of Becoming Ill. *142 pp.*

Stacey, Margaret, *et al.* Hospitals, Children and Their Families. *The Report of a Pilot Study. 202 pp.*

Monographs in Social Theory

General Editor Arthur Brittan

● **Barnes, B.** Scientific Knowledge and Sociological Theory. *About 200 pp.*

Bauman, Zygmunt. Culture as Praxis. *204 pp.*

● **Dixon, Keith.** Sociological Theory. *Pretence and Possibility. 142 pp.*

● **Smith, Anthony D.** The Concept of Social Change. *A Critique of the Functionalist Theory of Social Change. 208 pp.*

Routledge Social Science Journals

The British Journal of Sociology. *Edited by Terence P. Morris. Vol. 1, No. 1, March 1950 and Quarterly. Roy. 8vo. Back numbers available. An international journal with articles on all aspects of sociology.*
Economy and Society. *Vol. 1, No. 1. February 1972 and Quarterly. Metric Roy. 8vo. A journal for all social scientists covering sociology, philosophy, anthropology, economics and history. Back numbers available.*
Year Book of Social Policy in Britain, The. *Edited by Kathleen Jones. 1971. Published annually.*

Printed in Great Britain by Unwin Brothers Limited
The Gresham Press Old Woking Surrey
A member of the Staples Printing Group